THE
ELECTED
AND THE
CHOSEN

WHY AMERICAN PRESIDENTS HAVE SUPPORTED JEWS AND ISRAEL

From George Washington to Barack Obama

Preface by Professor Alan M. Dershowitz

DENIS BRIAN

gefen גפן
publishing house
JERUSALEM • NEW YORK   Est. 1981

Cover Design: Sherwin Soy
Typesetting: Benjie Herskowitz, Etc. Studios
Photo of author: Pam Rutter

ISBN: 978-965-229-598-9

1 3 5 7 9 8 6 4 2

Gefen Publishing House Ltd.
6 Hatzvi Street
Jerusalem 94386, Israel
972-2-538-0247
orders@gefenpublishing.com

Gefen Books
11 Edison Place
Springfield, NJ 07081
516-593-1234
orders@gefenpublishing.com

www.gefenpublishing.com

Printed in Israel   *Send for our free catalogue*

Library of Congress Cataloging-in-Publication Data

Brian, Denis.
The elected and the chosen: why American presidents have supported Jews
and Israel : from George Washington to Barack Obama / Denis Brian.
    p. cm.
ISBN 978-965-229-598-9
1. Presidents – United States – Relations with Jews. 2. Presidents –
United States – History. 3. United States – Foreign relations – Israel. 4. Israel
Foreign relations –United States. 5. Jews – United States – Attitudes toward
Israel. 6. Zionism – United States. 7. United States – Ethnic relations. I. Title.
E176.472.J47B75 2012
327.7305694 – dc23

                    2012030793

To my wife, Martine;
daughter, Danielle;
grandson, Alex;
and granddaughter, Emma;
with love.

Also by Denis Brian

The Seven Lives of Colonel Patterson: How an Irish Lion Hunter Led the Jewish Legion to Victory, 2008

The Curies: A Biography of the Most Controversial Family in Science, 2005

Pulitzer: A Life, 2001

The True Gen: An Intimate Portrait of Hemingway by Those Who Knew Him, 1988

Einstein: A Life, 1977

Contents

Preface, by Professor Alan M. Dershowitz   ix

Acknowledgments   xiii

Introduction   1

George Washington, 1732–1799   16

John Adams, 1735–1826   26

Thomas Jefferson, 1743–1826   32

James Madison, 1751–1836   39

James Monroe, 1758–1831   48

John Quincy Adams, 1767–1848   53

Andrew Jackson, 1767–1845   58

Martin Van Buren, 1782–1862   61

William Henry Harrison, 1773–1841   68

John Tyler, 1790–1862   69

James Knox Polk, 1795–1849   74

Zachary Taylor, 1784–1850   77

Millard Fillmore, 1800–1874   81

Franklin Pierce, 1804–1869   84

James Buchanan, 1791–1868   88

Abraham Lincoln, 1809–1865   92

Andrew Johnson, 1808–1875   105

Ulysses S. Grant, 1822–1885   111

Rutherford B. Hayes, 1822–1893   118

James A. Garfield, 1831–1881   126

Chester A. Arthur, 1829–1886   131

Grover Cleveland, 1837–1908   135

Benjamin Harrison, 1833–1901   141

William McKinley, 1843–1901   148

Theodore Roosevelt, 1858–1919   155

William Howard Taft, 1857–1930   168

Woodrow Wilson, 1856–1924   177

Warren Gamaliel Harding, 1865–1923   184

Calvin Coolidge, 1872–1933   190

Herbert Clark Hoover, 1874–1964   197

Franklin Delano Roosevelt, 1882–1945   205

Harry S. Truman, 1884–1972   224

Dwight David Eisenhower, 1890–1969   243

John Fitzgerald Kennedy, 1917–1963   260

Lyndon Baines Johnson, 1908–1973   276

Richard Milhous Nixon, 1913–1994   289

Gerald Rudolph Ford, 1913–2006   299

Jimmy Carter, 1924–   307

Ronald Wilson Reagan, 1911–2004   323

George Herbert Walker Bush, 1924–   332

William Jefferson Clinton, 1946–   343

George Walker Bush, 1946–   361

Barack Hussein Obama, 1961–   375

Bibliography   389

Index   399

Preface

BY PROFESSOR ALAN M. DERSHOWITZ

Many Americans are aware of the role played by American presidents in regard to the Jewish community and Jewish state.

Most know of George Washington's famous letter to the Jewish congregation in Touro in which he said:

> For happily the Government of the United States, which gives to bigotry no sanction, to persecution no assistance, requires only that they who live under its protection, should demean themselves as good citizens.... May the Children of the Stock of Abraham, who dwell in this land, continue to merit and enjoy the good will of the other inhabitants; while every one shall sit under his own vine and fig tree, and there shall be none to make him afraid.

We are aware of President Truman's bold decision to ignore the advice of several cabinet ministers by recognizing Israel immediately after its establishment. We know of the love expressed for Israel by several recent presidents, including George W. Bush and William Jefferson Clinton.

Many Americans are also aware of President Jimmy Carter's hatred of most Israeli leaders and of many Israeli politicians – a hatred that allowed him to use the despised word "apartheid" in a title of one of his books on Israel. Newspaper readers are also aware of President Nixon's mixed record: his overt anti-Semitism coupled with his strong support of Israel during the Yom Kippur War.

I think of myself as quite knowledgeable with regard to American and Jewish history, having read quite widely in both fields. I was shocked when I read this book to find out how much I didn't know – how almost every president of the United States had some connection to American Jews, the Jews who lived in Europe and Palestine, and to the Zionist Project that eventuated in the nation state of the Jewish people.

I was not aware of how many American presidents had close Jewish friends and advisors, how many were Christian Zionists, and how many did so much for the oppressed Jews of Russia, Romania, Palestine, and other places where Jews were subject to mistreatment.

I knew that former president Taft had opposed President Wilson's nomination of Louis Brandeis, the first Jewish justice appointed to the Supreme Court, and I believed that his vitriol was based on Brandeis's religion, but I now must reconsider that view, having learned of Taft's more positive actions towards Jews; while President Andrew Johnson – arguably the worst president in American history – was overtly and proudly anti-Semitic, with no redeeming qualities or actions.

I knew that General Grant had signed an order expelling the Jews from certain areas under his command during the Civil War, but I did not know that President Grant was a philo-Semite who appointed many Jews to high positions.

Nor did I know that when Theodore Roosevelt was police commissioner of New York and was asked to prevent an anti-Semitic pastor from speaking, he instead cleverly ordered the pastor to be provided with a large detachment of policemen – all of whom were Jewish.

These and other well-documented and hitherto unknown facts makes *The Elected and the Chosen* a remarkable read for anyone interested in American and/or Jewish history.

Michael Oren, in his brilliant book *Power, Faith, and Fantasy: America in the Middle East, 1776 to the Present,* has made a strong case for a close ideological and theological connection between the American and Israeli experiment. *The Elected and the Chosen*, with its plethora of anecdotes, personal letters, and other previously unknown documentation, fills out the story. Reading it helps you understand why Americans have remained closer to Israel than any other country on the face of the earth. It also puts the lie to such undocumented and un-academic screeds as *The Israel Lobby* by Walt and Mearsheimer. It proves that the reason why Congress is so supportive of Israel is not because of campaign contributions or political lobbying, but rather because there are deep historical, moral, religious, political, and military connections between our nation and the nation state of the Jewish people – and because most Americans admire Israel.

At a time when some – out of ignorance or malice – are questioning the legitimacy of the alliance between the United States and Israel, this book is a welcome anodyne to such naysayers. It is a must-read for all who care about maintaining a crucial alliance so important to both the United States and to Israel.

Acknowledgments

My thanks to the archivists at all the Presidential Libraries, the Library of Congress, and the National Archives. I would also like to thank the White House Press Office, Gerhard Peters and John T. Woolley, American Presidency Project; Jewish Virtual Library; American Jewish Historical Society; *New York Times*; *Washington Post*; *Associated Press*; *Reuters*; *Jerusalem Post*; *Haaretz*; *Jewish Press*; *Daily Mail*; *Daily Express*; *Sunday Times*; *American Jewish Historical Quarterly*; US Department of State, Foreign Relations of the United States; Israel Foreign Ministry; Israel State Archives; Ben-Gurion Archives; American Holocaust Museum; The David S. Wyman Institute for Holocaust Studies; Ohio Historical Society; Massachusetts Historical Society; Passaic County Historical Society; Pam Rutter; Peter Stockton; former New York Mayor Ed Koch; James C. Humes; Clifton Truman Daniel; Judith Apter Klinghoffer; History News Network; Claudia Anderson, Supervisory Archivist, LBJ Library; Allen Fisher, Jeff Stein, Embassy of Israel; Frederick J. Augustyn Jr., Library of Congress; Sonja P. Wentling; Jerry Klinger; Bob Clark; Randy Sowell; Sam Rushay; Liza Talbot; Michael D. Greco; Steven Altergood; Yehoshua Freundlich; David R. Sabo; David J. Haight; Herbert J. Pankratz; Zionist Archives; British Foreign Office Archives; Kings College Archives; M.I.5 Files; and British National Archives, Kew, London.

Thanks to my agent, Phyllis Westberg and her assistant, Karen Gormandy, of Ober Associates; my publisher, Ilan Greenfield, of Gefen Publishing House; editors Tziporah

Levine and Ita Olesker; production coordinator, Lynn Douek; and Sherwin Soy for his striking book jacket design.

Special thanks to Professor Alan M. Dershowitz for his remarkable preface, and to my wife, Martine, who helped, encouraged, and inspired me every step of the way.

Introduction

The rebellion in Tunis launched in late February 2011, which spread to Egypt, Libya, Yemen, Bahrain, and Syria, spurred President Obama to order a complete review of America's Middle East policy. Whatever the outcome of the rebellions and of Obama's political decisions, one thing is predictable with reasonable certainty: Israel will remain the only state in the region on which America can depend.

How did this relationship come about? And what does this book offer to explain the situation? It offers a fresh, insider's look at the lives of all the presidents – based on private letters, diaries, and previously secret documents – with an emphasis on the presidents' public and private interactions with American and foreign Jews, their handling of Middle East policy, and conversations and correspondence with fellow Americans as well as with Arab, Israeli, British, and Russian leaders. This book illustrates how the presidents' religious upbringing, their character, and their close friendships with Jews and Jewish leaders, as well as their knowledge of history and their unique access to information on international events, impacted their views and resulted in critical and often unexpected decisions. It explains why, almost without exception, American presidents have actively supported Jews at home and abroad, and since 1948 have ensured the creation and survival of the embattled State of Israel.

Chronologically, this book covers the Revolutionary War, in which Jewish support was vital to Washington's success; the founding of America; the Civil War; pogroms in Russia;

anti-Semitism in Europe and America; the rise of Zionism; World Wars I and II; the Holocaust; the creation of Israel; Arab attacks aimed at Israel's destruction; Israel's de facto alliance with the United States; the Suez War; the Vietnam War; Israel's attack on the USS *Liberty*; US political, military, and moral support; behind-the-scenes diplomacy with both Israeli and Arab leaders; the Israeli nuclear reactor; terrorism; Middle East peace negotiations; Desert Storm and the Gulf War; the disengagement from Gaza; and the current turmoil in the Middle East.

From their early days in America, inspired by the Bible, Puritans believed they would be fulfilling God's will by helping His chosen people, scattered as they were throughout the world, to return to Palestine, their promised and former homeland. This return, Puritans held, would foreshadow Christ's Second Coming.

America's political leaders, though less formally religious than the puritans, demonstrated the Bible's great influence on them at the Continental Congress in 1776: Benjamin Franklin wanted the seal of the American Union to portray Moses lifting up his staff and parting the Red Sea, while Pharaoh in his chariot was overwhelmed by the waves. Thomas Jefferson proposed that the seal should show the children of Israel in the wilderness en route to the Promised Land, guided by a cloud by day and a pillar of fire at night. Instead, they chose the Liberty Bell, with a quote from Leviticus 26:10 in the Old Testament: "Proclaim liberty throughout all the land unto all the inhabitants thereof."[1]

John Adams, the second American president, eagerly anticipated the prospect of Jews invading Palestine and wresting it from its Turkish rulers. As early as 1819, Adams wrote to Mordecai Noah, a Jewish-American author and former

---

[1] Peter Grose, *Israel in the Mind of America* (New York: Knopf, 1983), 316.

US consul to Tunis, "I could find it in my heart to wish that you had been at the head of a hundred thousand Israelites... marching with them into Judea and making a conquest of the country and restoring your nation to the domination of it. For I really wish the Jews again in Judea an independent nation."[2]

In 1840, President Van Buren helped to rescue Syrian Jews who, falsely accused of horrendous crimes, were being tortured and murdered by the Muslim authorities. With the help of like-minded European leaders, Van Buren stopped the massacre.

The next organized attempt to help persecuted Jews began over fifty years later. After visiting Palestine with his daughter in 1891, Protestant preacher William Blackstone returned to his Oak Park, Illinois, home an impassioned Zionist advocate. His fervent writings on the subject persuaded several hundred prominent Americans and a future president, William McKinley, to support a Jewish homeland in Palestine. Blackstone was seven years ahead of the Hungarian Jew Theodor Herzl – a lawyer-journalist who, incensed by the humiliations and callous treatment of fellow Jews, especially in anti-Semitic France, made the Zionist cause an effective worldwide movement.[3]

But it was not until World War I that a Jewish state in Palestine became a practical possibility. Then the British Balfour Declaration promised Jews that in return for their help in winning the war, Palestine (then ruled by the Turkish enemy) would be their homeland. Jews did help them win the war. So did the United States. And at the Versailles Peace Conference in 1919, after the Allies had won the war, American president Woodrow Wilson expressed his support for the Balfour Declaration. The newly created League of Nations, a forerunner of

---

[2] "John Adams Embraces a Jewish Homeland," Jewish Virtual Library, www. jewishvirtuallibrary.org/jsource/US-Israel/adams.html.

[3] Alex Bein, *Theodore Herzl: A Biography,* translated from the German by Maurice Samuel (Cleveland: World Publishing Company, 1962), 232.

the United Nations, agreed to let Britain rule Palestine (then called the Mandate) to prepare it to be a Jewish homeland.[4]

Britain and America were not alone in supporting a Jewish homeland in Palestine. At the San Remo, Italy, conference in April 1920, fifty-one nations – all the members of the League of Nations – unanimously approved a Jewish homeland in Palestine. As for Middle East Arabs, they were also given a homeland in Palestine: Transjordan, now known as Jordan, as well as what was left of the defeated Turks' Ottoman Empire – Syria, Lebanon, Mesopotamia (now Iraq), and all of Arabia.

Two years later, both Houses of Congress unanimously voted in favor of the Balfour Declaration.

However, the British failed to fulfill the terms of their Balfour Declaration, because during the 1920s and 1930s they were faced with an almost continuous revolution, as Arabs and Jews fought each other and both fought the British. Even one hundred thousand occupying British troops couldn't keep the peace. Having lost too much in blood and treasure, the British hoped to hand over the problem to some other country or organization.

Meanwhile, former Republican president Herbert Hoover promoted a pro-Jewish policy: to avoid the otherwise inevitable bloodshed and to provide Jews with a refuge, he suggested that Arabs should be encouraged to leave Palestine and helped to settle in the large Arab nations in the region.[5] World War II put the problem on hold. Defeating the Nazis became the main objective of both the British – with thousands of Jewish volunteers – and their American allies, all focused on winning the war.

During the war FDR, as Roosevelt was affectionately known, not only suggested putting a barbed-wire fence around

---

[4] Walter Laqueur, *The History of Zionism: From the French Revolution to the Establishment of Israel* (New York: Holt, Rinehart and Winston, 1972), 197.

[5] Herbert Hoover and Hugh Gibson, *The Problems of Lasting Peace* (New York: Doubleday, Doran and Co., 1943), 235–36.

Palestine, but also proposed gradually moving Arabs out of the contested country, until Jews became a 90 percent majority in control of their completely independent nation. Meanwhile, FDR undertook to find a way to provide land in other parts of the Middle East for the displaced Palestinian Arabs. But on a visit to Ibn Saud, the king of Saudi Arabia, FDR was disappointed to discover that the Arab monarch was adamantly opposed to a Jewish homeland in Palestine.

The British government should have warned FDR that he was on an impossible quest. In their foreign-office files was the report of a conversation, just before the war, between Ibn Saud and a British army lieutenant colonel, Harold Richard Patrick Dickson. In the report, the Arab monarch is quoted as saying, "For a Muslim to kill a Jew, or for him to be killed by a Jew, ensures him an immediate entry into Heaven and into the august presence of God Almighty."[6]

Toward the war's end in 1944, as in 1922, both Houses of Congress had unanimously voted to support the Balfour Declaration. But it was not until 1946 that the Zionist dream became a real possibility when President Harry Truman proposed an Anglo-American committee of inquiry, consisting of six British and six American delegates, to consider the future of Holocaust survivors and of Palestine itself. A pro-Zionist member of the committee, British Labor MP Richard Crossman, noted in his diary that Zionist leader Chaim Weizmann "suggested that the Palestinian problem was not a matter of right or wrong, but...between the greater or lesser injustice." As injustice was unavoidable, Weizmann suggested that "the Committee's task was to decide to be unjust to the Arabs of Palestine or to the Jews."[7]

[6] Ibn Saud to British Lieutenant Colonel H. R. P. Dickson, 1937, British Foreign Office file no. 371/20822 E 7201/22/31; and Elie Kedouri, *Islam in the Modern World* (London: Mansell, 1980), 69–72.

[7] Richard Crossman, *Palestine Mission: A Personal Record* (London: Hamish Hamilton, 1947), 123.

During the inquiry, Professor Philip Hitti, a prominent Arab-American historian at Princeton, testified that Muslim law required Jews and Christians to recognize the superior status of Muslims; that the Arabs were descendants of the ancient Canaanites who held the land before the Jews; and that Jerusalem is the Muslims' third holy city, toward which the early Arabs prayed. He stated that the land was given to the Arabs by Allah as the result of a jihad, or holy war, and that the Hebrews came and went, but the natives remained.[8]

Albert Einstein and his historian friend Erich Kahler disputed Hitti's views, pointing out in a Princeton newspaper that "one does not get very far with claims of historical right. Very few peoples of the world would be entitled to their present countries if such a criterion was applied. The fact is, that the Israelites came, but they never went. Jewish communities persisted in Palestine uninterruptedly throughout the ages."[9]

The committee learned how Jews were treated in various Arab countries: In Iraq it was high treason to support Zionism. In Yemen Jews had to live in ghettoes that were locked at night, were not legally allowed to leave the country, and were forced to get off the sidewalk when an Arab passed by.

While the inquiry continued, Republican Wendell Willkie, who had lost the presidential race to Franklin Roosevelt, made an around-the-world fact-finding journey with stops in Britain and the Middle East. On his return, he told Bartley Crum, a pro-Zionist member of the Anglo-American Committee of Inquiry, "The Arabs have a good case in Palestine. There is only one thing wrong with it. The Jews have a better case."[10]

---

[8] "Palestine Setting of Sacred History of Jewish Race," *Princeton Herald,* April 14, 1944, 1.

[9] Ibid., 6, 9.

[10] Bartley Crum, *Behind the Silken Curtain: A Personal Account of Anglo-American Diplomacy in Palestine and the Middle East* (New York: Simon and Schuster, 1947), 290–91; and Michael T. Benson, *Harry S. Truman and the founding of Israel* (Westport, CT: Greenwood, 1997), 17.

The committee decided unanimously that one hundred thousand Jews should be allowed into Palestine.

Despite fierce opposition to a Jewish homeland in Palestine from the Arab and Muslim world, and almost equally fierce opposition from the essentially pro-Arab US State Department – from President Truman's Secretary of State, George Marshall, and from most of his trusted advisers – as well as a growing American reliance on Arab oil, a defiant Truman helped to create the new State of Israel. How he pulled it off against great odds is a compelling chapter in American history. He later admitted that his biggest problem in office had not been whether or not to drop the atomic bomb on Japan, but whether to recognize Israel, when the overwhelming advice and pressure was to say no. This book will explain what brought him to say yes.

At the outset, Jews in the newly created Israel of 1948 faced a life-or-death situation when five Arab armies attacked – from Egypt, Iraq, Jordan, Lebanon, and Syria. To almost everyone's amazement the Israelis defeated them. David Ben-Gurion, Israel's first prime minister, called it a miracle.

If, as the historic record shows, American presidents, from Washington to Obama, have been Israel's most loyal supporters, how did Israel respond?

On June 17, 1981, for example, when Israeli F-16s destroyed Iraq's nuclear reactor near Baghdad, the world protested. But, thanks to the Israelis, when the Americans and their allies subsequently twice invaded Iraq, they were not threatened with a nuclear weapon.

As for political support, Reagan's UN ambassador Jeane Kirkpatrick said that in the UN in 1992, Israel voted with the US more often than any other country, "agreeing in 86.2 percent of the votes, as compared to 80.1 percent for Britain,

76.6 percent West Germany, 70.7 percent Canada, 67.9 percent Italy, and 67.2 percent Japan."[11]

Never free from attack or threat of attack, Israel found a new champion in President George W. Bush, and a new enemy in Iran. In April 2006, Bush pledged to defend Israel, while Iranian president Mahmoud Ahmadinejad not only denied the existence of the Holocaust, but threatened to wipe Israel off the map. Bush also refused to negotiate with Hamas or Hezbollah, the terrorist groups intent on Israel's destruction, which many Palestinian and Lebanese voters had chosen to represent them.

In my research for this book I uncovered surprising and little-known facts about American presidents and their positive attitudes toward Jews and, eventually, toward Israel:

- ❖ Lincoln's close friend and confidant was his Jewish chiropodist.
- ❖ Police commissioner Theodore Roosevelt encouraged Jews to join the almost all-Irish New York police force, and wrote that "the most astonishing courage was displayed by the seven Jewish Rough Riders (during the Spanish-American War).... One of the colonels among the regular regiments who did so well on that day, who fought beside me, was a Jew."[12]
- ❖ As a boy, Dwight Eisenhower believed that there were no Jews on earth. According to his understanding of the Bible, they were all angels in heaven. During World War II, because hostile Arabs of North Africa believed the rumor that he was Jewish and intent on turning the

---

[11] Wolf Blitzer, *Between Washington and Jerusalem: A Reporter's Notebook* (New York: Cambridge University Press USA, 1985), 8.

[12] *New York Times*, Sept. 13, 1899, 3; and Denis Brian, *The Seven Lives of Colonel Patterson: How an Irish Lion Hunter Led The Jewish Legion to Victory* (Syracuse, NY: Syracuse University Press, 2008), 90.

country into a Jewish state, Ike had to put out a pamphlet explaining that he was a Christian.

❖ John F. Kennedy saw a Japanese prisoner shoot to death a Jewish chaplain who was handing the prisoner a glass of water.[13]

❖ In his childhood, Lyndon Baines Johnson's Zionist aunt told him that he must always help the Chosen People. He took it to heart and as a politician secretly helped hundreds of Jews to escape from Hitler's Europe to America, including a future conductor of the Boston Symphony Orchestra.

❖ Ronald Reagan intentionally kept official American army documentary films of Nazi concentration camps at his home to show to Holocaust deniers.

❖ Despite their anti-Jewish remarks and reputations, both Richard Nixon and Jimmy Carter did as much as any other president to make sure Israel survived and flourished.

❖ George Henry Walker Bush played a major role in helping thousands of endangered Ethiopian Jews find a safe haven in Israel.

❖ On his deathbed, Bill Clinton's friend told him that God would never forgive him if he didn't stand by Israel, and Clinton wrote of his close friendship with Israeli prime minister Yitzhak Rabin, which led to his love for the man.[14]

Public, private, and previously secret sources used in this book show why, when much of the Western world made their lives intolerable, most American presidents attempted to help

---

[13] Michael O'Brien, *John Kennedy: A Biography* (New York: St. Martin's Press, 2005), 233.

[14] Bill Clinton, *My Life* (New York: Knopf, 2004), 353–54; and "Finish Rabin's Work," *New York Times*, opinion page, November 3, 2010.

those in peril and eventually encouraged the creation and survival of the embattled Jewish homeland.

The demands of politics and urge to be reelected naturally influenced the decisions of American presidents. But the early presidents had no incentive to court Jewish votes, because there were so few potential Jewish voters. The motives of these presidents were clearly religious, moral, or personal – or all three – often influenced by their childhood teachers and relatives, their encounters and friendships with Jews in peace and on the battlefield, and their considerable knowledge of Jewish history through the Bible.

Later, in the 1920s and 1930s, American presidents were confronted by homegrown admirers of Hitler and Mussolini, and by the poison of such anti-Semitic preachers as Father Charles Coughlin, who enthralled more than thirty million receptive listeners. Likeminded motor magnate Henry Ford promoted a provocative book, *The Protocols of the Learned Elders of Zion*, as evidence that Jews were conspiring to rule the world.

Not one American president fell for Coughlin's bigotry, or for *The Protocols*. President Taft ridiculed the book's claim, asking if Jews were so powerful, why were millions of them persecuted and poverty stricken? His skeptical view was confirmed the following year, in 1921, when a correspondent for *The Times* of London provided evidence that the book was anti-Semitic Russian propaganda.

Inevitably, after World War II and the Holocaust, President Truman responded to the needs of the survivors, an important aspect of which was to find them a refuge.

During the Cold War, between 1947 and 1997, the Soviet Union and the United States competed for influence in the Middle East, with the Russians backing and arming the Arabs bent on Israel's destruction, and American presidents sustaining or increasing their assistance to Israel.

Truman's mixed motives for recognizing and supporting Israel and his ambivalent attitude toward Jews is here covered in detail. Both his and Lyndon Johnson's critics considered it political suicide to support Israel when it was enormously outnumbered by militant anti-Israel Arabs, who held the oil on which US survival as a great power depended. But when their motives were questioned, both presidents gave the same answer: it was the right thing to do.

Here we explore the factors that made them reach this conclusion, as well as investigating accounts of their conversations and correspondence with Arab leaders such as Egypt's Anwar Sadat, the PLO's Yasser Arafat, Jordan's King Hussein, and King Ibn Saud and Prince Bandar of Saudi Arabia.

The overall political reason for the pro-Israel stance of American presidents is both practical and idealistic. They saw and continue to see Israel as a fellow democracy whose people share Western values of justice, tolerance, free speech, a free press, human rights, and religious freedom. They know that Israelis, living in a small and vulnerable country, are never free from the threat of attack by their neighbors. Because the American public and Congress largely and consistently share this view, it makes support for Israel an all-but-inevitable American policy.

Israel, in turn, has proved a loyal ally, voting in the UN in concert with the United States more often than any other nation. Economic aid the US sends to Israel is one of the most cost-effective investments in support of US international interests, because all the money returns to the US as debt repayment, and the money for military aid is required to be spent in the US, accounting for thousands of American jobs. Israel and the US also share military secrets and conduct joint military exercises. During Desert Storm Israel refrained from responding to Iraq's scud missile attacks to enable President Bush to hold onto his coalition, which included Arab states. In that same war, the US Air Force used Israeli-designed Pioneer unmanned reconnaissance aircraft and Israeli-made fuel tanks to extend the range of its F-15 fighters.

Today, Israel provides facilities for America to store and maintain military equipment and allows American troops to disembark at its ports and train on its soil. Israel is the only country in the area on which the US can rely to provide open access to its ports, especially Haifa, where about forty US Navy vessels dock every year. And to keep things going smoothly, some three hundred Department of Defense personnel travel to Israel every month.[15]

Even their biographers will be surprised to read of Hoover's and Roosevelt's plans to make Palestine a Jewish state; how Roosevelt helped to save some one hundred thousand Jews from probable slaughter; of the private conversations between JFK, Ben-Gurion, and other Israeli leaders over Israel's nuclear plant at Dimona, which reveal the personalities and characters of the participants, their subtle diplomatic exchanges, and Ben-Gurion's growing admiration for JFK. They will discover how LBJ probably broke the law to save Jews from Hitler's Germany and of his immediate and consistent response to Israel's attack on the USS *Liberty*, and how shortly before his death Ike admitted that he had made a mistake in supporting Egypt against Britain, France, and Israel during the Suez War. This book also tells of Ronald Reagan's remarkable private reaction to Israel's bombing of Iraq's nuclear reactor, which he publicly deplored.

Readers will learn that despite their anti-Semitic slurs, Truman and Nixon were great supporters of the Jewish state. Nixon's favorite novelist, attorney, judge, and the man he chose as his secretary of state were Jews, and Nixon rated

---

[15] Mitchell G. Bard, "The Evolution of Strategic Cooperation," Jewish Virtual Library, http://www.jewishvirtuallibrary.org/jsource/US-Israel/evolution_of_strategic_coop.html.

Golda Meir the world's greatest leader. Carter, despite his criticism of Israel's treatment of Palestinians, ensured Israel's survival with military hardware and the latest secret technical equipment. Although he considered Rabin weak and indecisive, Clinton had high praise for Rabin's political acumen – similar to his own – and grew to love him.

As a presidential candidate in 2008, Barack Obama promised to help Israel maintain its military edge so that it could repel attacks from as far away as Iran and as close as Gaza. He reassured some Israelis by choosing Joe Biden, a self-proclaimed Zionist, to be his vice president, though others thought Obama too concerned with placating the Arabs. A 2009 Rasmussen Report showed that 81 percent of Americans agreed with President Obama that as part of a future Middle East peace agreement Arab leaders must agree on Israel's right to exist.

Not all has been sweetness and light between the two countries. In 2010, eager to broker a Middle East peace agreement, Obama issued a tough ultimatum to Israeli Prime Minister Netanyahu: he must cancel approval of new housing units in disputed territory, freeze all Jewish construction in East Jerusalem, release hundreds of Palestinian prisoners to bring the Palestinians to the peace table, and agree to discuss the partition of Jerusalem and provide a solution to the problem of Palestinian refugees.

Shortly after, on March 20, 2010, when Netanyahu arrived at the White House, Obama had a further demand: that Israel move its troops back to where they were before the Second Intifada (Palestinian uprising in 2000). Netanyahu returned to Israel without committing himself.

Nevertheless, that same year the House and Senate Appropriations Committees approved Obama's request for $3 billion in military aid for Israel, more than half the combined total amount that went to other countries. Obama also approved the sale to Israel of the Lockheed Martin F-35 Lightning 11 nuclear-capable stealth fighter bombers, a decision that former head of the Israeli Air Force, Eitan Ben Eliyahu, called a key test of the close relationship between the two countries.[16]

As a senator, Obama had visited Israel, saw the damage and distress from thousands of Hamas rockets fired from Gaza, and expressed his support for Israel's military responses. Today, we are faced with the probability of new revolutionary governments taking over in the Middle East; how will it affect the close US-Israel relationship? One aim of this book is to give the likely answers.

On March 4, 2011, at a fundraiser in Miami, Obama said, "Our commitment to Israel's security is inviolable, is sacrosanct."[17]

At a press conference in Tel Aviv on March 24, 2011, US defense secretary Robert Gates said, "We have an unshakeable commitment to Israel's security. I cannot recall a time during my years in public life when our two countries have had a closer relationship. The United States and Israel are cooperating in areas such as missile defense technology, the joint Strike Fighter, and in training exercises such as Juniper Stallion." Later that afternoon, speaking with President Peres, he said, "President Obama is the eighth president I have worked for and I believe that the Defense relationship between America and Israel has never been stronger."[18]

---

[16] Luis Ramirez, "Israel Provider of Fighter Jet," VOA: Voice of America, August 17, 204f-fighter-jets-seen-as-litmus-test-for-continued-us-support-1008999349/124026. html.

[17] Sheryl Gay Stolberg, "Obama Upbeat about Israel's Future," *New York Times*, May 4, 2011, http://thecaucus.blogs.nytimes.com/03/04/obama.com/2011/03/04/obama-upbeat-about-israels-future/.

[18] *Vos Iz Neias*? The Voice of the Orthodox Jewish Community, "Jerusalem – Gates in Israel: No Other Nation Would Tolerate This," http://www.vosizneias. com/79479/2011/03/24/Jerusalem-again-israel-no-other-nation-would-tolerate-this-photos-video.

On May 22, President Obama addressed over ten thousand members of AIPAC, the most influential pro-Israel lobby in America, to frequent applause. He explained that his Middle East peace plan regarding national borders "allows the parties themselves to take account of the changes that have taken place over the past forty-four years," including "the demographic realities on the ground." Prime Minister Netanyahu responded, "I am a partner with the president's desire to achieve peace."[19]

Then, during his speech before a packed joint meeting of the United States Congress on May 24, 2011, when Netanyahu received twenty-nine standing ovations, he reaffirmed Obama's effective support for Israel.

Obama had requested Congress to give Israel $205 million for its Iron Dome defense system, and they approved by a vote of 410 to 4. In the spring of 2011, *Haaretz* reported that Iron Dome had intercepted and destroyed in midair nine rockets fired from Gaza.[20]

Here, then, is an account of what some have called a passionate friendship, and how the character, heritage, upbringing, experiences, and fundamental beliefs of American presidents have ensured their unfailing support of Jews, and since 1948, of Israel.

Even presidential biographers and Middle East experts will find much in this book that is new and revealing, some of it from previously secret documents and personal diaries and letters. It will also explain why American presidents have so wholeheartedly and consistently supported Israel, and indicate why future presidents are likely to follow in their footsteps.

---

[19] Hilary Leila Krieger, "At AIPAC Obama Defines His Formula for Mideast Peace," JPost.com, March 22, 2011, www.jpost.com/DiplomacyPolitics/Aericle. aspx?=221711.

[20] Anshel Pfeffer, "Iron Dome Makes World History Intercepting Nine Gaza Rockets," *Haaretz*, http://www.haaretz.com/print-edition/news/iron-dome-world-history-intercepting-nine-gaza-rockets-1.355033.

George Washington

1732–1799

⦿ First president, 1789–1797

⦿ Led the Continental Army to victory in the American Revolutionary War

⦿ Presided over the writing of the Constitution

The historical records do not reveal any meaningful contact between George Washington and the Jews or mention any comments he made about them until he became leader of the Revolutionary Army. Then Jews became vital to his success, and without their help America might still be a British possession. Later, as president, Washington put his pro-Jewish views on record, especially when he assured members of a Rhode Island synagogue that bigotry and religious persecution would not be tolerated in the United States.

George Washington was eleven years old in 1743 when his father, Augustus, a Virginia planter of English descent, died. He left his wife, Mary, and six children, a ten thousand acre estate in Virginia, and forty-nine slaves. George's half-brother,

Lawrence, fourteen years his senior, took over as his surrogate father, allowing George to continue at school in Fredericksburg until he was fifteen, when he hoped to join the British navy. But he changed his mind after a relative warned him that he'd be better off being "an apprentice to a Tinker" than joining the British navy, where his superiors would "Cut him and Slash him and & use him like a Negro, or rather, like a dog." [1]

His brother Lawrence had named their inherited estate Mount Vernon, and George sometimes surveyed their woods and fields armed with a compass and a surveyors' chain. Seeing him at it, a neighbor, Thomas Fairfax, hired him to survey his extensive acres in the Shenandoah Valley beyond the Blue Ridge Mountains. At the age of sixteen, in the spring of 1748, George set off on horseback on his first trip with Fairfax's young nephew. They rode together almost a hundred miles to the mountain gap through which they reached the vast country beyond. There, they were surprised to come across a – fortunately – friendly Indian war party celebrating victory by dancing around a fire, to the beat of a kettledrum, one of them brandishing a scalp.

Pleased with George's report, Thomas Fairfax kept him on as his surveyor for three years, and they became lifelong friends. Based perhaps on Fairfax's recommendation – and despite his lack of military experience – George Washington was then appointed a lieutenant colonel of a British colonial regiment. His mission was to lead a detachment of forty men with Indian aides and drive off a French force crossing the frontier into Virginian territory. The twenty-two-year-old set off in April 1754, and in the ensuing fight his men killed ten, wounded one, and took twenty-one prisoners, with the loss of only one of their own. That summer, two months later,

---

[1] Ron Chernow, *Washington: A Life* (New York: The Penguin Press, 2006), 18.
.

Washington faced a French and Indian force of about eleven hundred men, bent on revenge. They fought for hours in a blinding rainstorm and the contest ended in a truce, though Washington suffered many more casualties than the enemy. Subsequently, the French agreed to keep only as much territory as they already controlled.

Washington got more military experience as aide-de-camp to British Major General Braddock, who, with two thousand men at his command, was charged with destroying a French fort near what is now Pittsburgh. On the journey Washington became feverish with dysentery, but soldiered on, trying to ease his hemorrhoids with cushions on his horse's saddle. He made Braddock promise that despite his illness he would be allowed to join in the fighting. Before Braddock's men reached the French fort, however, they were attacked by a strong force of French and Indian fighters. The redcoats were outmatched by the Indians, who hid in the trees and picked off their targets with deadly accuracy. But Washington survived. Though musket balls penetrated his hat and shredded his coat, they didn't leave a mark on him. General Braddock, however, had four horses shot from under him before he fell, fatally wounded. Washington had him wrapped in blankets and buried on the side of the road, before joining the defeated, demoralized, and fearful remnants of the British army on their painful trek back to Virginia. On the way, Indians killed and scalped the wounded and the stragglers. Despite the disastrous and humiliating defeat, the word reached home of Washington's courage, and he was deservedly hailed as a hero.

In January 1759, he married Martha Curtis, a wealthy widow with four children. After sixteen years of peaceful existence, managing his estate at Mount Vernon and caring for his wife and four stepchildren, he was elected to the Virginia House of Burgesses.

As a representative of one of the thirteen colonies, he attended the Continental Congress in Philadelphia in March 1775 to discuss the violence – fueled by heavy taxes and oppressive laws – in Boston, Lexington, and Concord, that had escalated into full-scale battles against British forces. The delegates voted to join the rebels, raise an army, and fight for their independence. John Adams, a delegate from Massachusetts, nominated Washington to lead the rebel army into battle, and while Washington waited outside the room, they voted unanimously for him to lead the fight. Although he shared the rebels' grievances, he accepted the task reluctantly, well aware of the superior resources of the British army on whose side he had once fought, and afraid that the task was beyond him.

He arrived outside Boston on July 5, 1775, and with some trepidation took command of sixteen thousand rebels, to be known as militiamen or patriots. The British redcoats had early victories, but then the war became a stalemate. When it resumed, thousands of Americans, known as loyalists, joined the fight on the side of the British, who also hired thousands of German mercenaries.

Many of America's approximately two thousand Jews fought under Washington, including most of Charleston, South Carolina's adult Jewish males. And, but for a Jew providing money to support the war, it might well have been lost.

The first Jewish patriot killed in the Revolutionary War was South Carolina's Francis Salvador. At twenty-nine, Salvador, an elected member of South Carolina's General Assembly, recruited volunteers to repel attacks on the South Carolina–Georgia frontier by Cherokee Indians, who had been killing and scalping its colonial inhabitants. On July 1, 1776, he rode thirty miles on horseback to sound the alarm, then hurried back to rejoin the militia defending other settlements under siege. During the fighting on August 1, he was shot and fell from his horse into some bushes. As he lay there dying, an Indian scalped him. The militia commander, Major Andrew Williamson, drove off the Indians and came upon Salvador, who asked him, as Williamson recalled, "whether I had beaten the enemy. I told him 'Yes.' He said he was glad of it and shook me by the hand and bade me farewell, and said he would die in a few minutes." According to William Henry Drayton, later South Carolina's Chief Justice, Salvador had sacrificed his life in the service of his adopted country."[2]

Although the French, Spanish, and Dutch were willing to ship arms and supplies to Washington in secret, he hadn't the money to pay for them. Meanwhile, some of his starving and ill-equipped troops were reduced to fighting barefoot in the snow, and many were deserting. He was in imminent danger of losing the war. Until a Jew, Haym Salomon, came to his rescue. A Polish rabbi's son, he had been arrested by the British in New York City, in 1778, as a patriot suspected of spying and was sentenced to be hanged. But the German-speaking Salomon talked his German prison guard into letting him escape (the British used some Germans, known as Hessians, as mercenaries to help in their battle). When Salomon reached Philadelphia, not yet under British control, he ran such a respected brokerage business that the French minister made him paymaster general for French troops fighting alongside Americans.

Salomon also made personal loans to members of the Continental Congress, charging below the going interest rates. This spurred James Madison to admit that "I have for some time...been a pensioner on the favor of Haym Salomon, a Jew broker."[3] In a 1782 letter, James Madison admitted, "The

[2] Jerry Klinger, "How the Jews Saved the American Revolution," American Jewish History 1654–1770, *The Jewish Magazine*, http://www.jewishmag.com/80mag/usa3/usa3.htm.

[3] Michael Feldberg, "Haym Salomon: The Rest of the Story," 2001, American Jewish

kindness of my little friend in Front Street, Salomon, will preserve me from extremities, but I never resort to it without mortifications, as he obstinately rejects all recompense.... To a necessitous delegate he gratuitously spares a supply of money out of his private stock."[4] Salomon also gave much of his own money to pay the salaries of government officials and army officers.

For his financial support of the patriot army, Washington had reason to regard Salomon as a vital contributor to final victory. After the war, Salomon and Robert Morris, the superintendent of finance, later saved the newly created United States from financial disaster.

Salomon died broke at forty-five in 1785, leaving a widow and three children. Some 150 years after his death, America recognized his service and the Liberty ship SS *Haym Salomon* was named in his honor.[5]

In 1975 the Postal Service issued a ten-cent stamp naming him a "Financial Hero" and "Contributor to the Cause" of the American Revolution. On the back of the stamp is printed: "Financial Hero – Businessman and broker Haym Salomon was responsible for raising money needed to finance the American Revolution and later to save the new nation from collapse." Chicago also celebrated Salomon by erecting a group monument of him, George Washington, and Robert Morris, the first superintendent of finance.

Another American Jew, David Franks, Haym Salomon's brother-in-law, was on Washington's staff. Franks, as president of Montreal's Spanish and Portuguese Synagogue, had spent sixteen days in jail for defending the right of a protestor to call King George a fool and compare him to the pope. When Washington's men invaded Quebec to "liberate" it from the British,

---

Historical Society, www.jewishworldreview.com.

[4] Ibid.

[5] Haym Salomon, Congressional Record, March 25, 1975.

Franks joined them, and when the British drove them off, Franks retreated with them to Philadelphia. There, because he was fluent in French as well as German, Franks became the liaison officer for the Comte d'Estaing, commander of the French troops fighting alongside the Americans. Later, as a major, Franks was aide-de-camp to Benedict Arnold, the military governor of Philadelphia, then commander of the American garrison at West Point.[6]

In 1779, Arnold turned traitor, offering to surrender West Point to the British for £6,300 and a commission as an officer in the British army. (He got both and escaped to England.) Having once been his assistant, Franks was suspected of being in cahoots with Arnold, but a court-martial cleared him of any complicity in the treason. It didn't hurt that Benedict Arnold, safe in England, had written to Washington to say that Franks was totally innocent of any part in the traitorous affair. Washington came to the same conclusion and appointed Franks to his staff and promoted him to lieutenant colonel. But fellow officers acted as if they still didn't trust him. So Franks persuaded Washington to give him a second court-martial, which again exonerated him.

The war lasted eight years and 137 days. At war's end, in 1783, the much-maligned Lieutenant Colonel David Franks was given top-secret diplomatic assignments, as well as a copy of the peace treaty that gave Americans their independence, to take to Benjamin Franklin in Paris and to John Jay in Madrid. He was also appointed the American vice-consul in Marseilles, and in 1786 he joined the diplomatic team arranging a US-Morocco trade agreement.[7]

---

[6] Ibid.

[7] Robert Leslie Cohen, "A Profile of David Salisbury Franks," Passaic County Historical Society, http:www.lambertcastle.otg/David20%Salisbury20%Franks. html.

However, despite two trials that had cleared him of any part in Benedict Arnold's treachery, his political enemies revived the charges that he had been the traitor's ally and had him dismissed from the diplomatic corps. Washington still believed in him, Jefferson called him "honest and affectionate," and for his service to the country Congress gave him acres of land and a job at the Bank of the United States in Philadelphia.[8]

In 1789, Americans unanimously voted for Washington to be their first president. As president – a job Washington didn't want and feared he wasn't up to – he was as trusted and respected as he had been at the head of his troops.

Washington not only had positive contacts with Jewish fighters and financiers, but with the Jewish religious community. After his presidential election in 1789, and during his ceremonial visit to the Northeast, he received a letter from Moses Seixas, the warden of Newport, Rhode Island's Touro Synagogue, as it's known today, welcoming him to the area. It reads in part:

> Deprived as we heretofore have been of the invaluable rights of free Citizens, we now (with a deep sense of gratitude to the Almighty disposer of all events) behold a Government, erected by the Majesty of the People – a Government, which to bigotry gives no sanction, to persecution no assistance – but generously affording to ALL liberty of conscience, and immunities of Citizenship: deeming every one, of whatever Nation, tongue, or language, equal parts of the great governmental Machine. . .For all the Blessings of civil and religious liberty which we enjoy under an equal and benign administration, we desire to send up our thanks.[9]

---

[8] Ibid.

[9] Seixas's letter to George Washington, August 17, 1790, George Washington Papers, Library of Congress.

Washington's reply has since been read aloud every year in the Touro Synagogue. It reads in part:

> The Citizens of the United States of America have a right to applaud themselves for giving Mankind examples of an enlarged and liberal policy: a policy worthy of imitation. All possess alike liberty of conscience and immunities of citizenship.... For happily the Government of the United States, which gives to bigotry no sanction, to persecution no assistance [repeating Seixas's words], requires only that they who live under its protection, should demean themselves as good citizens. May the Children of the Stock of Abraham, who dwell in this land, continue to merit and enjoy the good will of the other inhabitants; while everyone shall sit under his own vine and fig tree, and there shall be none to make him afraid. May the father of all mercies scatter light and not darkness in our paths, and make us all in our several vocations useful here, and in his own due time and way everlastingly happy.[10]

A few months later, on December 19, 1790, Rabbi Manuel Josephson wrote to Washington on behalf of several Jewish congregations to express their support and high expectations.[11]

In his reply, Washington, brought up as an Episcopalian, proudly noted the unique characteristic of Americans in their political and religious toleration of fellow countrymen:

> Gentlemen: The liberality of sentiment towards each other which marks every political and religious denomination of men in this country, stands unparalleled in the history of nations. The affection of such people is a treasure beyond the reach of calculation: and the repeated proofs which my fellow-citizens have given of their attachment to me, and

---

[10] Abraham J. Karp, *From the Ends of the Earth: Judaic Treasures of the Library of Congress* (New York: Rizzoli, 1991), 268, 270.

[11] George Washington Papers, Library of Congress.

approbation of my doings; form the purest source of my temporal felicity.... The power and goodness of the Almighty were strongly manifested on the events of the late glorious revolution; and his kind interposition on our behalf, has been no less visible in the establishment of our present equal government. In war he directed the sword, and in peace he directed our councils, the agency of both has been guided by the best intentions and a sense of duty which I owe my country. And as my exertions have been hitherto rewarded by the approbations of my fellow-citizens I shall endeavour [British spelling] to deserve a continuance of it by my future conduct.... May the temporal and eternal blessings which you implore for me, rest upon your congregations.[12]

Washington's response was naturally heartening to Jewish Americans, many of whom had escaped from countries where Jews had endured centuries of bigotry, persecution, confinement to ghettos, pogroms, murders, forced conversions, and expulsions. A small but significant example of Washington's lack of bigotry was his hiring practice when in need of workmen for his Virginia home, Mount Vernon. Writing to an employment agent, on March 24, 1784, requesting a joiner and bricklayer, he explained: "They may be of Asia, Africa or they may be from Europe, Mahometans, Jews, or Christians of any Sect, or they may be Atheists."[13]

Washington caught a cold while riding on his estate, and it developed into pneumonia. He died at home in Mount Vernon, Virginia, on December 18, 1799. He was sixty-seven years old. In his will he freed all three hundred of his slaves.

---

[12] Ibid.
[13] Ibid.

John Adams

1735–1826

- ✪ Second president, 1797–1801
- ✪ Washington's vice president
- ✪ Negotiated peace with Britain to end the Revolutionary War

As a boy, John Adams had such a passion for hunting that he took his gun to school so that the moment he was let out he could begin hunting crows and squirrels.[1]

The son of a Harvard-educated farmer and deacon of his Congregationalist church, Adams was born in Braintree, now Quincy, Massachusetts, on October 30, 1735. Like his father, he went to Harvard, where he rejected his father's wish for him to be a clergyman, choosing instead to study law, and he became a Boston lawyer in 1758. His father died of flu in the epidemic of 1761. Three years later, John married his childhood sweetheart, a minister's daughter, Abigail Smith, and they had four children.

What became known as "The Boston Massacre," not "The Boston Tea Party," may have been the spark that set off the American Revolution, and it also made John Adams famous

---

[1] Anne Husted Burleigh, *John Adams: Man of Braintree* (Piscataway, NJ: Transaction, 2009), 9.

throughout the colonies. Bostonians resented the presence of British troops and at times insulted and harassed them. On the night of March 4, 1770, when a young man harassed a soldier guarding the Customs House on King Street, the guard struck him on the head with the butt of his musket. An angry crowd gathered and threatened to attack the guard. Six more redcoats and their officer, Captain Thomas Preston, came to his rescue, which enraged the crowd, now grown to several hundred. They pelted the soldiers with snowballs, rocks, and insults, calling them cowards and daring them to fire their muskets. When shots fired over the heads of the crowd failed to stop the attacks and one soldier was knocked to the ground, the redcoats fired directly into the crowd. Three died on the spot, eleven were injured, and two died later of their injuries. The crowd quickly dispersed, and the next day all British troops were withdrawn from the center of town. The eight soldiers, including Captain Preston, were charged with murder.

Afraid of public reaction, no Boston lawyer was willing to defend them, until Captain Preston pleaded with John Adams, who accepted the task. As he proudly noted in his diary on the third anniversary of the incident:

> The part I took in the defense of Capt. Preston and the soldiers, procured in me anxiety, obloquy enough. It was, however, one of the most gallant, generous, manly and disinterested actions of my whole life, and one of the best pieces of service I ever rendered my country. Judgment of death against those soldiers would have been a foul stain upon this country as the execution of Quakers or witches, anciently. As the evidence was, the verdict of the jury was exactly right. There is no reason the town should not call the action of that night, a Massacre, nor is it any argument in favor of the Governor or Minister, who caused them (the army) to be sent there. But it is the strongest proofs of the danger of standing armies."[2]

---

[2] L. H. Butterfield, ed., *Diary and Autobiography* of *John Adams* (Cambridge, MA: Harvard University Press, 1962), 79.

Adams' courage and skill led to the acquittal of Captain Preston and five soldiers. The two other soldiers escaped the death penalty and were found guilty of manslaughter. They had their thumbs branded with the letter M in open court, were discharged from the army, and sent home to England.

Despite his daring defense of the British, Adams was known as an outspoken promoter of American independence, and so the Massachusetts colony elected him their representative at the Continental Congress. There, at the second Congress, he successfully nominated George Washington to be commander-in-chief of the Revolutionary Army and persuaded Thomas Jefferson to write the first draft of the Declaration of Independence.

During the war Adams twice sailed to France and, with Benjamin Franklin, talked the French into supporting the American Revolution with both their ground troops and navy. After the war, Adams was America's first ambassador to Britain.

He had nominated George Washington to head the army and to be America's first president. Washington returned the favor by making Adams his vice president and successor.

From the first days of the United States, Adams and other Founding Fathers found inspiration for their decisions in the ancient history of the Jews. Benjamin Franklin joined Adams in recommending that the official seal of the United States should have an Old-Testament theme depicting the Jews crossing the Red Sea, and that the motto around the seal should be "Resistance to Tyrants Is Obedience to God." This also reflected the views of the early pilgrims in New England, who had escaped religious persecution in Europe and saw their emigration as a reenactment of the Jewish exodus from Egypt. In this scenario, "England was Egypt, the [English] king was

Pharaoh, the Atlantic Ocean was the Red Sea, America was the Land of Israel, and the Indians were the ancient Canaanites. They [the New England Puritans] were the new Israelites, entering into a new covenant with God in a new Promised Land."[3]

A direct descendant of Henry Adams, a Puritan who had escaped to America from religious persecution in England during the reign of King Charles I, John Adams did not believe in Christ's divinity. But he did believe in Christ's moral teachings and consequently had become a Unitarian. Unitarians are encouraged to follow their own spiritual path and to have shared values rather than accept creeds or dogmas. He greatly admired both the heroic Jews and prophets of the Bible and Jews he knew personally, and was puzzled by French philosopher Voltaire, who characterized Jews as "the most abominable people on earth...all of them born with raging fanaticism in their hearts, just as Bretons and Germans are born with blond hair." Voltaire also stated that Jews had contributed nothing toward civilization, in vivid contrast to John Adams, who almost idolized them.[4]

"The Hebrews have done more to civilize man than any other nation," Adams wrote to a correspondent, F. A. Van der Kemp, in 1808:

> If I were an atheist, and believed in blind eternal fate, I should still believe that fate had ordained the Jews to be the most essential instrument for civilizing nations. If I were an atheist of the other sect, who believe, or pretend to believe, that all is ordered by chance, I should believe that chance had ordered the Jews to preserve and propagate to all mankind the doctrine of a supreme, intelligent, wise, almighty Sovereign of

---

[3] Rabbi Ken Spiro, "Jews and the Founding of America," Crash Course in Jewish History no. 55, aish.com, http://www.aish.com/jl/h/48955806.html.

[4] *The Complete Works of Voltaire, 1778*, vol. 1 (The Voltaire Foundation of the University of Oxford), 150–59.

the universe, which I believe to be the great essential principle of all morality, and consequently of all civilization. They are the most glorious nation that ever inhabited the Earth. The Romans and their empire were but a bubble in comparison to the Jews. They have given religion to three quarters of the globe and have influenced the affairs of mankind more and more happily than any other nation, ancient or modern.[5]

Adams again raised the subject in 1818, when the multitalented Mordecai Noah, perhaps the most prominent Jewish American of the time, sent President Adams a copy of a speech he gave at the consecration of the Spanish and Portuguese synagogue in New York City. In it he stressed the worldwide persecution of Jews by non-democratic states and, as an early Zionist, he expressed the belief that Jews would only be free from persecution when they had their own homeland. Adams replied: "I have had occasion to be acquainted with several gentlemen of your nation and to transact business with some of them, whom I found to be men of as liberal minds, as much honor, probity, generosity, and good breeding as any I have known in any seat of religion or philosophy. I wish your nation to be admitted to all privileges of citizens in every country in the world. This country has done much. I wish it would do more, and annul every narrow idea in religion, government, and commerce."[6]

Noah had briefly been the US consul to Tunis in 1813 (to be described in the chapter on Madison) and wrote of his experiences in his book *Travels in England. France, Spain and the Barbary States,* published in 1818, a copy of which he sent to Adams.

---

[5] Charles Francis Adams, ed., *Works of John Adams* (Boston: Little, Brown, 1856), 609.

[6] Moshe Davis, ed., *With Eyes Toward Zion: Scholars Colloquium America–Holy Land Studies* (New York: Arno Press, 1977); American Jewish Historical Society.

Then former president Adams praised Noah's "judicious observations and ingenious reflections," but was disappointed that he hadn't "extended his travels to Syria, Judea, and Jerusalem," because it would then have been the most complete travel book he'd ever read. It was in his remarkable letter to Noah that Adams revealed himself to be a militant Zionist: Adams was the first American president to express Zionist views – and militant Zionist views – a century before the acknowledged father of Zionism, Theodor Herzl.

"If I were to let my imagination lose," he wrote to Noah, "I should wish you had been a member of Napoleon's Institute at Cairo, nay farther, indeed I could find it in my heart to wish that you had been at the head of a hundred thousand Israelites indeed, as well disciplined as a French Army & marching with them into Judea & making a conquest of that country & restoring your nation to the dominion of it. For I really wish the Jews again in Judea an independent nation." However, there was a proviso: "I believe [that] once restored to an independent government & no longer persecuted [the Jews] would soon wear away some of the asperities and peculiarities of their character & possibly in time become Unitarian Christians, for your Jehovah is our Jehovah, & your God of Abraham, Isaac, and Jacob is our God."[7]

John Adams died at ninety of arterioslosclerosis, in his Quincy, Massachusetts, home. Remarkably, both he and Jefferson died on July 4, 1826, the fiftieth anniversary of the adoption of the Declaration of Independence.

---

[7]   Davis, *With Eyes Toward Zion.*

Thomas Jefferson

1743–1826

- ✪ Third president, 1801–1809
- ✪ Principle author of the Declaration of Independence
- ✪ Initiated the Louisiana Purchase, doubling the size of the United States

Perhaps the most brilliant man of his time, at least in the Western world, and surely the most versatile, Thomas Jefferson was an architect who designed his own magnificent home, Monticello. He invented such wonders as a clock which ran on cannonballs and gravity. He was a lawyer, writer, scientist, scholar fluent in several languages, politician, diplomat, philosopher, astronomer, violinist, creator of his own Bible based on reason and minus the miracles, main author of the Declaration of Independence, and founder and designer of the University of Virginia.

The third of ten children, Thomas Jefferson was born in Shadwell, Virginia, on April 13, 1743, to a successful planter-surveyor-cartographer, Peter Jefferson, of Welsh descent, and his wife, Jane Randolph, who claimed descent from English and Scottish kings.

At first, Thomas was tutored by a Protestant clergyman and sometimes by his father and an older brother. At nine he was eagerly learning French, Greek, and Latin. His father died when he was fourteen. Three years later, he began to study mathematics, metaphysics, and philosophy at the College of William and Mary in Williamsburg, Virginia, graduating at nineteen with top honors, fluent in French and Italian. He also read in German, Greek, Latin, and Anglo-Saxon – when not studying for a law degree. After graduating, he was admitted to the Virginia bar and began his career as a lawyer. Five years later he married a young widow, Martha Wayles Skelton, daughter of a Virginia planter, and they had six children, only two of whom survived infancy.

As a delegate to the Second Continental Congress in 1775, he was the principal author of the Declaration of Independence. During the War of Independence, as Virginia's governor, he barely escaped capture by the British.

Raised as an Anglican, Jefferson grew up to be skeptical of all organized religions. He doubted Christ's divinity and didn't buy any of the Bible miracles. To retain Christ's teachings but eliminate what he regarded as fantasy, he created his own Bible by simply cutting out all the miracles. "I am a Christian," he wrote, "in the only sense he [Christ] wanted anyone to be, sincerely attached to his doctrines in preference to all others, ascribing to himself every human excellence, and believing he never claimed any other...." He wrote eloquently of Christ:

> 1. His parentage was obscure, his condition poor, his education null, his natural endowments great, his life correct and innocent: he was meek, benevolent, firm, disinterested, and of the sublimest eloquence. The disadvantages under which his doctrines appear are remarkable.

2. Like Socrates and Epictetus he wrote nothing down. But he had not, like them, a Xenophon or Arrian to write for him. . . On the contrary, all the learned of his country, entrenched in its power and riches, were opposed to him lest his labors should undermine their advantages, and the committing to writing his life and doctrine fell on unlettered and ignorant men who wrote, too, from memory, and not till long after the transactions had passed.

3. According to the ordinary fate of those who attempt to enlighten and reform mankind, he fell an early victim of the jealousy and combination of the altar and the throne, at about thirty-three years of age, his reason not having attained maximum of the energy, nor the course of his preaching, which was but of three years at most, presented occasions for developing a complete system of morals.

4. Hence the doctrines that he really delivered, have come to us mutilated, misstated, and often unintelligible.

5. They have been still further disfigured by the corruptions of sensationalizing followers, who have found an interest in sophisticating and perverting the simple doctrines he taught, by engrafting on them the mysticisms of a Grecian sophist, filtering them into absolutes, and obscuring then with jargon until they have caused good men to reject the whole in disgust and to view Jesus himself as an impostor.

Notwithstanding these disadvantages, a system of morals is presented to us which, filled up in the style and spirit of the rich fragments he left us, would be the most perfect and sublime that has ever been taught by man.[1]

---

[1] Bernard Mayo, ed., *Jefferson Himself: The Personal Narrative of a Many-Sided American* (Boston: Houghton Mifflin, 1942), 231–32.

Despite his jaundiced view of organized religions, Jefferson championed the rights of all – including Jews – to worship as they wished. He liked the fact that Jews did not try to convert others to their religious beliefs, but was puzzled how they could believe that "the God of infinite justice" punished "the sins of the fathers upon their children, unto the third and fourth generations."[2]

Yet he worked to achieve civil and religious freedom for Jews. His 1777 bill to establish religious freedom in Virginia was adopted in 1786, thanks to James Madison's strong support. It reads, "No man shall be compelled to frequent or support any religious worship, place, or ministry whatsoever, nor shall be enforced, restrained, molested, or [burdened] in his body or goods, nor shall otherwise suffer, on account of his religious opinions or beliefs; but that all men shall be free to profess...their opinion in matters of Religion, and that the same shall in no wise diminish, enlarge, or affect their civil capacities."[3]

He also agreed with fellow philosopher John Locke that "Neither Pagan nor Mahamedan nor Jew ought to be excluded from the civil rights of the Commonwealth because of his religion." When Virginia's law became the law of the land in 1789, Article 6 includes these Jefferson-inspired words: "No religious test shall ever be required as a qualification to any office or public trust under the United States."[4]

In 1801, the first year of his presidency, Jefferson appointed a Jew, Reuben Etting of Baltimore, who fought as a captain in the Revolutionary War, to be the US Marshall for Maryland.

Perhaps his greatest achievement as president was to buy Louisiana Territory from the French for $15 million, or three cents an acre, which doubled the size of the United States.

---

[2] *Jefferson's Works*, vol. 4, p. 325, Library of Congress,

[3] Statutes at Large of Virginia, vol. 12 (1828), 84–86.

[4] Ibid.

After he left the White House, he discussed Jewish history with Mordecai Noah, the Jewish-American author and early Zionist. Noah sent Jefferson the same speech he had mailed to former president Adams. Part of Jefferson's reply on May 28, 1818, reads:

> I have read [the speech] with pleasure and instruction, having learnt from it some valuable facts in Jewish history which I did not know before. Your sect by its sufferings has furnished a remarkable proof of the universal spirit of religious intolerance inherent in every sect, disclaimed by all while feeble, practiced by all when in power. Our laws have applied the only antidote to this vice, protecting our religions, as they do our civil rights, by putting all on an equal footing.

> But more remains to be done, for although we are free by the law, we are not in practice. Public opinion erects itself into an inquisition, and exercises its office with as much fanaticism as fans the flames of the Auto-da-fe. The prejudice still scowling on your section of our religion altho' the elder one, cannot be unfelt by ourselves. It is to be hoped that the individual dispositions will at length mould themselves to the model of the law, and consider the moral basis, on which all our religions rest, as the rallying point which unites them in a common interest....

> I should not do full justice in the merits of your Discourse, were I not...to express my consideration of it as a fine specimen of style and composition. I salute you with great respect and esteem.[5]

Jefferson showed his continued interest in the history of the Jews in his correspondence with Joseph Marx of Richmond in the summer of 1820, writing to him, "Th. Jefferson presents to Mr. Marx his compliments & thanks for Transactions

---

[5] Karp, *From the Ends of the Earth*, 230, 239–40.

of the Paris Sanhedrin, [an influential group of French Jews] which he shall read with great interest, and with the regret he has ever felt at seeing a sect, the parent and basis of those of Christendom, singled out by all of them for persecution and oppression, which prove they have profited nothing from the benevolent doctrine of him whom they profess to make the model of their principles and practice. He salutes Mr. Marx with sentiments of perfect esteem and respect."[6]

Through reading about the Sanhedrin, Jefferson would find that, although he despised the tyrannical French leader Napoleon Bonaparte, they shared similar liberal views about Jews and religion. In Paris in 1807, Napoleon met rabbis and Jewish scholars, members of a legal assembly known as the Sanhedrin, to discuss Jewish interests. After which Napoleon allowed Jews to worship freely, to have a synagogue built in the city, and to become French citizens. When asked by Dr. Barry O' Meara, his personal physician, why he had encouraged and supported Jews, the former emperor of France, now imprisoned on St. Helena, replied, "My primary desire was to liberate the Jews and make them full citizens. I wanted to confer upon them all the rights of equality, liberty and fraternity as was enjoyed by the Catholics and Protestants. It is my wish that Jews be treated like brothers as if we were all part of Judaism." [7]

Two months after Joseph Marx wrote to Jefferson, Jacob De La Motta, a Jewish doctor in Savannah, Georgia, having delivered the consecration address at the dedication of Savannah's new synagogue, sent Jefferson a copy. He replied on September 1, 1820: "Jefferson returns his thanks to Dr. De La Motta for the eloquent discourse.... It excites in him the gratifying reflection that his country had been the first to prove

---

[6] Papers of Thomas Jefferson, Princeton.

[7] Barry Edward O'Meara, *A Voice From St. Helena* (London: Simpkin and Marshall, 1922), 118.

to the world two truths...that man can govern himself, and that religious freedom is the most effective anodyne against religious dissention.... He is happy in the restoration of Jews, particularly, to their social rights, and hopes they will be seen taking their seats on the benches of science as preparatory to their doing the same at the board of government. He salutes Dr. La Motta with sentiments of great respect."[8]

However, Jefferson regarded men like Noah and De La Motta as exceptional Jews, and believed that for Jews as a whole to be respected and treated as equals they needed more secular learning. In historian Arthur Hertzberg's opinion, "Jefferson was thus expressing the view of the mainstream of the Enlightenment, that all men could attain equal place in society, but the 'entrance fee' was that they adopted the ways and the outlook of the 'enlightened.' Jefferson did not consider that a Yiddish-speaking Jew who knew the Talmud was equal in usefulness to society with a classically trained thinker like himself."[9]

He seems to have been reacting to a personal experience, when he expressed his sympathy for Jewish schoolchildren having to listen to the reading of the King James version of the New Testament in public schools, calling it "a cruel addition to the wrongs" Jews had historically suffered, "by imposing on them a course of theological reading which their conscience do not permit them to pursue."[10]

Jefferson died at sixty-seven of amoebic dysentery, causing dehydration, on July 4, 1826 – the same day and within hours of John Adams's death.

---

[8] Karp, *From the Ends of the Earth*, 202–43.

[9] Arthur Hertzberg, *The Jews in America* (New York: Columbia University Press, 1998), 87.

[10] American Jewish Historical Society.

James Madison

1751–1836

✪ Fourth president, 1809–1817
✪ Key champion and author of the United States Bill of Rights
✪ As president, led the country in the War of 1812

At five feet four inches, James Madison was the shortest and lightest president before or since. By contrast his wife, Dolly, who called him "my darling little husband," was a head taller and twenty-one years younger.

A precise, reserved, and scholarly Princeton graduate, Madison spoke in a whisper and weighed little more than a hundred pounds, so that he looked as if a puff of wind would blow him off the planet. But he was no lightweight in explaining why he had favored America becoming a secular state and why he despised Christianity as practiced through the ages.

"During almost fifteen centuries," he wrote, "has the legal establishment of Christianity been on trial. What has been its fruits? More or less in all places, pride and indolence in the Clergy, ignorance and servility in the laity, in both superstition, bigotry and persecution. What influence, in fact, have ecclesiastical establishments had on society? ...On many instances they have been upholding the thrones of political tyranny; in no instance have they been the guardians of the liberties of the people.... A just government, instituted to secure and perpetuate it, needs them not."[1]

Madison was born at Belle Grove Plantation, near Port Conway, Virginia, on March 16, 1751, the oldest of twelve children. His father, also James, was a tobacco planter and, with five thousand acres, the largest landowner in the county. His mother, Eleanor Rose Conway, was the daughter of a successful tobacco planter. Both of his parents were of English descent and brought up James as an Episcopalian.

His mother and grandmother taught him at home as a child, and by the time he was eleven he had read every book in his father's large library. From then until sixteen, a Scot, Donald Robertson, a University of Edinburgh graduate, taught him mathematics, geography, modern and ancient languages, and gave him a love of learning. From sixteen, he studied under the Reverend Thomas Martin, who also taught Jefferson, and at eighteen, in 1769, he entered the College of New Jersey, now known as Princeton. There he studied Latin, Greek, science, geography, mathematics, rhetoric (the effective use of language), history, and philosophy. After graduating, he stayed on at Princeton to learn Hebrew and political philosophy from the college president, John Witherspoon, a Scot who spoke of his pride in the spirit of liberty in America. Witherspoon would become the only clergyman and college president to sign the Declaration of Independence.

The extremely well-educated Madison also studied the law, and as a young lawyer worked with preacher Elijah Craig on constitutional guarantees for religious liberty in Virginia.

When elected to the Virginia State Legislature in 1776, Madison helped his closest friend, Thomas Jefferson, draft

---

[1] The James Madison Papers, Library of Congress, Manuscript Division, http://memory.loc.gov/ammem/collections/madison_papers.

the Statute for Religious Freedom, which disestablished the Church of England and excluded the state from having any compulsory power in religious matters. Before that, anyone in Virginia who questioned the existence of God was liable to be prosecuted.

Although he did not have a law degree, Madison is considered to be the Father of the American Constitution, which was signed into law in 1789.

Winning the presidency with 122 of the 175 electoral votes, he had been in the White House two years when the previously mentioned Mordecai Noah, the first prominent Jewish-American writer, expressed his political aspirations. Noah explained to Madison's secretary of state, James Monroe, that his appointment as a Jew to be an American consul would "prove to foreign powers that our government is not regulated in the appointment of their officers by religious distinction."[2]

Monroe agreed and offered Noah the post of consul to Riga, which he turned down, probably because he didn't speak the language or like the Russian climate. But he did successfully lobby to be the US consul to Tunis, where there were some sixty thousand fellow Jews among the mostly Muslim-Arab population, and the climate was more to his taste. So, in 1813, with President Madison's approval, Monroe appointed Noah the US consul in Tunis.

The small, frail, and sickly president had inherited a problem from the two previous administrations. For years, state-sponsored terrorists known as Barbary pirates, based in Lebanon, Algeria and Tunis, had been plundering and blackmailing American merchantmen in the Mediterranean, costing the American government huge sums in gold to ransom the men and their ships from the pirates.

---

[2] Karp, *From the Ends of the Earth*, 265–67.

Noah was in Tunis when the United States Congress declared war on the pirates and sent Stephen Decatur at the head of a flotilla of nine ships to the dangerous waters. On May 15, 1815, Decatur captured an Algerian frigate, whose captain was killed in the battle. A few days later Decatur entered the port of Algiers and aimed his forty-four guns at the Algerian governor's palace, a tactic that eventually resulted in a peace treaty.

Decatur then headed for Tunis and waited for Noah to join him aboard his flagship *Guerrier*, before handing him a letter from Secretary of State Monroe, which read:

> At the time of your appointment, as Consul to Tunis, it was not known that the religion which you profess would form an obstacle to the exercise of your Consular functions. Recently, information, on which entire reliance may be placed proved that it would produce a very unfavorable effect. In consequence of which, the President (Madison) has deemed it expedient to revoke your commission. On receipt of this letter, therefore, you will consider yourself no longer in the public service. There are some circumstances, too, connected with your accounts, which require a more particular explanation, [and] are not approved by the President. I am very respectfully, sir, Your obedient servant, James Monroe.[3]

Noah was furious and disappointed. He had already successfully carried out a secret mission – paying ransom to free two imprisoned Americans – and justifiably believed that he was an effective consul. So he decided to ignore the note, not tell Decatur that he had been fired, and to continue his efforts to free more American sailors and their ships, as well as to try to negotiate a peace treaty. With Decatur's help he went ashore and got an audience with the Bey of Tunis, the country's leader. Knowing that Tunisians feared the fighting

---

[3] Ibid., 264–65.

prowess of the British navy, Noah told the Bey – stretching the truth – that several American ships within sight and firing-range of the Bey's palace had been won in battle from the British Navy during the War of 1812. Noah then got the Bey to look though his telescope at the nine American fighting ships bristling with guns aimed at the palace. As the Bey focused on the guns, Noah warned him that unless he made his pirates stop attacking American ships and paid $46,000 to recompense American ship-owners for their losses, the flotilla would open fire. The threat worked.

Lebanon also signed a peace treaty with the United States on August 5, 1815, quickly followed by Algeria and Tunis.[4]

Having been fired, Noah reached home bitterly disappointed by his treatment, and spent the next three years trying to restore his reputation, mainly through his book recounting his travels and experiences as the US consul in Tunis, titled *Travels in England, France, Spain and the Barbary States in the Years 1813–1814 and 1815*. In it he pointed out: "My dismissal from office in consequence of religion, has become a document on file in the department of State. This may hereafter produce the most injurious effects establishing a principle, which will go to annihilate the most sacred rights of the citizen."

Three years after he had returned home, on May 6, 1818, Noah sent the now retired President Madison a copy of a speech he gave at the consecration of the Jewish Synagogue in Manhattan. But it seems that his main reason for writing was to get an explanation for being fired as America's consul in Tunis. In a covering letter, he expressed his gratitude to Madison and his fellow Founding Fathers, to whom

> the Jews in the United States owe many of the blessings which they now enjoy... and has created a sincere attachment toward this Country on the part of foreign Jews.... I have not

[4] Ibid., 205.

had the pleasure of seeing you since my return from the Mediterranean. It arose from a belief that my recall was the result of very unfavorable impressions made on your mind; if these impressions have existed, I do sincerely hope that they have been removed by subsequent explanations, for I wish you to be assured...that no infamy arose in Barbary to the public service from my religion as relating to myself, on the contrary my influence and standing abroad was highly creditable and flattering. I could wish not only for the sake of my coreligionists, but for that of your administration, that if my letter of recall cannot be erased from the Books of the Department of State...for as my accounts are adjusted, and a balance struck in my favor, the objections in that letter refer solely to my religion, an objection that I am persuaded you cannot feel, nor authorized others to feel.[5]

Eventually, Noah came to believe that he had not been fired from his job as US consul in Tunis because he was a Jew, but because he had spent too much to ransom American sailors at a time when the American public resented paying the Barbary pirate any ransom. As for the charge that he had spent too much, it turned out that the US government owed Noah money.

Despite his diplomatic disappointment, Noah had a bright future, and was highly respected in religious, political, playwriting, and journalistic circles.

Meanwhile, Noah's cousin, Uriah Levy, was having trouble with his career in the United States Navy, where being Jewish was a big obstacle to promotion. Furthermore, Levy was an outspoken and proud Jew, who responded to anti-Semitic remarks with his fists, or once, with a gun when challenged to

---

5 William Bryk, "The Jewish Commodore," Mr. Beller's Neighborhood, http://mrbellersneighborhood.com/2002/06/the-jewish-commodore; Cecil Roth, ed., *The Standard Jewish Encyclopedia* (Garden City, NY: Doubleday, 1959), 1201, s.v. "Uriah Phillips Levy."

a duel. Levy's turbulent life as a sailor began in 1802 when, at age ten, he ran away from his Philadelphia home in the night to join *The New Jerusalem* as a cabin boy. He left a note to his mother promising to return for his bar mitzvah – a promise he kept two years later.

He spent the next four years at sea, and at seventeen had saved enough to buy a share in a schooner, the *George Washington*, of which the co-owners made him the master. But when he took a brief trip ashore on the Isle of May in the West Indies, the mate and another crew member sailed off with the ship, $2,500, and the cargo of wine.

A British press-gang headed by a Royal Marine sergeant found Levy stranded on the island and arrested him, even though he had papers to prove he was an American sailor. The following conversation then took place:

Sergeant: You don't look like an American to me. You look like a Jew.

Levy: I'm an American and a Jew.

Sergeant: If the Americans have peddlers manning their ships, no wonder they sail so badly.

With that Levy punched the sergeant in the mouth.

He came to aboard a British ship, where an officer handed him a New Testament and ordered him to swear himself into the British Navy.

Levy refused, saying: "I am an American and cannot swear allegiance to your king. And I am a Jew and cannot swear on your Testament, or with my head uncovered."[6]

The frustrated officer took him to Admiral Sir Alexander Cochrane (eventually head of the British navy). Finding Levy's papers in order, the admiral let him go.

After making his way back to the United States, Levy returned to the West Indies where he pursued the men who

---

[6] Ibid.

had stolen his ship, captured them, and took the ringleaders to Boston, Massachusetts for trial. Convicted of "felony and piracy," they were sentenced to death. One was hanged, "but the other, who had some family influence, received a presidential pardon."[7]

When war broke out against the British in 1812, partly in the vain hope of seizing Canada from them, Levy volunteered to serve his country. President Madison accepted his offer. Soon after boarding the *Argus* as an acting lieutenant, he nailed a mezuzah outside his cabin door. His orders were to take American envoy, William Crawford, to France. On the trans-Atlantic journey, Crawford got to like Levy and gave him letters of introduction to several influential men, among them the famous Marquis de Lafayette, who became a friend. After dropping off Crawford in France, Levy and his crew joined the battle against the British, sinking more than twenty enemy merchant ships in the English channel, until the *Argus* was captured and its crew imprisoned in notorious Dartmoor Prison. There they stayed for sixteen months, enduring a winter so cold that the River Thames froze solid. Levy and other officers were allowed to lodge in a village near the prison, on their honor not to escape.

Freed at war's end, and back in the United States, Levy was promoted to lieutenant and stationed aboard the *Franklin*. The camaraderie of fellow sailors during the war was replaced by their resentment that a Jew had been promoted, and the crew behaved as if he didn't exist. Of some four hundred men aboard, the only one to speak with him was the ship's doctor.

During a navy ball, Levy trod on Lieutenant Peter Potter's foot. Despite his apology, Potter called him "a damned Jew!" and challenged him to a duel with pistols. Levy replied,

---

[7] James Morris Morgan, "An American Forerunner of Dreyfus," *Century Illustrated Monthly Magazine* 58 (1899): 756.

"That I am a Jew I neither deny nor regret," and accepted the challenge.

Early next morning, on June 21, 1816, they faced each other in a New Jersey meadow. Levy recited a Hebrew prayer, then suggested that they call off the duel as ridiculous. Potter called him a coward, apparently unaware that Levy was a crack shot. After walking twenty paces they turned and the duel began. Potter aimed to kill, firing four times and just missing each time, while Levy fired into the sky. When Potter's fifth shot grazed Levy's ear, it seemed likely that his next shot would kill or maim Levy. But Potter never made it. For his fifth shot, instead of aiming at the sky, Levy aimed at Potter, who fell dead. Tried for murder, Levy was found not guilty and returned to his post aboard the *Franklin*.[8]

During one of Levy's several court-martials, usually for fighting sailors who had insulted him, a Captain Gregory admitted that "the prejudices existing against him originated in his being a Jew." His own executive officer on the *Vandalia* was quoted as saying, "I'll be damned if this old Jew shall come here to order me about."[9]

James Madison, "The Father of the Constitution," died of heart failure on July 28, 1836, at age eighty-five.

Fortunately for Uriah Levy, the incoming President James Monroe – who as Madison's secretary of state had appointed Levy's cousin, Mordecai Noah, the US consul in Tunis – was to be more supportive than Levy's anti-Semitic shipmates.

[8] Ira Dye, *Uriah Levy: Reformer of the Antebellum Navy* (Gainesville, FL: University Press of Florida, 2006), 57–59, 136–37, 179.

[9] Mel Young, ed., *Uriah Phillips Levy, Captain, USN, and the Naval Court of Inquiry* (Lanham, MD: University Press of America, 2009), 92.

James Monroe

1758–1831

⊛ Fifth president, 1817–1825

⊛ Served as foreign minister to France and Britain, secretary of state, and secretary of war

⊛ Proclaimed the Monroe Doctrine, warning Europeans not to interfere in American affairs

James Monroe's father, Spence, was a planter of Scottish descent with a 600-acre Virginia estate, and his mother, the former Elizabeth Jones, was a Welsh architect's daughter.

Born on April 28, 1758, in Westmoreland County, Virginia, James and his sister and three brothers were raised as Episcopalians. At sixteen, shortly after both of his parents had died, he began to study at the College of William and Mary in Williamsburg, dropping out at eighteen to join Washington's Revolutionary Army as a lieutenant. At the Battle of Trenton, he was carried off the field with a near-fatal shoulder wound. When he recovered he returned to the battle and Washington, recognizing him as "a brave, active, and sensible officer," promoted him to lieutenant colonel.[1]

---

[1] Gary Hart, *James Monroe* (New York: Times Books, 2005), 11–12.

Resigning his commission in 1780, he returned to William and Mary to study law under Thomas Jefferson, who became his lifelong friend.

He was elected to the Continental Congress in 1783, and three years later Monroe married an attractive New York socialite, Elizabeth Kortright, the daughter of a British army officer. They had a good marriage and two daughters.

When Monroe resigned from Congress and moved to Fredericksburg to practice law, he also pursued a political career that led to the White House. He was successively US senator for Virginia, US minister to France, governor of Virginia, envoy to France to negotiate the Louisiana Purchase, minister to Britain, and finally, in 1817, president of the United States.

Monroe was the third president to see potential in the multitalented Jewish American Mordecai Noah, journalist, editor, playwright, and diplomat. He also helped Noah's proud and pugnacious cousin, Uriah Levy, to survive the attacks of his anti-Semitic enemies and rise to unprecedented heights – for a Jew – in the United States Navy.

As mentioned, Noah had convinced Monroe, when he was Madison's secretary of state, that as a Jew he would have rapport with the approximately sixty thousand Jews in Tunis, an Arab nation in North Africa. But Monroe had recalled him from Tunis with the excuse that being a Jew in an Arab nation was a handicap, so that Monroe had been in the awkward position of having hired and fired Noah for the same reason – that he was a Jew. Monroe's explanation at the time was that Muslims had complained about a Jew being the United States consul in Tunis. Noah finally accepted his fate, believing that losing the position had nothing to do with being Jewish, but was probably because, as previously mentioned, he had spent too much in ransom to free American sailors from a Tunisian prison.

Despite the Tunis disappointment, Noah was doing well, as a newspaper editor and successful playwright. That he and President Monroe were finally reconciled is indicated by the twenty-page letter Noah wrote to him on June 23, 1824, asking him to support his friend and presidential hopeful, William Crawford, Monroe's secretary of the Treasury, who was running against Andrew Jackson and John Quincy Adams in the upcoming presidential election. Crawford had an impressive record as a hero of the Revolutionary War, governor of Georgia, minister of war, and minister of finance. But he and Monroe almost came to blows while arguing at a cabinet meeting, and although Crawford apologized, they hardly spoke to each other after that. Crawford lost the election to John Adams's son, John Quincy Adams.[2]

Meanwhile, President Monroe had been making sure that Noah's cousin, Uriah Levy, stayed in the navy. As early as 1818, assigned to the frigate *United States*, Levy was court-martialed for fighting with a fellow lieutenant who had called him "a damned Jew!" Found guilty of ungentlemanly behavior, he was dismissed from the navy. But after President Monroe had taken a look at Levy's colorful record, and sought the advice of the secretary of the navy, he wrote on January 12, 1821, "Although Lieutenant Levy's conduct merited censure, it is considered that his long suspension from duty has been a sufficient punishment for his offense, the sentence of the court is therefore disapproved and he is restored to duty."[3]

Levy was then ordered to the Mediterranean as first lieutenant on the US brig *Spark*, where he stayed for less than a year, until in March 1822 he was ordered back to the US to serve at the Charleston Naval Station. There, during a hurricane, he spotted two men in turbulent water, clinging to a plank and in danger of being swept out to sea. Levy waded into

---

[2] Karp, *From the Ends of the Earth*, 267.

[3] Dye, *Uriah Levy*, 103.

the water and, grabbing the plank, eventually pulled then back to the shore and safety.

In October, he took command of US Gun Boat 158, *The Revenge*, used to suppress slave traders and punish pirates. Near Cuba, a Spanish war ship mistook *The Revenge* for a pirate ship and opened fire. Instead of returning fire, Levy moved close enough to have a shouted conversation with its crew, followed by the arrival of several heavily armed Spanish sailors aboard *The Revenge* to confirm Levy's claim that it was an American military vessel. That accomplished, Levy insisted on a written apology from the Spanish captain for firing on *The Revenge*, or face a duel with him. The Spanish captain ignored Levy's demand and simply left the scene. Soon after, *The Revenge* sank during a storm, but being close to the shore of Belize all the crew were saved.[4]

Having lost his ship, Levy faced a Court of Inquiry that also discussed the incident with the Spanish warship – about which Levy's enemies had called him a coward for not returning fire. President Monroe agreed with the not-guilty verdict on both counts, and wrote to Levy, "The circumstance under which the attack was made [by the Spanish ship on *The Revenge*] would have justified you in resisting it, and that the forbearance shown by you on that occasion was greater than your duty required." Monroe did not agree that Levy's actions were cowardly and was "disposed to pass it by without any particular censure."[5]

It didn't take long before Levy was court-martialed a third time, this time for swearing at another officer, and was again dismissed from the navy. Again, President Monroe supported Levy and had the sentence reduced to suspension without pay for several months. The lack of pay was hardly a punishment, as Levy was wealthy from

[4] Ibid., 120.

[5] Ibid., 131–32.

real-estate investments. When the sentence was completed, he returned to the navy. Two years later, he was again court-martialed for calling a fellow officer "a great many unsavory names." On this occasion his commanding officer merely reprimanded him.[6]

A proud and pugnacious man with no tolerance for anti-Semitism, Levy was also a man with a mission. Revolted by the common practice of flogging in the navy, he maintained that it was not only ineffective as punishment, but embittered the victims, and he determined to have it abolished.

James Monroe, the man who made Uriah Levy's astonishing career possible, died at seventy-three of tuberculosis in New York City, on July 4, 1831, ten months after his wife had died. He was the last of the five Founding Fathers and, along with Jefferson and Adams, the third president to die on July 4. He was succeeded by his secretary of state, who was also former president John Adams's son, John Quincy Adams.

---

[6] William Bryk, "The Jewish Commodore," Mr. Beller's Neighborhood, http://mrbellersneighborhood.com/2002/06/the-jewish-commodore.

John Quincy Adams

1767–1848

✪ Sixth president, 1825–1829

✪ Son of former president John Adams and Abigail Adams

✪ Served as an American diplomat,
senator, and secretary of state

John Quincy Adams was evidently a remarkable diplomat. George Washington appointed him his US ambassador to the Netherlands in 1794 and to Portugal in 1796. His own father, on succeeding Washington, made him his US ambassador to Russia in 1797. President Madison sent him back there in 1809, and to the United Kingdom in 1814. Madison's successor, President Monroe, made him secretary of state.

It didn't hurt that Adams spoke French and Dutch fluently, and that as a fourteen year old he had accompanied US envoy Francis Dana to Russia as his secretary and interpreter. Dana's task was to persuade the Russian government to recognize the US government. After more than a year the Russian government had not received Dana, so Quincy left and joined his father in Paris.

Born to John and Abigail Adams, in what is now Quincy, Massachusetts, on July 11, 1767, he followed in his father's footsteps to an extraordinary extent, not only by becoming president, but in adopting many of his ideas. Both were Harvard graduates and lawyers, both had been ministers to Holland and England, and they traveled much of the world together. They even looked alike: bald and overweight. They were also deeply religious Unitarians who admired Jews and sympathized with those who dreamed of a return to their ancient homeland. As John Quincy Adams wrote in his diary for December 20, 1834, after reading a speech given to members of the Hebrew Orphan Society in Charleston, South Carolina: "It is a good example of Jewish tenacity, coupled with a laudable zeal of charity."[1]

Tenacity was one of his own characteristics. In the White House, he rose each morning at five, read the Bible, and went either for a walk or for a swim in the Potomac. Once someone stole his clothes and the naked, dripping president persuaded a boy on the river bank to hurry to the White House to bring back fresh clothes.

John Quincy married Louisa Catherine Johnson, daughter of a businessman, in London on July 26, 1797, when he was the US ambassador to Russia, and they had three sons and a daughter.

During the first year of his presidency, he stated in a letter to Mordecai Noah – the former Jewish-American diplomat in Tunis – that he (like his father) supported the "rebuilding of Judea as an independent nation."[2]

---

[1] The Diaries of John Quincy Adams, volume 39, p. 463, Massachusetts Historical Society, http://www.masshist.org/jqadiaries/diaries.cfm.

[2] James H. Hudson, *The Founders on Religion* (Princeton, NJ: Princeton University Press, 2007), 127.

Now Noah had a more immediate plan: until they could return to their ancient homeland, he intended to provide the world's Jews with a safe and welcoming home in America – a city of their own on Grand Island in the Niagara River, near Buffalo. The thousands of acres he bought from the state were currently thickly wooded and inhabited by bears, foxes, and raccoons. He had already named this Promised Land in America "Ararat" – after the mountain on which Noah's ark is said to have come to rest after the flood – and to publicize his visionary venture he had a replica of Noah's ark built, loaded with wild animals, then floated down the river from Buffalo to New York City. To inaugurate Ararat he rented a Buffalo church and used his knowhow as a successful playwright to enthrall and inform his audience of reporters, politicians, socialites, and curious locals, among them Seneca Indian Chief Red Jacket, who arrived by boat.

Ararat, he said, as a city of Jewish refuge would be protected by the Constitution and laws of the United States and at first led by him for four years, after which a new leader of its government would be elected every four years. To Noah's disappointment, leaders of European Jewry declined to endorse his plan, and the European Jewish press ridiculed the idea. The Grand Rabbi of Cologne, Germany, wrote to Noah on behalf of himself and London's leading rabbis: "God alone knows the epoch with any political-national design is forbidden, as an act of high treason against the Israeliish [sic] restoration; and He alone will make it known to the whole universe, by signs entirely unequivocal." As for American Jews, they were apparently happy where they were. Still, Noah pressed on with his plan for eight years, until 1833 when he sold Ararat to a businessman who wanted the land for its timber.[3]

---

[3] "Mordecai M. Noah and the Mormon Zion," Spalding Research Project, http://olivercowdery.com/gathering/ararat1.htm.

Noah's sailor cousin, Lieutenant Uriah Levy, had also been having a tough time: frequently under arrest and always under suspicion by his anti-Semitic shipmates. In 1827, when his ship was docked for repairs near Rio de Janeiro, he saw a Brazilian press-gang in the harbor seize an American sailor. When the sailor called for help, a fellow American, Midshipman Moores, rushed to his aid but was pushed back by a Brazilian admiral. Moores moved in again and decked the admiral. That's when Lieutenant Levy hurried ashore and joined the fight. As a Brazilian officer slashed at Moores with a saber, Levy deliberately took the blow, which dislocated his finger. Midshipman Moores said later that in warding off the saber, Levy had saved his life. Levy talked the Brazilians into letting him, the American sailor, and Midshipman Moores go free.

Soon afterwards, the Brazilian emperor, having heard of the fight, visited the navy yard. He spotted Levy with his arm in a sling and said that he'd like to have such a brave officer in his own navy. He even offered him the command of a new sixty-gun frigate that had just arrived from the United States. Levy declined the offer, saying that he "loved his own service so well that he would rather serve it as a cabin-boy than as a captain in any other service in the world."[4]

It seemed obvious that the US Navy didn't want him, even as a cabin boy, because he faced his fifth court-martial that same year, when once more he was dismissed from the US Navy. As a civilian, he increased his considerable fortune in real-estate ventures. But he was determined to return to the navy.

The year Levy was dismissed from the navy, 1827, Quincy Adams left the White House, and became a Massachusetts

---

[4] Dye, *Uriah Levy*, 145–46; and Morgan, "An American Forerunner of Dreyfus," 797–800.

congressman. He still took a friendly interest in Jews, and when the British House of Commons was debating a bill in 1833 to give British Jews the right to vote, he wrote to Joseph Hulme, a British MP, encouraging him to support the bill. During the debate, Hulme, a Liberal representing Middlesex, stood in the House and said: "Look to other countries – look to France – look to America. I have a letter in my hand from Mr. John Quincy Adams, the late president of the United States, in which he bears testimony to the advantage of the admission of Jews to full civil rights and advantages, that no set of men can be better subjects." Although the bill passed in the House of Commons, it needed the approval of the conservative House of Lords, which took another quarter of a century.[5]

On February 23, 1848, having been a congressman for eighteen years, eighty-one-year-old former president John Quincy Adams suffered a stroke and collapsed and died in the House of Representatives.

---

[5] *Hansard*, April 17, 1833, vol. XVII, column 242; *Publications of the American Jewish Historical Society*, issue 22, http://www.ajhs.org/.

Andrew Jackson

1767–1845

- ✪ Seventh president, 1829–1837
- ✪ Major general in the War of 1812
- ✪ Nicknamed "Old Hickory" because of his toughness and aggressive personality

Andrew Jackson was brought up on the western edge of the South Carolina wilderness by his widowed mother. He was born in 1767 to Scots-Irish immigrants who had recently emigrated from Ireland. His father died of an accident at twenty-nine, before Andrew was born, and his mother died when he was fourteen. He taught himself law – between cockfighting, horseracing, and hell-raising – but despite his wild youth he was an avid Bible reader and often attended Presbyterian church services.

As a boy during the Revolutionary War, Jackson served as a courier for the patriots, and at age thirteen he was captured by the British. Because Andrew refused to clean a British officer's boots, the officer slashed at him with his sword, leaving a permanent scar on his hand.

After the war, at age twenty-nine, he was admitted to the North Carolina bar.

A tough, aggressive major general in the Tennessee militia, he became a national hero in the 1812 war against the British. He led successful attacks against the Creek Indians, Britain's allies, and defeated the British forces at New Orleans.

As a battle-scarred, lean six-footer with red hair, blue eyes, and a wicked temper, he first served in the House of Representatives, then in the Senate, before winning the presidency in 1838. (Jackson founded the Democratic Party, championed the underdog and was FDR's and Truman's favorite president.)

When tens of thousands of uninvited guests barged into the White House to witness his swearing in, he escaped from the mob by leaving through a window. To discourage future unwelcome visitors, he installed a resident parrot that cursed profusely.

President Jackson had inadvertently married his wife, Rachel Donelson Robards, before her divorce from her first husband became final, and he fought duels with men – killing one of them – who accused him of running off with another man's wife.

One of his most successful political fights was against the Rothschild family's influence in the Second Bank of the United States, not because they were Jews but because he resented European influence in America's financial affairs. It was a bad mistake, because it led to the biggest financial depression since the creation of the United States.

He indicated that he was pro-Jewish in 1829, the first year of his presidency, by appointing Mordecai Noah, the former US consul in Tunis, to be overseer of the port of New York, an important job he held for four years.[1]

While Noah still held that job in 1833, President Jackson sent Noah's naval officer cousin, Uriah Levy, recently restored to the navy, to deliver dispatches to the American minister in

---

[1] John and Alice Durant, *Pictorial History of American Presidents* (New York: A. S. Barnes, 1955), 59–60.

France. On his arrival, the minister invited Levy to a dinner to celebrate the Fourth of July. During the meal, when someone proposed to toast the United States president, a few guests groaned or hissed. Incensed, Levy slapped one in the face with his gloves and challenged him and others to duels. They all wisely backed down – he was a sure shot – and apologized.[2]

By 1837, the last year of Jackson's presidency, Levy had been court-martialed five times, but repeated attempts by his enemies to have him permanently dismissed from the navy had failed.

Jackson was succeeded as president by his vice president, Martin Van Buren. After which, he retired to his Tennessee home, where he lived for eight years before dying at seventy-eight, on June 8, 1845. His death was attributed to thrombosis, exacerbated by a musket bullet that had been left in his lung.

---

[2] Morgan, "An American Forerunner of Dreyfus," 796–800.

Martin Van Buren

1782–1862

- ✪ Eighth president, 1837–1841
- ✪ Secretary of state, ambassador to Britain, and vice president under Andrew Jackson
- ✪ A native Dutch speaker, he was the only president for whom English was a second language

The fifty-five-year-old son of a New York state tavern keeper had been a widower for eighteen years when he and his four sons moved into the White House. He was nicknamed the "Little Magician" – little because he was less than five feet six inches tall, and magician because of his political prowess as President Andrew Jackson's secretary of state, minister to England, and vice president.

Van Buren was born to Abraham and Maria Van Buren, both of Dutch descent, on December 5, 1782, at Kinderhook, New York, and brought up in the Dutch Reformed Church. He studied law from the age of fourteen and after six years was admitted to the bar. At twenty-five, in 1807, he married his childhood sweetheart, also a distant relative, Hannah Hoes, and they had four sons and a daughter.

He began to take an active part in New York politics at age seventeen. At age thirty-three, in 1815, he was New York state attorney general; in 1821, its US senator; and in 1829 its governor – but only for three months, until President Andrew Jackson appointed him secretary of state. Two years later, Jackson made him his ambassador to Great Britain, and in 1833, his vice president.

As president – the first one not to have been born a British citizen – he drove through the swampy, malaria-ridden streets of Washington, where pigs and chickens freely roamed, passing open sewers, in an olive-green coach with elegantly dressed footmen aboard, especially on his Sunday trip to attend Dutch Reformed Church services.

During Van Buren's second year as president, the much-court-martialed Jewish naval officer Uriah Levy took command of USS *Vandalia*, and flouted navy rules by banning flogging on his ship, replacing it with more humane punishments such as restriction of liberty, extra duties, and solitary confinement. As one of his officers attested, "There was less corporal punishment in the *Vandalia* under Captain Levy than in any ship I sailed in, except the *Preble*, which I sailed in later."[1]

Meanwhile, President Martin Van Buren had been hearing of the desperate plight of Jews in Syria where they were being tortured and killed. In 1840, news trickled through to America that, in response to false and atrocious rumors, Syrians were torturing and murdering Jews. When he heard of it, Rabbi Isaac Lesser of Philadelphia led a deputation of Jewish leaders from New York, Philadelphia, Richmond, and Cincinnati, to appeal for the president's help.

The arrest, torture, and killing of Jews in Damascus, Syria's capital, had followed the disappearance of a Jesuit priest, Father Tomaso de Camangiano, and his servant, Ibrahim

---

[1] Dye, *Uriah Levy*, 174.

Amara. When a search failed to find them, Tomaso's fellow priests accused the Jews of killing the men to use their blood in Passover matzos. This type of "blood libel," as Jews called it, began in medieval times, when Christians spread the false and fanciful rumor that Jews used Christian children's blood in unleavened bread to celebrate Passover, a celebration of the escape of the ancient Jews from slavery in Egypt. The blood-libel first arose in Norwich, England in 1144, and the rumor quickly spread throughout the Christian and Islamic worlds, becoming a rallying cry to incite and justify anti-Jewish pogroms.

In fact, not only does the Torah forbid observant Jews from consuming blood, they even refrain from eating rare meat.

Father Tomaso had been last seen on his way to the Jewish quarter in Damascus to deliver a leaflet to a synagogue. So the police searched the Jewish quarter, and even dug up graves in their hunt for the missing men. Their biggest find was a leaflet apparently left by Tomaso in a barber shop near the synagogue, and the police arrested the Jewish barber, Suleiman Negrin. Under torture, he said that seven of the most distinguished leaders of the Jewish community in Damascus, including several rabbis, had handcuffed Father Tomaso, then offered Negrin gold and silver to kill the priest. When he refused, according to Syrian court records, the rabbis "threw Father Tomaso on the ground, put his neck on a basin, and slaughtered him, careful that not a drop of blood was spilled. Then they moved him to another room, burned his clothes, and cut his body to pieces, which they put into a sack and threw into the sewage near the Jewish quarter."[2]

After their arrest, the seven accused men were burned and beaten, had their teeth pulled out, were immersed in water

---

[2] Judith Apter Klinghoffer, *The Damascus Affair, Descriptive Overview, "Blood Libel,"* History News Network, Trial transcript, and correspondence with Klinghoffer, www.facinghistory.org/node/239.

until they almost drowned, then made to stand for thirty-six hours, deprived of food, water, and sleep.

Under torture, Rabbi David Harari's servant confessed that Tomaso's servant had also been murdered in the presence of the seven Jewish leaders.

Syria's Sherif Pasha widened the net by ordering sixty-five boys at a Hebrew school, one as young as five, to be imprisoned, and fed only bread and water before they were interrogated. When one confessed to taking part in the priest's murder, seventy more Jewish men, including all the Jewish butchers and grave diggers in the city, were imprisoned.

Rabbi Moses Salomon's interrogators whipped him on the soles of his feet, drove thorns between his fingernails and toenails, paraded him through hostile street crowds, and told him that he was about to be decapitated.

Sherif Pasha reprieved him from the death sentence at the last moment, only to have him thrown into a tank of icy water. When he rose to the surface gasping for air, he was beaten unconscious. After he recovered consciousness, his torturers tied a rope around his genitals and dragged him around, finally tying him to two poles, and throwing him into the air to fall on the stone pavement.

Despite these horrendous tortures, the rabbi never incriminated anyone.

However, another rabbi, Moses Abulafia, subjected to similar torture while his wife and daughter looked on, not only confessed but converted to Islam and helped the prosecution.

Isaac Iccioto, an Austrian citizen who had escaped capture, sought refuge in the Austrian consulate. Despite Syrian pressure, Austrian consul Giovanni Meriato refused to turn him over to the Syrians, saying, according to Syrian court records, that the Arabs' methods were inhuman and barbaric and that they "were known for their brutalities and total disrespect for truth and justice." James de Rothschild, the honorary

Austrian consul in Paris, had already appealed to the French government to intervene, but it declined; he then reported the Damascus Affair to the European press. When the news reached America it spurred protest meetings by American Jews in several cities.

A New York Jewish delegation assured President Van Buren that if the priest and his servant had been murdered it was not "committed by the Jews of Damascus, or those of any other part of the world for the purpose of using blood or any part of a human being in the ceremonies of our religion." They handed him a petition that read in part, "The moral influence of the Chief Magistrate of the United States would be, under Heaven, the best aid we could invoke for the protection of our persecuted brethren under the Mohammedan domain."

Van Buren moved fast after he obtained confirmation of the horrors in Damascus from his secretary of state, John Forsyth. He first needed to pinpoint who was in charge of the country. Syria had been ruled by Turks since 1515 as part of the Ottoman Empire, but Egypt had recently defeated Turkey in battle, and since 1839 Syria had been governed by Egypt's Muhammed Ali.

So the American president instructed his consuls in both Alexandria, Egypt, and Constantinople, Turkey, to tell Muhammed Ali that the Americans were horrified by the "extravagant charges strikingly similar to those which, in less enlightened ages, were made pretexts for the persecution and spoliation of these unfortunate people." By contrast, Van Buren pointed out that America's liberal institutions "place upon the same footing, the worshippers of God, of every faith and form." This, he explained, was why he was intervening "on behalf of the oppressed and persecuted race, among whose kindred are found some of the most worthy and patriotic of [American] citizens."[3]

---

[3] Ibid.

On behalf of Van Buren, Secretary of State Forsyth wrote to John Giddon, the US consul in Egypt, on August 14, 1840:

> In common with all civilized nations, the people of the United States have learned with horror the atrocious crimes [against] the Jews of Damascus, the cruelties of which they have been the victims. The President fully participates in the public feeling, and he cannot refrain from expressing equal surprise and pain, that in this advanced age, such unnatural practices should be ascribed to any portion of the religious world, and such barbarous measures be resorted to, in order to compel the confession of imputed guilt; the offenses of which these unfortunate people are charged, resembles too much those which, in less enlightened time, were made the pretexts of fanatical prosecution or mercenary extortion, to permit a doubt that they are equally unfounded. The President has witnessed, with the most lively satisfaction, the effort of several of the Christian Governments of Europe, to suppress or mitigate these horrors, and he has learned with no common gratification, their partial success."[4]

Three Englishmen – Foreign Minister Lord Palmerston; the Sheriff of London, Sir Moses Haim Montefiore; and missionary John Nicolayson, head of the English Protestant mission in Jerusalem – also led a delegation to meet Muhammed Ali. Palmerston expressed his "deep sympathy with the Jewish nation," and "called on the British government to exercise its merciful interposition and powerful influence to help the victims and to prevent the recurrence of atrocities."[5]

Palmerston also "strongly" recommended that the Turks "hold out every just encouragement to the Jews of Europe to return to Palestine," and he "gave instructions to all the British

---

[4] Daniel Pipes, "On Behalf of Van Buren," *New York Post,* June 15, 2003; and Jonathan Frankel, *The Damascus Affair: "Ritual Murder," Politics, and the Jews in 1840* (New York: Cambridge University Press, 1997), 131.

[5] Albert M. Hyamson, *Palestine: The Rebirth of an Ancient People* (New York: Knopf, 1917), 54.

representatives in the Levant and Syria to place the Jews under their special protection," including non-British Jews. The British government also instructed James Finn, the British consul in Jerusalem, to protect "foreign Jews whose own Consuls refused to act for them." This was of some comfort to Russian Jews who had recently arrived in Palestine.[6]

Negotiations dragged on for weeks while mobs attacked Jewish institutions throughout the Middle East. Finally, on August 28, the Syrians agreed to the unconditional release and recognition of the innocence of the surviving nine prisoners out of the thirteen arrested. Several survivors were permanently crippled. Soon after, in Constantinople, Montefiore persuaded the Sultan to issue an edict to stop the spread of "blood libel" accusations throughout the Ottoman Empire. It read in part: "For the love we bear to our subjects we cannot permit the Jewish nation, whose innocence for the crime alleged against them is evident, to be worried and tormented as a consequence of accusations which have not the least foundation in truth."[7] Many Jews who had escaped from Damascus in fear for their lives never returned to Syria.

It was the first time that American Jews as a group had come to the rescue of threatened and persecuted Jews overseas. As Philadelphia's Rabbi Leeser remarked, "The Jews [of other lands] are not aliens among us, and we hail the Israelite as a brother, whether his home is in the torrid zone, or where the poles encircle the earth with impenetrable fetters of icy coldness."[8]

The fate of Father Tomaso and his servant is still a mystery.

At the end of his term in office, Van Buren retired to his Kinderhook, New York, home, where at age seventy-nine, on July 24, 1862, he died of bronchial asthma.

---

[6] Ibid., 55.

[7] Ibid.

[8] Ibid.

William Henry Harrison

1773–1841

- ❂ Ninth president, 1841
- ❂ Defeated Shawnee Indians in the battle of Tippecanoe
- ❂ Died in the White House after thirty-two days as president

As president, William Henry Harrison had little time to interact with Jews or with anyone else, because he was in office for just thirty-two days.

The father of five boys and four girls, he had enjoyed a distinguished political career and been a general during the War of 1812 against Britain.

After taking his oath of office, he gave a speech lasting one hour and 45 minutes on a cold January day, during a snowstorm, without wearing a hat or coat. He died of pneumonia thirty-two days later. His wife, Anna Tuthill Symmes, a judge's daughter, got the news of her sixty-eight-year-old husband's death on April 4, 1841, as she was about to leave home to join him in the White House.

Ironically, he had once planned to be a doctor, briefly studying medicine at the University of Pennsylvania, under the famous physician Dr. Benjamin Rush.

John Tyler

1790–1862

- ✪ Tenth president, 1841–1845
- ✪ Congressman, senator, and governor of Virginia
- ✪ William Henry Harrison's vice president, he assumed the presidency after Harrison's death

Harrison's vice president, John Tyler, was on his knees shooting marbles with a few of his many children in their Williamsburg, Virginia, home, when told that the president was dead. So he left immediately for Washington with his family and the family pets, two Italian wolfhounds and a greyhound.

A few days after his inauguration – his inaugural address cautiously limited to eight short paragraphs – he was criticized by Jacob Ezekiel, a prominent Jew in Richmond, Virginia, for using the words "Christian nation" in asking Americans to observe a day of mourning for the late president. In his reply on April 19, 1841, Tyler said that in using the word Christian he had not intended to exclude any of his fellow citizens. He wrote:

> The last paragraph is an invitation to all and excludes the idea of any especial invocation. For the people of whom you are one, I can feel no other than profound respect. The wisdom

which flowed from the lips of your prophets has in times past, and will continue for all time to come, to be a refreshing fountain to mankind – while Holy records bear witness of Divine favors and protection of the God of Abraham and of Isaac and of Jacob, God of the Christian and Israelite, to his chosen people – may I then hope, sir, that this explanation will remove all difficulties, and that your voice and the voices of all your brethren will ascend to our Common Father in supplication and prayer on the day I have suggested.[1]

James Tyler was born near Charles City, Virginia, on March 29, 1790. His father, also John, a friend of Thomas Jefferson, was a Virginia tobacco farmer and circuit court judge of English descent. His mother, Mary Armistead, died when he was seven. After graduating from William and Mary Preparatory School, he studied law at its college and at nineteen, in 1809, was admitted to the bar. Although raised as an Episcopalian, he, like several of the Founding Fathers, especially Jefferson, was a strong advocate of religious freedom and the separation of church and state.

After a five-year courtship, he married Letitia Christian in 1819, on his twenty-ninth birthday, and she gave him four daughters and three sons. Two years after her death in 1842, Tyler married Julia Gardiner, who gave him three daughters and five sons.

As president, he approved the appointment of Walter Cresson as American consul in Palestine. A Quaker from Philadelphia, during his four years in Jerusalem, from 1844 to 1848, Cresson not only converted to Judaism, but was circumcised, and changed his name to Michael Boiaz Israel ben Abraham. On his return to the United States as a Jew, his relatives thought he had gone mad and tried to have him

---

[1] President Tyler's letter to Jacob Ezekiel, *Publications of the American Jewish Historical Society*, no. 9 (1901): 161–62.

committed to a mental asylum. He escaped that fate by returning to Palestine, "where he lived a strictly Orthodox life, and
endeavored to promote Jewish colonization."[2] Cresson also
"proposed to relieve the existing distress among the Jews of
Palestine by employing them on the land, and the oppression
of Jews elsewhere by enabling them to settle in the Holy Land.
With that in mind he began agricultural work in the Valley of
Rephaim." Although his project eventually failed "it was of
considerable educational value and left seeds behind which
fructified."[3]

What President Tyler thought of Cresson is not on the
record, but what is on the record is Tyler's remarkable response
to the activities of another Jewish American, the naval officer,
Uriah Levy.

In 1837, after twenty years as a lieutenant, Levy had
been promoted to master commander, and the following year
took command of the USS *Vandalia*. But, because he continued his humane policy of banning flogging on his ship, he
was court-martialed for the sixth time. A Lieutenant George
Mason Hooe charged him with "scandalous and cruel conduct
unbecoming to an officer and gentleman." Instead of flogging
a sixteen-year-old boy on the ship for mimicking an officer,
Hooe charged that Levy had ordered that the boy be tied to a
gun, with his trousers lowered, to allow a mixture of tar and
parrot feathers to be applied to his buttocks. Levy was found
guilty of the charge and dismissed from the navy.

Fortunately, his dismissal was brought to President Tyler's
attention. After reading Levy's rocky record of facing and surviving five court-martials, Tyler decided that while Levy "had
resorted to an entirely disgraceful punishment, his motives
were good, the punishment drew no blood and caused no

[2] Cecil Roth, ed., *The Standard Jewish Encyclopedia* (Garden City, NY: Doubleday,
1959), 510.

[3] Hyamson, *Palestine*, 52–55, 174.

harm." Consequently, he reduced Levy's punishment to twelve-months' suspension and to everyone's astonishment, Levy included, promoted him to captain.[4]

President Tyler showed his knowledge of Jewish history when he replied to a letter from Joseph Simpson, a prominent Baltimore Jew, on July 3, 1843. Simpson had written to Tyler about the separation of church and state, and objected to General-in-Chief Scott, of the US Army, as a representative of the state, presiding at a conference of Christian missionaries.

In his reply, President Tyler, well aware of the persecution of Jews abroad, wrote:

> Whether General Scott is to preside over the meeting it will not and cannot be in his character as General in Chief of the army.... He will necessarily for the time being lay aside his sword and epaulets, and appear...as a distinguished citizen, but in no other light than as a citizen. Was he a Hebrew and of the same tribe with yourself, his right to preside in your synagogue if permitted or required by your laws would in no way affect him in his military character; nor would it make him obnoxious to the censure of the Government for so doing. The United States have adventured upon a great and noble experiment, which is believed to have been hazarded in the absence of all previous precedent – that of total separation of Church and State. No religious establishment by law exists among us. The conscience is left free from restraint and each is permitted to worship his Maker after his own judgment. The offices of Government are open alike to all....

> The Hebrew persecuted and downtrodden in other regions takes up his abode among us with none to make him afraid. He may boast, as well he can, of his descent from the

---

[4] Guide to the Uriah P. Levy Collection, Processed by Rachel Pollack, American Jewish Historical Society, Internet, 2003. Flogging in the Navy, Navy Department Library.

Patriarchs of Old – of his wise men in council, and strong men in battle. He may ever more turn his eye to Jude, resting with confidence on the promise made him of his restoration to that Holy Land and he may worship the God of his fathers, after the matter that that worship was conducted by Aaron and his successors in the priesthood, and the aegis of the Government is over him to defend and protect him. Such is the great experiment which we have tried, and such are the happy fruits which have resulted from it; our system of free government would be imperfect without it. The body may be oppressed and manacled and yet survive; but if the mind of man be fettered, its energies and faculties perish; and what remains is of the earth, earthy. Mind should be free as the light or the air. While I remain connected with the Government be assured Sir, that as far as the Executive action is concerned, the guarantees of the Constitution in that great particular will know no diminution.

For your kind expression of goodwill towards me personally, I beg you to accept my thanks, along with my best wishes for your health and happiness.

John Tyler[5]

When his term was up in 1845, Tyler became chancellor of his alma mater, the College of William and Mary, before retiring to his Virginia farm where, in 1862, at the age of seventy-one, he died of a stroke.

---

[5] "Correspondence of President Tyler: Religious Freedom," *William and Mary College Quarterly Historical Magazine* 13, no. 1 (July 1904): 1–3.

James Knox Polk

1795–1849

- ✪ Eleventh president, 1845–1849
- ✪ Congressman and governor of Tennessee and Speaker of the House
- ✪ Oversaw the opening of the US Naval Academy, the Smithsonian Institution, and the issuance of the first US postage stamps

Support by American Jews for Democrats grew during Van Buren's presidency, largely because of his coming to the aid of the tortured Syrian Jews in the Damascus Affair. The support continued under President James Knox Polk.

His time in the White House was largely spent in increasing the size of the United States, fighting the Mexicans to win Texas as the fruit of war, as well as successfully negotiating with the British for Oregon. However, Polk briefly met the father of Reform Judaism in the United States, Rabbi Isaac Mayer Wise, who also recalled in his autobiography, *Reminiscences*, that on his ten-day visit to Washington, he was the first visitor to arrive in the Senate to watch senators in action, and the last to leave.[6]

---

[6] Isaac M. Wise, *Reminiscences* (Cincinnati, OH: Leo Wise and Company, 1901), 71.

James Polk was the first of ten children, all brought up as Presbyterians. His father, Samuel, was a prosperous farmer of Scotch-Irish descent, and his mother, Jane Knox, was a descendant of the brother of the Scottish religious reformer, John Knox. As a boy, James was home schooled before attending the University of North Carolina, where he graduated with honors in 1818.

After studying law he was admitted to the bar in 1820. His first case was defending his own father, charged with fighting in public, and he got him off lightly – with a $1 fine.

At age twenty-eight, in 1824, he married twenty-year-old Sarah Childress, who was of great help to him throughout his political career, as a Tennessee congressman, Speaker of the House, and governor of Tennessee.

In 1845, during the first year of Polk's presidency, Mordecai Noah, the former diplomat and successful playwright and newspaper editor, published his *Discourse on the Restitution of Jews*. Anticipating Theodor Herzl by half a century, he wrote:

> I confidently believe in the restitution of the Jews and I consider it my duty to call upon the free people of this country to aid in any effort which it may be prudent to adopt.... Where can we plead the cause of independence for the children of Israel with greater confidence than in the cradle of liberty?... Here we can unfurl the standard and seventeen millions of people will say, "God is with you, go forth and repossess the land of your fathers." We have advocated the independence of South American republics. We have combated for the independence of Greece...if these nations were entitled to our sympathies, how much more powerful are the claims of that beloved people, before whom the Almighty swore they should be his people. The Jews are in a most favorable position to repossess the promised land, and to organize a free and liberal government.

The first step is to solicit from the Sultan of Turkey permission for Jews to purchase and hold the land. Those who desire to repose in the Holy Land will be aided by societies to reach their haven of repose. The valley of the Jordan will be filled by agriculturalists from Germany, Poland and Russia.[7]

The fifty-three-year-old President Polk was succeeded by President Zachary Taylor, and that same year, 1849, Polk is believed, while on a goodwill tour of New Orleans, to have contracted cholera from which he died.

His last words were to his wife: "I love you Sarah, for all eternity I love you."

She lived for another forty years.[8]

Harry Truman considered Polk a great president because he said what he intended to do and then did it.[9]

---

[7] Mordecai Noah, *Discourse on the Restoration of the Jews* (New York: Harper and Brothers, 1845); and Karp, *From the Ends of the Earth*, 268.

[8] *First Lady Biography: Sarah Polk,* National First Ladies' Library, Canton, Ohio.

[9] Robert H. Ferrell, *Off the Record: The Private Papers of Harry S. Truman* (Columbia, MO: University of Missouri Press, 1997), 390.

Zachary Taylor

1784–1850

⊛ Twelfth president, 1849–1850

⊛ Known as "Old Rough and Ready," he was a military leader in the War of 1812, Black Hawk War, Seminole War, and Mexican-American War

⊛ Died sixteen months after taking office

Zachary Taylor, James Madison's second cousin and a kinsman of Robert E. Lee, was a professional soldier for forty years, reaching the rank of brigadier general. He also owned a flourishing Mississippi cotton plantation and 118 slaves. As president, shortly before his death, he bought a sugar plantation with sixty-four more slaves.[10]

But he spent most of his life as a soldier, notably at Monterey in the war against Mexico, which gained the US an enormous amount of territory – to the great satisfaction of those who believed in America's Manifest Destiny: its God-given right to expand "from sea to shining sea." Jewish-American Lieutenant Henry Seeligson played a conspicuous part during

---

[10] *Encyclopedia Americana* (Scholastic Library Publishing, 2008), s.v. "Taylor, Zachary."

General Taylor's successful attack on Monterey, and the general congratulated him for his outstanding bravery.[11]

Another notable Jewish fighter of the time – though not in battle – was the previously mentioned Rabbi Isaac Mayer Wise. He fought in the Albany, New York, Beth El Synagogue, with its Orthodox president, Louis Spanier, over their respective religious views.[12] When Spanier punched him in the nose, as Wise recalled, "the people acted like furies. The Poles and Hungarians struck out like wild men. The young people jumped down from the choir galleries to protect me. Within two minutes the whole assembly was a fighting mass. The sheriff and posse who were summoned were belabored and forced out."[13] Wise later moved to Temple B'nai Jeshurun in Cincinnati.

Zachary Taylor's planter father, Richard, a graduate of the College of William and Mary, had served with Washington in the Revolutionary War. His mother, Sarah Dabney Strother, had been taught by tutors educated in Europe. Both were Episcopalians, of English-Scottish descent.

Born near Barboursville, Virginia, on November 24, 1784, Zachary was the youngest of three sons in a family of nine children. He had a spotty education, taught occasionally by tutors. The family soon moved from Virginia to a ten-thousand-acre plantation in Louisville, Kentucky.

Zachary chose the army as his career, married Margaret Mackall Smith in 1810, and they had one son and five daughters.

He was nominated for president as a hero of the Mexican-American War, and as a soldier whose efforts had helped to give the United States new territory in California, Nevada,

---

[11] Simon Wolf, *The American Jew as Patriot, Soldier and Citizen* (Philadelphia, 1895), 75.

[12] Max I. Dimont, *The Jews in America* (New York: Simon & Schuster, 1978), 123–24.

[13] Wise, *Reminiscences*, 134–137.

Utah, and parts of Wyoming, Colorado, Arizona, and New Mexico. He beat his political rivals, Louis Cass and Martin Van Buren, with over 47 percent of the popular vote.

As president, he welcomed the pugnacious Rabbi Isaac Mayer Wise to the White House for what turned out to be a friendly conversation. As Wise tells it:

> I visited William H. Seward [then a Republican US Senator for New York, an anti-slavery activist, and later Abraham Lincoln's Secretary of State] on the first morning of my arrival in Washington. He treated me like an old friend and declared his willingness to render me any service or favor.... I only asked the privilege of visiting him occasionally and being introduced by him to prominent personages. "Let us begin with this at once," said he. After changing his clothes, he invited me to walk with him. He offered me his arm, walked with me from the hotel to the White House, chatted in the most cordial manner imaginable...took me through the Treasury Building, then to the White House in the presence of the President....

> Seward hesitated at the door, then a voice within bade us enter. A fire was burning in the grate opposite the door, and a man sat in the front of the fire, with his back to the door. Without turning around to see who it might be, he called out, "Step up closer, gentlemen, it is cold today." We took up our positions on either side of the grate, and I knew that I was standing before the President. He extended his hand. He said, "I suppose you never have seen a President of the United States, and for that reason you have paid me a visit."

> "I beg your pardon, Your Excellency," said I, "I had the honor of speaking to your predecessor, James K. Polk. My object in coming has been to see the hero of Buena Vista [a famous battle in the Mexican-American War]."

Hereupon the old war-horse bowed graciously. "Mr. Seward," said he, "your friend seems to be very polite." The old man became so talkative that I ventured to say: "Your Excellency, it has afforded me the keenest pleasure to form the acquaintance of the hero-President – a unique and magnificent personality. Permit me, however, to say that I believe you have never met a person of my kind. "

He looked at me dumbfounded, "I have seen people of all sorts and conditions," said he, "and would like to know what you mean."

"Certainly," said I. "I am a rabbi."

"You are right: I have never seen a rabbi." [One reason that he had never seen a rabbi in his long military career was that Jews were not allowed to be chaplains in America's military forces, only Christians.] He now extended his hand a second time, and continued the conversation. All the Washington papers reported the visit the next morning, under the caption, "The First Rabbi to Visit the President."[14]

Sixteen months into his first term, on July 8, 1850, a hot day in Washington, Taylor drank a pitcher of iced milk and ate a bowl of cherries. Having survived yellow fever, dysentery, malaria, cholera, and many battles during his military career, sixty-six-year-old President Zachary Taylor died that night of gastroenteritis.

---

[14] Ibid., 137.

Millard Fillmore

1800–1874

- ✪ Thirteenth president, 1850–1853
- ✪ Congressman and comptroller for New York and chancellor of the University of Buffalo
- ✪ Zachary Taylor's vice president, he assumed the presidency after Taylor's death

The eldest son of the nine children of Nathaniel Fillmore, a poor farmer of Scottish descent, and his wife, Phoebe, of English descent, Millard Fillmore was born in Summerhill, New York, on January 7, 1800. Homeschooled in reading, writing, and arithmetic, and despite his lack of a college education, he was hired by a Quaker lawyer as a clerk and encouraged to become a lawyer. Called to the bar in his early twenties, with his rugged backwoodsman's looks, deep voice and confidence, he did well.

At twenty-six, he was wealthy, popular, respected, and married to Abigail Powers, a minister's daughter, who had briefly been his teacher, though only one year older. She gave him a son and a daughter. At thirty-one, in 1831, he rejected his Episcopalian upbringing in favor of Unitarianism. That same year, while living in Buffalo, New York, Fillmore was elected

81

to the US House of Representatives. In 1848 he became Zachary Taylor's vice president and less than two year later, after Taylor's death, the president.[1]

During Fillmore's first year as president, Uriah Levy's campaign against flogging in the navy played a large part in persuading Congress to ban the practice.

That same year, Fillmore faced a tricky problem. The Swiss government was putting American Jews in Switzerland at risk. This was exacerbated by the United States representative there who had already approved a treaty with the Swiss, the first clause of which restricted the Swiss government's protection to American Christians.

Nevertheless, Fillmore opposed the anti-Jewish clause, and he and public pressure caused the Senate not to ratify the Swiss treaty. French Jews living in Switzerland had also been discriminated against, but France's leader, Louis Napoleon, knew how to end Swiss bigotry: he threatened to deport all Swiss citizens living in France.[2]

In 1853, Fillmore emphasized his pro-Jewish attitude by giving US Senator Judah P. Benjamin of Louisiana the chance to be the first Jewish justice of the United States Supreme Court. The *New York Times* picked up the story, reporting on February 15, 1853, that "if the President nominates Benjamin, the Democrats are determined to confirm him."

But Benjamin turned it down, preferring to remain the first Jew in the United States Senate. He kept his Senate seat, reelected by Louisiana voters on a pro-slavery platform. Later, after Louisiana seceded from the Union, Benjamin was to serve under Confederate President Jefferson Davis in turn as attorney general, secretary of war, and as the Confederacy's secretary of state.

---

[1] Millard Fillmore's Obituary, *New York Times*, March 9, 1874, 1.

[2] "Made Swiss Accept Jewish Passports," *New York Times*, December 11, 1911, 5.

Fillmore's wife, Abigail, died in 1853, the year they left the White House; his daughter, Mary, died a year later. In 1855 he made an extensive tour of Europe, and in 1858 he married Caroline McIntosh, a wealthy widow.

He opposed Lincoln during the Civil War, and co-founded the private University of Buffalo, now the public State University of New York at Buffalo. On March 8, 1874, at age seventy-four, Millard Fillmore died of a stroke in his Buffalo home.

Franklin Pierce

1804–1869

- ✪ Fourteenth president, 1853–1857
- ✪ Successful lawyer and the only president from the state of New Hampshire
- ✪ Brigadier general in the Mexican-American War

Shortly before his inauguration as president, on January 6, 1853, Franklin Pierce, his wife, Jane, and thirteen-year-old son, Benjamin, were on a train from Andover to Lawrence, Massachusetts, when it derailed and rolled down an embankment. Pierce and his wife escaped injury, but their son, their only surviving child, was killed. Mrs. Pierce never recovered from her son's death and blamed it on her husband's political ambition.[1]

The son of Benjamin Pierce, a Revolutionary War general and New Hampshire's governor, of English descent, and Anna Kendrick, Pierce was born on November 24, 1804, in Hillsborough, New Hampshire, and raised as an Episcopalian.

While a student at Bowdoin College, Brunswick, Maine, he made lifelong friends of the future novelist Nathaniel Hawthorne and the future poet Henry Wadsworth Longfellow.

---

[1] Franklin Pierce's Obituary, *New York Times*, October 9, 1869, 3.

At age thirty, on November 19, 1834, he married Jane Means Appleton, the daughter of a Congregationalist minister, formerly a Bowdoin College president.

Pierce was an extremely successful attorney, and became a US congressman and then a US senator. Although a Northerner, he sympathized with Southerners, because he believed that the Constitution supported slavery. During the Mexican-American War he had served as a brigadier general, and his heroic record helped to get him elected president. His wife took little interest in his political career and none after their son's accidental death.

Among those attending his inauguration was the Jewish Senator for Louisiana, Judah Benjamin, who had declined President Fillmore's offer to make him a Supreme Court judge. Benjamin soon received an invitation from Pierce to dine at the White House, where he sat near Jefferson Davis, the secretary of war, and his wife, Valma. Benjamin made a strong impression on her, because thirty years later, in 1898, she wrote to Francis Lawley, a *London Times* correspondent:

> I first met him at dinner at President Pierce's house...it would be difficult to convey to you the impression his voice made upon me. It seemed a silver thread woven amidst the warp and woof of sounds which filled the drawing room; it was low, full, and soft, yet the timbre of it filled every ear like a silver trumpet. From the first sentence he uttered, whatever he said attracted and claimed the attention of his audience.... Sometimes, when they [Benjamin and Jefferson Davis] did not agree on a measure, hot words in glacial, polite phrases passed between them, and they had up to the year of secession little social intercourse; an occasional invitation to dinner was accepted and exchanged, and nothing more.[2]

---

[2] Eli N. Evans, *Judah P. Benjamin: The Jewish Confederate* (New York: The Free Press, 1988), 82–83.

Pierce was the first US president to appoint a Jew, August Belmont, as both United States charge d'affaires and ambassador at the Hague.

During Pierce's presidency, in 1855, the resilient Captain Uriah Levy's career was once more in jeopardy. Congress had enacted the Naval Reform Act to rid the navy of an overabundance of naval officers. Levy was among those cashiered as a cost-cutting measure.

But he had a chance to appeal his dismissal before a board of inquiry in November 1857. Anti-Semitism was still alive and well in the US Navy at the time, and Levy was one of the very few Jews to have made it his career. Because so many officers were willing to testify against him, making no attempt to disguise that their dislike of him was because he was a Jew and the fact of his six court-martials, the odds were heavily against him.

In his corner was his distinguished attorney, Benjamin F. Butler.

After a barrage of complaints about his client, he called on thirteen active-duty and nine retired naval officers for the defense. Without exception, they praised Levy for his courage and competence. Fifty-three character witnesses followed, governors, senators, congressmen, bank presidents, merchants, doctors, editors, and historian George Bancroft, who had been a secretary of the navy. Levy had been fired, said Bancroft, "because he was of the Jewish persuasion."

The odds were still very much against him.

Then, on December 19, 1857, Uriah Levy himself rose to speak in his own defense. He held the floor for three days and gave the men who had his fate in their hands the compelling if not spellbinding story of his life. He started with his childhood, when his "Israelite" parents had "nurtured me in the faith of my ancestors." The transcript of the hearing runs to nine hundred pages. When Levy concluded with "I am an

American, a sailor, and a Jew," the room exploded in applause and some threw their caps in the air.

On Christmas eve he was restored to active duty.[3]

Franklin Pierce's wife, Jane, died of tuberculosis in Concord, on December 2, 1863. Franklin Pierce himself died at age sixty-five, from cirrhosis of the liver, on October 8, 1869, also at his Concord, New Hampshire, home.

---

[3] William Bryk, "The Jewish Commodore," Mr. Beller's Neighborhood, http://mrbellersneighborhood.com/2002/06/the-jewish-commodore.

James Buchanan

1791–1868

- ✪ Fifteenth president, 1857–1861
- ✪ Ambassador to both Britain and Russia
- ✪ Strove to maintain peace between the North and the South, but only alienated both sides

America's only bachelor president and the only president from Pennsylvania, James Buchanan was the son of an immigrant from Donegal, Northern Ireland. A wealthy attorney at twenty-nine, worth $300,000, his fiancée, Ann Coleman, broke off their engagement when she believed the rumor that he was a womanizer. Before he could disprove the rumor, she became ill and died. Ann's physician, Dr. Chapman, diagnosed it as the first instance he ever knew of hysteria producing death, but later believed that the cause was a laudanum overdose.[4]

That appears to be the end of his romantic interest in women, although he admitted to being flirtatious.

---

[4] Jay Tolson, "The Ten Worst Presidents," *US News & World Report*, February 16, 2007, www.usnews.com/news/history/features/the-10-worst-presidents; Philip S. Klein, *President James Buchanan: A Biography* (University Park, PA: Pennsylvania State University Press, 1962), 303, 381, 387.

Buchanan's businessman father, James Sr., and his mother, Elizabeth Speer, were both of Scottish-Irish descent. James was born on April 23, 1791, the second of eleven children, in Franklin, Pennsylvania. He was raised as a Presbyterian and graduated with honors from Dickinson College, Carlisle, Pennsylvania, before studying law in Lancaster. He was admitted to the bar in 1812.

He became successively a Democratic congressman, a senator for Pennsylvania, Andrew Jackson's minister to Russia, James Polk's secretary of state, and Franklin Pierce's minister to Britain. When elected president in 1857 by defeating the Republican candidate, John Fremont – and with his fiancée having accidentally or intentionally killed herself – he adopted his auburn-haired, twenty-five-year-old orphaned niece and made her mistress of the White House.

In his first year Buchanan appointed a Jewish congressman, Emmanuel Hart, a colonel in the New York militia, to be surveyor of the port of New York, a job Hart held for four years. Hart later became treasurer of the Society for the Relief of Poor Hebrews.

On August 31, 1858, President Buchanan wrote to his Jewish friend, Judah Benjamin, then the US senator for Louisiana:

> I write for the purpose of tendering you the appointment of Minister of Spain and expressing a strong desire that you may accept it. I feel satisfied that the Country will unite with me in my opinion that this is an appointment eminently fit to be made. Indeed I am not acquainted with any gentleman who possesses superior, if equal, qualification to yourself for this important mission. Such being the case I think your Country has the right to the benefit of your services.... Assuring you

that I shall do all in my power to make it agreeable to yourself, useful to your Country, and promotive to your own fame."[5]

The Jewish press not only welcomed the prospect of a Jew representing America, but also of a Jew returning to Spain from which his ancestors had been banished. But Benjamin turned it down, preferring to stay in the Senate.

In 1859, despite persistent American protests, some Swiss cantons continued their anti-Semitic policies, specifically in the case of an American Jew, A. H. Goodman. As a Jew, he had been ordered to leave his home in the Swiss canton of Neuchatel, where he had run a business for five years. Protest meetings, newspapers throughout America, and a Jewish delegation from Baltimore pressed Buchanan to revoke the US-Swiss treaty that allowed such religious intolerance against an American citizen.

So Buchanan instructed his minister in Switzerland, Theodore Fay, to take up the case. Fay got the Swiss to let Goodman stay, but only as a special favor, not as a right. This spurred Fay to thoroughly investigate the Swiss treatment of Jews, and in 1859 he sent his critical "Israelite Note" to Switzerland's Federal Council. It was not only a rigorous defense of Jewish rights, but a detailed account of the American Constitution. After it was translated into French and German, the Council put it on sale; it was favorably reviewed in several Swiss newspapers, and caused several cantons to abolish their restrictions against Jews.[6]

Now the Jewish American naval officer, Uriah Levy, comes into the picture again. Having survived six court-martials and two Courts of Inquiry, and won the support of several US presidents – three times exonerated by President James

---

[5] Eli N. Evans, *Judah P. Benjamin: The Jewish Confederate* (New York: Simon & Schuster, 1988), 96.

[6] American Jewish Historical Society, No. 11, p-p. 7 et seq.

Monroe, and once by President Andrew Jackson – he got his final unprecedented promotion.

On February 21, 1860, forty-three years after President Monroe had made him a lieutenant in the United States Navy, President Buchanan promoted him to commodore (today's equivalent is admiral), the highest rank a Jew had ever reached, and gave him command of the Mediterranean Squadron. To celebrate the unique occasion, the American fleet and frigates in Sardinia's La Spezia harbor fired a thirteen-gun salute, and Levy's flagship, USS *Macedonian*, raised his pennant bearing a single star on its main mast.[7]

The day before leaving the White House, Buchanan told the incoming President Abraham Lincoln, "If you are as happy in entering the White House as I shall feel in returning to Wheatland you are a happy man."[8]

Buchanan was the first president to publish his memoirs, and just before his death, he said, "History will vindicate my memory."[9] He died at age seventy-seven on June 1, 1868, of respiratory failure and rheumatic gout.

---

[7] Uriah P. Levy, 133, ZB files, Navy Department Library.

[8] Jean H. Baker, *James Buchanan* (New York: New York Times Books, 2004), 140.

[9] "Buchanan's Birthplace State Park," March 28, 2009.

Abraham Lincoln

1809–1865

- ✪ Sixteenth president, 1861–1865
- ✪ Led the country during the American Civil War, preserving the Union while ending slavery
- ✪ First US president to be assassinated

As a child Abraham Lincoln knew that his world was a dangerous place. The woods near his one-room, log-cabin, dirt-floor home teamed with bears and other wild animals. Indians had killed his paternal grandfather while he was trying to clear part of a forest for farm land, and his beloved mother, Nancy, died at age thirty-four when Lincoln was nine. As an adult he confided to his law partner and biographer, William Herndon, that he was the son of a poor, almost illiterate Kentucky farming couple of English descent, and that his mother "was a bastard, the daughter of a nobleman so called of Virginia," adding, "I owe everything I am to her."[1]

A year after Nancy's death, Lincoln's father married Sarah Bush Johnson – a widow with two daughters and a son – a

---

[1] *The American Heritage Book of the Presidents and Famous Americans* (New York: Dell, 1967), 404.

stepmother Lincoln adored and called his "angel mother."[2] His parents were Calvinists, but Lincoln did not admit to any church membership. Although he appeared to be deeply religious, often quoted the Bible, and as president attended Presbyterian church services, he was evasive about his religious beliefs. When asked by an evangelist if he intended to go to heaven or hell, Lincoln replied, "I intend to go to Congress."[3]

He was a warm, witty, and mostly cheerful boy with moody episodes, which later developed into periods of deep depression. Abe, as he became known, was well liked by backwoods neighbors, especially as he willingly carried water for them, made fires to warm them, and baby-sat. Despite only eighteen months of formal schooling, he developed a lifelong passion for learning and was rarely seen without a book in his hand, among them *Robinson Crusoe*, *Aesop's Fables*, *Pilgrim's Progress*, a George Washington biography, the Bible, and the works of Shakespeare, Byron, and Robert Burns.

In 1830, the family moved to Illinois with the lean and muscular twenty-two-year-old Lincoln driving a team of oxen. After settling in, he canoed to New Salem, for fun, before taking a job delivering goods by flatboat from New Salem to New Orleans. There, he and his friends "saw Negroes chained, maltreated, whipped and scourged"; they "came in their rambles to a slave auction where a fine mulatto girl was being pinched and prodded and trotted up and down the room like a horse to show how she moved." Lincoln's "heart bled" at the sight of it, said a friend, John Hanks. "I can say, knowing it, that it was on this trip that he formed his opinion of slavery. I have heard him say so often."[4]

2   *Encyclopedia Britannica*, 15th ed., vol. 10, p. 965, s.v. "Lincoln, Abraham."

3   Franklin Steiner, *The Religious Beliefs of Our Presidents*, Free Presidential Library, 1996, ch. 8.

4   Lord Charnwood, *Abraham Lincoln* (New York: Henry Holt, 1917), 14.

At six feet four inches, the tallest man around and a skillful wrestler, he could split wood and fell trees like a lumberjack. He spoke in a somewhat high-pitched backwoods twang, and moved awkwardly, "with the long-sliding flat-footed, cautious manner of a plowman."[5]

Unlike most of his neighbors he did not hunt, reluctant to kill animals even for food, telling friends that "an ant's life is as sweet to it as ours to us."[6]

After various dead-end jobs, he spent a few months as a captain in the Black Hawk War against invading, heavily armed Indians, in which he saw no fighting but "had a good many bloody struggles with the mosquitoes," and helped to bury five men who had been scalped and killed. Still, he relished the camaraderie of his fellow soldiers.[7]

The war over, bored with running a small local store, and after three years as postmaster of New Salem, he won a seat in the state legislature. Having taught himself grammar and mathematics, he now tackled the law, and in 1836 he passed the Illinois bar exam. He moved to Springfield, Illinois, the following year, where, for the next twenty-five years he handled over five thousand civil and criminal cases, and earned the nickname "Honest Abe."

In Quincy, Illinois, in 1838 he befriended Abraham Jonas, a Jewish attorney who had served four terms in the Kentucky state legislature. Jonas had emigrated from England in 1819 to join his brother, Joseph, in Cincinnati. As the first Jewish settler in the area, people came from miles around to see if Joseph had horns. Jonas had then moved to Quincy, where he first met Lincoln.

---

[5]　*Encyclopedia Britannica*, 15th ed., vol. 10, p. 965, s.v. "Lincoln, Abraham."

[6]　Paul M. Angle, ed., *The Lincoln Reader* (New Brunswick, NJ: Rutgers University Press, 1947), 26.

[7]　*Encyclopedia Britannica*, s.v. "Lincoln, Abraham."

Lincoln seemed reluctant to marry, having broken off one engagement, but in 1842, at age thirty-three, he married Mary Todd, the high-spirited and well-educated daughter of a prominent slave-owning Kentucky family, and they had four sons.

In 1847, after a quarter of a century as a successful lawyer, and four successive terms in the Illinois House of Representatives, Lincoln was elected as a Republican to the US House of Representatives, where he was an outspoken opponent of slavery and of the Mexican-American War. The war had started in 1846 after the United States annexed Texas, which the Mexicans claimed was their land, but after their military defeat by the US in 1848 they never again claimed Texas.

Lincoln's strong and heartfelt objection to slavery was opposed by Senator Stephen Douglas, who, during a debate with him, proposed allowing slavery in Louisiana and letting the settlers in Kansas and Nebraska decide if they wanted it. Lincoln responded: "I cannot but hate it. I hate it because of the monstrous injustice of slavery itself."[8]

When Lincoln became a presidential candidate, among the Jews supporting him were Sigmund Kaufmann, publisher of several German-language newspapers in New York City, and Lewis Dembitz of Louisville, Kentucky. At the 1860 Republican National Convention, Dembitz was the first delegate to vote for Lincoln's nomination.

Because of his anti-slavery views, Lincoln already had many enemies, especially in the South, and winning the presidential election only increased their number. This caused his friend Jonas to write to him on December 30, 1860, of his "great anxiety in regard to your personal safety":

> I have a very large family connection in the South, and in New Orleans I have six children and a host of other relatives. I receive many letters from them, their language has to

---

[8] Lincoln at the Lincoln-Douglas debate, at Ottawa, Illinois, August 21, 1858.

be very guarded, as fears are entertained that the sanctity of the mails is not much regarded. Yesterday I received a letter from N. O. who is prudent, sound, and careful of what he writes, and among other things he writes, "Things are daily becoming worse here, God help us, what will be the result it is dreadful to imagine. One thing I am satisfied of, that there is a perfect organization, fearful in numbers and controlled by men of character and influence, whose object is to prevent the inauguration of Lincoln. Large numbers of desperate characters, many of them from this city, will be in Washington on the 4th of March and it is their determination to prevent the inauguration, and if by no other means, by using violence on the person of Lincoln. Men engaged in this measure are known to be of the most violent character, capable of doing any act necessary to carry out their vile measures."

The writer of this, I know, would not say what he does, did he not believe the statement above given to you. I cannot give you his name, for were it known that he communicated such matters to persons in the North, his life would be in danger – and I trust you will not communicate having received any such information from me.... Permit me to suggest – ought not the Governors of the free States, and your friends generally to adopt at once some precautionary measure – no protection can be expected from the damned old traitor [President James Buchanan] at the head of the Government or his subordinates – something should be done in time and done effectively. With great esteem and devotion, I am truly yrs, A. Jonas.[9]

Warned that there would be an attempt to assassinate him during his journey to Washington, Lincoln changed his route and arrived safely under guard at six in the morning of

---

9   Arnold Fine, "Abraham Lincoln and the Jews," Our Jerusalem, November 4, 2001, http://www.ourjerusalem.com/history/story/history20011104.html.

February 23, 1861, riding to his inauguration on March 4, 1861, in an open carriage.

On April 12, by firing on Union soldiers in Fort Sumter, Charleston, South Carolina, Confederates launched the Civil War.

Commodore (Admiral) Uriah Levy, now the highest ranking Jewish officer in the US Navy, offered Lincoln his entire substantial fortune for the war effort, which Lincoln declined. Levy also wanted to fight for the Union. Instead, noting how often Levy had survived his own court-martials, Lincoln appointed him to a place on the US Navy Court Martial Board, which he accepted.[10]

Once the war started, New York rabbi Arnold Fischel wanted to be a Union army chaplain, but Congress had restricted that calling to ordained Christian ministers. So the rabbi wrote to Lincoln on December 11, 1861, that the Chaplaincy Act violated the Constitution by establishing "a prejudicial discrimination against a particular class of citizens on account of their religious belief."

Lincoln replied: "I shall try to have a new law broad enough to cover what is desired by you on behalf of the Israelites." But it took almost two years before Congress permitted Jews to be chaplains."[11]

While visiting his troops, Lincoln got frostbitten feet and asked chiropodist Dr. Isachar Zacharie, a Jewish immigrant from England, to treat him. He was so pleased with the result that he gave him this testimonial: "Dr. Zacharie has operated on my feet with great success and considerable addition to my comfort." Zacharie did not confine his work to the feet of the famous, but by his own reckoning cared for those of some fifteen thousand Union soldiers for free. The anti-Republican

---

[10] Isaac Mafkens, *Abraham Lincoln and the Jews,* self-published, 1909, p. 53.

[11] Rabbi Fischel and Abraham Lincoln, accessed March 21, 2010, http://www.jewishjewels.org/newsletter/2004_02.htm.

press ridiculed Zacharie as the president's conniving "toe trimmer," who aimed to enrich himself by creating "a corps of corn doctors, or foot soldiers to put the army in marching order."[12]

It was evident that Jewish soldiers in the Union army were encouraged to practice their religion when, in the spring of 1862, twenty-one Jewish members of the 23rd Ohio Volunteer Regiment in Fayette, West Virginia, were given home leave to celebrate Passover, especially meaningful to Jews fighting to free others from slavery.[13]

In sharp contrast was General Grant's General Order Number Eleven. Issued on December 17, 1862, it ordered all Jews to be deported within twenty-four hours from Tennessee, Kentucky, as well as Mississippi, areas controlled by his army, because, as traitors to the Union they were trading with the Confederate enemy. This order was prompted by General Sherman's charge that Jews were buying or stealing thousands of bales of cotton to sell for huge profits in the North. Although Confederate spies had conclusive proof that the Union army itself was speculating in cotton, Southern Jews who had lived in Tennessee and Kentucky for decades, together with Jewish Union soldiers and their families, were threatened with expulsion and arrest if they disobeyed the order.

Grant even ignored pleas to rescind his order from his father-in-law, who had several Jewish friends.

Learning of this imminent exodus, many newspapers protested, including the *New York Times*. Northern Jews urgently petitioned Lincoln, and a delegation visited him with affidavits from leading Republicans and military men refuting Grant's charges. Jewish merchants from Paducah, Kentucky,

---

[12] Karp, *From the Ends of the Earth*, 250–52; Isachar Zacharie, *New York World*, editorial, September 24, 1864, http://www.jewishworldreview.com/herb/geduld_presidents_day.php3?printer_friendly.

[13] Rabbi Yaacov Polskin, "A Truly American Passover," http://www.jewishworldreview.com/0404/american_passover.php3.

sent Lincoln a telegram on December 29, saying that "they were insulted and outraged by the inhuman order that violated the Constitution."[14]

Henry Kutner, president of the St. Louis, Missouri, branch of B'nai B'rith, wrote to Lincoln on January 5, 1863:

> In the name of hundreds who have been driven from their houses, deprived of their liberty, and injured in their property *without* having violated any law or regulation. In the name of the thousands of our Brethren and their children who have died and [those] now willingly sacrificing their lives and fortunes for the Union and the suppression of the rebellion. In the name of religious liberty, of justice and humanity – we enter our solemn protest against this Order, and ask of you – the Defender and Protector of the Constitution – to annul that Order and protect the liberties even of your humblest constituents.[15]

The man who took immediate action was Cesar Kaskel of Paducah, who led a delegation to Washington. When Kaskel showed the president a copy of Grant's orders, Lincoln said, as if history were repeating itself. "The children of Israel were driven from the happy land of Canaan." Kaskel replied, "Yes, and that is why we have come to Father Abraham to ask for his protection." To the delegates' delight, Lincoln said, "And the protection they shall have at once."[16]

He wrote to General-in-Chief H. W. Halleck, who in turn sent this telegram to Grant: "A paper purporting to be General Order No. 11, issued by you December 17, has been presented here. By its terms it expels all Jews from your department. If such an order has been issued it will be immediately revoked."

---

[14] Brooks Simpson, *Ulysses S. Grant: Triumph Over Adversity 1822–1865* (New York: Houghton Mifflin, 2000), 165.

[15] Judaic Treasures of the Library of Congress: Order No. 11, Jewish Virtual Library.

[16] Karp, *From the Ends of the Earth*, 247.

Halleck also wrote privately to Grant that Lincoln had "no objection to expelling traitors and Jew peddlers, which I suppose was the object of your order, but as in terms of proscribing an entire religious class, some of whom are fighting in our ranks, the President deemed it necessary to revoke it." A few days later, when Rabbi Isaac Mayer Wise of Cincinnati thanked Lincoln for rescinding the order, Lincoln said that he made no distinction between Jews and gentiles and that "to condemn a class is, to say the least, to wrong the good with the bad."[17]

To augment his badly depleted forces, on January 1, 1863, Lincoln issued his Emancipation Proclamation declaring slaves in the secessionist Southern States to be free, and inviting them to join the United States army and navy. Nearly 189,000 former slaves joined the Union army and not only helped to identify the Union cause with the anti-slavery movement, but to win the war.

Soon after his Emancipation Proclamation, Lincoln met a Canadian Christian Zionist, Henry Wentworth Monk, who said that he hoped that oppressed Jews in Turkey and Russia would be emancipated "by restoring them to their national home in Palestine." Lincoln replied that it was a noble dream shared by many Americans.[18]

Armed with a quip for most occasions, Lincoln added that his chiropodist was a Jew who "has so many times put me upon my feet that I would have no objection to giving his countrymen a leg up."[19]

Later in the month he sent his chiropodist, Zacharie, now his close friend and confidant, to New Orleans, just captured by Union troops, to investigate conditions in the city and to

---

[17] Ibid.

[18] Mitchell G. Bard, "Roots of the U.S.-Israel Relationship," Jewish Virtual Library, http://www.jewishvirtuallibrary.org/jsource/US-Israel/roots_of_US-Israel.html.

[19] American Jewish Historical Society, www.ajhs.org.

mediate between the military government and the resident civilians. There, "Zacharie recruited a cadre of peddlers to send back vital information, such as Confederate troop movements, and did his own investigations as well, both to gauge Southern feelings and to watch out for contraband shipments. He also did what he could to help New Orleans' Jews withstand the shortages of food and medication during wartime." Lincoln had arranged for Zacherie to have safe passage to Richmond, the Confederacy capital, where he discussed peace terms with Judah Benjamin, the Confederacy's Jewish secretary of state. His meeting with Benjamin, Zacharie said, was "of the most friendly nature." According to the *New York Herald*, Zacharie made an extraordinary proposal: the federal government should pardon the Confederates and transport them to Mexico, where they would forcibly expel the French-supported government of Emperor Maximilian and proclaim Jefferson Davis the president of Mexico. The Southern states would then return to the Union. However, the *New York Herald* reported that Lincoln's radical cabinet members vetoed the idea, determined on unconditional surrender.[20]

The following year, the *New York World* revealed that the president's Jewish chiropodist, Dr. Zacharie, "enjoyed Mr. Lincoln's confidence perhaps more than any other private Individual [and was] perhaps the most favored family visitor to the White House." Thirteen letters from Zacharie to Lincoln are in the Library of Congress. One from Lincoln to him, on September 19, 1864, reads: "I thank you again for the deep interest you have taken in the Union Cause. The personal matter on behalf of your friend which you mentioned shall be fully and fairly considered when presented." Zacharie replied: "Dear Friend, Yours of the 19th came duly to hand, it has had the desired effect with a friend of the Prairie. I leave

---

[20] Lincoln Papers, Library of Congress; Karp, *From the Ends of the Earth* , 250–52.

tomorrow for the interior of Pennsylvania and may go as far as Ohio. One thing is to be done and that is for you to impress on the minds of your friends, not to be to[o] sure [about being reelected for a second term]."[21]

During the war, Lincoln appointed at least seven Jewish generals, among them Brigadier General Leopold Blumenberg, a fervent abolitionist, of the Maryland Volunteer Regiment; Hungarian-born Major General Frederick Kneher, commander of the 79th Indiana Regiment; Brigadier General Leopold Newman of New York; General Edward Salomon of Illinois – a commanding general at age twenty-nine – who led the 82nd Illinois Volunteer Infantry at Gettysburg, which included over a hundred Jewish soldiers; West Point graduate Brigadier General Alfred Mordecai, who joined the Army of Northeastern Virginia; General Phineas Horowitz of Baltimore, surgeon general of the Navy; and General William Meyer of New York, who received a letter of thanks from Lincoln for his efforts to diffuse the situation during the New York draft riots, violent disturbances by mostly German and Irish immigrants who resisted being drafted into the Union army.

There were no Jewish generals in the Confederate Army.[22]

Among other Jews in the First New York Lincoln Cavalry was Hungarian-born Joseph Pulitzer, later known as editor-publisher of the *St. Louis Post Dispatch* and the *New York World*.

In the winter of 1864 the war was all but over, with Grant winning in the West and Lee beaten at Gettysburg, and with the fall of Mobile, New Orleans, and Atlanta to Union troops. Lincoln wrote to his secretary of war on January 25, 1865, "About Jews. I wish you would give Dr. Zacharie a pass to go

[21] Herb Geduld, "Lincoln's Jewish Generals," Jewish World Review: Past and Present, http://www.jewishworldreview.com/herb/geduldI.asp.

[22] *The Collected Works of Abraham Lincoln* (New Brunswick, NJ: Lincoln Association, 1933), VIII, 238.

to Savannah, remain a week and return, bringing with him, if he wishes, his father or sisters or any of them. This will spare me trouble and oblige me – I promised him a long time ago that he should be allowed this whenever Savannah should fall into our hands."[23]

By war's end, on April 9, 1865, 620,000 soldiers had been killed as well as an untold numbers of civilians.

When Lincoln was reelected for a second term, one of his first acts was to hear a request from Zacharie to free Goodman Mordecai, a fellow Jew, from a Union prison. Although Mordecai was a Southerner who had fought for the enemy, Lincoln granted the request.[24]

Five days later, on April 14, 1865, actor and Confederate spy John Wilkes Booth, a pistol in one hand and a dagger in the other, fired a bullet into Lincoln's head as he and his wife, Mary, watched a play in a Washington theater. The wound was fatal and Lincoln died the next day, April 15, which was to have been a day of national prayer to mark the end of the Civil War.

Shortly after Lincoln's death, in the midst of Passover preparations, synagogues throughout the country draped their alters in black, and instead of tears of joy for the war's end many in the congregations wept for the death of their beloved president. The *Jewish Record* drew the analogy between Lincoln not having lived to see the reconciliation of North and South, and Moses dying...before he saw the Israelites enter the Promised Land.

Booth, the assassin, was a twenty-six-year-old white supremacist who believed that whites had a God-given right to own slaves. He broke his leg when he leapt onto the

[23] Ibid.
[24] "Isachar Zacharie," Jewish Virtual Library.

theater stage after shooting Lincoln, but was able to escape on horseback. However, he was discovered hiding in a Virginia bathhouse, where he was fatally shot.

Lincoln had a premonition of his death, telling his law partner, Herndon, that he "would come to some terrible end, he didn't know what; it was a fate that lurked ahead." He had also told his wife and a few friends that he woke from a nightmare deeply disturbed, and turned to the Old Testament for consolation. Leafing through its pages he found, to his surprise, that at least sixteen chapters were devoted to dreams and dream interpretations.[25]

Rabbi Morris Raphall of B'nai Jeshurun told his New York congregation that he met Lincoln only once, and then it was with a request: to let his son-in-law, C. M. Levy, rejoin the army and to promote him from second to first lieutenant. Even though Levy had been dismissed from the service on unspecified charges, Lincoln, said the rabbi, "had granted [the request] lovingly, because he knew he was speaking to a Jew and because he knew him to be a servant of the Lord."[26]

---

[25] Angle, *Lincoln Reader*, account by Ward Hill Lamont, 520–22.

[26] Karp, *From the Ends of the Earth*, 252.

Andrew Johnson

1808–1875

- ✪ Seventeenth president, 1865–1869
- ✪ Abraham Lincoln's vice president, he assumed the presidency after Lincoln's assassination
- ✪ Escaped impeachment by Congress by one vote

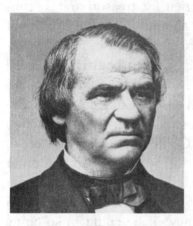

Andrew Johnson was and remains the only outspoken anti-Semitic US President, and the only one who never spent a day in school. His father, Jacob Johnson, a Raleigh, North Carolina, janitor of English descent, died in 1811 when Andrew was three, in a failed attempt to save the editor of the *Raleigh Gazette* from drowning. Andrew's widowed seamstress-washerwoman mother, Mary, became her four sons' sole supporter, with never enough to send any of them to school.

Andrew grew up in Greenville, East Tennessee where, barely able to read or write, he eked out a living as a tailor. However, at nineteen, in 1827, he married Eliza McCardle, an educated cobbler's daughter, who taught him elementary arithmetic, how to read and write, and encouraged his political aspirations. Dismissed by opponents as poor white trash, he overcame his lack of formal education and social graces as an energetic and pugnacious champion of the working class.

He talked his way into the job of his city's alderman at age twenty, its mayor two years later; was twice elected to the Tennessee House of Representatives at age twenty-seven and at twenty-nine, and to its senate at thirty-three. There he successfully supported small farmers and was a fierce opponent of slave-owning aristocrats. Elected to the US House of Representatives at thirty-five, he became Tennessee's governor at forty-five, and in 1857, at forty-nine, its US senator.

After Lincoln was elected president in 1861, Johnson said of the Confederates who wanted to break from the Union, "I would have them arrested and tried for treason and, if convicted, by the eternal God, they should suffer the penalty of the law and at the hands of the executioner."[1]

His anti-Semitism came to light when Louisiana seceded from the Union on January 20, 1861, and the state's Jewish US Senator, Judah Benjamin, joined the Confederacy. In discussing with an acquaintance those senators he considered to be traitors, Johnson singled out Confederate David Yulee, of Florida, as "a contemptible Jew," and added, "There's another Jew – the miserable Benjamin! He looks on a country and a government as he would a suit of clothes. He sold out the old one; and he would sell out the new, if he could in so doing make two or three millions."[2]

When, that same year, a convention of Southern states elected Jefferson Davis president of the Confederate States, Davis made his close friend and most trusted adviser, Judah Benjamin, his attorney general, then secretary of war, and ultimately the Confederacy's secretary of state.

---

[1] David C. Whitney and Robin Vaughn Whitney, *The American Presidents: Andrew Johnson* (Garden City, NY: Doubleday, 1993), 144.

[2] Eli M. Evans, *Judah P. Benjamin, the Jewish Confederate* (New York: Simon & Schuster, 1988), 111.

Andrew Johnson's own state of Tennessee joined the Confederacy on June 8, 1861, and he alone of twenty-two Southern Senators defied the overwhelming pro-Confederate sympathy of most Southerners and continued to support Lincoln and the Union cause. Viewed as a patriot by Northerners, many Southerners despised him as a traitor, hanging him in effigy, and a mob once stormed a railroad carriage in which he was traveling and threatened to lynch him, but left in a hurry when he drew his pistol.

In 1862, after Union troops had taken much of Tennessee, Lincoln appointed Johnson military governor of occupied Tennessee, as a brigadier general.

Meanwhile, Judah Benjamin had earned the reputation abroad as the most brilliant mind in America. Some called him the brains behind the Confederacy. Jefferson Davis praised him as the ablest and most faithful member of his advisory council, "a man who had no personal aspirations, no wishes that were not subordinate to the prosperity of the cause."[3]

Early in 1864, armed bands sympathetic to the Union cause burned bridges to delay Confederate forces and help Union troops in their advance through the Cumberland Gap. When Confederates captured some bridge burners, Benjamin sent this dispatch: "The insurrectionists not proved to be bridge burners are to be held as prisoners of war, while the others identified as burners are to be tried summarily by drumhead court martial, and, if found guilty, executed on the spot by hanging. It would be well to leave their bodies hanging in the vicinity of the burned bridges."[4]

After the hangings, Andrew Johnson, as military governor of Tennessee, cited the Old Testament to condemn Benjamin: "The blood of these men, like Abel, cried aloud from the ground against the author of their death, and succor to their

---

3 Ibid., 357.
4 Ibid., 133.

wives and little ones." He denounced Benjamin as among other things "a double-dyed traitor, every honorable-minded man would detest."[5]

It was hardly a surprise when Republican delegates chose Southern Democrat Andrew Johnson as Lincoln's running mate in 1864 because, although a Southern Democrat, his vigorous and courageous support of Lincoln and the Union cause was never in doubt. However, the nomination greatly disturbed Rabbi Isaac Mayer Wise, who recalled a speech in which Johnson, in lashing out at Senator Benjamin for threatening to leave the Union, had emphasized that Benjamin was a Jew, and described him as "one that understands something about the idea of dividing garments, who belongs to that tribe that parted the garments of our Savior, and for this venture... he was made attorney general [for the Confederacy]." As editor of the *Israelite* newspaper, Rabbi Wise asked his literary editor, H. M. Moos, who had Union credentials as a former guide for Union troops during the Civil War, to complain to the vice-presidential candidate about his anti-Semitic remarks.

Moos wrote to Johnson: "I cannot believe that you could have said that Benjamin was of that cursed race which stoned the prophets and crucified the redeemer of the world...leaving an impression upon the ignorant masses, calculated to have a baleful influence on those who are already too much prejudiced against my people.... Loose and uncalled for remarks against my race...will deprive us in the coming election of ten thousands of votes."[6] Apparently, Johnson did not respond, and he became Lincoln's vice president.

At Lincoln's second inauguration on March 4, 1865, Johnson gave such a maudlin and rambling speech, that his predecessor, Hannibal Hamlin, thought he was drunk, grabbed his coattails, and vainly tried to pull him back to his chair.

5   *New York Tribune*, April 30, 1864.
6   Evans, *Judah P. Benjamin*, 260–61.

Some suggested that Lincoln should fire Johnson as a drunk, but he refused, saying, "I've known Andy a great many years, and he ain't no drunkard."[7]

On April 14, 1865, after Lincoln's assassination, Andrew Johnson, now president, accused Jefferson Davis and Judah Benjamin of planning the murder and vowed, "They shall suffer for this."[8]

He was backed up by the *New York Times*, which recommended that the rebel leaders should die "the most disgraceful death on the gallows."[9] But Johnson had a change of heart, hanged a few Confederates, but pardoned most, including a Jewish attorney, Alfred Huger Moses, who had been sentenced to death.

Jefferson Davis escaped from the Confederate capital, Richmond, reportedly in his wife's dress, but was captured in Georgia and spent two years in prison.

There is no convincing evidence that he or Benjamin were involved in Lincoln's assassination.

Benjamin, a British as well as an American citizen, escaped capture with other Confederates, at first hiding in an ambulance pulled by a pair of old horses, which got stuck in the mud. After getting out of the mud, an ex-Confederate officer took him by boat to the Florida Keys. When a suspicious Federal gunboat captain approached the boat, Benjamin hurriedly donned a cook's apron, and covered his face with grease and soot. Benjamin's disguise as the boat's cook fooled the Yankee, whose parting shot was to say that it was the first time he'd seen a Jew doing manual labor. From Florida, Benjamin boarded a ship and crossed the Atlantic for England, where he resumed his legal career and became so successful and respected that Queen Victoria made him a Queen's

---

[7] Whitney and Whitney, *American Presidents*, 45.

[8] Evans, *Judah P. Benjamin*, 304.

[9] *New York Times*, May 1, 1865.

Counsel, which allowed him to practice law in the House of Lords.[10]

Meanwhile, President Andrew Johnson had been trying to adopt Lincoln's policy of reconciliation with the former enemy and to rebuild the devastated South, despite opposition from Minister of War Edwin Stanton. Johnson consequently fired Stanton and appointed General Ulysses S. Grant, who declined the offer, leaving Stanton still in charge. Enraged, Johnson again fired him and gave the job to Major General Lorenzo Thomas. Three days later, on February 24, 1868, the House impeached Johnson for high crimes and misdemeanors. Specifically the crimes were firing Stanton without their consent, expressing contempt for Congress, and resisting its attempts to impeach him. He survived by one vote. However, it wasn't the end of his contentious political career. When General Grant replaced him as president in 1868, Johnson retired, but after seven years he returned to Washington again as the US senator for Tennessee. He died that same year of a stroke at age sixty-six, in his daughter's Tennessee home.

Judah Benjamin suffered from diabetes and died of heart failure at seventy-three on May 6, 1884, in his Paris mansion.

---

[10] Evans, *Judah P. Benjamin*, 307–308, 311–313, 318–319.

Ulysses S. Grant

1822–1885

- ✪ Eighteenth president, 1869–1877
- ✪ Commander of the Union army in the Civil War
- ✪ Championed the Fifteenth Amendment, giving constitutional protection for African American voting rights

Ulysses S. Grant was called "Grant the Butcher" during the Civil War, because he fought to win at all costs – which meant massive casualties. Yet he deplored big-game hunting and would never kill an animal, except, of course, those of the human variety in wartime. Though he demanded unconditional surrender, when he beat the Confederates he was magnanimous: even letting the defeated men return to their homes with their horses and allowing the officers to keep their side arms. He also sent twenty-five thousand rations to starving Confederates.

Grant was born on April 27, 1822, in Point Pleasant, Ohio, to Jesse Root Grant, a tanner and strict abolitionist, and Hannah Simpson; he had three sisters and two brothers. He, like his parents, was a Methodist, an avid reader of the Bible, and a strong believer in the separation of church and state.

111

Although as a West Point graduate he sometimes drank himself under the table and spent much of his young life as a soldier at military outposts where cursing was the lingua franca, he never swore – drunk or sober – and was an avid Bible reader. Dismissed from the army because he couldn't hold his liquor, he took dull, dead-end jobs, finally as a clerk working for his young brothers who ran the family leather store in Galena, Illinois.

At twenty-six, in 1848, he married Julia Boggs Dent, a slave-owner's daughter. They had a good marriage, which produced three sons and a daughter.

He enlisted at the start of the Civil War and eventually became commander-in-chief of the United States armies and Lincoln's favorite general, because they had similar views on war strategy – to fight the enemy relentlessly.

Both sides in the war needed to keep the cotton trade alive: the North to supply its mills making uniforms and military tents for its Union army, the South to sell to the North for its economic survival. The US Treasury and the army issued licenses to engage in this trade, but the system led to unlicensed would-be traders bribing army officers to let them buy Southern cotton without a license.

General Grant was responsible for issuing cotton-trading licenses in parts of Mississippi, Tennessee, and Kentucky, while trying to capture the heavily defended town of Vicksburg, Mississippi, from the Confederates. As winning the fight was his main preoccupation, he was incensed when he learned that "every colonel, captain, or quartermaster [is] in secret partnership with some operator in cotton; every soldier dreams of adding a bale of cotton to his monthly pay." Believing that Jewish traders were most responsible for the problem, he issued several directives to stop it.

On November 9, 1862, he directed Stephen Hurlbut to refuse all those seeking permits to travel south of Jackson.

"The Israelites especially," Grant wrote, "should be kept out." The next day he ordered General Webster to instruct "all the conductors on the road that no Jews are to be permitted to travel on the railroad southward from any point. They may go north, and be encouraged in it, but they are such an intolerable nuisance that the department must be purged of them." This became necessary, he explained, because of "the total disregard and evasion of orders by Jews." He was further exasperated when his own father appeared at his headquarters seeking trade licenses for his friends, including several Jews.

On December 17, 1862, Grant wrote to C. P. Wolcott, assistant secretary of war, "Regulations of the Treasury Department have been violated, and that most likely by Jews and other unprincipled traders.... I have instructed the commanding officer at Columbus to refuse all permits to Jews to come South, and I have frequently had them expelled from the department, but they come in with their carpet-sacks in spite of all that can be done to prevent it. The Jews seem to be a privileged class that can travel everywhere.... If not permitted to buy cotton themselves they will act as agents for somebody else." That same day Grant issued Order Number 11, which read as follows:

> 1. The Jews, as a class are violating every regulation of the Treasury Department, and also department orders, are hereby expelled from the Department (Tennessee) within twenty-four hours from the receipt of this order.

> 2. Post commanders will see to it that all of this class of people be furnished passes and required to leave, and anyone remaining after such notification will be arrested and held in confinement until an opportunity occurs of sending them out as prisoners, unless furnished with a permit from headquarters.

3. No passes will be given these people to visit headquarters for the purpose of making personal application for trade permits.[1]

Many newspapers and several Jewish organizations protested the order, and a delegation from Kentucky led by Cesar Kaskel persuaded Lincoln to have the order revoked.[2]

After the war, when Grant was a Republican presidential candidate, many Jews refused to vote for him because of Order 11, but staunch Jewish Republicans, like Simon Wolf of Washington, did, and helped to make Grant the next president. Wolf had accepted Grant's explanation that a subordinate had written the order and he had signed it without reading it. True or not, President Grant demonstrated that far from being anti-Semitic, he was pro-Jewish.

He appointed a Jew, General Edwin S. Saloman, to be the governor of what became Washington state, and offered Jewish businessman Joseph Seligman, who declined the offer, the position of secretary of the Treasury. Eventually, Grant appointed more Jews to public office than any previous president.[3]

Grant had been president for three months when he invited Rabbi Hayim Schneerson, from Jerusalem, to the White House. A fervent Zionist and great-grandson of the founder of Lubavitch Hasidism, the rabbi was in Washington to improve the lives of Jews in Palestine and to stop the American consul in Palestine from attempting to convert a Jewish girl to

---

[1] All the information on Grant and Order Number 11 is from Karp, *From the Ends of the Earth,* 247–56; "General Grant's Infamy," Jewish Virtual Library, http://www. jewishvirtuallibrary.org/jsource/anti-semitism/grant.html; Dr. Yitzchok Levine, "General Grant's Expulsion of the Jews," March 5, 2008, http://www.jewishpress. com/indepth/columns/general-grants-expulsion-of-the-jews/2008/03/05/; and Lewis Regenstein, "Jews and Anti-Semitism in the American Civil War," The Jewish Magazine, Jan. 2007, http://www.jewishmag.com/110mag/civilwar/civilwar.htm.

[2] Simpson, *Ulysses S. Grant,* 165; Karp, *From the Ends of the Earth,* 247.

[3] Harold Shafman, *The First Rabbi* (Santa Barbara, CA: Pangloss Press, 1988), 527–31.

Christianity. The rabbi had complained about it to Secretary of State, Hamilton Fish, who had arranged for him to meet President Grant.

Dressed in colorful oriental clothes, he told Grant:

> The Israelites in Palestine possess no political or civil rights, are often deprived of protection by the representatives of civilized nations, which the Christians enjoy, and are exposed to violence and arbitrary rule. The only shelter the Israelites occasionally find is in the courts of the different European Consulates, where one of their coreligionists is employed as interpreter or deputy Consul. This free Republic alone [the United States], whose banner covers the oppressed, whose foundation is based on equality, toleration, and liberty of conscience, has no Israelites employed near the consul at Jerusalem. I do pray, therefore, your Excellency, to turn your attention to the deplorable condition of my brethren of the Orient, that the principles of this Government be embodied in its representatives abroad. And that your Excellency may show me that favor which will enable my brethren in the Holy Land in the hour of need to seek refuge under the Stars and Stripes.

According to Washington's *National Intelligencer*, Grant, "deeply moved by the Rabbi's sincere and telling words, inquired with interest as to the circumstances affecting the Jews in Jerusalem which might be guarded by the American Consulate, and replied, with his wonted quick decision, 'I shall look into the matter with care.'" Soon after, Grant recalled "the erring diplomat [back to the United States] to the satisfaction of Palestinian Jewry and the delight of the rabbi who accomplished it." Why Grant and Fish willingly met the oddly clad foreigner is unclear, even though the global responsibilities of American presidents were not very taxing. Curiosity or cordiality aside, the new president desired to please Jewish opinion, which had shown during the presidential campaign of 1868 that it remembered his anti-Jewish General Order Number 11 of Civil War days.

The rabbi traveled on to California, lecturing in various cities, telling a Cincinnati audience that the time was not far off when Israel (in Turkish control as part of the Ottoman Empire) would be restored to the Jewish people. He had twice visited Romania in the 1860s where, he said, life for the half a million Jews was intolerable, their property confiscated, farmers expelled from their farms, Jews arrested because they were Jews, and forced to leave the country. While in Chicago, he wrote to President Grant on January 19, 1870, thanking him for appointing a Jewish American consul in Jerusalem. He then went on:

> I feel myself encouraged in again praying to the great American people and their chosen chieftain. Five hundred thousand souls in Rumania are subject to the malicious [actions of the non-Jewish Rumanians in control of the country]. Their crime is their belief in One God, their sin that they are sons of the stock of Abraham. The children of Israel live there as a scattered flock of defenseless sheep – as helpless orphans.... On all the earth there is no Israelite the occupant of a throne or in any position of might, whence he could speak a weighty word for these unfortunates. The influence of the United States can be exerted in two different ways...in appointment of consuls friendly toward our race in that country; but more especially would such an appointment prove efficacious...if a Jewish citizen were sent there as consul.[4]

If anything Rabbi Schneerson had understated the plight of Romanian Jews. They were beaten, maimed, and robbed. Only Christians could be citizens, and some two hundred restrictive laws applying to Jews made it next to impossible

---

[4] Ibid., 531.

for them to earn a living. In 1872 the US consul in Paris confirmed the rabbi's report, characterizing Romanian treatment of Jews as "a disgrace to Christian civilization."

That and the rabbi's advice doubtless persuaded Grant to appoint a Jewish American attorney and political journalist, Benjamin Franklin Peixotto of San Francisco, as the unpaid US consul in Bucharest, Romania's capital, where he gave Jews hope of a brighter future.

Back in New York, lecturing at Cooper Union, Rabbi Schneerson stressed the need to buy land and buildings before God would restore their country to the Jews, and pointed out that the Old Testament tells how Abraham had bought land there even though God had promised it to him. Quite a prophet, the rabbi felt that America would be the chosen agent to restore Israel to the Jews.[5]

On July 31, 1870, President Grant, as guest of honor, sat for three hours at the dedication of a new synagogue, Adas Israel, at the corner of Sixth and G Streets in Washington, and contributed ten dollars to its funds. It is now the largest Conservative synagogue in the city. Although he never publicly apologized for Order 11, privately he conceded that it was an "obnoxious order."[6]

After leaving the White House, he and his wife, Julia, went on a two-year world tour, which included Jerusalem. The trip had been expensive, his investments failed, and by 1885 he was broke and suffering from throat cancer. But he managed to complete his memoirs, regarded by many as a masterpiece, just days before he died at age sixty-three, on July 23, 1885, at Saratoga Springs, New York.

---

[5]   Roth, *The Standard Jewish Encyclopedia,* s.v. "Rumania."

[6]   Grant Papers, Library of Congress.

Rutherford B. Hayes

1822–1893

- ✪ Nineteenth president, 1877–1881
- ✪ Oversaw the end of Reconstruction and the country's entry into the Second Industrial Revolution
- ✪ Elected president in one of the most hotly contested elections in American history

No one would have expected a heroic life for Rutherford Hayes, a frail and sickly boy who, according to the *New York Times*, was "as timid and nervous as a girl, with an aversion to the rough and mischievous ways of healthy schoolboys."[1] Yet he grew up to be a Union army general, a daring, much battle-scarred war hero, and finally, the nineteenth president of the United States.

When his storekeeper father, of Scottish Puritan stock, died ten weeks before his birth in Delaware, Ohio, on October 22, 1822, his mother's brother, Sardis Birchard, became his

---

[1] Rutherford Hayes's Obituary, *New York Times*, January 18, 1893, 1.

guardian. Hayes's delicate health kept him from school in his early years.

He was educated in a professor's Middletown, Connecticut, home before attending Ohio's Kenyon College. There he overcame his timidity and at nineteen considered a career in public office, confiding to his diary his ambitious plans:

> I do not intend to leave here until about a year after I graduate, when I expect to commence the study of law. Before then I will become a master of logic and rhetoric and obtain a good knowledge of history. To accomplish these objects I intend to study hard...and believe I can make, at least, a tolerable debater. It is another intention of mine, that after I have commenced in life, whatever may be my ability or station, to preserve a reputation for honesty and benevolence, and if ever I am a public man I will never do anything inconsistent with the character of a true friend and good citizen. To become such a man I shall necessarily have to live in accordance with the precepts of the Bible [he was a Methodist] which I firmly believe, although I have never made them strictly the "rule of my conduct" – Thus ends this long dry chapter on self."[2]

Finishing college at the top of his class, Hayes entered Harvard Law School, where he was still not one of the boys, as he admitted in another diary entry: "More faults to cure.... Trifling remarks, boyish conduct, etc., are among my crying sins.... Mend, mend!... I was quite lame from scuffling, and all my fingers stiffened from playing ball. A pretty business for a law student."[3]

He graduated in 1845, became a successful Cincinnati lawyer, and at thirty married twenty-one-year-old Lucy Ware

---

2 The Ohio Historical Society, Hayes Diary, June 19, 1841, http://www.ohiohistory. org/onlinedoc/hayes/quotes.html.

3 Durant, *Pictorial History of American Presidents*, 162–67.

Webb, a doctor's daughter and also a college graduate. During their long, happy marriage, they had seven sons and a daughter.

As an ardent Lincoln supporter, when the Civil War broke out Hayes volunteered for the Union army and was a major in the 23rd Ohio Regiment. Their task was to protect the Baltimore and Ohio Railroad from potential enemy attacks at Clarksburg, West Virginia. He proved a good soldier, and in October 1861 was promoted to lieutenant colonel.

The following year, one of his men, Private Joseph Joel, asked him if he and twenty fellow Jews in the regiment could be temporarily excused from duty to celebrate Passover. Hayes said yes.

There were no matzos to be found in the area, but a friendly Jewish trader returning to Ohio offered to buy matzos there and ship them back south. On the morning of the eve of Passover the men anxiously awaited the matzos. To their delight, Joel recalled, a supply train arrived at the camp, and there were not only seven barrels of matzos, but their thoughtful friend "had enclosed prayer books." The men divided into two groups, one to build a wooden hut and the other to forage for food. The food foragers came back with "two kegs of cider, a lamb, several chickens, and some eggs.... There, in the wild woods of West Virginia, away from home and friends, we consecrated and offered up to the ever-loving God of Israel our prayers and sacrifice.... Since then a number of my comrades have fallen in battle in defending the flag they volunteered to protect with their lives. I myself have received a number of wounds all but mortal, but there is no occasion in my life that gives me more pleasure and satisfaction than when I remember the Passover of 1862."[4]

---

[4] "Joseph Joel, 23rd Ohio Volunteer Infantry," Rutherford B. Hayes Presidential Center, Paper Trail, January 2006, http://www.rbhayes.org/hayes/manunews/paper_trail_display.asp?nid=102&subj=manunews.

The following summer, at Parisburg, Virginia, Hayes's forces were attacked by a much greater Confederate force. Keeping a cool head, he extracted his men from what could have been a disaster.

Ordered to Maryland in August, he led his regiment in the Battle of South Mountain, where he was severely wounded and carried off the field. His wife and her doctor brother, Joseph Webb, took care of him for several weeks in a makeshift hospital in Middletown, Maryland. When he recovered from his wounds, he returned to the battle, leading raids to destroy Confederate stores and disrupt their lines of communication in Southern Virginia. In the fall of 1864, Hayes was promoted to Brigadier General "for gallant...services in the battles of Winchester [where he led a daring charge]," and soon after he was made a major general "for gallant and distinguished services during the campaigns of 1864."[5]

Learning of his exploits, Ohio voters nominated him for Congress, but got a sharp rebuke, when he wrote from the camp of Sheridan's army on August 24, 1864, "Your suggestion about getting a furlough to stump was certainly made without reflection. An officer fit for duty who at this crisis would abandon his post to electioneer for a seat in Congress ought to be scalped. You may feel perfectly sure I shall do no such thing."[6]

Instead, in 1865, he commanded an attack on Lynchburg. Soon after, General Robert E. Lee surrendered and the war was over. Hayes was lucky to have survived: in total, four horses had been shot from under him in battle, and he had been wounded four times. That same year an adoring Ohio public elected him to Congress, where he served for two years and

5   Hayes's obituary, *New York Times*, January 18, 1893.

6   "Memorable Quotes from the Diary and Letters of Rutherford B. Hayes," Rutherford B. Hayes Presidential Center, http://www.ohiohistory.org/onlinedoc/hayes/quotes.html.

was respected for his honesty and efficiency. He resigned from Congress to serve as Ohio's governor from 1868 to 1872.

While governor he received a letter from Joseph Joel, the soldier who had obtained his permission to observe Passover. Joel wrote to announce the birth of his daughter. Hayes replied:

> My Dear Joel; I was much gratified to receive your kind letter of the 10th. Chills and fever, and as a consequence, inflamed eyes have prevented an earlier reply. I went up the Shenandoah Valley two weeks ago, visiting the battle scenes of 1864, hoping to benefit my health, as well as to revive recollections of stirring events. I am now nearly well again. I congratulate you and Mrs. Joel on your new happiness. We also have another boy, now three and a half months old. A healthy, well-behaved little fellow.... I am looking forward to a release from public life and to freedom as hopefully as a schoolboy to his coming vacation, or a soldier to a furlough. I retire absolutely. I shall make no attempt to go higher. If I ever accept public employment again it will be incidental and for special reasons.... I shall always cherish you as one of the true friends, and shall be interested in whatever befalls you.[7]

Joel eventually moved with his family to Staten Island and became an editor and publisher. He wrote to Hayes again to say that his wife had given birth to their first son, and they named him Rutherford B. Hayes Joel.

Hayes's uncle, Sardis Birchard, died in January 1874, leaving him a fortune. Now able to retire, his supporters persuaded him two years later to serve again as governor, and that same year at the Republican convention in Cincinnati, he was named Ohio's favorite son. To the surprise of political experts, Hayes won the presidential nomination. Even more unexpected was his victory over his rival, Democrat Samuel Tilden,

---

[7] Rutherford B. Hayes Presidential Center, http://www.rbhayes.org/hayes/manunews/ paper_trail_display.asp?nid=102&subj=manunews.

because Tilden had several hundred thousand more popular votes. Hayes's win was bitterly disputed by the Democrats, but an election commission voting along party lines favored Hayes the Republican.

Outgoing President Grant feared that angry Democrats would disrupt the inauguration ceremony, so Hayes was first privately sworn in at the Red Room of the White House on March 5, 1877, and later on the same day in public on the East Portico of the US Capitol.

After a little over a year in office, he noted in his diary for August 9, 1878, "Nothing brings out the lower traits of human nature like office seeking. Men of good character and impulses are betrayed by it into all sorts of meanness."[8]

Concerned about the mistreatment of Romanian Jews, in 1879 President Hayes got his secretary of state, William Evarts, to write to the US representative there: "As you are aware, this government has ever felt deep interest in the welfare of the Hebrew race in foreign countries, and has viewed with abhorrence the wrongs to which they have at various periods been subjected by followers of other creeds in the East."[9]

US appeals to the Romanians to act humanely failed.

Meanwhile, in the United States, Alexander Graham Bell spoke to President Hayes using his recent invention, the telephone, and the president had one installed in the Oval Office.

Apart from his attempt to improve the lives of Romanian Jews, Hayes's interaction with Jews seems to have been limited to letting twenty-one Jewish soldiers under his command celebrate Passover. That is, until 1880, when he was told that, despite a US-Russian treaty of 1832 guaranteeing citizens of each country "the same security and protection as natives of the country in which they reside," for no apparent reason the

---

[8]   Ohio Historical Society, http://www.ohiohistory.org/onlinedoc/hayes/quotes.html.

[9]   Seymour Martin Lipset, *America Exceptionalism: A Double-Edged Sword* (New York: W. W. Norton, 1997), 139.

Russians threatened to expel an American Jew, Henry Pinkos, his wife, and child living in St. Petersburg.[10]

After John Foster, the American representative there, put pressure on the Russian foreign minister, he explained that there had been an attempt to assassinate Czar Alexander the Second, and many of the suspects were Jews. Foster replied that Pinkos was a businessman and had not been accused of any crime, and that "in the view of this government the religion professed by one of its citizens has no relation to the citizen's right to the protection of the United States."[11]

The Russian official pointed out that the anti-Jewish laws that existed in Russia before the 1832 treaty with the United States were still in force, and that his country granted no greater rights to American Jews than they did to their own Jews.

US Secretary of State William Evarts replied, "We ask treaty treatment for our aggrieved citizens, not because they are Jews, but because they are Americans."[12]

Eventually, Pinkos was given a three-month extension to sell his business in Russia, before he booked his and his family's passage back to America. But the Russians said their passports were invalid and they couldn't leave. The captain of the ship in which they planned to sail refused to return the passage money, so Pinkos had to accept charity to enable them to return to America. His parting words, a reporter noted, were, "Russia is no place for one of my creed."[13]

Hayes also helped a Jewish woman on home ground, who had been refused a job in the Interior Department because she insisted on observing her Sabbath and refused to work

---

[10] *Jewish Year Book*, 1904–5, p. 287.

[11] Ibid., 290.

[12] Cyrus Adler and Aaron M. Margalith, *With Firmness in the Right: American Intercession on Behalf of Jews in the Diplomatic Correspondence of the United States, 1840–1938*, p. 179.

[13] Ibid., 180.

on Saturdays. Hayes ordered the department to hire her, and it became law that Jews could not be denied employment as Federal civil servants because they intended to observe their religious practices.

Rutherford Hayes died of complications from a heart attack on January 17, 1893, at the age of seventy-one, three years after the death of his beloved wife, Lucy.

James A. Garfield

1831–1881

- ✪ Twentieth president, 1881
- ✪ Major general in the Civil War and an outstanding speaker and debater
- ✪ Second president to be assassinated

In sharp contrast to Rutherford Hayes, James Garfield was a tough kid, enjoying nothing more than a fistfight. The youngest of five siblings, he was born to an Ohio farmer, Abram, and his wife, Eliza, on November 19, 1831. His father died from an infection and exhaustion after fighting a forest fire when Garfield was not yet two, and his widowed mother then ran the farm with the help of her older children. As a boy, Garfield not only loved to fight but also to read about famous battles. His favorite book was *The Jewish War* (against the Romans) by Jewish historian Josephus, a book that he won as a school prize. His boyhood ambition was to go to sea, but the closest he got, at seventeen, was as a "tow boy," driving horses and mules on the tow path to pull boats on the Ohio Canal. It was a hazardous job and he often fell into the canal, experiencing, as he once calculated, "fourteen almost marvelous escapes from drowning."[1]

At eighteen he attended Gealuga Seminary, but dropped out for a semester to teach at a country school – after beating up the school bully who had driven away the previous teacher. He taught there for only a few months before returning to the seminary to prepare for his application to Hiram Electric Institute (later Hiram College), founded by the Disciples of Christ. There, he excelled at Greek and Latin, and, as an ambidextrous linguist he used a unique party trick to entertain friends, simultaneously writing in Greek with one hand and Latin with the other.

A benefactor paid for his education at Williams College in Massachusetts, and in his free time he taught at Vermont's North Pownal school, replacing, by an odd coincidence, Chester Arthur – who would be his successor as US president. He did so well at Williams, graduating with honors, that Hiram hired him as its professor of Greek and Latin, and the next year, at age twenty-six, he became the college president.

Soon after, he married Lucretia Rudolph, a farmer's daughter. With her encouragement, he prepared for a political career by studying law, while on Sundays he preached at the Disciples of Christ church. Through teaching and preaching he developed into an outstanding speaker and debater, which accounts for his election in 1859 as a Republican Ohio State Senator. Three years later, at the start of the Civil War, he joined the Union army as a colonel.

In command of the 42nd Ohio Infantry Volunteers, he drove the Confederate forces out of eastern Kentucky, and in September 1863, though his horse was shot from under him, he managed to deliver a message on foot that saved a large Union

---

[1] Whitney and Whitney, *American Presidents*, 165.

force from disaster. For this, at age thirty-two, he was promoted to major general, the youngest general in the Union army.

While still in the army he was elected to Congress, and at President Lincoln's request he left the battlefront to serve as a congressman.

He happened to be in New York City shortly after Lincoln's assassination when an angry mob gathered near the Exchange Building on Manhattan's Wall Street, and killed one man and severely injured another for expressing anti-Lincoln sentiments. By chance Congressman Garfield was in the Exchange Building, saw the dangerous situation from a balcony, and watched several men vainly try to calm the mob. A reporter must have been in the crowd to record what happened next. Garfield got the mob's attention, and as if preaching a sermon to the Disciples of Christ on God's eternal presence, began: "Fellow citizens, clouds of darkness are around about Him! His pavilion is dark waters, and thick clouds of the skies! Justice and judgment are the establishment of his throne! Mercy and truth shall go before his face! Fellow citizens, God reigns and the Government at Washington still lives."[2] His words and air of command calmed the mob that moments before had been threatening to attack the nearby building of the Democratic *New York World*.

The blue-eyed, fair-haired, six-foot-tall Garfield was described by friends as genial, easygoing, and warmhearted – but not toward unrepentant Confederates. When nominated for president in 1880, he stated his inflexible condition for renewing friendship with the South: Southerners must admit "forever and forever more, that in the war for the Union, we were right and they were wrong."[3]

---

[2] *The American Heritage Pictorial History of the Presidents of the United States*, vol. 2, "James Abram Garfield" (American Heritage Publishing Co., Inc., 1968), 521.

[3] Whitney and Whitney, *American Presidents,*, 165.

Just before he became the twentieth president of the United States in 1881, the New York Times published a feature headed "Russian Hatred of Jews: Facts about Persecuted American Citizens." It revealed that the US State Department's 142-page "Executive Document 470" gave details of Russian persecution of Jews, and America's attempts to stop it.[4]

In that document, the US consul in St. Petersburg reported that "the amount of suffering undergone by over 15,000 people – men, women, and children – destitute of food and lodging, is painful to contemplate." He estimated that in the whole of Russia, while five million Russian Jews were clamoring to be freed from all the special restrictions imposed on them, there were, on the other hand, "85,000,000 other Russian subjects who were clamoring to have the 5,000,000 expelled from the empire."[5]

President Garfield's denunciation of a pogrom in Russia early in 1881 initiated "a pattern of protests about the treatment of Russian Jews which persisted until World War 1"[6] – and throughout the twentieth century.

By July 2, 1881, only months into his presidency, Garfield was at Washington's Baltimore and Potomac railroad station, en route to Williams College for his class's twenty-fifth anniversary, where he intended to show his two sons his alma mater.

Waiting for him at the station was Charles Guiteau, an armed and mentally unbalanced, disgruntled office seeker, who shot Garfield in the arm and back. Guiteau was arrested and taken to prison while his mortally wounded victim was carried to the White House. There the inventor of the telephone,

---

4   "Russian Hatred of Jews," New York Times, November 9, 1880, 2.

5   Whitney and Whitney, American Presidents, 167.

6   Lipset, American Exceptionalism, p. 159.

Alexander Graham Bell, used his induction-balance device to locate the bullet in Garfield's back.

It didn't help: the forty-nine-year-old president died on September 19, 1881, and his vice president, Chester Arthur, succeeded him.

The assassin was hanged nine months later.

Chester A. Arthur

1829–1886

- ✪ Twenty-first president, 1881–1885
- ✪ James A. Garfield's vice president, he assumed the presidency after Garfield's assassination
- ✪ Finally completed civil service reform initiated by Hayes

Chester Arthur's father, William, was an Irish-born Baptist minister and farmer, and his mother, Malvina, was part Native American. Chester was born in Fairfield, Vermont, on October 5, 1829. A boyhood friend recalled that even in his youth, Arthur showed leadership. When he and his friends decided to build a dam across a stream, for example, Arthur would order one to collect sticks, another stones, and a third mud, while he never got his hands wet or dirty. Yet they all obeyed him without question or protest.[1]

A graduate of Union College, he became successively a New York City attorney, a brigadier general during the Civil War, and collector for the port of New York. When that job ended, he resumed the practice of law in Manhattan.

---

[1] *New York Post*, April 2, 1900.

At thirty, on October 25, 1859, he married twenty-one-year-old Ellen Herndon. Their first son died at age two of a brain disease. A second son was born in 1864, and a daughter in 1871. When his wife died of pneumonia at age forty-two, on January 12, 1880, he vowed never to remarry – a promise he kept.

A year later he was President Garfield's vice president, but only for six months – an assassin killed the president and Arthur took over.

He was soon confronted with the problems of Jewish Americans wishing to travel to Russia, to work or settle there. Instead of asking them customary questions – if they had a criminal record or suffered from an infectious disease – Russian officials who issued visas simply asked them their religion. Those who said "Jewish" were automatically denied visas. When this was brought to President Arthur's attention, he told his ambassador in St. Petersburg to advise his Russian counterpart:

> The Government of the United States concludes its treaties with foreign states for the equal protection of all classes of American citizens. It can make absolutely no discrimination between them, whatever be their origin or creed.... Any unfriendly or discriminatory act against them on the part of a foreign power would call for our earnest [protests], whether a treaty existed or not.... You can go further and advise him that we can make no new treaty with Russia, nor accept any construction of our existing treaty which shall discriminate against any class of American citizen on account of their religious faith."[2]

It had no effect: the Russians continued to discriminate against Jews. Arthur shared his frustration with congressmen

---

[2]   "Russia Hoodwinking US about Passports for Jews," *New York Times*, July 1, 1911, 1.

on December 6, 1861, informing them that American Jews who wanted to go to Russia were subjected to the same discrimination as Russian Jews, despite energetic official American protests. Almost exactly a year later, on December 4, 1883, Arthur told Congress, "There is no reason to believe that the time is not far distant when Russia will be able to secure toleration to all faiths within her borders." This aroused a skeptical Congress to pass a resolution asking to see the correspondence between the US and Russia on the sensitive subject. So, on May 2, 1882, President Arthur sent this special message to Congress: "In answer to the resolution of the House of Representatives...calling for correspondence respecting the condition of Israelites in Russia, I transmit herewith a report from the Secretary of State [James Blaine] and his accompanying papers." The Russians remained intolerant.

Soon after, Arthur had a new secretary of state, Frederick Frelinghuysen, who stepped up the diplomatic pressure on Russia. He wrote to the American representative there, "The prejudice of race and creed have in our days given way to the claims of our common humanity. The people of the United States have heard with great respect the suffering of the Jewish Russians.... It can scarcely be doubted that much has been done which a humane person must condemn.... Should you be of the opinion that a more vigorous effort might be put forth for the prevention of this great wrong you will...state with all proper deference that the feeling of friendship which the United States entertains for Russia prompts the hope that the Imperial Government will find means to cause the persecution of these unfortunate fellow-beings to cease."[3]

Friendly persuasion also failed to work: the Imperial Government remained unmoved.

---

[3]   "The Policy of Humanity," *New York Times*, November 2, 1902, 6.

Meanwhile, in America, a group of volunteers led by Clara Barton met in the Washington, DC, home of Adolphus Solomon, a Jewish American printer and philanthropist with special concern for Russian Jews. As well as helping to establish Mount Sinai Hospital and the Montefiore Home for Chronic Invalids, he funded the Jewish Protectory and Aid Society, and the Russian Jews Immigration Aid Society. In Solomon's home the group drew up the constitution for a new organization called the American Red Cross. They elected Barton president, and Solomon vice president, a position he held for seven years.

When in 1884 President Arthur was asked to appoint the first American delegates to the International Congress of the Red Cross in Geneva, he chose Barton and Solomon. Delegates from thirty-seven nations took part, electing Solomon vice president of the convention. Adolphus Solomon also helped to create the American Jewish Historical Society, where he is still celebrated as "The Red Cross's Jewish Star."

When Chester Arthur entered the White House the public mistrusted him, but greatly respected him when he left. A year later, in 1886, at age fifty-seven, he died of kidney disease.

Grover Cleveland

1837–1908

- ✪ Twenty-second and twenty-fourth president, 1885–1889 and 1893–1897
- ✪ Only president to serve two non-consecutive terms
- ✪ A divisive politician nonetheless renowned for his honesty and good character

At three-hundred pounds, Grover Cleveland, known to his nephews as "Uncle Jumbo," was not only a formidable figure because of his weight, but because of his record as New York's sheriff who doubled as the state's hangman.

The first of nine children, his father was a congregational minister and his mother a bookseller's daughter. Of Anglo-Irish ancestry, Cleveland had been an assistant teacher for the blind, an assistant district attorney for Erie County, New York, the county's sheriff and hangman, and mayor of Buffalo.

Cleveland was governor of the state when nominated by Democrats to be their next president.

Once dubbed the "veto mayor" due to his relentless and successful battle against Buffalo's corrupt politicians, he was regarded as a man of integrity, especially by his Democratic supporters, who called him "Grover the Good." However, when a rumor spread through the nation that he had fathered a child out of wedlock, the odds against his becoming president seemed insurmountable. Cleveland told his campaign staff to tell the truth, which was that as a lawyer in Buffalo he and several friends had enjoyed the company of a woman who gave birth to a son she named Oscar Folsom, after Cleveland's law partner. She was in the habit of asking the men in her life to give her money or she would expose them as the boy's father. As the only bachelor among them, although he did not believe the boy was his, Cleveland agreed to acknowledge that he was the father and paid for his support.

Joseph Pulitzer, a Hungarian Jew who served in the Union army, came to his rescue. As owner of the powerful *New York World*, Pulitzer had Cleveland's claims investigated and confirmed as true, then backed Cleveland as an honest man who "saved the honor of two families by taking on himself the sins of other men." It did the trick: Cleveland won the presidential election.[1]

On June 2, 1886, at forty-nine, Cleveland became the first and only president to marry in the White House; his bride was a twenty-two-year-old college graduate, Frances Folsom, daughter of his former law partner. Later that year he attended the unveiling of the Statue of Liberty in New York Harbor. A gift from France, its erection was only possible because of the financial contributions of thousands of readers of Pulitzer's *New York World*.

In 1887, Cleveland appointed Oscar Straus, a Jewish graduate of Columbia Law School, as the American minister to Turkey. Straus was well aware that the Turkish government welcomed Jewish Americans into all the extensive territory

---

[1]   Denis Brian, *Pulitzer: A Life* (New York: Wiley, 2001), 88, 90.

they ruled, with one exception – Palestine. Nevertheless, on learning that the Turks intended to expel several Jewish Americans from Palestine, Straus told them that the American Constitution did not recognize any distinction between its citizens because of their religion. The Turks then relented: Jewish Americans were allowed to stay in Jerusalem for a month. Straus got them to make it three months. As he mentioned in his memoir, *Under Four Administrations: From Cleveland to Taft*, the Turkish Grand Vizier explained to him that Jews were kept out of Palestine for their own protection, because at Easter religious fanaticism reached such a peak that Jews living in Palestine had to stay in their homes to avoid being attacked, or even murdered, by Christians. Furthermore, he said, there were reports that Jews throughout the world were planning to "strengthen themselves in and around Jerusalem with a view to reestablishing their ancient kingdom at some future time."

Straus advised the Grand Vizier that the Easter problem could be solved by employing a strong police force, that a few enquiries would reassure him that there was no such plan among the Jews of the world with regard to Jerusalem, and that rather than American Jews it was Jews from Romania and Russia who wanted to immigrate to Palestine.[2] His conversation with the Grand Vizier took place nine years before the appearance of Herzl's 1896 pamphlet promoting the Zionist idea of a Jewish homeland in Palestine.

After leaving Turkey to see for himself what was happening in Jerusalem, Straus found that hundreds of Jewish immigrants had been imprisoned there. He quickly got them released and also ensured that the rights of Jewish Americans in Turkey were protected.[3] After two years abroad as

---

[2]   Oscar S. Straus, *Under Four Administrations: From Cleveland to Taft* (Cambridge, MA: Houghton Mifflin, 1922), 80–81.

[3]   Review of Straus, *Under Four Administrations*, by *New York Times* Book Review,

an American diplomat, Straus returned to the United States, where he appealed to American Jews to help Russian Jews whose lives were in danger.

Straus was on good terms with President Cleveland, whose first term ended in 1889. Benjamin Harrison succeeded him and was president until 1893, when Cleveland ran and won again, to become America's twenty-fourth president. During his second term, his State Department frequently protested against the Russian practice of asking Americans applying for entry visas to state their religion and then refusing to issue visas to those who said "Jewish."

Two years later the Russians were still at it, and the American minister in Russia, Clifton Breckenridge, warned them that they were endangering relations with the United States.[4] Yet they remained inflexible, following the lead of their new czar, Nicholas II, who regarded almost any reforms as "nonsensical dreams."[5]

In Cleveland's third annual message to Congress on December 2, 1895, he said that Russian officials were still questioning Americans about their religion in order to ban Jews, and that he would continue to protest against the "obnoxious practice."[6]

On November 30, Thanksgiving, 1905, the now former president Cleveland attended a celebration of the 250th anniversary of Jews living in America. Jacob Schiff, a prominent Jewish-American banker and philanthropist, kicked off the event by leading other distinguished American Jews down an

November 19, 1922; US Department of State, US Foreign Relations, 1887, 1888, 1889.

4   US Department of State, US Foreign Relations, 1887, 1888, 1889.

5   US Department of State, US Foreign Relations, 1895.

6   Barbara Tuchman, *The Proud Tower: A Portrait of the World Before the War, 1890–1914* (New York: Bantam Books, 1979), 128.

aisle to the stage of Manhattan's Carnegie Hall, as the New York Symphony Orchestra played Mendelssohn's "March of the Priests," and the packed house of five thousand applauded. Schiff had given much of his fortune to help Russian Jews immigrate to America, and had successfully lobbied Congress and President Cleveland to prevent legislation that would have stopped the massive influx to America of Jews desperate to escape from Russia. Referring to a recent pogrom in Odessa, when four hundred Jews were slaughtered, Schiff said: "Racial prejudice and hatred are still rampant. The Jew still remains a martyr whose life must be sacrificed so that freedom and enlightenment, for which he has ever battled, will still triumph even in darkest Russia."[7]

Cleveland followed, saying:

> All nationalities have contributed to the composite population of the United States, many of them in greater number than the Jews. And yet I believe that few if any of those contributing nationalities have, directly and indirectly, been more influential in giving shape and direction to the Americanism of today.... Columbus on his voyage in search of a new world was aided by Jewish support and comrades help.... The Jews among us have in their care and keeping the history and traditions of an ancient Jewish commonwealth astonishingly like our own Republic in its democracy.... The ancient commonwealth was ordained by God for the government of His chosen people; and we should not close our minds to a conception of the coincidence in divine purpose discoverable in the bestowal, by the Ruler of the Universe, of a similar plan of rule, after thousands of years, upon the people of the United States, who also had their beginning in willing

---

7   American Presidency Project, Grover Cleveland, http://www.presidency.ucsb.edu/ws/?phd=4327.

submission to God's sovereignty and the assertion of freedom in His worship.[8]

On June 24, 1908, the seventy-one-year-old Cleveland died of heart and kidney disease, with his wife at his side. His last words were, "I have tried to do right."[9]

[8] Addresses delivered at Carnegie Hall, Thanksgiving Day, November 30, 1905, *New York Times*, December 1, 1905, 1, 4.

[9] Mark Wahlgren Summers, *Rum, Romanism, and Rebellion: The Making of a President, 1884* (Chapel Hill, NC: North Carolina Press, 2000), 6.

Benjamin Harrison

1833–1901

✪ Twenty-third president, 1889–1893

✪ Great-grandson of a signer of the Declaration of Independence and grandson of President William Henry Harrison

✪ Known for economic legislation and annual federal spending that reached $1 billion for the first time

Benjamin Harrison was born in North Bend, Harrison County, Ohio, on August 20, 1833. He was the fourth president born in that state. The great-grandson of a signer of the Declaration of Independence and a grandson of former president William Henry Harrison, Benjamin was the second son of eight children. His parents, John Scott Harrison, a farmer and congressman, and Elizabeth Ramsey Irwin, were both Presbyterians of English descent.

Tutors taught Harrison as a boy to prepare him for Farmer's College, where he studied for two years. He went on to Miami College, Oxford, Ohio, in 1850, where he was so strongly influenced by Robert Bishop, a Presbyterian minister who taught him history and political science, that after graduating Harrison wrote to him, "Whenever you may see anything in my course [in life] which you may deem reprehensible, be assured any course that may suggest itself [to you, will meet] with a hearty welcome."[1]

He left Oxford to study law in Cincinnati, and at age twenty, in 1853, married Caroline Scott, a daughter of the president of Farmer's College. Harrison was admitted to the bar the following year and moved to Indianapolis, where he became the city attorney, as well as a court reporter and the father of a son and daughter.

During the Civil War he served as a colonel in the Seventieth Regiment of Indiana Volunteers, riding into battle in Atlanta with General William T. Sherman. After three years, he was honorably discharged as a brigadier general, having been admired by his troops for his ability, energy, and courage.

The retired general did not immediately return to political life, though he was active in philanthropic work, taught Bible classes to men and women in his Presbyterian church, and was superintendent of its Sunday school.

In 1881, Indiana elected him to the US Senate, but despite his intelligence and debating skill, after six years he had little to show for it. When he was not reelected in 1887, he feared that his political career was over. Two years later he was president of the United States, having defeated Cleveland, the sitting president. Although his rival won the popular vote, Harrison had 233 electoral votes to Cleveland's 168.

Although courageous on the battlefield, in the White House he was afraid of being shocked by the recently installed electric lights. So he left it to the newly hired electrician to turn the lights on and off.[2]

---

[1] Ebenezer Presbyterian Church, Lexington, Kentucky, spiritual leader: Robert Bishop.

[2] Durant, *Pictorial History of American Presidents*, 189.

That first year in office, while Harrison was avoiding light switches, American Methodist missionary William Blackstone launched the first significant movement to promote the Zionist cause. Just back home from a trip to Palestine with his daughter, he was determined to alleviate the plight of Jews as victims of pogroms incited by Russian czar Alexander.[3]

Blackstone believed that Jews were "a people chosen by God to manifest His power and His love to…a world steeped in deepest idolatry," and that Jews would only be safe from persecution by returning to their ancient homeland.[4] Now, with the slaughter of Russian Jews in the headlines, Blackstone organized a "Conference on the Past, Present and Future of Palestine," held at Chicago's First Methodist Episcopal Church, where he encouraged Christian and Jewish leaders to become Zionists.

Strong support came from the more than a hundred thousand Yiddish-speaking immigrants who had arrived in Chicago in the 1880s and 1890s after escaping from Russia, Lithuania, and Poland. They had formed a group called the Knights of Zion, which bought land in Palestine for Jews willing to settle there. Energized by their support and the Chicago conference, Blackstone published a petition titled "Palestine for the Jews," which read in part:

> What shall be done for the Russian Jews? Why not give Palestine back to them again? According to God's distribution of nations, it is their home, an inalienable possession from which they were expelled by force. Why shall not the powers which under the Treaty of Berlin in 1878 gave Bulgaria to the Bulgarians, and Servia [Serbia] to the Servians, now give Palestine back to the Jews? The title deed to Palestine is

---

[3] "Chicago: Incubator of American Zionism," American Jewish Historical Society, http://www.ajhs.org/.

[4] William Blackstone, *Palestine for the Jews* (New York: Arno, 1977), 1.

recorded...in the hundreds of millions of Bibles now extant in more than three hundred languages of the earth.

[As for the Russian Jews] where shall 2,000,000 of such poor people go? Europe is crowded and has no room for more peasant population. Shall they come to America? This will be a tremendous expense, and require years.

Let us now restore to them the land of which they were cruelly despoiled by our Roman ancestors. To this end we respectively petition His Excellency Benjamin Harrison, President of the United States, and the Honorable James G. Blaine, Secretary of State, to use their good offices and influence with the Government of their Imperial Majesties, Alexander III, Czar of Russia; Victoria, Queen of Great Britain and Empress of India; William II, Emperor of Germany; Francis Joseph, Emperor of Austro-Hungary; Abdul Hamid II, Sultan of Turkey; His Royal Majesty, Humbert, King of Italy; Her Royal Majesty Marie Christiana, Queen Regent of Spain; and the Government of the Republic of France and with the Governments of Belgium, Holland, Denmark, Sweden, Portugal, Roumania, Servia, Bulgaria, and Greece. To secure the holding at an early date of an international conference to consider the condition of the Israelites and their claims to Palestine as their ancient home, and to [alleviate] their suffering condition.[5]

Blackstone sent copies of his petition to religious, political, and business leaders throughout the United States and got 413 supportive signatures, including those of Melville Fuller, chief justice of the US Supreme Court; Thomas Reed, Speaker of the House of Representatives; Robert Hill, chairman of the House Committee on Foreign Affairs; Ohio congressman and future US president William McKinley; William Russell, governor of Massachusetts; John D. and William Rockefeller;

---

[5] Papers of William Eugene Blackstone, Wheaton College, Illinois, http://www2.
wheaton.edu/bgc/archives.

J. P. Morgan; Cardinal Gibbons; the publisher of the *Chicago Tribune*; as well as a few American rabbis and a few leading American Jews. Reform Jews were notably absent from the list.[6]

On May 5, 1891, Secretary of State Blaine introduced Blackstone to the president, and Blackstone asked him to try to persuade world leaders to hold an international conference to consider the Jews' claims to Palestine as their homeland. The conference never occurred, though a similar one took place in 1947, fifty-six years later, when members of the United Nations fulfilled Blackstone's dream and Israel was created.

President Harrison did appeal to Czar Alexander to stop mistreating Jews, as he reported in his Third Annual Message, on December 9, 1892:

> The Government has found occasion to express in friendly spirit, but with much earnestness, to the Government of the Czar its serious concern because of the harsh measures being enforced against the Hebrews in Russia, by the revival of anti-Semitic laws, long in abeyance, great numbers of those unfortunate people have been constrained to abandon their homes and leave the Empire. The immigration of these people to the United States – many other countries being closed to them – is largely increasing and is likely to assume proportions which may make it difficult to find homes and employment for them here and to seriously affect the labor market.
>
> It is estimated that over a million will be forced from Russia within a few years. The Hebrew is never a beggar, he has always kept the law – lived by toil – often under severe and oppressive civil restrictions. It is also true that no race, sect,

---

6   Hilton Obenzinger, "In the Shadow of 'God's Sun-Dial': The Construction of American Christian Zionism and the Blackstone Memorial," *SEHR* 5, no. 1, Contested Politics, February 27, 1996, www.stanford.edu.

or class has more fully cared for its own than the Hebrew race. But the sudden transfer of such a multitude under conditions that tend to strip them of their small accumulations and to depress their energies and courage is neither good for them or for us.

The banishment, whether by direct decree or not less certain indirect methods, of so large a number of men and women is not a local question. A decree to leave one country is...an order to enter another – some other. This consideration, as well as the suggestion of humanity, furnishes ample ground for the [protests] which we have presented to Russia. While the historic friendship for that Government cannot fail to give assurance that our representations are those of a sincere well-wisher.[7]

Czar Alexander's callous response was to remove all Jews, sometimes forcibly, from Moscow, St. Petersburg, and Kiev, and into outlying regions far from the cities. However, his reign soon ended. His father had been assassinated and he himself had survived an assassination attempt, but his death in 1894 was from natural causes. By then a new president, Grover Cleveland, was back in the White House for a second term.

Meanwhile, Blackstone continued his campaign by sending his family Bible to an Austrian Jewish journalist, Theodor Herzl, who had experienced virulent anti-Semitism especially in France, in 1896. Then, Alfred Dreyfus, a Jewish officer in the French army, was sentenced to life in prison on Devil's Island for spying, a crime of which he was innocent. Herzl's response was to publish a pamphlet titled "The Jewish State,"

---

[7] Woolley and Peters, American Presidency Project, Benjamin Harrison, www. presidency.ucsb.edu/benjamin_harrison.php.

in which he called for Jews to have their own country, when and where to be decided by a council of nations.

Blackstone had marked the Bible he sent to Herzl, to indicate the many verses prophesying that the restored Jewish state should be in Palestine, its ancient homeland; this Bible can be seen today in Israel's Herzl Museum.

Herzl continued his mission by convening and chairing the First Zionist Conference in Basle, Switzerland, in August 1897. There, some two hundred wildly enthusiastic Jewish delegates from seventeen countries elected him the first president of the World Zionist Organization.

By that time, Benjamin Harrison was finished with world affairs. Approached to make another run for the presidency in 1896, he had declined, saying, "Why should a man seek that which to him would be a calamity?"[8]

He died of pneumonia at age sixty-seven in his Indianapolis home, on March 13, 1901.

---

[8] *American Heritage Pictorial History*, "Benjamin Harrison," 592.

William McKinley

1843–1901

⊛ Twenty-fifth president, 1897–1901
⊛ Led the nation to victory in the Spanish-American War
⊛ Third president to be assassinated

As a US congressman for Ohio in 1891, William McKinley was one of 413 influential Americans who had signed William Blackstone's petition to restore the Jewish homeland in Palestine. McKinley biographer Margaret Leech partly explained his Jewish sympathies, describing him as "a man who, in a day of sharp sectarian prejudice...was devoid of bigotry, possessing as a grace of his nature the tolerance that is unaware of its virtue."[1]

The seventh in a family of nine children (as was President Cleveland), McKinley was born in Niles, Ohio, on January 29, 1843. His father, William Sr., of Scottish-Irish-English descent, managed a blast furnace. His mother, Nancy, was of German-English descent.

At seventeen, William attended Allegheny College in Meade, Pennsylvania, but left after one term because of illness. When fit enough to return, his parents couldn't afford

---

[1] *In the Days of McKinley* (New York: Harper and Brothers, 1999), 12.

it, so he taught in a country school, then clerked in the local post office, until the Civil War gave him a chance to show his mettle. On June 11, 1861, eighteen-year-old McKinley joined the Twenty-third Ohio Volunteer Infantry, in which Rutherford Hayes, also a future United States president, was his commanding officer.

Only about twelve hundred Jewish Americans fought for the Confederacy, while about eight thousand fought for the Union, among them Captain Daniel Mayer, a surgeon in civilian life. He and McKinley met during the early fighting in West Virginia and struck up what became a lifelong friendship.

McKinley's outstanding courage at the Battle of Antietam was vividly recalled by Major Rutherford Hayes:

> The bloodiest day of the war, the day on which more men were killed and wounded [23,000] than on any other day of the war, was the seventeenth of September 1862, in the Battle of Antietam, better known as the Battle of Sharpsburg. The battle began at daylight. Without breakfast, without coffee, the men went into the fight and continued until after the sun went down. Early in the afternoon they were famished and hungry. The commissary department of the brigade was under Sergeant McKinley's administration and a better choice could not have been made, for when the issue came he performed a notable deed of daring at the crisis of the battle…. After filling up two wagons with necessary supplies he drove them through a storm of shells and bullets to the assistance of hungry and thirsty fellow soldiers.

> The mules of one wagon were disabled, but McKinley drove the other safely through and was received with hearty cheers, and from his hands every man in the regiment was served with hot coffee and warm meals, a thing that had never

occurred under similar circumstances in any other army in the world.[2]

McKinley's courage under fire won him a battlefield promotion to lieutenant. Later, by showing his own fearlessness he rallied panic-stricken Union troops near Winchester, West Virginia. At another time his horse was killed under him, but he kept fighting on foot.

President Lincoln promoted him to major "for gallantry and meritorious services at the battles of Opiquan, Cedar Creek and Fisher's Hill."[3]

At war's end, the twenty-two-year-old McKinley was serving on Rutherford Hayes's staff. And as president Hayes remembered him well, recalling, "When I became commander of the regiment I learned to know him like a book, and love him like a brother."[4]

After the war McKinley studied at Albany Law School, and in 1889 was prosecuting attorney for Stark County, Ohio. He also taught Sunday School in the Methodist Church and was attracted to a banker's daughter, Ida Saxton, who taught Sunday School in the nearby Presbyterian Church. They often met and chatted at the street corner between the two churches, which led to their marriage in January 1871.

The deaths of their infant daughters in 1871 and 1873 devastated them, and so severely affected Ida's health that she became a lifelong invalid, suffering from epilepsy and phlebitis. McKinley spent as much time as he could with her despite the demands of his promising career as Ohio's US representative. In 1890 he was elected the Republican leader in the House. Some time during the following two years he learned

---

[2]   Colonel T. W. Townsend, *Our Martyred President: Memorial Life of President McKinley,* Memorial Volume, 1901, p. 38.

[3]   Ibid., 69–70.

[4]   "Federation of Zionists," *The New York Times,* June 19, 1899, 2.

of William Blackstone's campaign to get people to endorse his petition titled "Palestine for the Jews." In it, as if having a conversation with his reader, the Christian Zionist had written, "But perhaps you say, 'I don't believe the Israelites are to be restored to Canaan and Jerusalem rebuilt.' Dear reader! Have you read the declarations of God's word about it? Surely nothing is more clearly stated in the Scriptures."[5]

As a devout Methodist, McKinley was familiar with the Old Testament account of God promising Palestine to the Jews. Perhaps as persuasive to McKinley the politician was Blackstone's report of the current situation, with some "2,000,000 Russian Jews piteously appealing to our sympathy and desperate for a shelter in Palestine."[6]

When elected Ohio's governor in 1891 McKinley focused for the next four years on domestic problems, especially the financial depression, when he paid out of his own pocket for a railroad car full of food and other supplies to be sent to impoverished miners.

Jews almost unanimously supported McKinley in his successful presidential bid against the Democratic contender, William Jennings Bryan.

In 1897, his first year as president, he accepted the invitation of a Jewish friend, Simon Wolf, to attend groundbreaking ceremonies for Washington Hebrew Congregation's building on 8th Street (later the site of the New Hope Baptist Church). That same year the Christian Zionist William Blackstone sent his family Bible to Theodor Herzl, who soon afterwards, on August 28, 1897, presided over the first International Zionist Congress in Basle, Switzerland, "to restore for Jews all over the world a legally-secured home and protect those living in

---

[5] Hilton Obenzinger, "In the Shadow of 'God's Sun-Dial': The Construction of American Christian Zionism and the Blackstone Memorial," *SEHR* 5, no. 1, Contested Politics, February 27, 1996, www.stanford.edu.

[6] Ibid.

Russia and other countries where they are exposed to persecution." The 208 delegates from sixteen countries gave the tall,
intense Herzl a standing ovation, shouting approval in many
languages. When one of them pleaded with him to stick with
the enterprise despite anticipated attacks and setbacks, there
were renewed cries of approval and Israel Zangwill, a prominent English Jew who had been something of a skeptic, "stood
on a table and applauded with all his strength."[7]

On returning to his home in Vienna, Herzl noted in his
diary: "If I were to sum up the Basle Conference: In Basle I
founded the Jewish state. Were I to say this [in public] I would
be greeted with universal laughter. But perhaps in five years
hence, in any case in fifty years hence, everyone will recognize
it."[8]

He was out by just one year.

In response to Herzl's conference, the Central Committee
of American Rabbis, representing some five thousand Jewish
Americans, denounced Zionism most fervently, especially the
Orthodox Jews among them who believed that the recreation
of Israel must first await the Messiah's arrival. The following year, Reform rabbis Stephen S. Wise and Gustav Gottheil
started the pro-Zionist movement in the United States and
within one year they had some ten thousand members.

President McKinley had kept in touch with his Civil War
Jewish friend, Captain Daniel Mayer, and in 1898 appointed
him the US consul to Argentina.

That year two rival newspaper titans, Hearst and Pulitzer,
infected their readers with war fever. McKinley succumbed to
public pressure and, on April 25, asked Congress to declare

---

[7] Alex Bein, *Theodore Herzl: A Biography,* translated by Maurice Samuel (New
York: World, 196), 242.

[8] Max Dimont, *The Jews in America: The Roots and Destiny of American Jews* (New
York: Simon & Schuster, 1952), 197.

war on Spain in order to help Cuban rebels drive their Spanish rulers from their land. Congress approved that same day what became known as the Spanish-American War. It lasted less than four months and ended with the American flag flying over Cuba, Puerto Rico, and, after a much longer fight, the Philippines.

When fellow Republican Julius Kahn, a Jew, was elected to Congress in 1899, McKinley entertained him and his wife, Florence, as his White House dinner guests. (Kahn died in 1924, after twenty-nine years in Congress, and his wife replaced him in a special election, the first Jewish congresswoman.)

McKinley began his second term in 1901, with Theodore Roosevelt, a hero of the Spanish-American war, as his vice president. In the fall he was hoping to attend Buffalo's Pan-American Exposition, but because of rumors that pro-Spanish Cubans planned to assassinate him, his secretary, George Cortelyou, advised him to cancel the visit. Discounting the rumors, McKinley replied: "Why should I? No one would wish to hurt me."

Among those waiting in line to meet the president at the exposition on September 6 was anarchist Leon Cozolgosz. He held a revolver concealed in a handkerchief to make it seem that his hand was bandaged, and when the president held out his hand in greeting, the assassin fired two bullets into him. In the ensuing uproar, the wounded McKinley was helped to a chair, and the enraged crowd began to kick and punch the would-be killer. But McKinley said, "Don't let them hurt him," then whispered to his secretary, "My wife, be careful, Cortelyou, how you tell her – oh, be careful!"[9]

Vice President Theodore Roosevelt had been climbing a mountain in the Adirondacks when, on September 15, he was told that the president was dying. On reaching Buffalo the

---

[9]   Leech, *In the Days of McKinley*, 584, 595–596.

next day he found McKinley dead. Roosevelt was then sworn in as the twenty-sixth president of the United States.

Just before the assassin's electrocution in Auburn Prison on October 29, 1901, he said, "I killed the president because he was the enemy of the good people. The good working people. I am not sorry for my crime." Vernon Briggs, director of the Massachusetts Department for Mental Health, studied the Cozolgosz case and interviewed his family. He discovered that the assassin, an unemployed factory worker, was one of seven children of Polish immigrants, born in Alpena, Michigan, in 1873 and baptized in St. Albertus Catholic Church. Briggs concluded that he was insane.[10]

Ida McKinley died less than six years after her husband.

---

[10] Jeffrey Seibert, *I Done My Duty: The Complete Story of the Assassination of President McKinley* (New York: Heritage Books, 2002), 430.

Theodore Roosevelt

1858–1919

- ✪ Twenty-sixth president, 1901–1909
- ✪ William McKinley's vice president, he assumed the presidency after McKinley's assassination, becoming the youngest US president
- ✪ A hero of the Spanish-American War, he was know for his exuberant personality

By sheer willpower Theodore Roosevelt changed himself from a scared and sickly child into a tough, tenacious, and trailblazing war hero, apparently afraid of nothing and no one, until he finally made it to the top as president of the United States. Even a would-be assassin's bullet that remained in his chest failed to slow or intimidate this human dynamo.

Born in New York City on October 27, 1858, the son of a wealthy Presbyterian banker of Dutch descent, Theodore Roosevelt was a nearsighted child, wracked with asthma, and afraid of everything. He idolized his father, and remembered how he carried "me in my distress, in my battles for breath,

155

up and down a room all night...I could breathe, I could sleep, when he had me in his arms."[1]

At thirteen, recovering in the country from an asthma attack, two bullies taunted him for his city ways and eyeglasses. He reacted in rage with flying fists, but lost the fight and felt humiliated. So he resolved to toughen up by working out at a gym in his home, learning to box and strengthening his muscles. "There were all kinds of things of which I was afraid," he admitted in his autobiography, "but by acting as if I was not afraid I gradually ceased to be afraid."[2]

The sickly, scared boy developed into a physically and morally courageous and ambitious man, eagerly tackling both mountain lions and mountaintops.

Having graduated from Harvard in 1880, at age twenty-one he married Bostonian Alice Lee. He then began to study at Columbia Law School and to take an interest in politics. The following year voters elected TR, as he became known, to the New York State Assembly.

His seemingly unquenchable spirit was tested in February 1884, when, within twenty-four hours, his mother died of typhus and his young wife of a kidney disease, just two days after giving birth to their daughter, also Alice. The distraught twenty-five-year-old widower finished his term in the State Assembly, left his baby to the care of his sister, Anna, and headed for the wild Dakota Territory. There, at his Elkhorn ranch, he hoped to conquer his grief through exhausting labor, working with the ranch hands, branding steers, riding hard, and controlling stampedes.

Back in New York two years later he made a failed bid to be the city's mayor, and that December he married Edith Kermit Carow. As a child in New York she had lived next door

---

[1] *American Heritage Pictorial History*, 624.

[2] Ibid.

to TR; she had been his early playmate and his younger sister's best friend. They were to have four sons and a daughter.

At his next job, at the Civil Service Commission, his reputation for exposing blackmail in the New York Custom House prompted Mayor William Strong, whose police department was rife with corruption, to make TR the president of the Board of Police Commissioners. Strong was not disappointed. TR established a merit system for both hiring and promoting policemen, fired crooked and illiterate cops, and equipped those left with bicycles to catch fleet-of-foot felons and stop runaway horses. Often around midnight he would leave a dinner party and go out to battle evil. His friend, muckraking reporter Jacob Riis, who knew the territory, sometimes joined him on these late-night expeditions to keep the cops awake and on their toes.

New York City police were overwhelmingly Irish, until TR allowed Jews and women to join the department. He further earned the respect of the Jewish community by his treatment of Pastor Hermann Ahlwardt, who had arrived from Germany on a Jew-baiting lecture tour. At first TR disappointed Jews eager to muzzle the pastor when he said that he lacked the authority to prevent Ahlwardt from speaking. Then he delighted them by ordering a large detachment of exclusively Jewish cops and plainclothes detectives to protect the bigot.

On December 12, 1895, Ahlwardt, a pastor and politician – a member of the Reichstag – stood on the stage of the Cooper Union, where Abraham Lincoln had spoken on his first visit to the city. The audience saw a heavy-set, red-faced man with a double chin, wearing a dinner jacket, white gloves, and a perpetual smile. A *New York Times* reporter described the audience as a mix of Italians, Germans, Hebrews, Americans, and cops in and out of uniform. He counted 150 men and three women, and estimated that over one-third were cops.

Ahlwardt told them that he planned to tour America to inflame the smoldering anti-Semitism. When he wondered why New York City was not called New Jerusalem, it aroused a chorus of hissing. When the hissing faded, he said that Jews lived by cunning and tricking others, that no Jews worked, and he challenged his audience to name one Jew in the Old Testament who had worked; he then gave his negative view of Jewish history from Pharaoh to the present, frequently interrupted by shouts of dissent and language the *New York Times* found not fit to print. When a little old man in the front row stood and threw three rotten eggs at him, he dodged them all with surprising agility for a heavyweight. As detectives escorted the little man out, Ahlwardt said, "Only a Jew would have done that!" followed by a shout from a man at the back, "Anyone else would have thrown straight." Just before midnight, six Jewish cops surrounded Ahlwardt for his protection and walked him out of the building.[3]

The next day, six Christian clergymen at Manhattan's Allen Memorial Church on Rivington Street told a packed house of mostly "Hebrews" that they admired the Jews and denounced the views of the "Jew-baiting" anti-Semite.[4] A reporter for a Milwaukee newspaper noted:

> [Ahlwardt's] appeals are intentionally directed to the densest ignorance and the vilest prejudices of which humanity is capable. Ahlwardt asserts that the Hebrews are "encroaching on the wealth of the world, and are a menace to the prosperity of other races." His avowed belief is that they should not hold office, enjoy the rights of citizenship, or have any share in public affairs. It is an affront to the people who boast of the Declaration of Independence and who cherish the liberal principles embodied in the Constitution of the United States

---

[3] *New York Times*, December 13, 1895, 2.

[4] "Herr Ahlwardt Denounced: Christian Clergymen Repudiate His Ideas," *New York Times*, December 15, 1895, 9.

for a man with Ahlwardt's narrow and reactionary views to come among them expecting to be accorded sympathetic audience."[5]

In his autobiography TR noted that Ahlwardt "made his harangue against the Jews under the active protection of some forty policemen, every one of them a Jew! It was the most effective possible answer; and incidentally it was an object-lesson to our people, whose greatest need is to learn that there must be no division by class hatred, whether that hatred be of creed against creed, nationality against nationality, section against section, or men of one social or industrial condition against men of another social or industrial condition. We must ever judge each individual on his own conduct and merits."[6]

When Hermann Ahlwardt's mission fizzled, he returned to Germany and, in 1914, was killed in a car crash.

TR continued to encourage Jews to join the police force. He met one, for example, Otto Raphael, while visiting the Bowery YMCA. There he was told that Otto and his father had rescued twelve women and children from a burning tenement. TR persuaded Otto to take the tests to join the police. Out of the 350 applicants, he came top in the physical tests and tenth in the written test, to become one of the eighty-five recruits accepted. TR described him as "a powerful fellow with a good-humored, intelligent face.... Otto's parents had come over from Russia, and not only in social standing but in pay a policeman's position meant everything to him. It enabled Otto to educate his brothers and sisters who had been born in this country, and to bring over from Russia some of his kinsfolk."[7]

---

[5] The *Milwaukee* newspaper report reprinted in the *New York Times*, December 9, 1895, 3.

[6] Theodore Roosevelt, *An Autobiography* (Cambridge, MA: DeCapo Press, 2000), 12–13.

[7] Ibid., 5.

During his career Raphael arrested a serial killer guilty of fourteen murders, was shot when making an arrest, and injured while saving children in the path of a runaway horse. He rose to the rank of lieutenant.

Impressed by TR's record in improving the police department, President McKinley appointed him assistant secretary of the navy. Soon after, fighting broke out in Cuba, a Spanish colony, between the US and Spanish forces on the island. The Spanish-American War was a successful struggle by the US and Cuban revolutionaries to free Cuba from Spanish rule. TR resigned from the naval office and joined the First Regiment of US Cavalry Volunteers, chiefly ranchers, cowboys, and Indians from the Far West and adventurous, horse-riding "bluebloods" from Eastern universities, known as the Rough Riders.

As a lieutenant colonel in the regiment, TR led his men in a successful attack on San Juan Hill, one of the war's most famous battles. The first Rough Rider fatality was a sixteen-year-old Jewish cowboy from Texas, Trooper Jacob Wilbusky. TR said that the seven Jewish Rough Riders under his command displayed "the most astonishing courage." At another time, discussing the charge up San Juan Hill, he mentioned that "one of the best colonels among the regular regiments who did so well on that day, who fought beside me, was a Jew."[8] About five thousand American Jews served in the war; twenty-nine were killed, forty-seven wounded, and twenty-eight died from disease.

After the war, TR's goal was to become governor of New York State, and he hoped for Jewish support. He wasn't disappointed. In October, 1898, Jewish supporters on Manhattan's Lower East Side flooded the area with leaflets in Yiddish, reminding potential voters of his heroic role during

---

[8]   Edmund Morris, *Theodore Rex* (New York: Random House, 2001), 244.

the Spanish-American War. Potential Jewish voters were also reminded how the Spaniards had mistreated Jews in the past, expelling them from Spain or burning them at the stake if they refused to convert to Catholicism.

He won the election.

As New York State's governor he was a great innovator and fighter against corruption. He continued to be a vigorous opponent of anti-Semitism at home and abroad, outraged by the mistreatment of army captain Alfred Dreyfus, a French Jew falsely convicted of treason and imprisoned for life on Devil's Island.

Speaking to a crowd of ten thousand in Walton, New York, on September 13, 1899, TR said: "We have watched with indignation and regret the trial of Captain Dreyfus. It was less Dreyfus on trial than those who tried him. We should draw lessons from the trial. It was due in part to bitter religious prejudices of the French people. Those who have never wavered from the doctrine of the separation of Church and State should ponder on what happened.... You cannot benefit one class by pulling another class down."[9]

Dreyfus had been imprisoned for twelve years when evidence of his innocence and pressure from his supporters forced the French government to free him.

In 1900 TR was named President McKinley's vice president. On September 13, 1901, while hunting and mountain climbing in the Adirondacks he was told that the president had been shot by a fanatic and was dying. When McKinley died the following day, TR took over. One of his first acts as president was to hire a Jew, William Loeb Jr., as his executive secretary and adviser.

In his second year as president, TR traveled south to settle a border dispute between Louisiana and Mississippi. While

---

[9] "Speech by Gov Roosevelt," *New York Times*, September 13, 1899, 3.

there he joined a bear hunt. After five days no one had bagged a bear, but one hunter had captured a small injured and stunned bear, which he had tied to a tree and invited TR to set free and to hunt. TR said that it would be unsporting. "Put it out of its misery," he suggested, and someone did.[10] When Rose Miehorn, a Jewish immigrant in the toy business, read about it, she made a bear doll and displayed it in her Brooklyn shop window. It became so much in demand she made and sold many more, then sent the original to TR, who was also known as "Teddy," asking if she could name it after him. He agreed, and in his successful 1904 reelection campaign Republicans used the Teddy Bear as their symbol.[11]

Despite the protests of successive American presidents, there had been no end to the Russian pogroms against Jews. One had started in the Russian city of Kishinev in April 1903, when a Christian boy was murdered by a relative who was eventually arrested. But before his arrest, an anti-Semitic Russian newspaper, *Bessarabian*, implied that Jews had murdered the boy. Another Russian paper, *World*, alleged that he had been murdered to use his blood to make matzos (the discredited, age-old blood libel). The false accounts in the newspapers incited a pogrom in the city, which raged for three days before the authorities made any attempt to stop it. Either forty-seven or forty-nine Jews were murdered, ninety-two severely injured, and some five hundred slightly injured; about seven hundred homes were destroyed, six hundred stores and businesses looted, and two thousand families ruined. The *New York Times* reported: "The anti-Jewish riots in Kishinev, Bessarabia, are worse than the censor will permit to publish. There was a well laid-out plan for the general massacre of the Jews on the day following the Russian Easter. The mob was led

---

[10] Morris, *Theodore Rex*, 173.

[11] Sermon by Rabbi Melanie Aton, Shir Hadash Congregation, July 1, 2006 (confirmed by phone conversation, April 10, 2010).

by priests, and the general cry, 'Kill the Jews!' was taken up all over the city. The Jews were taken wholly unaware and were slaughtered like sheep.... Those who could make their escape fled in terror, and the city is now practically deserted of Jews."[12]

A delegation of six American Jews entered the White House on June 1, with Louis Levi as the spokesman. As TR biographer Edmund Morris tells it, they were "escorted by John Hay, courteously veiling his usual jocular anti-Semitism ('The Hebrews – poor dears!'). One could not mock their present distress. All over America, Christians as well as Jews were collecting funds to help the surviving victims of the Kishinev pogrom." Donors included Hay, who made an unpublicized donation of $500 to the Kishinev Relief Fund, according to Morris. Levi accused the Russian authorities of total ignorance, superstition, and bigotry, which resulted in the carnage. TR wondered if it would do any good for him to speak out on behalf of the Jews, then answered himself that "it would be very much like the Czar expressing his horror of our lynching Negroes."

TR told the Jewish delegation that he had never known of a more immediate and deeper expression of sympathy by Americans for the victims of the pogrom. Then "he recited some lines from Longfellow's 'The Jewish Cemetery at Newport,' and paid tribute to the American Jews who had fought in the Revolution and the Civil War."[13] The State Department sent a petition to Russia with thousands of signatures protesting the pogrom, but the czar refused to accept it. (It is now in the US National Archives.)

After the pogrom, Russian Jews created self-defense leagues to combat future attacks, and thousands of others left for the West or for Palestine. Nevertheless, there were some

---

[12] *New York Times*, April 28, 1903, 6.

[13] Morris, *Theodore Rex*, 243–244, 253.

three hundred pogroms in Russia in the following three years, which strengthened the appeal of the Zionist cause.

Twenty-four men were punished for their part in the Kishinev pogrom: one got seven years in prison, another got five, and twenty got one or two years.

When TR was awarded the Nobel Peace Prize for helping to mediate peace between the Russians and Japanese – the first American to get a Nobel prize in any category – he told his family that keeping the money would be like accepting a reward for rescuing a drowning man. Instead, he gave it to various charities, including $4,000 (10 percent) to the Jewish Welfare Board.

When on November 30, 1905 (Thanksgiving), Jews celebrated their 250 years in America at Manhattan's Carnegie Hall, former president Cleveland, as mentioned, addressed the celebrants. This is part of the letter from TR that Cleveland read aloud:

> The lamentable and terrible suffering to which so many of the Jewish people in other lands have been subjected, makes me feel it my duty, as the head of the American people, not only to express my deep sympathy for them, but to point out what fine qualities of citizenship have been displayed by the men of Jewish faith and race, who, having come to this country, enjoy the benefits of free institutions and equal treatment before the law.... Even in our colonial period the Jews participated in the building of the country.... During the Revolutionary period they aided the cause of liberty by serving in the Continental army and by substantial contributions to the empty treasury of the infant Republic. During the Civil War, thousands served in the armies and mingled their blood with the soil for which they fought. While the Jews of the United States, who now number more than a million, have remained loyal to their faith and their race traditions, they

have become indissolubly incorporated in the great army of American citizenship."[14]

In 1907 TR became the first US president to appoint a Jew, Oscar Straus, to a cabinet position as secretary of commerce and labor. Straus had been President Cleveland's minister to Turkey, and President McKinley had kept him on in the same position and had been considering him as a potential secretary of state after Hay retired. According to Straus, TR believed that his appointment "would provide an object lesson to Russia and other countries in which unreasonable discrimination and prejudice against Jews prevailed."[15]

TR and Ernest Hemingway were among the admirers of a book titled *The Man-Eaters of Tsavo* by an Irishman, John Henry Patterson. In it he told how the British government sent him to British East Africa (today's Kenya) to deal with two lions that were terrorizing and killing laborers working on a railroad from the coast to Uganda. A tragic event later in Patterson's life inspired Hemingway's *The Short Happy Life of Francis Macomber*. TR sought Patterson's advice on big-game hunting and had entertained him as his guest at the White House. They continued to write to each other during World War I when Patterson, a British army colonel in Gallipoli, commanded the Zion Mule Corps of Jewish volunteers. Later in the war, Patterson commanded the Jewish Legion, also volunteers – and the first such fighting force in two thousand years – who helped to drive the Turks from Palestine.

Patterson wrote about the Jewish Legion to TR on April 12, 1915: "I have been in Egypt...organizing a corps of Russians from various parts of the Russian empire, mostly Jews. They are a very useful body of men and we are off to the front

---

[14] *New York Times*, December 1, 1905, 1, 4.
[15] Newton Fuessle, *New York Times* Book Review, review of *Under Four Administrations*, Oscar S. Straus, 1922.

in a day or two.... Not one of us has the slightest doubt about our being able to lick Germany. We will do it handsomely in time."

TR replied: "I was intensely interested in your organizing a corps of Russian refugees and the fact that these are mostly Jews. A cousin of Mrs. Roosevelt's is a captain in the Artillery and he informs me that his three best gun-crews are exclusively Jews, either born in or sons of men born in Russia."

On December 11, 1918, a month after the war's end and three weeks before he died, TR congratulated Patterson on the success of the Jewish soldiers he commanded in the Jewish Legion. TR's letter reads in part: "To have the sons of Israel smite Ammon on the hip and thigh under your leadership is something worthwhile."[16]

Patterson's commander-in-chief, Major General Sir Edmund Chaytor, told him that the men of the Jewish Legion had been among the bravest he had ever commanded: "So few have heard of the Battalion's good work or of the very remarkable fact that in the operations...a Jewish force was fighting on the Jordan within a short distance of where their forefathers under Joshua (the leading character in the sixth book of the Old Testament, who led fellow Jews out of exile in Babylonia back to the Promised Land they had once possessed) had first crossed into Palestine.... The way you smashed up the Turkish rearguard when it tried to counterattack across the Jordan made our subsequent advance up the hills of Moab an easy matter." [17]

Theodore Roosevelt confirmed that he was a Zionist in two of his letters and a speech. In the first letter, to James Bryce, on August 7, 1918, he wrote: "The Turk should be driven from Europe, Armenia made independent under a

---

[16] Denis Brian, *The Seven Lives of Colonel Patterson: How an Irish Lion Hunter Led the Jewish Legion to Victory* (Syracuse, NY: Syracuse University Press, 2008), 90.

[17] Ibid., 138.

guarantee of the Allies; the Jews given Palestine; the Syrian Christians protected; the Arabs made independent." In the second letter, written on September 16, 1918, he replied from his Oyster Bay, Long Island, home to a letter from Rabbi Julian H. Miller of Chattanooga, Tennessee, "I am very much pleased with your letter and very much pleased with your sermon. It seems to me that it is entirely proper to start a Zionist state around Jerusalem."[18]

During a speech on September 8, 1918, between writing those letters, he said, "Armenia must be freed, Palestine made a Jewish state, the Greeks guaranteed their rights, and the Syrians liberated – all of them, Mohammedans, Jews, Druses, being guaranteed an equal liberty of religious beliefs, and required to work out their independence on the basis of equal political and civil rights for all creeds."[19]

TR predicted that he would die at sixty, which he did, of a heart attack in his sleep in his Oyster Bay home. The date was January 6, 1919, just two months after the end of World War I.

[18]   TR's letter to James Bryce, August 7, 1918: *The Letters of Theodore Roosevelt*, vol. 8 (Cambridge, MA: Harvard University Press, 1951–1954), 1359; TR's letter to Rabbi Julian Miller, September 16, 1918: ibid., 1372.

[19]   Mem. Ed., XX1, 409; Nat. Ed., X1X, 371. Theodore Roosevelt Association, Oyster Bay, accessed April 21, 2010, www.theodoreroosevelt.org.

William Howard Taft

1857–1930

- ✪ Twenty-seventh president, 1909–1913
- ✪ Was also chief justice of the Supreme Court, the only person to have served in both offices
- ✪ Sought to further economic development in Latin America and Asia through Dollar Diplomacy

Outweighing even President Cleveland at over three hundred pounds, William Howard Taft had no fire in his considerable belly to be president of the United States. He and his mother, Louisa, were firmly against it, but his ambitious wife, Helen, and several other family members were all for it, and they prevailed.

Early in life Taft had developed a positive attitude toward Jews. As he once explained, "My father was a Unitarian, and I was brought up in that faith. Across the street from the Unitarian Church in Cincinnati was the Jewish synagogue of which the Rev. Isaac M. Wise was rabbi. Our clergymen exchanged pulpits, so in my boyhood days I sat at the feet of Dr. Wise in the Unitarian Church and listened to sermons which he delivered from the pulpit of that church. It is therefore, not to be supposed that there is any prejudice of any sort in my mind or that there was anything but impatience at the suggestion of prejudice that may exist in narrow minds."[1]

As a Unitarian, like his parents, he followed no creed, welcomed people of all religious faiths or of none, and believed that the highest religious goal was to lead an ethical life. Taft believed in God, but not in the divinity of Jesus Christ.

The son of Alphonso Taft, a prominent attorney and diplomat of English descent, and Louisa Torrey, a Holyoke College graduate, Taft was born in Cincinnati, Ohio, on September 16, 1857. He not only developed into an outstanding high-school student and athlete, but proved unbeatable at boxing and wrestling, and his proud father boasted that he was better than the then current world champion boxer, John L. Sullivan.

Graduating from Yale in 1874, second in a class of 121, he earned a law degree from Cincinnati Law School in 1880. Two years later, President Chester Arthur appointed Taft's father the ambassador to Austria-Hungary. So Taft put his legal career on hold to savor the high life in Europe, which included a visit with his parents to the spectacular court of the ruling Hapsburgs in Vienna. A few months later he returned home to join his father's law firm.

In 1886 he married Helen Herron, daughter of the law partner of former president Rutherford Hayes, a lifelong love match that produced two sons and a daughter. Taft was also in love with the law and served successively as a Cincinnati Superior Court judge between 1887 and 1890; the US solicitor general from 1890 to 1892; then a US Circuit judge, a job he held from 1892 to 1896. He resigned to be professor and dean of the University of Cincinnati's law department. But his ultimate aim was to be a US Supreme Court judge, which

---

[1] *New York Times*, January 7, 1913, 3.

he compared to being in heaven. "I love judges," he once said, "and I love courts. They are my ideals, that typify on earth what we shall meet hereafter in heaven under a just God."[2]

Consequently, he was disappointed in 1901 when President McKinley appointed him to be the first civil governor of the Philippines, a country that Spain had ceded to America after losing the Spanish-American War. Despite his reluctance to be there, Taft proved a great success, endearing himself to some of the men by calling them his "little brown brothers." His more significant achievement, however, was to benefit the native population by getting Pope Louis XIII to sell hundreds of thousands of acres of Vatican-owned Philippine farmland at the bargain price of $7 million. The land was then sold to Filipinos on easy terms.

Because of the hot climate and his immense weight – he was the heaviest president before or since – Taft rarely got a good night's sleep, and he sometimes dropped off during a meeting, snoring gently. He once even slept through a terrifying, thunderous typhoon, and on another occasion his wife nudged him awake during a funeral service. Hearing a false rumor that he was seriously ill, Elihu Root, the US secretary of war, inquired after his health. Taft cabled back that he was fine and had just completed a twenty-five-mile ride on horseback. Root shot back, "How's the horse?"[3]

President Theodore Roosevelt called Taft "the most lovable personality I have ever come in contact with," and after Taft had served three years overseas as governor, he appointed him secretary of war.[4]

Roosevelt backed Taft to be his successor, trusting him as a fellow Republican to continue his radical reforms. With his enthusiastic and energetic support, Taft easily defeated

---

[2] *American Heritage Pictorial History*, "William Howard Taft," 663.

[3] Durant, *Pictorial History of American Presidents*, 218.

[4] Ibid., 220.

his opponent, William Jennings Bryan, getting over a million more popular votes. Soon after his inauguration on March 4, 1909, Taft reappointed Oscar Straus, a Jew, as the US ambassador to Turkey.

Two months later Taft accepted an invitation from Rabbi Leonard Levy to address his congregation at Rodef Shalom. The first US president to speak to a Jewish congregation at a Sabbath service, he said, "I esteem it a great privilege to appear before this intelligent and patriotic audience, at the instance of your leader, your rabbi, who was a warm friend of my predecessor [Roosevelt].... The prayer to which we have just listened, full of liberality and kindness and humanity, makes me feel ashamed of all narrowness and bigotry in religion, and it makes me glad to say that never in the history of this country, never in any circumstances or in any crisis, have the Jewish people failed to live up to the highest standard of citizenship and patriotism."[5]

Knowing that they would have a sympathetic ear in Taft, a delegation from the American Association of Foreign Newspapers confronted him at the White House on February 28, 1910, to complain about pending bills in Congress to restrict immigration. He indicated that he opposed the congressional bills when he replied that in a visit to New York's East Side he was exceedingly impressed to find "that there was no part of the country in which the real, true spirit of patriotism prevailed more deeply than there. That threw a somewhat new light on my general view of the situation with respect to the laws of immigration, and how they ought to be enforced."[6]

Taft had another chance to express his opinion of Jews shortly after at a B'nai B'rith Convention, when he said: "There is no people so much entitled to become the aristocrats

---

[5] Taft's speech to Rodef Shalom Congregation, Pittsburgh, Pa., May 29, 1909, accessed March 23, 2010, http://rodefshalom.org/who/history/more%20information/..

[6] "Taft Tribute to Jews," *New York Times*, March 1, 1910, 3.

of the world, and yet who make the best Republicans. I have profound admiration for the Jewish people, because they are essentially aristocrats, because they make excellent citizens, and are in favor of law and order. I am glad to have them come to this country. They have the profoundest appreciation of our institutions of liberty and education." His audience gave him a standing ovation.[7]

In the same supportive spirit, when anti-Jewish riots broke out in Poland in June 1910, Taft not only condemned them but, according to Zionist leader and US Supreme Court Justice Louis Brandeis, he "issued a qualified statement of support for Zionist aims."[8] Nothing was more important to Brandeis than helping to restore a Jewish homeland in Palestine as "the living culmination of thousands of generations of Jewish history," which he visualized as becoming a miniature California, where "Jews would achieve their age-old dream of democracy and social justice."[9]

Throughout Taft's presidency Russia was still treating American Jews like Russian Jews, as second-class human beings, which incited the US House of Representatives to vote 300 to 1 to end the 1832 US-Russian trade treaty. At first Taft hesitated to end the treaty, fearing a backlash against Russian Jews, but with pressure from American Jews, especially from banker and philanthropist Jacob Schiff, he agreed to go along with Congress. As a result there was some temporary improvement in the lives of Russian Jews.

Taft personally helped one Jewish family to escape from Russia. For four years, Wolf Fanmich, a Jewish cobbler living in Pennsylvania, had been separated from his wife and three

---

[7] Ibid.; "Taft Praises the Jews," Bnai B'rith, April 8, 1910.

[8] Melvin I. Urolsky and David W. Levy, eds., *Letters of Louis D. Brandeis* (University of Oklahoma Press, 2002), 365.

[9] Philippa Strum, *Louis D. Brandeis: Justice for the People* (New York: Schocken Books, 1984), 273.

young children, who were trapped in Russia. When he arrived at the Russian border to take them home with him, he was told that although he was an American citizen and his passport was in order, as a Jew he was not allowed to enter the country; deeply disappointed, he returned to the United States. Taft heard of the problem and got his American representative in St. Petersburg to investigate. As a result, the Russians let the family leave Russia. However, when they reached Ellis Island, a doctor found that the wife had an eye disease. Normally she would have been refused entry, but Taft ordered doctors to treat her while her children stayed with her. She was cured after forty days, and she and her children joined Fanmich in their Pennsylvania home. [10]

Taft's good deeds did not go unnoticed. On January 7, 1914, International Order of B'nai B'rith delegates arrived at the White House to give him a gold medal for trying to improve the lives of Russian Jews and for his services to the Jewish race. In thanking them, he said:

> Those of us who are not of the Jewish people have to be humble. The genius, the strength of your race, the patience and the persistence with which you pursue your purpose to maintain your rights and exalt your race – all make yours an exceptional history in the history of the world. The persecutions to which you have been subjected because of your religion have in a sense doubtless developed the character and tenacity of your race, but it needs a free country like the United States to develop the flower and enable you to show to the world at large the wonderful capacity of the race as supporters of law and order in a Government of freedom and a Government that insists on equality before the law. [11]

---

[10] *The New York Times*, December 16, 1911, 1.

[11] *American Heritage Pictorial History*, 668.

Due to a generous immigration policy and the high birth rate among Jewish Americans during Taft's presidency, they had increased to almost three million, many of whom enjoyed a lively and flourishing Yiddish press, theater, and cultural life.

Less dynamic than Roosevelt and eager to please everyone, Taft failed in his attempt for a second term and was succeeded in 1913 by a Democrat, former Princeton University president and New Jersey State governor Woodrow Wilson.

After the Russian revolution and overthrow of the czar in 1917, "jubilant New Yorkers staged mass meetings to celebrate," and Taft used the situation to praise Jews "for having maintained their racial identity in the face of centuries of persecution."[12] In 1920, to Taft's great delight, President Warren Harding, who had succeeded Woodrow Wilson, appointed him chief justice of the United States Supreme Court – Taft's idea of heaven on earth.

At the time, motor magnate Henry Ford, one of America's leading anti-Semites, published a newspaper, *The Dearborn Independent*, with a circulation of seven hundred thousand, and in November 1920 he published a book titled *The International Jew: The World's Foremost Problem*. It claimed that Russian pogroms were simply Jewish propaganda and blamed the troubles in American baseball on Jews. Ford maintained that there was a Jewish conspiracy to control the world, and he republished much of *The Protocols of the Learned Elders of Zion* to support his view. Strangely, he denied disliking Jews and being an anti-Semite. He even sent his Jewish neighbor, Rabbi Leo Franklin, a new Ford car as a gift. But the rabbi returned it, to Ford's apparent puzzlement. "What's wrong, Dr. Franklin?" Ford wrote to him. "Has something come between us?"[13]

---

[12] Naomi W. Cohen, *Jacob H. Schiff: A Study in American Jewish Leadership* (London: Brandeis University Press, 1999), 208.

[13] Neil Baldwin, *Henry Ford and the Jews: The Mass Production of Hate* (New York:

Outraged by the publication of *The International Jew*, thousands of Jewish Americans sent letters of protest to Ford, and on September 1920, the Anti-Defamation League published a pamphlet titled "The Poison Pen: The Perils of Racial Prejudice," urging all who influenced public opinion "to strike at *The International Jew* as un-American, un-Christian agitation." More than a hundred prominent non-Jewish Americans signed the pamphlet, among them President Woodrow Wilson, W. E. B. Dubois, Clarence Darrow, William Jennings Bryan, and former presidents Theodore Roosevelt and William Howard Taft.[14]

Taft regarded Ford's bigotry with contempt and in an address to the Anti-Defamation League in Chicago on December 23, 1920, the ex-president said:

Anti-Semitism is a noxious weed that should be cut out. It has no place in America. One of the chief causes of evil and suffering in the world today is race hatred and any man who stimulates that hatred has much to answer for. When he does this by the circulation of unfounded and unjust charges and the arousing of mean and groundless fears, his fault is to be more condemned. How much of the article (in *The Dearborn Independent*) is due to Mr. Ford's initiative and how much he has yielded to the recommendations of others in consenting to its publication, one cannot say. But of course he is responsible for the effect.

Responding to charges in *The Protocols of the Learned Elders of Zion* that Ford was promoting – that there was an international conspiracy of Jews to dominate the world – Taft said:

Public Affairs, 2001), 133.

[14] "The International Jew," June 27, 2009, The Jewish Virtual Library, www.jewishvirtuallibrary.org/jsource/anti-semitism/ford.html.

No existence of this world-controlling power is cited as proof. The conclusion of the author rests on his own assertion and the further comprehensive and entirely satisfying assurance that "everybody knows it."

If it is true that the international bankers and capitalists are Jews alone, if it is true that they wield a world power that controls governments and nations and wars and peace and economic law, can the author of these articles in *The Dearborn Independent* explain why it is that more than half of the 13,000,000 Jews in the world are still suffering not only from persecution and oppression, but the bitterest penury and starvation? The tales of Baron Munchausen [a fictional teller of tall stories] are the only things in literature that should be classed with these protocols, for they are not more preposterous. There is not the slightest ground for anti-Semitism among us. It has no place in free America.[15]

Taft was proved right the following year when a *London Times* correspondent revealed that *The Protocols* was anti-Semitic Russian propaganda with no foundation in fact. Its fabricator had used the plot of an old satirical French novel, *Dialogue in Hell between Machiavelli and Montesqueu* by a French lawyer, Maurice Joly. *The Protocols* was translated into several languages, and in time this anti-Semitic propaganda became a tool of the Nazis to demonize Jews.[16]

On March 8, 1930, a month after resigning as the chief justice at age seventy-two, Taft died of a heart attack with his wife at his side. He was buried in Arlington National cemetery.

---

[15] "Taft Flays Story of Zion Protocols," *New York Times*, December 14, 1920, 4.

[16] Philip Graves, "The Protocols of Zion – An Exposure," *The London Times,* August 16 to 18, 1921, 9,10, and *Protocols of the Learned Elders of Zion,* translated from the Russian of Nilus by Victor E. Marsden, former Russian correspondent of *The Morning Post,* The Britons Publishing Society, London, England, 1934, 1,75.

Woodrow Wilson

1856–1924

- ✪ Twenty-eighth president, 1913–1921
- ✪ Led the nation through World War I
- ✪ For his sponsorship of the League of Nations, he was awarded the 1919 Nobel Peace Prize

Woodrow Wilson was the son, nephew, and grandson of Presbyterian ministers of Scottish-Irish ancestry. His mother, Jessie, daughter of another Presbyterian minister, was born in England. He chose academia and politics as his career, but was as devoted a Presbyterian as his forebears: reading the Bible every day, wearing out three Bibles during his life, praying on his knees first thing in the morning and last thing at night, saying grace at every meal, and believing that God guided him.

His critics claimed that he thought he was God himself, or at least believed that it was God's will for him to become president. Although he appeared cold and aloof in public, he was, in fact, an emotional and passionate man, and unlike the God of his Bible, he had a great sense of fun. He often amused his wife and three daughters with imitations of drunks, pompous

177

Englishmen, stage villains, and of President Teddy Roosevelt shaking his fists defiantly and orating with flamboyant and patriotic fervor.

Wilson loved limericks, and in private, in a lighthearted mood, would break into a jig while singing a vaudeville favorite such as, "Oh, you beautiful doll! You great, big, beautiful doll!"[1]

Woodrow Wilson was born in Stanton, Virginia, on December 26, 1856. As a child he battled dyslexia and was unable to read well until he was about ten, but he caught up as a teenager by teaching himself shorthand, which helped him to advance academically. Stubborn, highly intelligent, and highly ambitious, he became in turn an attorney, a history teacher, the president of Princeton University, and New Jersey's governor. It was Wilson who appointed Samuel Kalisch, the first Jew to the New Jersey Supreme Court.

When the Democratic Party nominated him their presidential candidate, Wilson invited a Jewish Boston attorney, Louis Brandeis, to discuss politics with him. A former Harvard Law School professor (and destined to be a US Supreme Court justice), Brandeis was known as "The People's Lawyer" because he fought for the underdog, at times without pay, supported civil liberties, and opposed big business monopolies. At their first meeting, Wilson was so intrigued with his views and personality that their conversation lasted several hours, during which Brandeis convinced him that huge industrial monopolies had to be regulated to "prevent them from doing evil."[2]

Fresh from their meeting, Brandeis wrote to a friend: "Wilson has all the qualities for an ideal president – strong,

---

[1] Colonel Edmund Starling, as told to Thomas Sugrue, *Starling of the White House* (Chicago: Peoples Book Club, 1946), 36.

[2] August Heckscher, *Woodrow Wilson: A Biography* (New York: Scribner's, 1991), 256.

simple and truthful, able, open-minded, eager to learn and deliberate."[3] The voting public was also impressed, and in 1913 Woodrow Wilson beat the incumbent Taft for the presidency on a platform, which included some of Brandeis's views.

Wilson's wife, Ellen Louise Axson, with whom he had three daughters, died in 1914, and a year later he married Edith Gault.

Like many previous presidents, Wilson compared the Jews of the Old Testament with the colonists and the early history of America:

> Recalling the previous experiences of the colonists in applying the Mosaic Code to the order of their internal life, it is not to be wondered at that various passages in the Bible that serve to undermine royal authority, stripping the Crown of its cloak of divinity, held up before the pioneer Americans the Hebrew Commonwealth as a model government. In the spirit and essence of our Constitution, the influence was paramount in that it was not only the highest authority for the principle 'that rebellion to tyrants is obedience to God,' but also because it was in itself a divine precedent for a pure democracy, distinguished from monarchy, aristocracy or any other form of government.[4]

Brandeis, his political adviser, who was also the leader of the Zionist movement in America, "felt free to call upon Wilson and members of his administration for the support of Zionist activities."[5] Rabbi Stephen Wise thought that no other American Jew equaled Brandeis in supporting Wilson "with such disinterestedness and limitless devotion to the

---

[3] Ibid.

[4] Mitchell G. Bard, "Roots of the US-Israel Relationship," Jewish Virtual Library, http://www.jewishvirtuallibrary.org/jsource/US-Israel/roots_of_US-Israel.html.

[5] Strum, *Brandeis*, 216.

ends of his terms of office."[6] It was a case of mutual admiration. "Wilson showed continuous friendship for Brandeis and used his influence to get Brandeis membership in Washington's exclusive Cosmos Club," where he had previously been excluded as a dangerous radical.[7]

On the death of Wilson's childhood friend, US Supreme Court Justice Joseph Lamar, in 1916, he nominated Brandeis to replace him. But the prospect of a Jew on the Supreme Court aroused frantic opposition from anti-Semites, Conservatives afraid of Brandeis's radical views and bankers reluctant to have the government supervise their financial operations. Brandeis had supported the supervision of banks in his 1914 book, *Other People's Money, and How the Bankers Use It.*

Conservatives, wealthy businessmen, and especially anti-Semites who deplored Brandeis's outspoken Zionist views were a formidable opposition. Among them were six former presidents of the American Bar Association and, surprisingly, former US president Taft. In May, with the nation's anti-Semites in full cry, Wilson wrote to the chairman of the Senate Judiciary Committee, "The propaganda in this matter has been very extraordinary, and very distressing to those who love fairness and value the dignity of the great professions.... [Brandeis] is a friend of all just men and a lover of the right."[8]

While in Detroit in October, Brandeis wrote to his brother: "Anti-Semitism seems to have reached its American pinnacle here, the New Athlete Club with 5000 members – and no Jews need apply."[9] Still, he assured a young American Jewish lawyer in Philadelphia, who had suffered from anti-Semitism, that Jewish talent would be recognized "even if not necessarily at 100 percent of its value."[10]

---

[6] Ibid.

[7] Heckscher, *Woodrow Wilson*, 395–97.

[8] Strum, *Brandeis*, 234.

[9] Ibid.

[10] Warren Bass, *Support Any Friend: Kennedy's Middle East and the Making of the*

Although the majority of the American Bar Association gave Brandeis a no-confidence vote, Wilson's resolute support finally won the approval of the Senate Judiciary Committee, but only by a two-vote majority, 10 votes to 8, and then by a more impressive positive Senate vote of 47 to 22.

Wilson was reelected to a second term in November 1916, on the soon-to-be discredited campaign slogan, "He kept us out of the war."

In December 1916, US Secretary of State Robert Lansing asked Wilson, "Will not the Mohamedans of Syria and Palestine and possibly of Morocco and Tripoli rely on [Wilson's promise of self-determination]? How can it be harmonized with Zionism, to which the president is practically committed? The phrase is simply loaded with dynamite."[11] Despite the dire warning, Wilson continued to support the Balfour Declaration, details of which he had learned from Balfour himself on the British Foreign Secretary's visit to Washington.

When the German practice of unrestricted submarine attacks on shipping caused the sinking of several American merchant ships, despite his promise to keep America out of the fighting Wilson asked Congress to declare war on Germany. After the Senate obliged with 82 votes to 6, and the House with 373 to 50, war was officially declared against Germany and its allies on April 6, 1917. The US did not declare war on Turkey, but on April 23, 1917, Turkey severed relations with the United States.

Soon after, Wilson appointed Bernard Baruch, one of his Jewish friends and counselors, as head of the War Industries Board.

On October 16, 1917, on the advice of Brandeis and others, Wilson officially approved the British Balfour Declaration.

US-Israel Alliance (New York: Oxford University Press, 2003), 17–18.

[11] Meyer W. Weisgal and Joel Carmichael, eds., *Chaim Weizmann: A Biography by Several Hands* (New York: Atheneum, 1962), 163.

On November 22, 1917, Wilson became the first president to endorse a national Jewish philanthropic organization when he wrote to Jacob Schiff to encourage public support for the United Jewish Relief Campaign to raise funds for European war relief. Toward the end of the war, Wilson appointed another Jew, Henry Morgenthau, ambassador to the about-to-be-defeated Turkey.

The war ended with an Allied victory on November 11, 1918. A week later, Wilson announced that he would lead the US delegation at the Paris Peace Conference. Europeans welcomed him as if he were the Messiah. Deeply distressed by the deaths of millions, Wilson's heart was set on the creation of the League of Nations, an organization dedicated to the prevention of future wars and making the world safe for democracy. To achieve this goal Wilson had prepared a list of fourteen points; the French leader, Clemenceau, ridiculed it with his "Mr. Wilson bores me with his Fourteen Points. Why, God Almighty has only ten."[12]

In fact the fourteen points were quite reasonable. Number twelve, for example, was "Self-determination for the people of the Turkish Empire," which, of course, included Palestinian Jews. Among those supporting this point was Felix Frankfurter, a Harvard Law School professor, in Paris as Wilson's legal adviser. Frankfurter was also a Zionist delegate and he energetically lobbied Wilson to include the Balfour Declaration in the peace treaty.

On March 3, 1919, Rabbi Stephen Wise headed a Zionist delegation to meet Wilson in the White House, where the president stated that, "the allied nations with the fullest concurrence of our government and people are agreed that Palestine should be the foundation of a Jewish Commonwealth."[13] This, despite the outspoken disapproval of both Wilson's

---

[12] *American Heritage Pictorial History*, 716.

[13] Heckscher, *Woodrow Wilson*, 540n.

secretary of state Robert Lansing, and Edward House, his confidential adviser. Lansing had protested that the US was not at war with the Turkish occupiers of Palestine and "many Christian sects and individuals would undoubtedly resent turning the Holy land over to the absolute control of the race credited with the death of Christ."[14]

Defying his doctor's advice, Wilson gave forty speeches across America in a desperate but futile attempt to sell membership in the League of Nations (a prototype of the United Nations) to the American public. As Winston Churchill succinctly put it, "The United States abandoned President Wilson's offspring."[15]

On October 16, Wilson suffered a stroke that left him partly paralyzed, and for the next several months he was virtually isolated in the White House, his condition hidden from all but a trusted few, and it is generally believed that for the last months of his presidency, Wilson's wife, Edith, ran the country.

In 1920 James Cox of Ohio, a League of Nations supporter, ran for president, but he was defeated by Republican Warren Harding, also of Ohio.

Woodrow Wilson died four years later. His last word: "Edith."[16]

After his death, Brandeis said that "he knew not fear." That is what the two men had in common. The Zionist president and the Zionist Supreme Court justice had also "recognized and appreciated each other's cold, objective intelligence and the sense of moral certitude that gave them each the courage to fight for unpopular causes."[17]

---

[14] Bass, *Support Any Friend*, 15, 17.

[15] Winston D. Churchill, *The Second World War, 1919–1940* (Boston: Houghton Mifflin, 1948), 13.

[16] *The American Heritage Book of the Presidents and Famous Americans*, vol. 9 (New York: Dell, 1967), 742.

[17] Strum, *Brandeis*, 223.

Warren Gamaliel Harding

1865–1923

> ✪ Twenty-ninth president, 1921–1923
> ✪ An influential newspaper editor and publisher, the only newspaper publisher to be elected president
> ✪ Advocated civil rights for African Americans

Warren Harding's presidency was overshadowed by the crimes of his political cronies and by his miserable marriage. In his bid for the White House he had to fight false accusations that he was an anti-Semite, his critics apparently unaware of his active support of Jews and their Zionist aspirations. His friends proved to be his worst enemies, and the cause of his death is still a mystery.

Born in Marion (now Blooming Grove) Ohio, in 1865, in time he would be the seventh Ohio-born president (Grant, Hayes, Garfield, Benjamin Harrison, McKinley, Taft, and Harding). Of English descent, Harding was one of eight children whose parents were both doctors, as their midwife mother eventually got her medical degree. Harding was more fragile than he looked, having had a nervous breakdown at twenty-four. He had no clear career goal, working in turn selling insurance, as a teacher, newspaper reporter, and owner of a small local newspaper, the *Marion Daily Star*.

At age twenty-six, on July 8, 1891, he married Florence Kling DeWolfe, a divorcée with a young son, the daughter of a banker who was known as the richest man in town. Theirs was not a happy union, and led to his romantic encounters, at times in a White House closet, with his mistress Nan Britton. She was thirty-one years his junior, and their liaison led to the birth of a daughter, Elizabeth Anne. Harding also had another long and passionate affair with Carrie Phillips, the daughter of a close friend.

After their marriage Mrs. Harding ran the newspaper's circulation department, keeping a firm hand on the delivery boys, and her haughty, take-charge nature justified her nickname, "The Duchess."

Though a generally friendly, outgoing man, Harding disliked foreigners, especially "the Poles, Slavs, and Huns," who worked in the eastern Pennsylvania coalmines in the 1890s. He blamed them for the violent and sometimes deadly strikes, but he liked and admired Jews of all national origins (presumably there were few if any Jewish coalminers in eastern Pennsylvania) and was that rarity for a man of his time, class, and heritage: pro-Jewish.[1]

For example, he eulogized Jewish philanthropist Baron Maurice Hirsch, who gave millions to help needy Jews throughout the world and for Russian Jews to emigrate, as "indisputably one of the greatest philanthropists of the age."[2]

When the anti-Semitic propagandist Dr. Hermann Ahlwardt began his lecture tour in New York City, Harding called

---

[1] Randolph C. Downes, *The Rise of Warren Gamaliel Harding, 1865–1920* (Columbus, OH: Ohio State University Press, 1970), 93–94.

[2] Ibid., 95.

him "a Jew-baiter" and "a bump on a log," and wrote, "The doctor may as well return [to Germany]. America has found the Jews to be among her most patriotic and devoted adopted citizens."[3]

The voters made Warren Harding an Ohio state senator between 1900 and 1904, and their lieutenant governor from 1904 to 1906. Although he had produced no significant new legislation, he worked hard and made no major mistakes. Popular among fellow Republicans, Harding also got on well with news reporters, having been one, and over the next few years he indicated that he was willing and able to run for the US Senate. He won the race in 1914 and served as Ohio's US senator for six years, when the Republican Party nominated him for president.

To his puzzled dismay, Jewish newspapers attacked him as an anti-Semite, citing his opposition to Woodrow Wilson's successful proposal to make Louis Brandeis the first Jew on the US Supreme Court. To prove the newspapers wrong, Harding invited influential Jewish friends to his Marion, Ohio, home, where Oscar Straus, Jacob Schiff, Louis Marshall, Julius Rosenwald, and Rabbi Louis Wolsey publicly denied the charge that Harding was an anti-Semite.

Members of B'nai B'rith had also denounced Harding as a Jew hater, which he had a chance to refute when he attended the dedication of the Marion lodge of B'nai B'rith, telling its members that he hoped "all Americans would catch the spirit of the organization in campaigning against ignorance, intolerance, and defamation."[4]

An influential Cleveland rabbi, A. H. Silver, urged his congregation not to believe the anti-Semitic slurs against Harding, and Liberal Rabbi Stephen Wise of New York's First Synagogue, was so incensed by the false charge, he announced

---

[3]   Ibid., 94.
[4]   Ibid., 531–32.

that although he intended to vote for Harding's Democratic rival, James Cox, "thinking Jews knew that Harding was no more opposed to Brandeis because he was Jewish, than did Wilson appoint him because he was Jewish."[5]

Harding himself said that he had opposed Brandeis because of his "extremely radical tendencies."[6]

One Jewish newspaper did back Harding, the *American Israelite*, the oldest and largest-circulation Jewish newspaper in America. In his October 6, 1920, editorial titled "Keep Religion Out of Politics," its editor, Leo Wise, wrote that Jewish newspapers, especially those "printed in the Yiddish jargon," were absurd to believe that Harding was anti-Jewish. Harding voted against Brandeis, Wise asserted, because his political convictions were not compatible with the American government and its economic institutions."[7]

To secure more Jewish votes, on October 27, the Hardings attended a Silver Jubilee celebration of Cleveland Independent Society, a group that helped Jewish immigrants adapt to life in America.

Harding's campaign worked: he defeated his Democratic opponent, Ohio Governor James Cox, whose vice-presidential choice had been the assistant secretary of the navy, Franklin Delano Roosevelt. Although a staunch Republican, Harding got more than 40 percent of Jewish votes despite the overwhelming number of Jewish Americans – almost 75 percent – who called themselves liberal or moderate.

One of his first decisions was to approve a joint congressional resolution giving American support to the British Balfour Declaration, telling the *Cleveland Plain Dealer* that he understood that Jews "wanted to establish their own

---

[5] Ibid.

[6] Ibid., 532.

[7] Ibid., 533–34.

homeland," because they had been "buffeted from nation to nation for centuries."[8]

Like President Taft, Harding personally helped Jews find refuge in the United States. As the *New York Times* reported on November 9, 1921:

> President Harding gave Rabbi Simon Glazer, Kansas City, Kansas, executive permission to adopt five children who are now in Rumania. The rabbi has already five children and the new additions are Jewish children who were left orphans by the death of their mother in one of the massacres in the Ukraine in 1920 and the death of their father. Immigration restrictions would have prevented them from coming to the United States, but President Harding agreed to allow Rabbi Glazer to adopt them and to legalize their entry. The oldest is 17 and the youngest 9 years and a collection has been taken up in Kansas City to pay for their transportation expenses.[9]

On May 11, 1922, Harding showed his strong commitment to a Jewish homeland in Palestine when he said: "I am glad to express my approval and hearty sympathy for the effort of the Palestine Foundation Fund in behalf of the restoration of Palestine as a homeland for the Jewish people. I have always viewed with an interest, which I think is quite as much practical as sentimental, the proposal for the rehabilitation of Palestine and the restoration of a real Jewish nationality, and I hope the efforts now being carried on in this and other countries in this behalf will meet the fullest measure of success."[10]

He had not long to live when, in a 1923 speech, he promised to rid his administration of corruption. Later in the year, on August 2, during a campaign trip to San Francisco with his

[8]   Ibid.

[9]   *The New York Times,* November 19, 1921, 1.

[10]   Eli E. Hertz, "Myths and Facts," UNM Israel Alliance, July 13, 2009, http://unmia. com/?p=318.

wife, Florence, and his friend Jesse Smith, he died aboard a ship. What killed the fifty-eight-year-old Harding is a mystery. Not even doctors were sure. There were three possibilities: a heart attack, a stroke, or food poisoning. Because his wife refused to allow an autopsy, unsubstantiated rumors suggested that she had poisoned him.

It was more likely that the antics of his prison-bound political "friends" and colleagues, known as the "Ohio Gang," helped to kill him, judging by his complaint to journalist William Allen White just two months before he died: " My God, [this is] a hell of a job. I have no trouble with my enemies. I can take care of my enemies in a fight. But my friends, my goddamned friends, they're the ones that keep me walking the floor nights."[11]

Warren Harding was a better president than some historians acknowledge. During his twenty-nine months in office he obtained an arms reduction agreement, created the Bureau of the Budget, was, according to subsequent investigators, not involved in the corrupt activities of his colleagues, and lived down his unjustified anti-Semitic reputation. In fact, he gave consistent support to the Jewish community.

---

[11] James D. Barber, *The Presidential Character: Predicting Performance in the White House* (Upper Saddle River, NJ: Prentice Hall, 1972), 191.

Calvin Coolidge

1872–1933

✪ Thirtieth president, 1923–1929

✪ Succeeded to the presidency upon the sudden death of Warren G. Harding

✪ Elected in his own right in 1924, he gained a reputation as a small-government conservative and a man of few words

At the height of a Boston police strike in 1919, as mobs looted stores and criminals took over the unprotected city of seven hundred thousand, the ineffectual mayor, Andrew Peters, confronted Massachusetts governor Calvin Coolidge, and insisted that he compromise with the strikers' demands. When Coolidge refused, the mayor punched him in the eye. Coolidge characteristically held his tongue, cupped a hand over his bruised eye, didn't hit back but stood his ground, while state troopers grabbed the mayor and led him away.[1]

The cops went on strike after Coolidge refused their demands for increased pay, better working conditions, and the right to join a union. When union leader Samuel Gompers

---

[1] "The Strike That Made a President," *American Heritage* 14, no. 6 (October 1963): 91, 93.

protested, Coolidge replied: "There is no right to strike against the public safety by anybody, anytime, anywhere."[2]

Because the police commissioner had fired all the striking police, Coolidge called on the state militia to protect the city, raised the minimum wage for new police recruits to $1,400 a year, and helped many fired cops find other jobs.[3] His humane and effective handling of the strike put him in the national spotlight as a credible presidential candidate.

Calvin Coolidge was born on Independence Day, July 4, 1872, in Plymouth, Vermont, where his father was a farmer, sometime teacher, and justice of the peace. When Coolidge was six, his grandfather gave him a forty-acre farm and taught him how to run it. His invalid mother, Victoria, whom he adored, died when he was twelve, probably from tuberculosis, and he kept her photo in his wallet for the rest of his life.

After school at nearby Black River Academy, he studied at Amherst College, graduating at age twenty-three in 1895 as an average student. His first job as a law clerk in Northampton, Massachusetts, lasted two years. A year later he was admitted to the bar and became the city's solicitor.

At thirty-three, in 1905, the shy bachelor amazed his friends by becoming engaged to one of the more attractive and vivacious women in town, twenty-six-year-old Grace Good-hue. A lip-reading teacher at Northampton's Clarke School for the Deaf, she first glimpsed him when watering flowers outside the school and glanced into the large open window of a boarding house opposite. There was Calvin Coolidge shaving in front of a mirror, wearing nothing but long underwear and a hat. Her laughter at the sight made him turn to look at her. They met on a more dressy occasion soon after, and it was a

---

[2] Whitney and Whitney, *American Presidents*, 252.

[3] Durant, *Pictorial History of American Presidents*, 243.

case of opposites attracting – she charming and outgoing, he shy and introverted. Soon after they married.[4]

A loyal Republican and a dogged worker, he steadily rose through the political ranks as a member of the state legislature, mayor of Northampton, state senator, president of the state senate, and two terms as lieutenant governor.

As Senate president he showed his dry sense of humor when a fellow senator asked for his ruling on the colleague who had told him to "Go to hell!" Coolidge replied, "I've looked up the law, and you don't have to go there."[5]

In 1919, voters chose him as governor of Massachusetts – confirming their wisdom when, that same year, he calmly handled the Boston police strike. Even so, he was somewhat surprised when presidential candidate Senator Warren Harding chose him as his running mate. Again, perhaps, a case of opposites attract. Harding won the presidency in a landslide.

In 1920, Turkey, having lost the recent war, renounced all rights and titles over parts of their Ottoman Empire, which included Mesopotamia (now Iraq) and Palestine. The British took control of Palestine with the approval of the League of Nations (which had been formed to try to keep the peace after World War I), having promised in their Balfour Declaration to hand Palestine over to the Jews when the time was ripe. Though the US was not a member of the League of Nations, most Americans agreed with the plan. On October 21, 1922, a joint session of the US House and Senate officially and unanimously endorsed the Balfour Declaration.[6]

As mentioned, Warren Harding also endorsed it, and so did Vice President Coolidge, who spoke of his "sympathy with

---

[4] Robert Sobel, *Coolidge: An American Enigma* (Washington, DC: Regnery, 1998), 55.

[5] Peter Hannaford, Calvin Coolidge Memorial Foundation, August 5, 2001.

[6] "US Congress Endorses the Balfour Declaration," Public Resolution 73, 67th Congress, Second Session.

the deep and intense longing which finds such expression in the Jewish National Homeland in Palestine."[7]

While Coolidge was enjoying a vacation with his family in Vermont, a messenger woke him shortly after midnight on August 3, 1923, with the news that President Harding was dead, and he needed to go through the ritual to make him the president. So, at 2:47 a.m. with his wife, Grace, as a witness, his father, a notary public, swore him into office. Then they all went back to bed.

As the new president serving the last few months of Harding's term, Coolidge fired many of the corrupt administration, and three months later, in November, he won the presidential election.

His time as president was overshadowed by the death of the youngest of his two sons, sixteen-year-old Calvin Jr., who died from blood poisoning caused by a blister he got while playing tennis on the White House lawn. As Coolidge wrote in his autobiography, "When he went, the power and glory of the Presidency went with him…I don't know why such a price was exacted for occupying the White House."[8]

During Coolidge's second year in the White House, on March 19, 1924, Rabbi Abraham Isaac Kook, Palestine's Chief Rabbi, and a delegation of rabbis arrived in New York to raise funds for Jewish charities in Palestine and Europe. It was known as the Central Committee for the Relief of Jews Suffering through the War, or the Central Relief Committee (CRS). Thousands of Jews, among them hundreds of rabbis, greeted the group's arrival – singing *Hatikvah*, which became Israel's national anthem. One non-Jewish reporter who interviewed Kook wanted to call him the "Jewish Pope," but Kook explained that the Jews don't have such a position.

---

[7] Mitchell G. Bard, "Roots of the US-Israel Relationship," Jewish Virtual Library. http://www.jewishvirtuallibrary.org/jsource/US-Israel/roots_of_US-Israel.html.

[8] Whitney and Whitney, *American Presidents*, 255.

Despite an impending cabinet meeting on April 15, and though it wasn't his day to receive visitors, Coolidge made an exception for Kook, who "thanked him for his government's support of the Balfour Declaration, and told him that the return of the Jews to the Holy Land would benefit mankind. According to the Talmudic sages, Kook explained, peace can only be expected when the Jews return to the Holy Land. Kook also thanked the American government on behalf of Jews throughout the world, for its relief work during the war. He praised America for its dedication to liberty as engraved on Philadelphia's Liberty Bell: 'And you shall proclaim liberty throughout the land for all its inhabitants.'"

Coolidge assured Kook that America would assist Jews whenever possible, and acknowledged the valuable contribution of Jews in the War of Independence, saying, "The Jews... were true to the teachings of their prophets. The Jewish faith is predominantly the faith of liberty."[9]

Coolidge, reputedly a man of few words, had earned the nickname "Silent Cal." But on May 3, 1925, when he laid the cornerstone of a projected Jewish community center in Washington DC, he showed that if interested he could refute his reputation. This is a small part of his speech at the center's dedication:

> From the beginnings of the conflict [The War of Independence] between the colonies and the mother country, the Jews were overwhelmingly on the side of the rising revolution.... There is romance in the story of Haym Salomon, a Polish Jew Financier of the Revolution. He negotiated for Robert Morris all the loans raised in France and Holland, pledged his personal faith and fortune, enormous amounts, and personally advanced large sums to such men as James Madison, Thomas

---

[9] Joshua Hoffman, "Rav Kook's Mission to America," *Orot*, vol. 1, 1991, http://www.tzemachdovid.org/gedolim/ravkook.html.

Jefferson, Baron Steuben, General St. Clair, and other patriot
leaders, who testified that without his aid they could not have
carried on in the cause.... When Baron de Kalb was fatally
wounded in the thickest fighting of the Battle of Camden,
the officers who were at hand to bear him from the field were
Major Nones, Captain Jacob de Leon, all of them Jews. The
patriots who laid the foundation of this Republic drew their
faith from the Bible. May they give the credit to the people
among whom the Holy Scriptures came into being.[10]

Soon after, speaking on the phone to a meeting of the Federation of Jewish Philanthropies of New York City, Coolidge
said: "You are demonstrating the supremacy of the spiritual life and helping others establish the Kingdom of God on
earth."[11]

His genuine distaste for small talk and long conversation
caused a contemporary to quip that Coolidge could be silent
in five languages. A story also made the rounds that a woman
told Coolidge she had bet with a friend that she could make
him say more than two words. "You lose," Coolidge reportedly
replied.[12]

Surprisingly, as president he gave 529 press conferences,
more than any other president before or since. However, only
a few reporters attended; questions had to be handed to his
press secretary in advance and then Coolidge choose those he
wanted to answer on the record. Off the record he could be
quite talkative.

His reputation for brevity was enhanced in August 1927,
when he gave reporters this ten-word statement: "I do not
choose to run for President in 1928." [13] Just before he left the

---

[10] *New York Times*, May 4, 1925, 1–2.

[11] John T. Woolley and Gerhart Peters, Calvin Coolidge, The American Presidency
Project.

[12] Whitney and Whitney, *American Presidents*, 255.

[13] Ibid.

White House, he shared with the incoming president, Herbert Hoover, his former secretary of commerce, his secret method for silencing garrulous visitors: "If you keep dead still they will run down in three or four minutes. If you even cough or smile, they'll start up again."[14]

With the substantial royalties from his autobiography, he bought "The Beeches," a mansion in Northampton, where he and his wife lived largely in seclusion, but with the welcome company of their dogs, cats, two canaries, Nip and Tuck, and a pet raccoon named Rebecca. The First Lady was evidently an animal lover: while in the White House she had fed a family of mice with crackers.

Coolidge died at sixty from a heart attack while shaving in his bathroom, on January 5, 1933, and was buried in the graveyard of his birthplace in Plymouth, Vermont.

In 1939, at the start of World War II in Europe, Coolidge's widow, Grace, campaigned for the Wagner-Rogers Bill to allow twenty thousand more fatherless and homeless Jewish child refugees under fourteen from Nazi Germany than the quota system permitted. Polls showed that the American public opposed the bill and it didn't even reach the floor for a vote; the bill failed.[15]

During the war, Grace Coolidge worked for the Red Cross and civil defense. She died in 1957 at age seventy-eight and was buried next to her husband.

Ronald Reagan, a Calvin Coolidge fan, considered him greatly underrated and hung his portrait in the Cabinet Room.

---

[14] Ibid.

[15] Dr. Rafael Medoff, "Grace Coolidge and Anne Frank." *Rutland Herald*, May 7, 2007, www.rutlandherald.com.

Herbert Clark Hoover

1874–1964

⊗ Thirty-first president, 1929–1933

⊗ A professional mining engineer, he was the first president to be born west of the Mississippi River

⊗ His policies could not overcome the economic despair of the Great Depression

Best known for failing to cure his country's deep financial Depression, the worst in the nation's history; less known for his extraordinary humanitarian and philanthropic ventures, President Herbert Hoover is hardly known at all for his radical Zionist views. Yet the thirty-first president of the United States believed that there was an effective way to avoid the otherwise inevitable bloodshed and to make Palestine a viable Jewish homeland. And that entailed encouraging Palestinian Arabs to resettle in Iraq.

Before he expressed these radical views he was faced, only a few months after his inauguration as president, with a financial disaster that spread to the whole world. In America bankrupt bankers jumped to their deaths from skyscrapers, countless men stood in breadlines to feed their impoverished families, and six thousand sold apples on New York City street corners. In the winter some of the homeless slept with newspapers for blankets.

Although Hoover was wealthy and had weathered the financial storm, he had had a tough start in life. Born in West Branch, Iowa, on August 10, 1874, his father, Jesse Clark Hoover, was an Iowa blacksmith and farm implement store owner of German-Swiss descent who died of typhus when Hoover was six. His mother, Hulda Minthorn, a former Canadian schoolteacher of Scots-Irish descent, died of pneumonia when he was eight. His aunts and uncles, who like his parents were devout Quakers, raised him. Hoover, too, became a member of this pacifist Christian group that follows no creed, but believes that a person should be directed by conscience alone and can have direct contact with God – without any go-between – through one's inner voice.

Putting himself through Stanford University by delivering laundry and newspapers and working for the head of the Geology Department, he earned a degree in geology. However, his first jobs out of college were inconsequential, such as pushing a car for ten hours, seven days a week in a California gold mine. When able to apply his gift for mining engineering, his career took off and he was in great demand, first in Australia and then China. In Australia he did the job required despite "red dust, black flies, white heat," whirlwinds and dust storms.[1]

He stopped working in 1899 long enough to marry Lou Henry, his college sweetheart and a banker's daughter, who, like Hoover, also had a Stanford degree in geology.

---

[1] Herbert Hoover Biography, Herbert Hoover Presidential Library and Museum, http://www.ecommcode.com/hoover/hooveronline/hoover_bio/index.htm.

The following year they moved to China. It was unfortunate timing. The Boxer Rebellion, an uprising by peasants, was in full force. They were intent on driving out all foreigners, killing those who stayed, and destroying everything foreign made. These formidable fighters were called Boxers because they believed that boxing and other physical exercises gave them such supernatural powers that they were bullet proof.

The Hoovers were trapped with other foreign families in Tiensin, protected by a small, desperately outnumbered contingent of soldiers from several countries. Hoover's task was to direct the building of barricades and to find food for his fellow foreigners, as well as six hundred anti-Boxer Chinese trapped with them. The group held out for several weeks until, in August 1900, an international military force of twenty-one hundred came to their rescue, and soon after, the Hoovers left for England.

When the rebellion was put down, Hoover returned to China, turned a failing mining business into a success, and became a millionaire at age twenty-seven, after which he was "delighted to get out of China into a larger engineering world."[2]

The Hoovers' two sons, Herbert Jr. and Allan, were both born in London, and between 1902 and 1907 the family of four circled the earth five times, with Hoover in demand as one of the world's most respected and rewarded mining engineers. By 1911, at age forty, he was worth several million.

His relief work during the Boxer Rebellion had been widely reported, and when World War I broke out in Europe, President Woodrow Wilson asked him to help Americans stranded in the war zone. Hoover accepted the challenge, and as head of a London-based committee he fed and found lodgings for 120,000 Americans, and got them safely back home. The

---

[2] Herbert Hoover, *Memoirs of Herbert Hoover: Years of Adventure, 1874–1920* (New York: Hollis and Carter, 1932), 65.

committee lent them more than a million dollars, of which all but $300 was repaid.

When America entered the war in 1917, President Wilson recalled Hoover to the States to be US food administrator, providing food for both American and allied armed forces and civilian populations. After the war Hoover worked without pay as chief of the Supreme Economic Council of the Allies to prevent a post-war famine. It meant feeding millions of Europeans, including – at the president's insistence – former enemies: Germans and eventually Russians.

To raise the money to feed ten million Belgians in their war-devastated country every day, and to get trucks, ships, and trains to carry the food to them, he created a charity, Committee for Relief of Belgium, which raised a billion dollars. For four years he and several colleagues worked without pay. Several Jewish Americans helped, among them Louis Marshall and Felix Warburg, like him wealthy Republican philanthropists. So did another Jewish American, Admiral Louis Strauss, who had once been Hoover's private secretary. Strauss said that he admired Hoover because he "appreciated talent. He didn't care whether the man who had it was of his political persuasion. He was absolutely color-blind as to race, and he didn't care anything about denomination."[3]

Walter Hines, America's ambassador to England, called Hoover a man "who began his career in California and will end it in Heaven, and he doesn't want anyone's thanks."[4]

Hoover's reputation as a problem-solving humanitarian made him an attractive presidential candidate, and after his landslide defeat of presidential rival, Al Smith, in 1928, Hoover became America's thirty-first president. Seven months

[3] Sonja P. Wenting, "The Engineer and the Shadlamin: Herbert Hoover and American Jewish Non-Zionists, 1917–1928," *American Jewish History* (Sept. 2000): 377–406.

[4] Herbert Hoover Presidential Library and Museum, http://www.ecommcode.com/hoover/hooveronline/hoover_bio/index.htm.

later he faced the Great Depression, the first immense problem he couldn't fix. Unfortunately, this man of action chose to do little except let the market take its disastrous course.

However, he remained active in support of Zionist causes. On June 30, 1929, he told Detroit Zionists that he hoped their deliberations might be "as always...really fruitful in their spiritual wisdom for which the Jewish race has been noteworthy in all ages."[5]

Riots broke out in Palestine in August 1929, as Arabs and Jews clashed over access to the Western Wall, and within a few days 133 Jews and 116 Arabs were killed and hundreds wounded on both sides. Hearing that Herman Bernstein, a Jewish American, had been to Palestine to find out the facts, Hoover invited him to the White House. There Bernstein said that after interviewing Arab leaders he could refute the anti-Jewish and anti-British propaganda spread by Arab sources. On leaving the White House, Bernstein told reporters that Hoover had been "deeply moved by the tragic events, and assured me that the American government was alive to the situation and doing all in its power in the matter."[6] Meanwhile, the American consul in Jerusalem, Paul Knabenshue, was protecting Jewish American women and children in the US consulate.

Early in 1932, Hoover wrote to Emanuel Neumann of the Zionist Organization of America, "I am interested to learn that a distinguished group of men and women is to be formed to spread knowledge and appreciation of the rehabilitation which is going forward in Palestine under Jewish auspices, and to add my expression to the sentiment among our people in favor of the age-old aspirations of the Jewish people for the restoration of their national homeland."[7]

---

[5]   Herbert Hoover, The American Presidency Project.

[6]   "Britain to Protect American Citizens," *The New York Times*, August 29, 1929, 1.

[7]   Herbert Hoover, The American Presidency Project, http://www.presidency.ucsb.edu/ws/print.php?pid=23121.

On November 3, 1932, the fifteenth anniversary of the Balfour Declaration, Hoover told the President of the Zionist Organization of America: "I have watched with genuine admiration the steady unmistakable progress made in the rehabilitation of Palestine which, desolate for centuries, is now retrieving its youth and vitality through the enthusiasm, hard work, and self-sacrifice of the Jewish volunteers, who toil there in the spirit of peace and social justice. It is very gratifying to note that many American Jews, Zionists as well as non-Zionists, have rendered such splendid service to the cause which merits the sympathy and moral encouragement of everyone."[8]

That same year, Hoover appointed Judge Benjamin Cardozo – a member of the Zionist Organization of America – to the US Supreme Court, the second Jewish judge on the court after Brandeis.

In 1933, President Franklin Roosevelt replaced Hoover in the White House, but out of office he retained a close interest in the future of Palestine. During World War II, after discussing Palestine with author and Zionist Eliahu Ben-Horin, Hoover put his ideas into his 1943 book, *The Problems of Lasting Peace*. In it he pointed out that after the war European nations would have mixed populations on their borders, which was a frequent cause of wars. The "heroic remedy," he suggested, was "the transfer of populations," which, though a great hardship on those transferred, "is less than the constant suffering of minorities and the constant recurrence of war."[9]

Taking the advise of T. E. Lawrence (of Arabia), Winston Churchill had already given the eastern part of Palestine – previously promised to the Jews in the Balfour Declaration – to

---

[8]   American Presidency Project. http://www.presidency.ucsb.edu//ws/index.php?pid=23326&st=palestine&stl=.

[9]   Herbert Hoover and Hugh Gibson, *The Problems of Lasting Peace* (New York: 1943), 235–36.

the Hashemite Arabs from Arabia, as a reward for their help in defeating the Turks in World War I. Today it's known as Jordan. What was left of "Palestine itself," Hoover suggested, "could be turned over to Jewish immigrants in search of a homeland." He considered this might be "the model migration in history – transferring Arabs to an Arab nation; restoring agricultural prosperity to the ancient valleys of the Tigris and Euphrates, and providing persecuted Jews with a refuge and a beacon. It would be a solution by engineering instead of by conflict."[10]

Iraq's prime minister, Nuri Said, proposed his own version of Hoover's plan: to exchange Baghdad's Jews for an equal number of Arabs from Palestine.

The *New York World-Telegram* gave Hoover's idea front-page treatment, headlined "Hoover Urges Resettling Arabs to Solve Palestine Problem," with a subhead, "Says Irrigation Could Provide Good Iraqi Land."[11]

Soon after the end of World War II, in December 1945, Hoover offered his "constructive humanitarian solution" to the Anglo-American Committee of Inquiry on Palestine "by which both Jews and Arabs would benefit materially," and which could help in "settling the Palestine question and providing ample Jewish refuge."[12]

His solution wasn't accepted, but three years later a Jewish state became a reality – and was immediately attacked by five Arab armies. During the fighting half a million Arabs fled or were driven out. Many hoped to return as victors, but when Israel won the fight, they were doomed to become refugees. The following year, Hoover again suggested that Arabs living in Palestine be resettled in Iraq, "which would give permanent

---

[10] Moshe Kohn, "The International Roots of Transfer," *The Jerusalem Post*, November 20, 2001.

[11] *New York World-Telegram*, November 19, 1945, 1.

[12] Bruce Brill, "Herbert Hoover's Mid-East-Solution," The Jewish Magazine, November 2004, http://www.jewishmag.com/84mag/humanitarian/humanitarian.htm.

solution to the problem of these unfortunate people" and "strengthen the economy of Iraq."[13]

When his Zionist friend and fellow author, Eliahu Ben-Horin, sent Hoover greetings on his eightieth birthday in August 1954, Hoover replied, referring to their Palestinian plan of population transfer, "We were on the right track!"[14]

On October 20, 1964, ninety-year-old Herbert Hoover died in Manhattan's Waldorf Towers, with his two sons at his bedside. In a tribute to him, Dr. Max Nussbaum, President of the Zionist Organization of America, called Hoover a fellow Zionist who had suggested and promoted a plan to transfer Arabs from Palestine to create a safe homeland for the Jews.[15]

[13] Ibid.

[14] Chaim Simons, *A Brick for the Bridge,* unpublished autobiography, 185–86; Chaim Simons, "A Historical Survey of Proposals to Transfer Arabs from Palestine, 1895–1947," 2004, http://www.geocities.com/ChaimSimons/transfer15.html?20092.

[15] Central Zionist Archives, www.Zionistarchives.org.il/ZA/pMainE.aspx.

Franklin Delano Roosevelt

1882–1945

✪ Thirty-second president, 1933–1945
✪ Provided a safety net for older Americans with Social Security
✪ Led the Allies to victory in World War II

Franklin Delano Roosevelt inherited the Great Depression. It did not end until eight years after his election, and then the end was largely due to the massive employment and military spending for World War II. Meanwhile, the ebullient and charismatic FDR, though crippled with polio, brought hope and Social Security to the nation.

Roosevelt was born to wealth in a Hyde Park, New York, mansion, on January 30, 1882. When he was five his father took him to meet President Cleveland in the White House, where the president placed his hand on FDR's head and said, "I have a strange wish for you, young man, that you never become president of the United States."[1]

---

[1] Sara Delano Roosevelt's diary, April 12, 1887, FDR Presidential Library, www.fdrlibrary.marist.edu.

The only child of James Roosevelt, of Dutch descent, and Sara Delano, of French descent, as boy he was baptized as an Episcopalian and brought up by governesses and tutors, although he often traveled with his parents to Europe. At age twenty-three, in 1905, he married twenty-year-old Eleanor Roosevelt, his fifth cousin once removed, who was given away by her uncle, his fifth cousin, President Theodore Roosevelt. His career path was onward and upward and almost duplicated that of his cousin Theodore's: from Harvard and Columbia Law School to the New York state Senate (1911–1913), assistant navy secretary (1913–1920), New York City lawyer (1921–1929), governor of New York (1929–1933), and US president (1933–1945).

Despite contracting polio at age thirty-seven, which left him dependent on a wheelchair for the rest of his life – and needing a helping hand whenever he wanted to stand – he remained ebullient, ambitious, and optimistic.

On July 16, 1933, just months after his inauguration as president, FDR discussed the persecution of Jews in Hitler's Germany with William Dodd Jr., his ambassador in Berlin. "The German authorities are treating the Jews shamefully," FDR told him, "and the Jews in this country are greatly excited. But this is also not a governmental affair. We can do nothing except for American citizens who happen to be made victims." Even in such cases, according to Dodd, FDR rejected the use of diplomatic pressure in favor of "unofficial and personal influence" on the Nazi government.[2]

The following month, FDR's politically active wife, Eleanor, invited her friend Alice Hamilton to the Roosevelts' Hyde Park home. Recently back from three months in Germany, Alice told them of witnessing German brutality against Jews.

---

[2]   Ambassador Dodd's diary, Laurel Leff and Rafael Medoff, the David D. Wyman Institute for Holocaust Studies, www.wymaninstitute.org/articles/2004-04-fdrdocs.php.

Other friends, among them FDR's Jewish neighbor – who was also his treasury secretary – Henry Morgenthau Jr., urged him to condemn Hitler's persecution of Jews.[3]

The American Jewish Committee, B'nai B'rith, and other Jewish organizations, had also urged FDR to intercede. On his behalf, Secretary of State Cordell Hull sent this timid message to Ambassador William Dodd in Berlin: "Unfortunate incidents have indeed occurred and the whole world joins in regretting them." Hull was cautious because he believed that reports of anti-Jewish violence were probably exaggerated.[4]

Hitler's political manifesto, *Mein Kampf*, recently published in English as *My Struggle*, glorified the "Aryan" race and claimed that Jews were trying to rule the world. One critic of the book, New York City's feisty Mayor Fiorello LaGuardia, son of an Italian Catholic father and a Jewish mother from Trieste, called its author a "perverted maniac."

In a prophetic speech the following year, LaGuardia warned that Hitler intended to annihilate the Jews in Germany. Three years later, in 1937, addressing the Women's Division of the American Jewish Congress, LaGuardia began a war of words with the Nazi government. He damned a German pavilion planned for the New York World's Fair as "a chamber of horrors for that brown-shirted fanatic." The Nazi-controlled German press hit back, denouncing him as "a dirty Talmud Jew," "a shameless Jewish lout," and "a warmonger." The German ambassador complained about LaGuardia to Cordell Hull, who "very earnestly depreciated the utterances which have given offense to the German Government," but explained that in America, LaGuardia was free to speak his mind.

When Cordell Hull complained to FDR that LaGuardia was poisoning German-American relations, the president

---

[3] Ibid., July 23, 2011.

[4] American Jewish Committee Twenty-Eighth Annual Report, N.Y., 1935, 46–50.

asked him, "What would you say if I should say that I agreed completely with La Guardia?" On LaGuardia's next visit to FDR, according to New York's mayor, "The president smiled as I entered his office. Then he extended his right arm and said, '*Heil*, Fiorello!' I snapped to attention, extended my right arm and replied, '*Heil*, Franklin!' and that's all that was said about it."[5]

As almost 15 percent of FDR's top appointments were to Jews, bigots called his New Deal political platform the Jew Deal, and suggested that he was a Jew. He wasn't. He was an Episcopalian of Dutch and French ancestry.

Convinced that reports of Germany's persecuted Jews were not exaggerated as Hull thought, Mrs. Roosevelt founded the International Rescue Committee to help anti-Nazi artists, intellectuals, and labor leaders, many of them Jews, to find safety in the United States. One of them, novelist Thomas Mann, told FDR that he now believed that the Nazis would be beaten because for the first time he had met someone who realized Hitler was evil.[6]

Hitler's draconian Nuremberg Laws gave only a hint of how far he would go to settle "The Jewish Problem." From January 1, 1936, his laws "protected German blood and honor," by forbidding marriages and extramarital intercourse between Jews and non-Jewish Germans; stripped Jews of German citizenship; banned them from state schools after age fourteen; and forbade them from working as lawyers, doctors, or journalists. Jews were also banned from public hospitals, public parks, libraries, and beaches. They could not collect

---

[5]   "Fiorello LaGuardia (1882–1947)," Jewish Virtual Library, http://www. jewishvirtuallibrary.org/jsource/biography/LaGuardia.html.

[6]   "America, Franklin D. Roosevelt and the Holocaust," historian William J. Vanden Heuvel's lecture on October 17, 1996, University of Chicago, Franklin and Eleanor Roosevelt Institute, http://newdeal.feri.org/feri/index.htm.

lottery winnings and their names were to be removed from war memorials.

Germans with four grandparents of "German blood" were classified as white. Germans with three or four Jewish grandparents were classified as Jews. Those with one or two Jewish grandparents were classified as crossbreeds or of mixed blood. The penalty for breaking the Nuremberg Laws – passed unanimously by the Nazi parliament – was prison.

Swiss officials insisted on a provision in the laws – obviously anticipating and attempting to prevent a flood of Jewish refugees into their country – which stated that Jewish women applying for a passport must use "Sara" as a middle name, and Jewish men, "Israel." To emphasize their Jewish identity, a large letter J had to be stamped on their passports, which could only be used to leave Germany, not to return.

Appalled by this official anti-Semitic action, FDR modified a rule requiring refugees to have their financial security guaranteed before they could enter the United States. Consequently, in 1936 America accepted 10,895 German refugees, compared with 6,346 the previous year; and in 1937 it accepted 17,199.

In FDR's developing Zionist views he was influenced by US Supreme Court judge Louis Brandeis. Like President Wilson, FDR admired Brandeis as a visionary, and when Rabbi Stephen Wise mentioned him during a conversation, FDR said, "Grand man! You know, Stephen, we of the inner circle call him Isaiah."[7]

Meanwhile, in Palestine, Arabs attacked a busload of Jews. The British response was to suspend Jewish immigration until they had resolved the problem. Rabbi Wise then persuaded FDR to accuse the British of breaching the conditions of their Palestinian Mandate. British prime minister Stanley Baldwin

---

[7] Strum, *Brandeis*, 384.

then allowed Jews to continue to enter Palestine, while a British Peel Commission investigated the overall situation. It concluded that control of Palestine had failed and that, rather than remain a British mandate, the land should be divided into a Jewish state and an Arab state, with an international zone surrounding and including Jerusalem. But neither Jews nor Arabs accepted the proposal.

On February 6, 1937, during that year's United Palestine Appeal, FDR publicly expressed his Zionist sympathies when he said:

> The American people...have watched with sympathetic interest the effort of the Jews to renew in Palestine the ties of their ancient homeland, and to establish Jewish culture in the place where for centuries it flourished and where it was carried to the far corners of the world. This year marks the twentieth anniversary of the Balfour Declaration.... These two decades have witnessed a remarkable exemplification of the vitality and vision of the Jewish pioneers in Palestine. It should be a source of pride to Jewish citizens of the United States that they, too, have had a share in the great work of revival and restoration.[8]

The Nazis began their military operations on March 12, 1938, by invading and occupying Austria, putting its 185,000 Jews in jeopardy.

That summer, FDR proposed an international conference in Evian, France, "to facilitate the emigration from Germany and Austria of political refugees." Representatives from thirty-two countries attended, but the most consequential outcome was more bad news for Jews: the Nazi poison had spread to Poland and Romania, whose delegates claimed the same rights as Germans to expel their Jewish populations. The only offer of a lifeline came from the Dominican Republic, which

---

[8] FDR Library.

agreed to accept one hundred thousand Jews. Soon after, five thousand Dominican visas were issued, but, due to internal political problems, only 645 Jewish refugees were able to enter the country.[9]

Privately, FDR was much more engaged in trying to help the Jews than he indicated in his non-committal press conferences. As Brandeis told Felix Frankfurter after speaking with the president in October 1938, "FDR went very far in our talk in his appreciation of the significance of Palestine – the need of keeping it whole and of making it Jewish. He was very interested – and wholly surprised – in learning of the great increases in the Arab population [there] since the War [World War I]; and of learning of the plentitude of land for Arabs in other Arab countries…. Possible refuge for Jews elsewhere he spoke of as 'satellites.'"[10]

In late October 1938, US senator Willard Tydings of Maryland brought up Palestine in a letter to FDR. The president replied:

> I have on numerous occasions, as you know, expressed my sympathy in the founding of a National Home for the Jews in Palestine, despite the set-backs caused by the disorders there during the last few years. I have been heartened by the progress which has been made by the remarkable accomplishments of the Jewish settlers in the country. As I have had occasion to inform a number of Members of Congress within the past few days, we have kept constantly before the British Government, through our Ambassador in London [Joseph Kennedy], the interest which the American people have in Palestine and I have every reason to believe that that Government is truly cognizant of public opinion on the matter

---

[9] *Encyclopaedia Judaica*, 1971, vol. 6, "The Evian Conference," 987.

[10] Strum, *Brandeis*, 385.

in this country.... You may be sure that we shall continue to follow the situation with the closest interest. "[11]

Sir Ronald Lindsay, the British Ambassador to the United States, discussed Palestine with FDR on October 15, 1938, and reported that the president was "impressed by the fact that the Arab population [there] had increased by 40,000 since the Mandate." FDR also told Lindsay that by starting a well-digging operation across Jordan, a large quantity of water would be made available to irrigate and cultivate the land thus created and "should be set apart for Arabs from Palestine. They should be offered land free, and that ought to be enough to attract them; and failing the attraction, they should be compelled to emigrate to it. Palestine could thus be relieved of 200,000 Arabs, at an estimated cost from twenty to thirty million pounds, but we ought to be able to find that money for the purpose."[12]

A few days after their conversation, German police forced some fifteen hundred Jews from their homes, seized their property, allowed them to take only one suitcase each, and dumped them across the Polish border at gunpoint.

As FDR and his staff discussed the Jewish situation, seventeen-year-old Herschel Grynszpan, living in Paris, got a postcard from his father saying that theirs was one of the Jewish families forced across the Polish border. Distraught at the thought of his family's distress, he went to the German embassy and fatally shot a Nazi official. (He was arrested and died in a concentration camp several years later.)

In reprisal, the following night, for what propaganda chief Joseph Goebbels called an attack by international Jewry against Hitler, the Nazis launched a devastating pogrom

---

[11] "Roosevelt to Senator Tydings on the Palestine Situation," Jewish Virtual Library,. www.jewishvirtuallibrary.org/jsource/US-Israel/fdr101938.html.

[12] Letter to Lancelot Oliphant, British Foreign Office, November 3, 1938 (PRO FO 371/21883 E6606/10/31.), The National Archives, Kew, England.

throughout Germany. Storm troopers murdered some fifteen hundred Jews, sent tens of thousands to concentration camps, destroyed 1,574 synagogues, and more than seven thousand Jewish businesses. It became known as *Kristallnacht* (Crystal Night) because of the multitude of smashed windows.

FDR recalled his ambassador from Germany and extended the visitors' visas of some twelve thousand Jewish refugees already in the US. Two days after Crystal Night, his ambassador to Poland, Anthony Drexel Biddle Jr., warned FDR that "the plight of the Jewish populations as a whole in Europe is becoming untenable."[13]

But when FDR asked Samuel Rosenman, a member of the American Jewish Committee, if he should allow more Jewish refugees into the United States, Rosenman said no, because "it would create a Jewish problem in the US."[14]

US assistant secretary of state Adolf Berle recalled that "the President was full of Palestine. He had suggested to Ronald Lindsay that they call a conference of Arab princes, that they lay down, say $200,000,000 to buy a farm for every Arab who wishes to leave Palestine, the money chiefly to be used in digging wells, which is perfectly possible in the Hedjaz."[15]

Seeking another way to help endangered European Jews, FDR advised the British to get Arabs to leave Palestine to allow more Jews in. But British Foreign Office official Lacy Baggalay discounted FDR's idea of drilling for water in Jordan, because experts had agreed that it was unlikely to yield much water, and even if it did, "it is now out of the question that any Arabs should be 'compelled' to emigrate to land thus brought into cultivation. Whatever else may remain uncertain about the

---

[13] November 1938, FDR Library, www.fdrlibrary.marist.edu/contact.html; Drexel Biddle warns FDR re Crystal Night, November 10, 1938, FDR Library.

[14] Doris Kearns Goodwin, *No Ordinary Time: Franklin and Eleanor Roosevelt: The Home Front in World War II* (New York: Simon & Schuster, 1994), 455.

[15] Lacy Baggalay, Minutes, British Foreign Office, November 19, 1938 (PRO FO 371/21883E6066/10/31). National Archives, Kew, England.

problem of Palestine, the impossibility of compulsion on this scale is now beyond dispute. Finally and in general, the President's suggestion, on which he has doubtless been coached by the Zionist leaders of America, is based on the old fallacy that the problem of Palestine, which has now become a political and sentimental issue of the first importance to the whole Arab and indeed the whole Moslem world, can be solved by economic sops and financial assistance."[16]

FDR strongly disagreed, again discussing the subject with Lindsay at the end of November, when he suggested that "the British should call in some of the Arab leaders from Palestine and some of the leaders from the adjoining Arab countries [and] explain to them that they, the Arabs, had within their control large territories ample to sustain their people." He said that Jewish immigration to Palestine and Jordan would not harm the Arabs, since there was plenty of room for everyone, and that "some of the Arabs on poor land in Palestine could be given much better land in adjoining Arab countries."

When Lindsay cited the Arab and Muslim objections to these proposals, FDR "belittled the opposition and thought it was largely due to British indecision and conflicting policy." He maintained that "if a plan was devised for a settlement of 100,000 (Palestine Arab) families costing $3,000 a family, or $300,000,000," it might be paid for "by the American Government, the British and French Governments, and private subscription – largely Jewish. Each of these bodies would contribute $100,000,000."[17]

On December 20, FDR received a British government memo stating that it was beyond its powers to compel Arabs to emigrate "with the object of vacating land in Palestine for settlement by Jews.... The morality of attempting such coercion

---

[16] Baggalay, ibid.

[17] Franklin D. Roosevelt Presidential Library and Museum, www.fdrlibrary.marist. edu/contact.html .

would be questioned in Britain, India and the Moslem world."
The memo concluded that "redistribution of the Arab and
Jewish communities in Palestine and across the Jordan" was
not a matter of finance but of politics.[18]

The next day, Brandeis sent FDR a news clipping reporting that a Bedouin Arab tribe had agreed to be transferred to
Jordan to make way for Jewish villages. In return, FDR sent
Brandeis a copy of the British memo with a note saying that he
had been informed by the French "that land in Arabia across
the Red Sea from Djibouti and back of the coastal range of
mountains, had all kinds of possibility for settlement – and
that the Iraqi people are entirely willing to take a large Arab
population for settlement on their newly irrigated lands." In
his reply Brandeis called the British attitude "deplorable. But
ultimately – if we insist – folly will yield to reason and the
right." On October 24, 1939, after resigning from the Supreme
Court, and six weeks after the start of World War II in Europe,
Brandeis spoke with FDR and afterwards described him "as
sympathetic as in the past; and as interested in all I was able
to tell him about the present in Palestine."[19]

France fell to the Nazis in June 1940, but southern France
remained unoccupied and some Jews escaped to neutral Spain
and Portugal. They were helped by American journalist Varian
Fry, who was leader of the International Rescue Committee,
an organization Eleanor Roosevelt supported.

In his last letter to FDR, on April 26, 1941, Brandeis
deplored the British decision not to allow Palestinian Jews
to be armed, despite the movement of victorious Nazi troops
across North Africa toward Palestine. "A word from you to the
British," he wrote, "manifesting your desire to be assured that
the Jews of Palestine will be afforded the necessary means for
self-protection, would be of the greatest help. Nor would it

---

[18] Strum, *Brandeis*, 384–85.
[19] Ibid., 385.

be irrelevant for you to suggest that the measure would help the British." FDR agreed and sent Brandeis's suggestion to the British.[20]

British Prime Minister Winston Churchill, himself an ardent Zionist, enthusiastically supported the idea, but it took eighteen months before it happened. Then, over thirty thousand Palestinian Jewish men and women volunteered for the British armed forces. Now, many had arms to protect themselves.

On June 22, 1941, Hitler invaded the Soviet Union, and his special SS death squads began to slaughter 1,500,000 Russian Jews.

A month after Japan's sneak attack on the US fleet at Pearl Harbor – on December 7, 1941 – and America's entry into World War II, Hitler announced that war could end in two ways, either by the extermination of the Aryan peoples or by the disappearance of Jews from Europe.

In the summer of 1942, Gerhart Riegner, the World Jewish Congress representative in Switzerland, learned from a contact in top Nazi circles of Hitler's plan to annihilate Europe's Jews. Knowing it was from a reliable source, he asked Howard Elting Jr., the American vice consul in Geneva, to inform the US and other Allied governments. At first, the US State Department believed it was just a "fantastic" war rumor and did nothing. But the British Foreign Office gave the information to a Jewish member of parliament, Samuel Silverman, who passed it on to Rabbi Stephen Wise in the United States. Wise is said to have wept on getting the news of the mass murders, then reported it to Sumner Welles, undersecretary of state. Welles asked him not to tell the press until the State Department had confirmed

---

[20] British Foreign Office, PRO file 371/30917, accessed March 28, 2010, http://www.fpp.co.uk/Auschwitz/docs/Riegner/dossier1942.html.

the news from sources available to the Czech and Polish governments in exile. This took almost three months.[21]

On November 28, Rabbi Wise and other Jewish leaders asked FDR to warn Hitler and the German people that after the war they would be individually held responsible for their crimes against the Jews. FDR agreed and made a statement to that effect in the US Congress; it was repeated in the British Parliament, and repeated frequently during the rest of the war.

Henry Morgenthau Jr. noted on December 3, 1942, that during their conversation the president had not only raised the subject of a Jewish homeland, but outlined how it could be achieved:

> Well, what I think I will do is this. First I would call Palestine a religious country. Then I would leave Jerusalem the way it is, and have it run by the Orthodox Greek Catholic Church, the Protestants, and the Jews – and have a joint committee run it. They are doing it all right now and we might as well leave it that way.... I actually would put barbed wire around Palestine, and I would begin to move the Arabs out.... I would provide land for the Arabs in some other part of the Middle East, and I know there are plenty of places. Each time we move out an Arab we would bring in another Jewish family.

Morgenthau asked if Jews should be the majority in Palestine, and FDR replied: "Yes, ninety percent of them should be Jews, but I don't want to bring in more than they can economically support, and I think that point has been reached." When Morgenthau wondered what the new Palestine would be, FDR said: "It would be an independent nation like any other nation – completely independent. Naturally, if there are ninety percent Jews, the Jews would dominate the government. There are lots of places to which you can move the Arabs. All you have to do is dig a well, because there is this

---

21 British Foreign Office., PRO File 371/30917.

large underground water supply, and we can move the Arabs to places where they can really live."[22]

The Nazis had killed at least two million Jews by December 1942, when Rabbi Wise wrote to FDR: "Dear Boss, I do not want to add an atom to the awful burden you are bearing with magic and, as I believe, heaven-inspired strength at this time. But you do know that the most overwhelming disaster in Jewish history has befallen the Jews in the form of Hitler's mass-massacres." Soon after, when the rabbi gave FDR a twenty-page document titled "Blue Print for Extermination," he promised that the United States would do all it could to rescue the surviving European Jews and to end the killings.[23]

How to save the endangered Jews was by winning the war, one aspect of which was the ongoing Manhattan Project to produce atomic weapons.

In August 1943, the *New York Times* published an "'extermination list' detailing, country by country, the 1,700,000 persons who had died from organized murder, the 746,000 who had died from starvation or disease."[24] That summer in Switzerland, Gerhart Riegner proposed a rescue plan for endangered Romanian and French Jews: by buying their lives. This would be done through Jewish organizations in the United States, transferring their funds to accounts in neutral Switzerland, which would then be sent to the Nazis. FDR approved the idea, and the necessary licenses to provide the rescue money had been issued, but nothing happened. Until outraged Treasury Department staffers told their boss, Treasury Secretary

---

[22] Presidential diaries, December 3, 1942, Papers of Henry Morgenthau Jr., FDR Library, www.fdrlibrary.marist.edu/contact.html.

[23] James MacGregor Burns, *Roosevelt: The Soldier of Freedom, 1940–1945* (New York: Harcourt Brace Jovanovich, 1970), 395.

[24] Burns, *Roosevelt*, 396.

Morgenthau Jr., that the State Department was guilty of trying to prevent the rescue of Jews from Hitler.[25]

Days after Morgenthau told FDR about it, on January 16, 1944, he created the War Refugee Board – funded mostly by Jewish groups and Treasury staff members – to rescue and transport to safety the victims of enemy oppression, and to provide temporary refuge for them.

In the spring of 1944, FDR sent a War Refugee Board official to neutral Sweden to find someone to undertake a risky assignment. He or she had to rescue Hungarian Jews otherwise destined for the death camps.

Raoul Wallenberg, first secretary of the Swedish embassy, a slim, pleasant-looking thirty-one-year-old, accepted the mission. He arrived in Budapest, the Hungarian capital in July, and rented thirty-two buildings, declared them protected by diplomatic immunity, put such signs on the front doors as "The Swedish Research Institute," and "The Swedish Library," and flew large Swedish flags from the buildings. At any one time the buildings held ten thousand Jews with Swedish passports provided by Wallenberg identifying them as Swedish citizens. He sheltered some in the Swedish embassy, and even got the Hungarian authorities to allow Jews under his protection to dispense with wearing the otherwise mandatory yellow Star of David, identifying them as Jews. One of those saved, Tom Lantos, reached America and became a respected and effective member of the US House of Representatives.

Wallenberg's most daring feat occurred after he learned that a trainload of Hungarian Jews were about to leave the railroad station for Auschwitz. He hurried to the railroad station and, according to his driver, "he climbed up on the roof of the train and began handing passports through the doors which were not yet sealed. He ignored orders from Germans

---

[25] British Foreign Office, PRO File 371/30917.

for him to get down." Arrow Cross men (members of a far right pro-German and anti-Semitic National Socialist Party), appeared on the scene and began shooting and shouting at him to get away. He ignored them, too, and calmly continued to hand out passports to the hands that reached out for them. "I believe the Arrow Cross men deliberately aimed over his head, so that not one shot hit him, which would have been impossible otherwise," said Wallenberg's driver. "I think that they did this because they were so impressed by his courage. After Wallenberg had handed over the rest of his passports he ordered all those who had one to leave the train and walk to the caravan of cars parked nearby, all marked in Swedish colors. I don't remember exactly how many, but he saved dozens off that train, and the Germans and Arrow Cross men were so dumbfounded they let him get away with it."

With the help of 350 other members of FDR's War Refugee Board, Wallenberg is believed to have saved the lives of some two hundred thousand European Jews and twenty thousand non-Jews. His fate is uncertain, because he disappeared after the war. Many leaders of the Arrow Cross Party were executed after the war for war crimes.[26]

After the concentration camps were freed, FDR hoped to get the king of Saudi Arabia to use his considerable influence to help homeless Jews find a home in Palestine, but the US ambassador to Saudi Arabia, William Eddy, warned him that the king had told him that "if America should choose in favor of the Jews, who are accursed in the Koran as enemies of the Muslims until the end of the world, it will indicate to us that America has repudiated her friendship with us."[27]

---

[26] Jan Larsson, "Raoul Wallenberg's Biography," The International Raoul Wallenberg Foundation, accessed March 28, 2010, http://www.raoulwallenberg.net/?en/wallenberg/raoul-wallenberg-s-biography.611.htm .

[27] Colonel William E. Eddy to US State Department, Feb. 1, 1945, FRUS Vol. 8, 680-683.

At the Yalta meeting between Churchill, FDR, and Stalin in February 1945, to determine the shape of the postwar world, FDR told the Soviet leader "that he was a Zionist and asked Stalin if he was one. Stalin said that he was one in principle, but that there were difficulties."[28]

Later in the month, FDR met Arabia's king Ibn Saud aboard the ship *Quincy*, hoping to persuade the monarch to help Jews. The British Foreign Office should have warned FDR that he was on a hopeless quest. Shortly before the war, Ibn Saud told H. R. P. Dickson, a British army colonel, and Dickson told his Foreign Office, "For a Muslim to kill a Jew... ensured him immediate entry into heaven and into the august presence of God Almighty."[29]

FDR did not know of Ibn Saud's implacable bigotry, so that after lunch he informed the king that Germany would be defeated, and he wanted to rescue and rehabilitate the remnant of Jews in Europe, who had suffered indescribable horrors at the hands of the Nazis. Then he asked, "What would the king suggest?"

"Give them and their descendants the choicest lands and homes of the Germans who had oppressed them," the king replied.

FDR explained that the Jews had a sentimental desire to settle in Palestine, and a dread of remaining in a country where they might suffer again. The king agreed that the Jews had good reason to mistrust the Germans, but he expected the Allies to be strong enough not only to destroy Nazi power forever, but to defend the Jews who remained in Germany. He could not conceive a country leaving a defeated enemy with the strength to strike back. When FDR asked him to support the admission of more Jews into Palestine, pointing out that even then they'd only be a small percentage of the Arab world, the king

---

[28] Burns, *Roosevelt*, 577–78.
[29] Colonel H. R. P. Dickson, Foreign Office File No. 371/2082E7201/22/31/.

replied that the Jews had only made the desert bloom because of the millions they got from British and American capitalists. He complained that Palestinian Jews who had joined the British army were fighting Arabs rather than Germans.

FDR stuck to his guns, saying that he was counting on Arab hospitality and the king's help in settling Jews in Palestine, but the king insisted that the enemy and oppressor of the Jews should be made to pay, "that is how we Arabs wage war. Amends should be made by the criminal, not by the innocent bystander. What injury have the Arabs done to the Jews of Europe? It is the Christian Germans who stole their homes and lives. Let the Germans pay." The king also pointed out that the Allies had fifty countries to which the Jews might go, whereas small, land-poor Palestine had already got its quota of European refugees.[30]

FDR was disappointed and perhaps even more so when they exchanged gifts: the king got a twin-engine Douglas transport airplane with an American crew and a spare wheelchair FDR had aboard, which delighted the king, who had crippling arthritis in his legs. In return the king gave FDR a jewel-encrusted sword, a dagger, and ceremonial Arab costumes.

Back in the White House, FDR answered a letter from the king, who was concerned about Palestine's future, assuring His Majesty that "he would make no decision without consulting both Arabs and Jews," and that he would take no action "which might prove hostile to the Arab people."[31]

FDR did not live long enough to see at least part of his plan fulfilled; he died of a massive stroke on April 12, 1945. On that same day in Germany, General Eisenhower made a

---

[30] Burns, *Roosevelt*, 578–579; Lewis Lipkin, "The Intriguing Meeting of FDR and Ibn Saud," Think-Israel, accessed March 28, 2010, http://www.think-israel.org/lipkin.roosevelt.html.

[31] Ibid.

traumatic visit to the first concentration camp liberated by the US army.

Louis Brandeis was one of FDR's greatest admirers. In a conversation about him with Felix Frankfurter, he said that although he considered Jefferson, Cleveland, and Wilson to have been great presidents, "none of them could match this fellow." In fact, he rated FDR "greater than Jefferson and almost as great as Lincoln."[32]

With FDR's death, the vice president, the relatively unknown Harry Truman, moved to the White House.

---

[32] Strum., *Brandeis*, 387.

Harry S. Truman

1884–1972

- ✪ Thirty-third president, 1945–1953
- ✪ FDR's vice president, he succeeded to the presidency when President Roosevelt died in office
- ✪ Ended war against Japan with nuclear weapons

Born on a Missouri farm in 1884 to a family of Baptists of English, Scots-Irish, French, and German origin, Harry Truman said of them, "We're a little bit of everything. If you shook the family tree, anything might fall out." A cousin interested in genealogy failed to convince him that he was descended from a French aristocrat, but Truman quipped, "As long as we don't find that Captain Kidd, Morgan the Pirate, or J. P. [Morgan, the robber baron] either, for that matter, is 'in the line' I'm satisfied." He sometimes claimed to be descended from the man who established "Truman's Brewery" in England in 1665.[1]

He had a rare eye problem known as "flat eye," and from the age of eight wore thick glasses in order to read. At ten he

---

[1] Phone conversation with Clifton Truman Daniel March 16, 2010; Niel and Verna Gail Johnson, "Rooted in History: The Genealogy of Harry S. Truman," Truman Library, http://www.trumanlibrary.org/geneology/?m=g_.essay.

developed diphtheria and was paralyzed for several months, when he was moved around in a baby carriage.

Harry shared the bigoted attitude of many unsophisticated Americans of his time and place, who casually called Jews "kikes," the Irish "Micks," Italians "Wops," and African-Americans "niggers" or "nigras." His bigotry did not extend to his neighbors, the Viners, an Orthodox Jewish family whom he sometimes helped during the Shabbos or Shabbat, holy days when their religion required them not to work. Then, he kept their fires alight in winter and did other household chores. In time, Harry and the Viners' son, Abe, became friends.

Consequently, when it came to writing a high school report on Shakespeare's Shylock in *The Merchant of Venice*, Harry had the advantage over the playwright. At least he knew some Jews. Shakespeare probably never met any, as they were banned from England during his lifetime. In 1900, as a sixteen-year-old high school student, Harry Truman wrote his view of the controversial character:

> We cannot blame Shylock for getting money as a means of revenge upon those who persecuted him. He was not a miser, and if one of his own nation had been in trouble, he would have helped him as quickly as a Christian would help a Christian.... I never saw Jew, Christian, or any other man who, if he had the chance, wouldn't take revenge. No one except the Hebrews has ruled the world, then, when they fell, remained a distinct people. After 2,000 years the Jews are a nation apart from nations, persecuted for their religion and still waiting for a leader to gather their scattered people.[2]

A voracious reader and admirer of some Old Testament Jews he had read about in the family Bible, Truman revered at least one New Testament Jew, Jesus Christ. In fact, after *The*

---

[2] Truman's High School essay on Shylock, Truman Library (copy in author's collection).

Lives of Great Men and Famous Women by Charles Francis Home, the Bible was his favorite book, leading him at eighteen to become a born-again Christian.

In his twenties Truman was in love with Bess Wallace, a blue-eyed blonde he first met as an eight-year-old when he sat next to her in school, in adoring silence. The adoration lasted a lifetime. He confirmed his bigotry in this June 22, 1911, letter to her: "I think one man's as good as another, so long as he's not a nigger or a Chinaman. Uncle Will says the Lord made a White man from dust, a nigger from mud, then threw up what was left and it came down a Chinaman. He does hate Chinese and Japs. So do I. It's race prejudice, I guess. But I am strongly of the opinion Negroes ought to be in Africa, Yellow men in Asia, and White men in Europe and America."[3]

Bess rejected his first marriage proposal, but they eventually married on June 26, 1919, seven months after the end of World War I.

Twenty years later, as a US senator for Missouri, he still called Jews "kikes," and in a December 21, 1939, letter to his wife, disdainfully dismissed Miami as a city of "hotels, filling stations, Hebrews, and cabins."[4] Yet he could truly say that one of his best friends, Eddie Jacobson, was a Jew or "Jew clerk" as he sometimes called him. The team of Captain Harry Truman and Sergeant Eddie Jacobson in charge of the Thirty-fifth Division regimental canteen at Camp Doniphan, Oklahoma, during World War I had worked so well that after the war, they became friendly partners in a Missouri haberdashery store. Even after they went bankrupt, they remained lifelong friends. Fortunately for the Jews, Truman's actions

---

[3] Truman's letter to Bess on June 22, 1911, Truman Library, www.trumanlibrary.org/hstpaper/fbpa.htm.

[4] Truman letter to Bess on December 21, 1939, Truman Library, www.trumanlibrary.org/hstpaper/fbpa.htm.

proved that his bigotry was superficial. His moral compass was stuck on what was almost his mantra: Do the right thing.

By the time Hitler had intensified his anti-Semitic campaign and country-grabbing spree in the late 1930s, Truman had paid all his debts due to bankruptcy and risen to local prominence as a Jackson County judge, and then as a US senator for Missouri, with a reputation as a straight shooter.

Because of the situation in Nazi Germany, many desperate European Jews saw Palestine as their only hope of escape or even survival. Their chance to go there was threatened when shortly before the British declared war on the Nazis in 1939, their Parliament approved a so-called "White Paper" by 268 votes to 179. It stated that because over 450,000 Jews were already in Palestine, the promise of a Jewish homeland in the Balfour Declaration had been fulfilled. The White Paper recommended an independent Palestine within ten years, governed jointly by Arabs and Jews, and limiting Jewish immigration to seventy-five thousand over the next ten years. After that, future Jewish immigrants would need Arab approval. Which meant, of course, no more Jews.

World War II forced the British to concentrate on winning the war, especially after their defeat at Dunkirk, the fall of France, and in 1941 the imminent Nazi invasion.

Shortly after Pearl Harbor and America's entry into the war on Japan and Germany, US senator Harry Truman told a Chicago crowd of twenty thousand, "No one can any longer doubt the horrible intentions of the Nazi beasts. We know that they plan the systematic slaughter throughout all of Europe, not only of Jews, but of vast numbers of other innocent peoples.... Today – not tomorrow – we must do all that is humanly possible to provide a haven and a place of safety for all those who can be grasped from the hands of the Nazi butchers.... This is not a Jewish problem. It is an American problem – and we must and we will face it squarely and honorably."[5]

Early in 1945, FDR made Truman his vice president. After FDR's sudden death barely three months later, on April 12, 1945, Truman was sworn in as his successor. Four days later, in concluding a speech to a joint session of Congress, he said, "As I have assumed my heavy duties, I humbly pray Almighty God, in the words of King Solomon, give therefore thy servant an understanding heart to judge thy people, that I may discern between good and bad; for who is to judge this so great people? I ask only to be a good and faithful servant of my Lord and my people."[6]

Less than four months later, on August 14, 1945, on Truman's return from a swim in the White House pool to his Oval Office, he learned that his plan to end the war had worked: Japan had been atom-bombed into surrender. World War II was over.[7]

Ten days after the war's end, Loy Henderson, the pro-Arab director of the US State Department's Near East Agency, warned Truman that if he supported a Jewish homeland in Palestine, the United States would lose prestige in the Middle East and alienate the Arab world. That same day Truman was so shocked by a report on the desperate condition of Holocaust survivors that he told General Eisenhower that "we appear to be treating the Jews as the Nazis treated them, except that we do not exterminate them. They are in concentration camps in large numbers under our military guard instead of SS troops. One is led to wonder whether the German people, seeing this,

---

[5] David McCullough, *Truman* (New York: Simon and Schuster, 1992), 286–87.

[6] President Truman before a Joint Session of Congress, April 16, 1945, Truman Library, www.trumanlibrary.org/ww2/stofunio.htm.

[7] Truman's Secretary's Files, August 14. 1945, Truman Library. www.trumanlibrary.org/library.htm.

are not supposing that we are following or at least condoning Nazi policy."[8]

On December 4, 1945, Truman first met Zionist leader Chaim Weizmann, who told him that the 1.5 million Jews who wanted to immigrate to Palestine could be absorbed by irrigating the desert. Truman said that many American Jews did not share Weizmann's aspirations, that he objected to a theocratic state in Palestine, preferring a democracy with equal rights for Arabs, Jews, and Christians. Exactly what Weizmann wanted.[9]

To be more fully informed, Truman instructed an Anglo-American Committee of Inquiry – six American and six British diplomats, scholars, and politicians – to conduct a fact-finding mission. They started early in January 1946 and questioned scores of witnesses. The committee members reported that the Palestinian Arabs shared the view of King Ibn Saud that, as they were not responsible for the Holocaust, they should not have to pay for it. They wanted an independent Arab state in Palestine, and a ban on land sales to Jews. However, committee members were deeply moved by the plight of Jewish refugees and unanimously recommended that one hundred thousand of them be allowed to enter Palestine as soon as possible.

Meanwhile, Republican Wendell Willkie, who lost the presidential race to FDR, had been on a world tour and had visited Palestine. When he got back, he told US attorney Bartley Crum, a Committee of Inquiry member, "The Arabs have a good case in Palestine. There is only one thing wrong with that. The Jews have a better case."[10]

---

[8] Michael T. Benson, *Harry S. Truman and the Founding of Israel* (Westport, CN: Praeger, 1997), 80.

[9] Zionist Archives, www.zionistarchives.org.il/ZA/pMain.E.aspx.

[10] Bartley Crum, *Behind the Silken Curtain: A Personal Account of Anglo-American Diplomacy* (New York: Simon & Schuster, 1947), 290–91.

Truman agreed and decided that one hundred thousand Jewish refugees should be allowed to settle in Palestine. But he didn't move fast enough for Rabbi Abba Hillel Silver, who, with a delegation of fellow Zionists, confronted Truman in the Oval Office on July 2, 1946, shouting and pounding on the president's desk, Truman shouted back: "No one, but no one, comes into the office of the President of the United States and shouts at him, or pounds on his desk. If anyone is going to do any shouting or pounding in here, it will be me." After Silver and his delegation left, the infuriated president told his staff never to "admit them again, and what's more, I also never want to hear the word Palestine mentioned again."[11]

On October 4, 1946, on the eve of Yom Kippur, Truman told a Jewish audience that the US supported the creation of a Jewish state. That spurred the State Department's Loy Henderson to complain that Truman had turned over Middle Eastern policy-making to the Zionists. Advised that Henderson had a pro-Arab bias, Truman called him into the Oval Office to explain himself, with advisers Clark Clifford and David Niles also present. Henderson said that all US legations and consular offices in the Middle East and all State Department Middle East experts shared his views. When Niles and Clifford joined in the discussion it became too hot – not for Henderson – but for Truman, who, with an "Oh hell, I'm leaving!" left.[12]

In mid-October, King Ibn Saud accused Truman of failing to live up to FDR's promise to consult with the Arabs about Palestine's future, and to make no decisions the Arabs would regard as hostile. Truman replied, "Among the survivors in the displaced persons centers in Europe are numbers of Jews, whose plight is particularly tragic inasmuch as they represent the pitiful remnants of millions who were deliberately selected

---

[11] McCullough, *Truman*, 598.
[12] Ibid., 605.

by the Nazi leaders for annihilation. Many of these persons look to Palestine as a haven where they hope among people of their own faith to find refuge, to begin to lead peaceful and useful lives, and to assist in the further development of the Jewish National Home." He stated that nothing would be done to alter the basic situation in Palestine without consulting both Arabs and Jews, pointing out that "during the current year there have been a number of consultations with Arabs and Jews."[13]

By February 1947, the British, in charge of Palestine for some thirty years, with a military force of one hundred thousand, were unable to keep the peace. Both Jews and Arabs frequently attacked them and each other with deadly effect, except during a brief period in World War II when many Palestinian Jews and some Palestinian Arabs fought alongside the Allies against the Germans.

With the British about to hand the problem over to the United Nations, the stage was set for one of the most dramatic events in modern history. UN delegates from fifty-seven countries were to vote whether or not to partition Palestine into two potential states. A two-thirds majority voting for the proposition meant that Palestine – a sliver of land half the size of Lake Michigan and with fewer people than the city of St. Louis – would be remade into an Arab state and a Jewish state, with a small international zone around and including Jerusalem. The Zionist General Council had accepted this partition in principle, but not the Arabs, who were unwilling to have the territory divided.

Lobbying by both sides for or against Resolution 181 now went into overdrive. Dean Rusk, head of the US State Department's UN desk in Washington, said afterwards that when he got a concession from the Zionists to reduce their

---

[13] Truman Library, http://www.trumanlibrary.org/publicpapers/index.php?pid=17877 ST=&STI.

immigration demands to 2,500 Jews a month, he approached the head of the Arab delegation, Saudi Arabia's Prince Faisal, with the offer. "Impossible! Impossible! " Faisal responded. "If we agree to 2,500, the Jews will simply bring in 2,500 pregnant women, and that will mean 5,000."[14]

The vote, on November 29, 1947, was thirty-three countries including the US in favor of partition, thirteen against, ten abstentions, and one absent. The proposition was adopted. Hearing the news, Jews throughout the world celebrated, but the Arab delegation stormed from the hall and Arab leaders spoke of "driving the Jews into the sea," and of "the Zionist plague."[15]

Truman's friend Eddie Jacobson knew that the British soon planned to leave Palestine and it would become a battleground. He also knew that Truman was so exasperated by the pressure from Zionists and anti-Zionists, not even Weizmann was welcome at the White House. As the only one likely to persuade Truman to meet Weizmann, Jacobson caught the next plane to Washington. Truman reluctantly agreed to see him, but only if he promised not to mention the Middle East. Jacobson agreed. But when he entered the Oval Office, he had tears streaming down his cheeks, and Truman, who knew the cause, greeted him with: "Eddie, you son-of-a-bitch, you promised me you wouldn't say a word about what's going on over there."

"Mr. President," he replied, "I haven't said a word, but every time I think of the homeless Jews, homeless for thousands of years, I start crying." Truman began to complain so bitterly about Zionists who had insulted and infuriated him in promoting their cause that Jacobson feared that "his dear

[14] Dean Rusk, *As I Saw It: A Secretary of States Memoirs* (New York: I. B. Tauris, 1991), 128.

[15] Benny Morris, *1948: The First Arab-Israeli War* (New Haven, CN: Yale University Press, 2008).

friend, the President of the United States, was at that moment as close to being an anti-Semite as a man possibly could be." Then Jacobson noticed the bust of Truman's hero, Andrew Jackson, on his desk, and said, "My people has its Founding Father, too. I admire him more than anyone else. He's old, ill, and has come all the way, thousands of miles, to see you, and you won't see him just because you are insulted by some of our American Jewish leaders, even though you know that Weizmann has absolutely nothing to do with these insults.... It doesn't sound like you, Harry, because I thought you could take this stuff they have been handing out."

Truman turned his back on his friend and stared out at the White House rose garden for a long time without speaking.

Jacobson had all but given up hope, when Truman turned to face him and, using "the most endearing words" Jacobson had ever heard, said, "You win, you baldheaded son-of-a-bitch. I will see him. I ought to have you thrown right out of here for breaking your promise. You knew damn good and well I couldn't stand to see you cry." Still crying, now tears of joy, Jacobson thanked his friend and left.[16]

During his meeting with Weizmann on March 18, Truman agreed to support the inclusion of the Negev and the port city of Aqaba in the proposed Jewish state and promised that if, after the imminent departure of the British, Zionists declared their homeland to exist, he would immediately recognize it. When Truman realized that the Jews would soon declare the country their homeland, he told American lawyer Bartley Crum that to prevent the Russians from gaining prestige in the area, he hoped to beat Russia to the punch, by being the first to recognize the Jewish state.[17]

---

[16] Merle Miller, *Plain Speaking: An Oral Biography of Harry S. Truman* (New York: Berkley), 234–35.

[17] Truman Library, John Shelsinger, *Truman, the Jewish Vote, and the Creation of Israel* (Hoover Press, 1974), 23.

Meanwhile, things were going seriously awry at the UN. Warren Austin, the US representative, was influenced by the French and Chinese delegates, who now regretted their pro-partition votes, having realized that partition without a peacekeeping force would lead to uncontrolled, widespread bloodshed. So now Austin called for a UN trusteeship rather than a partitioned Palestine, while much of the rest of the General Assembly listened in astonishment to this reversal of American policy. Without telling Truman, the US State Department had already drafted a trusteeship plan that assured "the territorial integrity of Palestine," and called for a plebiscite to determine the views of the majority of the registered members of both the Arab and Jewish communities of Palestine."[18]

Truman was furious when he heard of it, telling his counsel, Clark Clifford, "I assured Chaim Weizmann that we were for partition and would stick to it. He must think I'm a plain liar. Find out how this could have happened."[19]

He recorded his bitter feelings in this diary entry for March 19, 1948, "The State Department pulled the rug from under me today.... [It] has reversed my Palestine policy. The first I know about it is what I see in the papers! Isn't that hell? I am now in the position of a liar and double-crosser.... There are people on the third and fourth levels of the State Dept. who have always wanted to cut my throat. They've succeeded in doing it."

The *New York Times* of March 20 confirmed his suspicion that State Department underlings had double-crossed him. He was further enraged when he read of a "shocking, inept,

[18] Harry S. Truman, *Years of Trial and Hope* (New York: Doubleday, 1950); Weisgal and Carmichael, Truman diary, March 19, 1948, Truman Library, http://trumanlibrary.org/diary/transcript.htm; Stanley Meisler, *United Nations: The First Fifty Years* (New York: Atlantic Monthly Press, 1997), 44; McCullough, *Truman*, 509–611; Rusk, *As I Saw It*, 127–28.

[19] Clark Clifford and Richard Holbrooke, *Counsel to the President: A Memoir* (New York: Random House, 1991), 10.

uncertain, and confused lack of liaison and common purpose between the State Department, the UN American delegation, and the White House, all of them apparently utterly at sea."

A desperate Weizmann wrote to Truman on April 9 that partition was unavoidable, and already existed in much of Palestine: "The choice for our people, Mr. President, is between Statehood and extermination."[20]

In fact, Jews had already been fighting Arabs for control of the land as the British were preparing to leave. By May 7, Jewish forces had captured Jaffa and 170,000 of its Arab inhabitants had fled.

Now Truman had to face a formidable opposition to recognizing a Jewish state. Against him was the entire Arab and Muslim world, all of his Joint Chiefs of Staff, the recently created CIA, and most of his pro-Arab State Department – and those who feared that recognizing a Jewish state could unleash World War III. He had to counter the opposition of Dean Rusk, his director of the Office of UN Affairs; George Marshall, his secretary of state; Robert Lovett, the undersecretary of state; George Kennan, chief of the Policy Planning Staff; Loy Henderson, the director of Near Eastern and African Affairs, and James Forrestal, the secretary of defense.

On the brink of a nervous breakdown, Forrestal tried scare tactics to get Clark Clifford to share his views, telling him: "You fellows over at the White House are just not facing up to the realities in the Middle East. There are thirty million Arabs on one side and six hundred thousand Jews on the other. It is clear that in any contest the Arabs are going to overwhelm the Jews. Why don't you fellows face up to the realities? Just look at the numbers!" The president knows the numbers, Clifford replied, but feels that the Jews "have a moral and ethical right to their own homeland."[21]

---

[20] Benson, *Harry S. Truman*, 187.

[21] Clifford and Holbrooke, *Counsel to the President*, 4.

Backing Truman and Clifford was a small group of Zionists in the White House, mostly low-level officials.

Truman asked his counsel, Clark Clifford, to prepare to "make the case in favor of the recognition of the new state... as though you were making an argument before the Supreme Court.... Consider it carefully, Clark, organize it logically.... Be as persuasive as you possibly can be." At the start of the critical meeting on May 12, 1948, Marshall's assistant, Robert Lovett, said that "although the Jewish army [the Haganah] had gained substantial ground [in Palestine] in recent weeks, there was no guarantee that in the long range the tide might not turn against them," and if that happened, they could not count on American help.

Now Clifford had to make the case for recognizing a Jewish state. First, he said it would be a humane act consistent with the president's foreign policy and a symbol of what the US should represent in world affairs. Furthermore, a Jewish state was inevitable, other nations would recognize it, and the US should do so before the Soviet Union. Marshall interrupted Clifford to complain: "Mr. President, I thought this meeting was called to consider an important and complicated problem in foreign policy. I don't even know why Clifford is here. He is a domestic adviser, and this is a foreign policy matter."

Truman said, "He's here because I asked him to be here."

Marshall then objected to Clifford giving an emotional rather than an objective opinion, which he, Marshall, was providing with international repercussions in mind. Furthermore, he said, support for a Jewish state would be a blatant attempt to win a few Jewish votes in the upcoming presidential election. He concluded by saying that if Truman followed Clifford's advice, then he would not vote for Truman in the coming election.

The threat directed at the president made the room grow silent. Everyone froze for as long as twenty seconds, until

Truman broke the ice by saying that he was aware of the dangers involved and of the political risks for himself. Lovett and Clifford met again that evening, when Clifford insisted that nothing would change Truman's decision to recognize the Jewish state. Marshall finally compromised: he couldn't support the president's position, but he wouldn't oppose it.[22]

On May 17, 1948, in a Tel Aviv building, as a fierce fight between Arabs and Jews raged nearby, Ben-Gurion announced to some four hundred fellow Jews their Declaration of Independence, proclaiming the rebirth of Israel. Eleven minutes later, Eliahu Elath arrived in the Oval office with a document stating that Ben-Gurion's government was the de facto authority of the country. Elath had crossed out "Jewish State" and written in "Israel." Truman inserted "provisional" before the word "government," and signed his approval. His next move was to phone his adviser on Jewish affairs, David Niles, to say, "Dave, I want you to know that I've just announced recognition. You're the first person I called, because I knew how much this would mean to you."[23]

As he spoke, the armies of Lebanon and Syria attacked the newborn state from the north, Iraq and Jordan attacked from the east, followed soon after by Egypt attacking from the south. Prime Minister Ben-Gurion feared that his country had only a fifty-fifty chance of surviving the five-army onslaught. An optimistic assessment, considering that Israel did not have one cannon or tank, and the Israeli air force consisted of nine obsolete planes. But help was on the way. Secret shipments of weapons from Czechoslovakia, with the Soviet Union's approval, were trickling into Israel. Nothing officially came from the United States. Again, help was on the way from thousands of Jewish volunteers from all over the world, some with fighting skills and their own weapons.

---

[22] Ibid., 6–8, 10–21.

[23] Abba Eban, *An Autobiography* (New York: Random House, 1977), 113–14.

Truman had placed an arms embargo on *all* countries in the Middle East, which put Israel at a great military disadvantage. The Arab armies were organized and well armed and the Jews had a poorly equipped ragtag citizen army, including recently arrived refugees from Hitler's concentration camps speaking several languages, most of whom had never even held a gun before. But Truman feared that arming Israel might start an arms race and possibly bring on World War III.

Two weeks after the five Arab armies attacked, the UN Security Council obtained a ceasefire. Fierce fighting resumed in July, when Israeli forces with heavy weapons from Czechoslovakia resumed the fight and captured Nazareth. After six days another truce was ordered, but was broken several times.

Throughout the following month of September, Truman was preoccupied with his election campaign. When political rival Thomas Dewey accused him of vacillating on whether the Negev belonged to Israel or the Arabs, Truman told an audience of eighteen thousand at Madison Square Garden, that both the Negev and Galilee should be Israel's, and that he was expediting loans to Israel. They showed their approval by singing, "I'm Just Wild about Harry!"[24]

A New York delegation warned him that unless he raised the arms embargo on Israel he would lose New York votes in New York State, he replied, "If you believe for one second that I will bargain my convictions for the vote you imply would be mine, you are pathetically mistaken."[25]

With gamblers betting fifty to one against Truman winning the election, and 65 percent of the nation's press supporting Dewey, to almost everyone's amazement he beat the odds and won. To sustain public support for Israel, Truman then sent his vice president, Alben Barkley, on a lecture-tour of America, inciting the State Department's anti-Zionist Edwin Wright to

---

[24] Madison Square Garden Press Release.

[25] Margaret Truman, *Harry S. Truman* (New York: William Morrow, 1972), 390.

accuse Barkley of insulting Arab leaders by calling Israel, "An oasis of freedom in a sea of tyranny."[26]

By year's end, the Israelis had driven most enemy forces back, and hundreds of thousands of Palestinian Arabs fled or had been driven out of the country. There were 6,373 Israelis killed fighting for their country, almost 1 percent of the Jewish population of 650,000. An estimated five thousand to fifteen thousand Arabs had been killed fighting for what they believed should be their country.

Israel's chief rabbi visited Truman in the White House in 1949, and said, "God put you in your mother's womb, so that you could be the instrument to bring about the rebirth of Israel after two thousand years." It moved Truman to tears.[27]

On his first visit to the White House, Israeli ambassador Abba Eban carried a large envelope containing his speech and his diplomatic credentials from President Weizmann. To Eban's gleeful surprise, the president grabbed the envelope, glanced at its contents and said, "Let's cut out all the crap and have a good talk." For the next forty minutes, Truman told him how Weizmann had talked him into giving the Negev to Israel, and how the State Department's "striped-pants boys" still opposed his pro-Israel policies.[28]

Truman remained in high spirits, and when Eddie Jacobson introduced him to a group at New York's Jewish Theological Seminary as "The man who helped create the State of Israel," Truman objected. "What do you mean, 'helped create'? I am Cyrus. I am Cyrus!" King Cyrus the Great of ancient Persia (today's Iran), overran the Babylonian Empire and let Jewish

[26] Wright, Oral History Interview, Interviewed by Richard D. Mackenzie on July 26, 1974, Truman Library, http://www.trumanlibrary.org/oralhist/wright/htm.

[27] Alfred Steinberg, *The Man From Missouri: The Life and Times of Harry S. Truman* (Putnam's, 1962), 308.

[28] Eban, *Autobiography*, 155–56.

exiles return to their homeland, Palestine, and rebuild their Temple.[29]

Retired to his Missouri home in 1954, Truman worked on his memoirs, campaigned across country for Democratic hopefuls and, after a daily brisk morning walk, supervised the building of his Presidential Library in Independence.

In his younger days, Truman had called New York City "kike town." Then, in a 1957 letter to his wife, the former president referred to it as "the US capital of Israel." Did that mean he was anti-Semitic? Rafael Medoff, director of the David S. Wyman Institute for Holocaust Studies, thinks that what's really important is that his actions spoke louder than his words.[30]

That's apparently how Ben-Gurion saw it. Meeting Truman by chance in 1961, the Israeli prime minister told him, "In the eyes of the Jewish people you will live forever!" Ben-Gurion relates, "As I said that, tears suddenly sprang to his eyes. And his eyes were still wet when he bade me good-bye. I had rarely seen anyone so moved."[31]

TV producer David Susskind met Truman about the same time to work on a TV series about the president, and was puzzled why Mrs. Truman, who always answered the door of their Missouri home, never asked him inside. Soon, Truman would emerge to discuss their plans as they strolled along the sidewalk. After several such visits, Susskind asked why he was never invited inside. To his astonishment, Truman replied, "Well, David, you're Jewish." Susskind said he couldn't believe that someone who supported the recognition of Israel and civil rights should have that attitude. "This isn't the White House.

---

[29] Warren Bass, "To Err Is Truman," *Jewish News of Greater Phoenix* 55, no. 48 (July 25, 2003); Benson, *Harry S. Truman*, 189.

[30] David Wyman Holocaust Studies.

[31] Dan Kurzman, *Ben-Gurion: Prophet of Fire* (New York: Simon & Schuster, 1983), 416.

It's the Wheelers' [his mother-in-law's maiden name] house,"
Truman replied. "And my wife and mother-in-law would never
have a Jew in the house. Not even my friend Eddie Jacobson."[32]

Considering the bigoted attitude of his wife and mother-in-law to Jews, Truman wondered why he, as a Midwest
Baptist, got so emotionally upset over Palestine and the fate of
the Jews. "It was my attitude," Truman wrote, "that the American government could not stand idly by while the victims
of Hitler's madness were not allowed to build new lives....
It's estimated that he killed six million Jews – burned most
of them up in furnaces. It was a horrible thing, and I dream
about it even to this day. On that account, the Jews needed
some place where they could go."[33]

He gave Israeli Foreign Minister Sharett another answer:
It stemmed from reading about Israel's history in the Bible,
from the days of Abraham, and from his careful study "of the
promises [Balfour Declaration] made to the Jewish people in
the First World War. Those promises must be kept."[34]

Harry Truman died of heart failure at eighty-eight on
December 26, 1972, in Kansas City's Research Hospital and
Medical Center. His wife, Bess, died ten years later.

Not all Israelis regarded him with uncritical admiration.
Moshe Dayan, in turn chief of staff of the Israeli Defense
Forces, minister of defense, and foreign minister, saw Truman
as "without doubt a sincere friend and supporter of the State
of Israel, but he had been unwilling to help us with arms in
1948, even during the grimmest hours when we were fighting
for our independence and our very survival."[35]

---

[32] James C. Humes, *Confessions of a White House Ghostwriter: Five Presidents and Other Political Ventures* (Washington, DC: Regnery, 1996), interview with Humes, January 22, 2007.

[33] Benson, *Harry S. Truman*, 63.

[34] Isaac Alteras, *Eisenhower and Israel: US-Israel Relations, 1953–1960* (Gainsville, FL: University of Florida, 1993), 20.

[35] Moshe Dayan, *Story of My Life: An Autobiography* (New York: Warner Books, 1977), 621.

In Israel itself they have named a village and a forest after him. Israel also issued a Truman stamp in 1966, and established the Harry S. Truman Center for the Advancement of Peace at Hebrew University. At its dedication, Hebrew University president Eliahu Elath – who had brought the document recognizing Israel to the White House for him to sign – said that Truman's recognition of Israel would be engraved "in golden letters in the four thousand years' history" of the Jewish people.[36]

---

[36] Benson, *Harry S. Truman*, 190.

Dwight David Eisenhower

1890–1969

- ✪ Thirty-fourth president, 1953–1961
- ✪ Five-star general during World War II and supreme commander of NATO forces in Europe, he ended the Korean war
- ✪ The first term-limited president in accordance with the 22nd Amendment

Reading the Bible from cover to cover as a boy convinced Dwight David Eisenhower that Jews were supernatural beings. It was when he reached Isaiah that Ike, as he became known, first learned that "the Children of Israel" were legendary beings known as cherubim and seraphim, some with six wings apiece. Naturally he assumed that Jews were not part of the real world – angels, in fact – and no longer to be found on earth.

His parents were unlikely to contradict anything in the Bible, especially his deeply religious mother, Ida, who delivered religious tracts from door-to-door and learned by heart

1,365 Bible verses. She encouraged Ike and his five brothers to read every word of the book at least once.

Dwight Eisenhower was born on October 14, 1890, in Denison, Texas, but his family soon moved to Abilene, Kansas, where apparently there were no Jewish inhabitants to put him right.

When he became president of the United States, he confirmed his early picture of ethereal Jews during a conversation with Israeli diplomats Moshe Sharett and Abba Eban. As Eban recalled in his autobiography, "There were even some [Americans] whose religious memories made it difficult for them to grasp the prosaic aspects of Israel's modernity. At a meeting in Paris in 1953, Eisenhower had told Sharett and me that as a boy...he had believed that Jews, or more accurately, the Children of Israel, were angels, cherubim and seraphim, the creations of legend. He was surprised and disconcerted to find that they existed in real life, if not in Abilene, then at least in Texas, and most unmistakably in New York."[1]

As he told the two Israelis, he had really believed that Jews were "an extinct species, until I came to New York and I found out how wrong I was."[2]

Ike's forebears were German Protestants. Both of his parents were college dropouts, and his father, David Jacob Eisenhower, like Harry Truman, ran a store into bankruptcy. As Jehovah's Witnesses, Ike and his five brothers were taught that man did not evolve, but was created. Based on their reading of the Old Testament, Witnesses also believe that Armageddon – the end of the world – isn't far off, and then

---

[1] Eban, *Autobiography*, 186; Jerry Bergman, Ph.D., Northwest State College, "Why President Eisenhower Hid His Jehovah's Witness Upbringing, *JW Research Journal* 6, no. 2 (July–December 1999).

[2] Abba Eban, *Personal Witness: Israel through My Eyes* (New York: Putnam, 1992), 225.

144,000 people will join God in heaven to enjoy everlasting life.

Despite his early historical misconceptions, his high school classmates predicted that he would "wind up as a professor of history at Yale." Instead, he chose to be a soldier. At twenty-one, in 1911, Ike defied the Witnesses' pacifist teaching and – to his mother's despair – left home for West Point.

A copy of his West Point Yearbook of 1915 is produced and cited on the Internet as iron-clad evidence that he was Jewish. The article, with a photo of him, begins: "This is Senior Dwight David Eisenhower, the terrible Swedish-Jew, as big as life and twice as natural. He claims to have the best authority for the statement that he is the handsomest man in the Corps and is ready to back-up his claim at any time."

An Eisenhower Library archivist explained that the West Point Yearbook is not a repository of facts; its contributors were fellow students willing to write almost anything for a laugh. Though if the "terrible" referred to his temper, that was true. According to his biographer, Carlo D'Este, as a child in a temper tantrum Ike used an apple tree as a punching bag, and as a young man, after losing a tennis match, he banged his head against a wall.[3]

His first significant contact with Jews was as General Douglas MacArthur's chief of staff in the Philippines, where he helped to train the Philippine army. In his book, *At Ease: Stories I Tell to Friends*, Ike recalled, "There was a considerable Jewish community in the city [about 200 in Manila]. And I had good friends among them," including Alex Frieder, a Pennsylvanian importer of Manila cigars.[4]

What Ike doesn't mention but Isaac Alteras does, in his book *Eisenhower and Israel*, is that "at a party in Manila [Ike]

---

[3] West Point Yearbook, accessed April 21, 2010, www.eisenhower.archives.gov/.

[4] Dwight D. Eisenhower, *At Ease: Stories I Tell My Friends* (New York: Doubleday, 1967), 229.

was outraged on hearing US businessmen express admiration for Hitler. Impressed by his condemnation of Nazism, his Jewish friends asked him to take the job of relocating Jewish refugees from Nazi Germany to China, Indochina, Indonesia and elsewhere in Asia."

Ike later wrote, "It would have been a wonderful thing to resettle those poor people who were driven out of their homelands."[5] However, he declined the opportunity because he intended to make the army his career.

Eventually, in 1937, Alex Frieder and his brother, Philip, helped hundreds of European Jews "who had struggled to Manila's port from Shanghai and heard harrowing tales from them of the fate of 17,000 Jews in Shanghai, who were looking to flee the Japanese after they had fled the Nazis." The Frieders asked their buddies to help fleeing Jews find a haven in the Philippines. One buddy, Paul V. McNutt, was the American high commissioner for the Philippines; another was a young officer named Col. Dwight D. Eisenhower. "McNutt succeeded in finessing the US State Department bureaucrats to turn a blind eye and quietly allow Jews to enter Manila at a rate of 1,000 a year."[6]

World War II brought Ike near the top, first as a general in the North African campaign and then as the commanding general of the European Theater of Operations. When the fighting ended in North Africa with an Allied victory, he was concerned by the growing tension in the region between Jews and Arabs. The Jews were outnumbered by about forty to one, and as Ike found,

> ...to placate the Arab at the expense of the Jew, repressive laws had resulted and the Arab population regarded any suggestion for amelioration of such laws as the beginning of an effort to

[5] Alteras, *Eisenhower and Israel*, 28.
[6] Pacific News Service, March 10, 2006, http://news.pacificnews.org.

establish a Jewish government with consequent persecution of themselves. Remembering that for years the uneducated population had been subjected to intensive Nazi propaganda calculated to fan their prejudices, it is easy to understand that the situation called more for caution...than it did for precipitate action and possible revolution.

The country was ridden, almost ruled, by rumor. One rumor was...that I was a Jew sent into the country by a Jew, Roosevelt [in fact, an Episcopalian of Dutch ancestry], to grind down the Arabs and turn over North Africa to Jewish rule. The political staff was so concerned...that they published material on me in newspapers and in special leaflets to establish evidence of my [non-Jewish German] ancestry. Arab unrest, or even worse, open rebellion, would have set us back for months and lost us countless lives.[7]

Toward the end of the war in Europe, on April 12, 1945, Ike was traumatized by his first visit to a concentration camp – a section of Buchenwald where sixteen-year-old Elie Weisel had been rescued after his father had died in the bunk above his. The day of his visit Ike wrote to his wife, Mamie, in the US, "I never dreamed that such cruelty, bestiality and savagery could really exist in this world!"[8] He also sent a telegram to his chief, George Marshall:

The most interesting though horrible sight that I encountered during my trip was a visit to a German concentration camp near Gotha. The things I saw beggar description. When I was touring the camp I encountered three men who had been inmates and by some ruse or another had made their escape. I interviewed them through an interpreter. The visual evidence and the verbal testimony of starvation, cruelty and

---

[7] Dwight D. Eisenhower, *Crusade in Europe* (Garden City, NY: Permabooks, 1952), 152.

[8] Eisenhower Library, www.eisenhower.archives.gov/.

bestiality were so overpowering as to leave me a bit sick. In one room, twenty or thirty naked men were piled up, killed by starvation.... I made the visit deliberately in order to be in a position to give firsthand evidence of these things, if ever in the future there develops a tendency to charge these things to propaganda.[9]

So Ike invited British members of parliament and American congressmen to be witnesses, and the world's press to bring their cameras to record the awful scenes. Many responded, and they have made it possible to refute Holocaust deniers.

Soon after, Ike encouraged his adviser on Jewish affairs, Lieutenant Judah Nadich, the US army's senior Jewish chaplain in Europe, to visit Displaced Persons camps in the American sector of Germany and to suggest improvements. At a DP camp at Fielding, near Munich, he found forty poorly fed survivors in rooms built for six, with leaking roofs. After visiting Fielding, Nadich got a telegram from David Ben-Gurion, head of the Jewish Agency for Palestine, asking for permission to visit DP camps in Germany. Nadich needed Ike's approval for the visit, so he took Ben-Gurion to meet Ike in his Frankfurt office, saying on entering, "General, if there were a Jewish state in Palestine, I should be introducing you to the prime minister, Mr. David Ben-Gurion." Ike lent them an army car and driver, and welcomed their suggestions for improvements. What impressed Ben-Gurion about Ike was his "reaction of cold fury to the horrors of Nazism which unfolded before him when the forces under his command entered the concentration camps."[10]

Nadich and Ben-Gurion arrived at the packed auditorium of Zeilsheim DP camp near Frankfurt on the afternoon

---

[9] Ibid.

[10] Kurzman, *Ben-Gurion*, 262–63.

of October 19, 1945. As they walked onto the stage, everyone stood and began to sing *Hatikvah* (The Hope), now Israel's national anthem, voicing the hope that some day Jews will return to "the land of Zion and Jerusalem." Many cried openly, Nadich and Ben-Gurion among them. As Nadich recalled, "Here in the DP camp on the accursed soil of Germany, the land of Israel had come to them in the person of Ben-Gurion! For the first time they believed that the nightmare was over, they were really free! ...Ben-Gurion assured them that they had never been forgotten, that the Jews the world over now knew about them and that the Jews in Eretz Yisrael [the Land of Israel] awaits them and will do everything possible to bring them to their midst."[11]

Meantime, General George Patton had given the Nazi Party his imprimatur by calling it equivalent to America's Democratic or Republican Parties. Ike quickly fired and then replaced him with General Lucian Truscott, who was tasked with improving the wretched lives of Jewish DPs. To ensure their continued welfare, an adviser on Jewish affairs was stationed at every DP camp with direct access to Judge Simon Rifkind, who had replaced Nadich as Ike's Jewish adviser.

After the war, in October 1945, Ben-Gurion thanked Ike "for his role in defeating Nazism and for his humaneness toward the survivors of the Holocaust. Eisenhower also expanded educational and agricultural programs in Hebrew to prepare them for a meaningful life in Palestine. Each week he sent military planes to Palestine to bring back Hebrew books, agricultural tractors, and teachers to the camps."[12]

Ike was still army chief of staff when he had a spirited conversation with two members of the Haganah, the Jewish

---

[11] Nadich obituary, *New York Times*, August 29, 2007; Judah Nadich, *Eisenhower and the Jews* (Twayne, 1953).

[12] Ike's Diary Entry, March 8, 1956, Eisenhower Library. www.eisenhower.archives. gov/.

underground army in Palestine. Years later, in 1956, he noted in his diary that "in 1946 or 1947, I was visited by a couple of young Israelites who were anxious to secure arms for Israel [it was not yet Israel]. They belittled the Arabs in every way, cited the ease in which the Turkish empire was dismembered following World War I, and in spite of a lot of talk about holy war, the Arabs, [they said,] due to their laziness, shiftlessness, lack of spirit, and low morale, did nothing. They boastfully claimed that Israel needed nothing but a few defensive arms and they would take care of themselves forever and without help of any kind from the United States." Having spoken to several Arab leaders, Ike warned the young Jews that "they were stirring up a hornet's nest and if they could solve the initial question peacefully and without doing unnecessary violence to the self-respect and interests of the Arabs, they would profit immeasurably in the long run." Ike added to his diary entry, "I'd like to see those young Israelites, today."[13]

His sympathy for Jewish victims of the Nazis did not translate into enthusiasm for President Truman's plan to recognize Israel. On September 29, 1948, as the US army's chief of staff, he advised the US joint chiefs of staff against action that would commit US troops to Palestine or "orient the peoples of the Middle East [Arabs] away from Western Powers, as the United States has vital security interest in that area." He also mentioned significantly that "a great deal of our military strength and our standard of living is based on oil."[14]

After Truman recognized Israel, Ike told B'nai B'rith president Philip Klutznick that "Now that it was done, we'll have to live with it."[15]

---

[13] Foreign Relations of the United States: Diplomatic Papers, 1948–1957, US State Department, September 29, 1948, 1450.

[14] Ibid., October 18, 1948.

[15] Alteras, *Eisenhower and Israel*, 32.

Ike was briefly Columbia University's president before leaving to command NATO (North American Treaty Organization) in Europe, until 1952, when he decided to run as a Republican for president of the United States against Democratic contender Adlai Stevenson. With this in mind, he lunched with wealthy Jewish supporters at New York's Commodore Hotel. There he told them that although Israel's existence was an established fact, its future depended upon "its ability to make peace with its Arab neighbors," and that the US government must do everything in its power to achieve that peace, including helping Arab refugees to integrate into Arab countries.[16]

Ben-Gurion sent Ike this supportive telegram: "When I had the privilege of meeting you in Frankfurt in the aftermath of your great victory [World War II], I was deeply impressed by your humane attitude toward the Jewish displaced persons, the victims of Nazism, and your willingness to assist them by every possible means." Privately, Ben-Gurion predicted, "Until now there was only one conduit to the White House – the Israeli; from now on there will be an Arab one as well. Eisenhower adores his young brother, Milton, who is close to the pro-Arab group of Dorothy Thompson [a prominent left-wing journalist wife of novelist Sinclair Lewis]. Efforts must be made to influence Milton in our direction."[17]

The widely read Thompson was critical of Zionism and the State of Israel. But her influence on Milton and his influence on Ike remain a mystery because, as Eisenhower Library archivist Thomas Branigar told this writer, Milton destroyed all his personal files, not wanting anyone to know how he had influenced political affairs.[18]

---

[16] Ibid.

[17] Ben-Gurion Archives.

[18] Author's phone interview with library archivist Thomas Branigar, July 16, 2008.

Irving Berlin was one of Ike's Jewish supporters in the presidential race, and Berlin's song, "I Like Ike," enlivened the campaign. Zionist Rabbi Abba Hillel Silver, though a Democrat, also backed Ike, and – when he won with a healthy but not a majority of Jewish votes – accepted his invitation to give a special prayer at the January 20, 1953, inauguration, following a Protestant minister's invocation, and preceding a Catholic priest's benediction. Neither Ike nor his five brothers remained Jehovah's Witnesses. Twelve days after he took the oath of office, Ike became a Presbyterian. He also changed the half-hearted view he held about Israel in 1948, judging by his reassuring statement on April 28, 1953, to Dr. Israel Goldstein, president of the American Jewish Congress: "Israel is a fact, a certainty, and it must remain so."[19]

A year later, he announced his intention to provide Israel with $70 million worth of military aid. This prompted Egypt's President Nasser to buy $80 million worth of weapons from the Soviet Union. The French, angered by Nasser's support of Algerian rebels who were fighting the French for an independent Algeria, then sold Israel two hundred tanks.

Ike hoped that Nasser and Ben-Gurion would resolve their differences in face-to-face discussions. But Nasser sought revenge for his country's two humiliating military defeats by the Israelis. The first was Egypt's failed attempt to destroy the Jewish state at its birth in 1948. The second was Israel's successful 1955 attack on the Gaza Strip (then occupied by Egypt), in response to Egyptian raids on Israel from Gaza.

To punish Nasser for starting a Middle-East arms race, Ike withdrew his offer to finance Nasser's cherished Aswan High Dam project. Nasser responded by blockading the Gulf of Aqaba, an Israeli lifeline, and by nationalizing the Suez Canal (jointly owned by the French and British) , expecting its

---

[19] American Jewish Congress.

revenues to pay for the dam. If "the imperialistic powers don't like it," he taunted, they can "choke on their rage."[20] Instead of choking, Britain, France, and Israel decided to change his mind by force.

Nasser's belligerence strengthened Ike's sympathy for Israel, which he now characterized in his diary as "a tiny nation, surrounded by enemies nevertheless is one we have recognized and on top of that it has a very strong position in the hearts and emotions of the Western world because of the tragic suffering of the Jews throughout two thousand years of history."

In the early afternoon of October 29, 1956, four Israeli fighter pilots flying Mustangs over the Sinai below radar, at a death-defying height of twelve feet, used their planes' wings and propellers to cut the phone lines linking Egyptian military units. Despite the Egyptians massive superiority in Soviet weapons, the Israeli ground forces made lightning advances, while the British and French belatedly joined in the fight many days later.

On first getting news of the surprise Israeli attack, an enraged Ike instructed John Foster Dulles, his secretary of state, to tell the Israelis "Goddamn it we are going to apply sanctions, we are going to the United Nations, we are going to do everything that there is to stop this thing."[21]

He complained to his son, John, "If the Israelis keep going...I may have to use force to stop them.... Then I'd lose the election. There would go New York, New Jersey, Pennsylvania, Connecticut at least."[22]

---

[20] William Stadiem, *Too Rich: The High Life and Tragic Death of King Farouk* (New York: Carroll and Graf, 1991), 346.

[21] Alteras, *Eisenhower and Israel*, 224.

[22] Stephen Ambrose, *Eisenhower: Soldier and President* (New York: Simon & Schuster, 1990), 353.

Nevertheless, he warned the Israelis that if they didn't withdraw immediately, the US might investigate the tax-exempt status of the United Jewish Appeal and other charities that gave Israel vital financial aid, and he would cut off their oil supplies.

Afraid that the fighting might lead to a nuclear war, Ike got American Zionist leader Rabbi Silver to tell Ben-Gurion that if he announced that "since the Israeli forces had now completed their mission, namely the liquidation of *fedeyeen* bases, they would return to their previous boundary, Eisenhower would include in his upcoming national radio broadcast a statement of deep appreciation for and friendship toward Israel."[23]

Bedridden with influenza, Ben-Gurion replied that he would have to consult with his government and with his French and British allies. When he responded it was to say,

> We must repeat our urgent request to the United Nations to call upon Egypt, which has consistently maintained that it is in a state of war with Israel, to renounce this position, to abandon its policy of boycott and blockade, to cease the incursions into Israeli territory of murder gangs and, in accordance with its obligations under the United Nations Charter to live at peace with member-States, to enter into direct peace negotiations with Israel.... I know your words of friendship stem from the depth of your heart and I wish to assure you that you will always find Israel ready to make its noble contribution at the side of the United States in its efforts to strengthen justice and peace in the world.[24]

What he did not confide to Ike was Israeli troops' recent astonishing victory. In a little over a week they had killed over one thousand of the enemy and taken nearly six thousand prisoners, with a loss of only 171 of their own men and one

---

[23] Eban, *Autobiography*, 217.
[24] Ibid.

taken prisoner. Israeli troops had also captured $50 million worth of military equipment. "At first, the military outcome looked like a daydream," Ben-Gurion wrote in his diary for November 7, "then like a legend, and finally like a series of miracles."

Ike was still furious, not only because he feared Soviet military intervention, but because he had been kept in the dark about Israel's intention to go to war. He again warned Ben-Gurion that unless his forces withdrew, he would destroy his economy and deprive him of oil. Ike's threats, applied to the French and British, and persuaded them to call it quits and leave the battlefield. The prowess of the Israeli troops who kept fighting, eventually prompted Ike to tell an American Jew, "The one thing I learned from that lesson, watching the way Israel's forces performed and the way Britain and France performed [is that] perhaps we've got the wrong allies."[25]

Ben-Gurion agreed to withdraw his troops, and by March 16, 1957, Israeli forces had returned to their previous borders.

Because of Ike's intervention, Nasser was still in power with the Suez Canal under his control. Furthermore, the French and British had lost and the Soviet Union had gained influence in the Middle East.

Nasser eventually allowed international shipping, including Israeli vessels, to use the Suez Canal, but showed no gratitude to Ike for saving him from another humiliating military defeat and continued to follow a pro-Soviet policy. To counter the growing Soviet threat, Ike persuaded Congress to accept "The Eisenhower Doctrine," which promised to help any Middle East country threatened by international Communism. The Israelis regarded the Arabs rather than the Russians as their biggest threat, but the explicit promise of US protection was irresistible. Israel accepted the offer.

---

[25] Alteras, *Eisenhower and Israel*, 295.

Soon after, Dulles assured Ben-Gurion that "the United States is committed to Israel's existence and would fight for her should an attack by the Soviet Union compel her to do so." Ike not only sold Israel one thousand recoilless guns and aircraft-detection equipment, but secretly funded Israel to buy tanks from Britain. The money provided was almost seven times the amount the US had ever previously sent Israel for military equipment.

Ike had only a few months left in the White House when the CIA told him that their U2 spy plane had detected something suspiciously like the start of a nuclear plant in the Negev Desert. Ike knew that the Israelis had a small program to produce nuclear energy for peaceful purposes near Tel Aviv. In fact, starting in 1958, the United States had helped Israel to build it in line with Ike's atoms-for-peace program.[26]

Ben-Gurion agreed to allow American inspection of the Negev complex, but not just yet. In fact, it had been built to produce nuclear weapons in the event that Israel's existence was at stake. Ben-Gurion had made the decision to build it after a sleepless night during the early days of Israel's existence, when his country had faced an overwhelming combined attack from five Arab armies. It was then he had decided that to survive, Israel must have "a nuclear option."[27]

The French had sent 150 French technicians to work at the Dimona plant in the Negev Desert. The British had sold Israel heavy water needed to produce a bomb. By December 1960, the American State Department knew "that a significant atomic installation was in fact built near Bersheeba. Six days later, the CIA told Ike that 'Israel was constructing, with French assistance, a nuclear complex in the Negev [that] cannot be solely for peaceful purposes.'" On December 22, 1960, a London newspaper, the *Daily Express*, reported:

---

[26] Eisenhower Library.

[27] Michael Bar-Zohar, *Ben-Gurion* (Zemora-Bitan, 1987), 136.

"British and American intelligence authorities believe that the Israelis are well on their way to building their first experimental nuclear bomb."[28]

Ben-Gurion had claimed that the nuclear plant was for peaceful purposes. It was, at the time. What he did not say was that he planned to develop it into a nuclear bomb factory capable of producing one nuclear bomb a year. Ike took Ben-Gurion's word that it was not a nuclear weapons plant, but left it to the incoming president, John Fitzgerald Kennedy to verify.

His presidency over, Ike moved with his wife, Mamie, to their Gettysburg, Pennsylvania, farm, where he kept abreast of the news and discussed the political problems of the day with his successors, John Kennedy and later Lyndon Johnson. He wintered in California's Palm Desert, where he played golf and, like his friend Churchill, painted. He had already written of his part in World War II in *Crusade in Europe* (1948), and gave an account of his presidency in *Mandate for Change* (1963) and *Waging Peace* (1965). He also produced a light-hearted memoir, *At Ease: Stories I Tell My Friends*, published in 1967. He never mentioned in any of his writings that he once thought Jews were angels, or that he had been a Jehovah's Witness. Nor did his son, John, in his *General Ike: A Personal Reminiscence*, published in 2003.

Though Ike never publicly admitted making the wrong decision in the Suez Canal crisis, when he sided with two dictatorships, Egypt and the Soviet Union, against three democracies, two of them close allies, his retrospective regret is on record.

On August 2, 1967, Max Fisher, head of the United Jewish Appeal, called at Ike's Gettysburg home to invite him to address the UJA. As Fisher was about to leave, Ike said, "You

---

[28] *Bulletin of the Atomic Scientists*, Eisenhower Library, International File Box 3, Israel; *Daily Express*, Dec. 22, 1960.

know, Max, looking back at Suez, I regret what I did. I never should have pressured Israel to evacuate the Sinai. If I'd had a Jewish adviser working for me, I would not have forced the Israelis back."[29]

In his memoirs, Richard Nixon, Ike's vice president, confirmed that Ike believed that his Suez decision was a mistake.[30] However, he consoled himself with the thought that he had eventually restored good relations with Britain, France, and Israel.

A whistleblower leaked a secret CIA report to the *Washington Post* in 1962, which revealed that during Ike's presidency, "Israeli intelligence agencies had blackmailed, bugged, wiretapped, and offered bribes to US government officials in an effort to obtain sensitive intelligence and technical information." At the same time, the US had used "sophisticated eavesdropping operations within Israel proper and against Israeli institutions abroad. Several of these were detected by Israel." There was also "an American effort to use American Jews to obtain sensitive information about Israel.... When the two countries discovered what each was up to, instead of driving them apart, Ike and Ben-Gurion agreed that their countries would end covert operations against each other. It led, soon after, to American and Israeli intelligence sources exchanging secret information, like the loyal allies they would become.[31]

Discussing Israel's preemptive Six-Day War against Egyptian forces in June 1967, Ike showed his pro-Israel attitude:

> I was certainly surprised by the speed of the victory. Naturally, when I saw the claims of Israel I said right away this

---

[29] Peter Golden, *Quiet Diplomat: A Biography of Max M. Fisher* (Cornwall Books, 1992); Eisenhower Library. Christian Herter Papers, File Box 8, March 25, 1960.

[30] Richard Nixon, *The Memoirs of Richard Nixon* (New York: Grosset and Dunlap, 1978), 179.

[31] Blitzer, *Between Washington and Jerusalem*, 96.

looks like an Israeli surprise attack. But I don't know what they could have done except that, with those Arab armies on their borders and Nasser talking of a total war to drive Israel into the sea. Try and make an analogy for this country. Suppose I had been president and some combination of enemies, much bigger than us, had been gathered on the seas and in Canada and Mexico, promising our extinction. If I hadn't attacked first while I had the chance I would have been tried for treason....

As a military man I was amazed that the Egyptians could have been caught that way after bragging so much about what they were going to do. I was surprised that they could be caught tactically like that with their planes parked together on airfields. . . But that surely was some harvest the Israelis got. I never had a harvest like that in World War II – 340 planes in one night.[32]

Eisenhower biographer Isaac Alteras believes that the "Eisenhower administration did not renege on its moral commitment to the legitimacy and survival of Israel; what was missing was...the public demonstration of sympathy, warmth and support that Truman exhibited.... But the change from Truman's attitude was more in tone than in substance. Neither Eisenhower nor Dulles ever tried to impose any solutions that would endanger Israel, despite cold-war calculations and Arab pressures to do so. Furthermore, economic aid and grants increased during the Eisenhower years."[33]

---

[32] S. L. Sulzberger, *An Age of Mediocrity: Memoirs and Diaries 1963–1972* (New York: Macmillan, 1973), 358.

[33] Alteras, *Eisenhower and Israel*, 290.

John Fitzgerald Kennedy

1917–1963

- ✪ Thirty-fifth president, 1961–1963
- ✪ Resolved the Cuban missile crisis
- ✪ The only Catholic president and the fourth president to be assassinated in office

His father, Joe Kennedy, was the driving force in the young life of John Fitzgerald Kennedy, later known as JFK. The Harvard-educated son of an Irish-American Boston saloonkeeper, Joe was a man of spectacular achievements. At twenty-five he was president of a Boston bank, at thirty-seven, a millionaire stockbroker; in his early forties he made more millions in the liquor distribution business and in real estate. With a wife, four sons, and five daughters, he also found time to be a Hollywood movie mogul with, among numerous mistresses, movie star Gloria Swanson.

Hungry for more power and prestige, he accepted President Roosevelt's offer to serve as chairman of the Securities and Exchange Commission (to oversee the stock market), and in the late 1930s , at age forty-nine, to be the United States ambassador to Great Britain. Joe, like Truman, called Jews "kikes," but unlike Truman did not share their Zionist aspirations or have any close Jewish friends.

JFK's friend and biographer, Ben Bradlee, noted that Joe Kennedy's "reputation was secure as a womanizer, who had been anti-war and seen as pro-German while he was Ambassador to Britain during World War II, and pro-[Joseph] McCarthy during the fifties."[1]

Interviewed by Joe Dinneen for his book *The Kennedy Family*, Joe Kennedy admitted, "I have a low opinion of some Jews in public office and in private life. That does not mean that I...believe they should be wiped off the face of the earth.... Jews who take unfair advantage of the fact that theirs is a persecuted race do not help much.... Publicizing unjust attacks on Jews may help to cure the injustices, but continually publicizing the problem only serves to keep it alive in the public mind." JFK persuaded Dinneen to remove this quote from the manuscript that was finally published.[2]

Joe scorned "the Jew media" in the United States, believed that the Nazis would beat the British in a war that seemed inevitable, and that the United States should stay out of it. It's hardly surprising that the German ambassador in Britain, Herbert von Dirksen, told Hitler that Kennedy was Germany's best friend in London.[3]

However, as the American ambassador to Britain, in November 1938, Joe Kennedy told US undersecretary of state Cordell Hull of attacks on Jews in Germany, and of the world's indifference to their plight. He also suggested that FDR should

[1] Michael O'Brien, *John F. Kennedy: A Biography* (New York: St. Martin's Press, 2005), 344.

[2] Seymour Hersh, *The Dark Side of Camelot* (Boston: Back Bay Books, 1998), 64.

[3] Edward Renehan Jr., "John Kennedy and the Jews," George Mason University History News Network, May 29, 2002.

support his proposal to settle six hundred thousand European Jews in some sparsely populated part of Britain's African empire. But neither Roosevelt nor the British were interested. He then asked Malcolm MacDonald, Britain's colonial secretary, "why in heaven's name England doesn't show more interest in governmental relief as she had all the land." In fact, MacDonald was in favor of resettling Jewish refugees in British North Rhodesia. Joe Kennedy continued to badger British officials, saying that although everyone seemed sorry for the Jews, no one was doing anything to help them. The officials replied that they were allowing seventy-five Jews to enter Britain every day.[4]

John Fitzgerald Kennedy had a lot in common with his father: multiple women, ambition, drive, and a strong work ethic, but not his bigotry. Throughout his political career, from congressman to president, he proved to be a friend of Jews and an outspoken and consistent supporter of Israel.

John F. Kennedy was educated at Choate, the London School of Economics, and Harvard. At twenty-two years old, in 1939, he visited Palestine during a six-month tour, which took in the Soviet Union, Romania, Turkey, Lebanon, Syria, Greece, France, Germany, Czechoslovakia, and Italy. While in Palestine, he wrote to his father that it should be divided into "two autonomous districts giving them both self-government to the extent that they do not interfere with each other, and British interest is safeguarded. Jerusalem, having the background that it does, should be an independent unit. Though this is a difficult solution, yet it is the only one that I think will work...I have never seen two groups more unwilling...to work out a solution that has some hope of success than these two groups."[5]

---

[4] Herbert M. Druks, *John F. Kennedy and Israel* (Westport , CN: Praeger, 2005), 1–2.

[5] Kennedy Library, Box 135, Special Events Series, President's Office Files.

Kennedy was back in the United States just days before Hitler's attack on Poland and the start of World War II on September 3, 1939. When America entered the war he joined the navy and served in the Pacific, until a Japanese destroyer sliced in two the ship he commanded and he returned home as a wounded war hero.

In what might have been a criticism of his father, he told a Boston crowd in 1944, "Every time an American voices expressions of anti-Semitism he is fighting for our enemies." And he described a horrifying wartime incident in the South Pacific when he saw a Japanese prisoner grab a gun and shoot "a Jewish chaplain to death, just as the chaplain was giving the prisoner a glass of water."[6]

With his father's advice and enthusiastic encouragement he chose a political career as a Democrat, and on November 5, 1946, he was elected to Congress. Representing Massachusetts, he supported Truman's decision to vote for the partition of Palestine, telling listeners at the 27th convention of the New England Zionist Region: "A just solution requires the establishment of a free and democratic Jewish Commonwealth in Palestine, the opening of the doors of Palestine to Jewish immigration, and the removal of land restrictions, so that those Jews who desire to do so, may work out their destiny under their chosen leaders in the land of Israel. If the United States is to be true to its own democratic traditions it will actively and dynamically support the policy."[7]

In the fall of 1951 he toured the world for ten weeks with several of his staff and family, including brother Robert. In Israel, they traveled only in daylight for fear of Arab terrorists. After meeting Israeli prime minister Ben-Gurion in Tel Aviv, he noted in his diary: "On every side signs of tremendous

---

[6] O'Brien, *John F. Kennedy*, 233

[7] Ronald Kessler, *Sins of the Father: Joseph P. Kennedy and the Dynasty He Founded* (New York: Warner Books, 1996), 294.

construction, clearing, growing, transporting... Soldiers appeared tough, rugged, and cocky.... You can feel a sense of dedication...and willingness to endure hardship...Jews very aggressive – confident. Arabs fear expansion. Say it is inevitable result of Jews encouraging immigration."[8]

One night, while in Jerusalem, President Chaim Weizmann's wife, Vera, showed them the difference between the Jewish and Arab world by indicating the dividing line across the city between the darkness in the Arab section and "the bright lights of Jewish-held Jerusalem."[9]

As a Congressman he favored giving Israel $76 million to help absorb its Jewish immigrants, called the country "a beacon of inspiration to all free men everywhere," and praised the tenacity with which Israel maintained its policy of unlimited immigration, which, in three years, increased the population from 600,000 to more than 1,200,000. He concluded that "for the peace of the world it is important that the Arab states recognize the reality of the existence of Israel."[10]

Six months after becoming a senator in 1952, Kennedy married Jacqueline Lee Bouvier; and they had a daughter, Caroline, and a son, John Jr.

In February 1953 he lived up to his pro-Israel campaign speeches by backing a resolution condemning Soviet Russia for persecuting Jews, and called for President Eisenhower to lift his arms embargo against Israel and to balance the arms that Egypt and other Arab nations were getting from Soviet Russia. "It is time," Kennedy declared, "that all the nations of the world...realized that Israel is here to stay. She will not

---

[8] Druks, *John F. Kennedy and Israel*, 22.

[9] Myer Feldman interview, Oral History Collection, 1966, 1967, 1968, Kennedy Library, 693.

[10] Warren Bass, *Support Any Friend: Kennedy's Middle East and the Making of the U.S.-Israel Alliance* (Council of Foreign Relations Book, 2008), 52.19.

surrender – she will not retreat – and we will never let her fall."[11]

The transformation of Palestine into Israel had astonished Kennedy. As he told an audience at Yankee Stadium celebrating Israel's eighth anniversary in 1954:

> A nation had been born – a desert had been reclaimed – and a national integrity had been redeemed, after 2,000 years of seemingly endless waiting. Zion had at last been restored and she had promptly opened her arms to the homeless and the weary and the persecuted. It was the 'Gathering of the Exiles.' They came from concentration camps and ghettoes, from distant exile and dangerous sanctuary, from broken homes in Poland and lonely huts in Yemen.... And Israel received them and fed them, housed them, cared for them, bound up their wounds and enlisted them in a struggle to build a new nation.... From Haifa to the Gulf of Aqaba, from Gaza to the Dead Sea, I found a revival of an ancient spirit. I found it in Israel's gift to world statesmanship, David Ben-Gurion, I saw it in the determined step of the soldiers and workers; I heard it in the glad voices of women in the fields, I saw it in the hopeful eyes of refugees.... The barren land I had seen in 1939 had become the vital nation of 1951.... But in the midst of our rejoicing we do not forget your peril. We know that no other nation in the world lives out its days in an atmosphere of such constant tension and fear. We know that no other nation in this world is surrounded on every side by such violent hate and prejudice.[12]

Back pain from a war injury forced Kennedy to seek relief in a hospital, where he completed a book he was writing. The surgery didn't help, but the book, *Profiles in Courage*, won

---

[11] McGeorge Bundy, *Danger and Survival* (New York: Vintage, 1990), 510; Avner Cohen, "Stumbling into Opacity: The United States, Israel and the Atom, 1960–1963," *Security Studies* 4, no. 2 (Winter 1994/1995): 213–15.

[12] Kennedy Library, www.JFKlibrary.org>...>Archives>ReferenceDesk.

him a Pulitzer Prize. In 1959 he was at work on another book, *The Strategy of Peace*, which included, "Israel is the bright light now shining in the Middle East. The survival and success of Israel and its peaceful acceptance by other nations of the Middle East is essential."[13]

During his presidential campaign, on August 26, 1960, Kennedy assured members of the Zionist Organization of America that fifty years after Theodor Herzl "proclaimed its inevitability," Israel was a triumphant reality. He spoke of Palestine in 1939, when he saw "great neglect and ruin" left by the Turkish empire, but where Jewish settlers worked to transform the country "under conditions of the utmost difficulty, by labor and sacrifice.... The ideals of Zionism have, in the last half century, been endorsed by both parties, and by Americans of all ranks and in all sections. Friendship for Israel...is a national commitment."[14]

On his first day in the White House, after narrowly winning the presidential race against Republican Richard Nixon, Kennedy was warned by Ike's secretary of state, Christian Herter, that India and Israel were the next two countries likely to develop nuclear weapons. Herter advised him to insist on an early inspection of Dimona, the name of Israel's nuclear plant, which a U2 spy plane had recently photographed. Although he decided to take the advice, he "found himself in a dilemma," as author Avner Cohen revealed: "He had a deep personal commitment to the cause of nuclear non-proliferation, but he also had a strong commitment to the security and well-being of Israel."[15]

Like Truman, Kennedy had a Jewish adviser, Myer Feldman. In his early days as president, when he had asked

---

[13] Druks, *John F. Kennedy and Israel*, 24.

[14] Ibid., 552.

[15] Avner Cohen, "Israel's Nuclear Capacity: A Political Genealogy," accessed April 4, 2010, http://members.tripod.com/alabaster_archive/nuclear_opacity.html.

Feldman to advise him on Middle East affairs, he replied that as a Jew he had an "emotional bias" in favor of Israel. "So do I," said Kennedy, "but I want all points of view fairly and forcefully represented."[16]

Kennedy could also expect pro-Israel input from Abe Ribicoff and Arthur Goldberg, two members of his cabinet who were acknowledged Zionists.

He was as concerned as Ike had been over the proliferation of nuclear weapons, and ten days after he entered the White House, Dean Rusk, his secretary of state, brought him a speculative account of what the State Department knew about Dimona. The next day, January 31, Kennedy discussed the problem with Ogden Reid, the US ambassador to Israel, who advised him that an American inspection of Dimona was possible, but only if done secretly.

Aware of Kennedy's growing concern about Dimona, Ben-Gurion decided that to save the project, he would let Americans inspect the nuclear facility. Kennedy chose two Jewish American nuclear physicists to inspect it, Eugene Wigner and I. I. Rabi, both Nobel Prize winners. Ready to inspect the plant on May 20, 1961, they might just as well have been blindfolded. The vital parts were underground, but the inspectors were shown only above-ground buildings, with simulated control-room panels to put the visitors off the scent. Elevators leading to the underground area, where plutonium was reprocessed, were carefully bricked over.

The inspectors reported to Kennedy that although there was no clear scientific reason to justify such a large reactor for a peaceful nuclear power program, they found no evidence of "weapons-related activity" such as a plutonium reprocessing plant.[17]

---

[16] Ibid.

[17] Walter D. Farr, "The Third Temple's Holy of Holies: Israel's Nuclear Weapons," The Counter-proliferation Papers, Maxwell Air-force Base, Alabama, September,

The positive report made it possible for Kennedy to meet Ben-Gurion soon after on friendly terms, in the president's suite at the Waldorf Astoria Hotel. Here is a partial account from the notes by Myer Feldman, who recorded their conversation:

KENNEDY: As some nations are concerned about Israel having a large reactor with the capacity for producing plutonium, on the theory that a woman should not only be virtuous but also have the appearance of virtue, our problem is how to document information about the nature of the reactor in such a way as to remove any doubts other nations might have as to Israel's peaceful purposes.

BEN-GURION: I want us to discuss the reactor in the context of Israel's problems – especially the almost insoluble one of Israel's serious shortage of fresh water. The only solution is desalinization, which is technically possible, but would only be commercially possible if very cheap power were available.... In three or four years we might have need for the plant to process plutonium.... I do not believe Russia wants to give atomic capacity to Egypt, but in ten or fifteen years presumably the Egyptians could achieve it themselves.

KENNEDY: Because we are close friends, the United States is sometimes suspect in matters dealing with Israel. So, wouldn't it be helpful for neutral scientists to inspect Dimona?

BEN-GURION: What do you mean by neutral?

KENNEDY: Scandinavians and Swiss.

BEN-GURION: I have no objection to them.

BEN-GURION: (after raising the question of Israel's security) Egypt has more planes and tanks than Israel, as well as two hundred Russian instructors. Nasser has declared that his aim

---

1999, accessed April 4, 2010, http://www.fas.org/nuke/guide/israel/nuke/farr.htm; Steven Altergood, and Hans M. Kristensen, "Israel's Nuclear Weapons Program, WMD Around the World," Federation of American Scientists, 2007, accessed April 4, 2010, http://nuclearweaponsarchive.org/Israel/ishist.html.

is to destroy, not just to defeat Israel. If they should defeat us, they will do to the Jews what Hitler did.... On my last meeting with President Eisenhower I had asked for defensive weapons because Egypt had twenty-six airfields to our four. And I was promised Hawks, but none has yet been sent.

KENNEDY: The problem is that, though Hawk is a defensive weapon, it could also be used as a missile, and by introducing missiles into the Middle East, other military weapons will escalate fast. Still, I don't want Israel to be at a disadvantage, and if Israel is faced with a critical breakthrough of weapons on the other side, we would know what to do.

BEN-GURION: Egypt has three hundred fighter planes and could get two hundred more from other Arab countries. Although Israel has sixty French Mirage planes on order it will take a year before all of them are delivered.

KENNEDY: The United States will not allow Israel to get in such a position of inferiority that it would encourage an attack.

Kennedy then asked Ben-Gurion for his views on Nasser's relations with the Russians.

BEN-GURION: They are very close. Nasser is not a Communist, but he relies on Russian support to get into Africa. The African leaders are not Communists but they are pro-Communist. Nasser is working very hard on those countries. His efforts help to bring the Russians into African countries, also.

KENNEDY: Because of the Russian threat to drive us out of Berlin, I'm not sure if our security problems aren't as great as Israel's. And we have to assume that Nasser will make our lives as difficult as possible.

BEN-GURION: For people in the uncommitted world freedom does not mean what it does to us. What makes an impression is better standards of living, and health and education. It's not just money they want, but to feel that they are treated as human beings. This is why Israel is working with Africans. If you succeed with the Peace Corps idea – with Americans going out, not as superior beings, but to help others – the psychological factor will be more important than the large amounts of money you give away.

Turning to Palestinian refugees, Kennedy spoke of repatriations, compensation, or their resettlement in Arab countries or elsewhere.

BEN-GURION: Egypt and other Arab countries regard the refugees as the best weapon at hand. If they can get hundreds of thousands of Arabs into Israel we would... still be surrounded by many millions of other Arabs.... I do not hate Arabs, but regard them as human beings, and we want you to help them.

KENNEDY: We want to maintain some influence with them.

Ben-Gurion left, relieved that he had not been subjected to the third-degree on Dimona, or over the refugee problem, and was reasonably confident that Hawk missiles would be on their way.

Kennedy's national security adviser, McGeorge Bundy, concluded that the American inspections of Dimona were not "as seriously and rigorously conducted as they would have to be to tell the whole story.... Their "inspection" was, in fact, a guided tour and they had reported, "No evidence of weapons-related activity."[18]

When the first promised Hawk missiles arrived in Israel – the United States having lent Israel $74 million to buy them – they were placed around Dimona.

The following year, 1962, Kennedy met Israeli foreign minister Golda Meir, and to her delight he said that the United States had a special relationship with Israel only comparable to that of the United States and Britain, but at the

---

[18] Bundy, *Danger and Survival*, 510; Avner Cohen, "Stumbling into Opacity," 213–15; Israeli transcript, "Appendix: The Atomic Reactor," Israel State Archives, Foreign Ministry Record Group, File 1w30.01/3294/12; US transcript, "Conversation Between President Kennedy and Prime Minister Ben-Gurion," LBJ Library National Security Files, Box 21.

same time needed to maintain its friendship with Arab States. In giving Kennedy a picture of the Arab refugee problem, she explained that just a year after Israel's creation, the Israelis – even though still officially at war with the Arabs – had offered to take back up to one hundred thousand refugees, and did take forty thousand. At the same time there were as many as 240,000 Arabs already living in Israel, "some 11 percent of the total population, not all of them peaceful citizens."

Kennedy conceded that Israel could not accept a flood of refugees, but that the problem was a threat to world peace and costing the United States money. He was confident that a solution was possible, and assured her that "we are interested that Israel should keep up its sensitive, tremendous, historic task. Our relationship with Israel is a two-way street. Israel's security in the long run depends in part on what it does with the Arabs, but also on us."

As with Ben-Gurion, he brought up Dimona, saying, "We're opposed to nuclear proliferation. Our interest is not in prying into Israel's affair, but we have to be concerned because of the overall situation in the Middle East."[19]

Kennedy had another chance to discuss Dimona on April 2, 1963, when Shimon Peres was chatting with Myer Feldman, the president's Middle East adviser. He invited them to join him in the Oval Office, knowing that Peres was in charge of its still top-secret nuclear project. Their conversation went as follows: JFK told Peres, "You know that we follow very closely the discovery of any nuclear development in the region. This could create a very dangerous situation. For this reason we monitor your nuclear effort. What could you tell me about it?"

Peres did not know that the previous week CIA Director John McCone had briefed Kennedy on Israel's nuclear project at Dimona, as a result of which Kennedy had issued a National

---

[19] Foreign Relations of the United States, 1961-1963, XV11, 262-263.

Security Action memo titled "Middle Eastern Nuclear Capabilities," instructing his administration to make the subject a top priority and to suggest plans to halt the arms race in the Middle East.

Reluctant to lie to Kennedy, Peres could not betray state secrets, so he came up with this vague response, similar to Ben-Gurion's to Eisenhower: "I can tell you most clearly that we will not introduce nuclear weapons into the region, and certainly we will not be the first."[20]

Two months later, on June 13, 1963, Golda Meir chaired a meeting with her top policy staff on US-Israel relations, focusing on Kennedy's attempt to learn more about Dimona. "There is no need to stop the work in Dimona," she said. "The issue is whether we should tell the truth or not.... I was always of the opinion that we should tell them the truth and explain why.... If we deny that Dimona exists, then it cannot be used as a source for bargaining, because you cannot bargain over something that does not exist."[21]

In the summer of 1963, Kennedy was trying to get Germany and China to agree not to produce atomic bombs, so that he felt bound to put the pressure on Israel to keep Dimona free of nuclear weapons.

Meanwhile, overwhelmed by domestic and foreign problems, most recently the arrest of Israeli spies in Egypt, Prime Minister Ben-Gurion had resigned.

Kennedy told Ben-Gurion's successor, Levi Eshkol, on July 5, 1963, "If Israel's purposes are to be clear beyond reasonable doubt, I believe that the schedule which would best serve our common purposes would be a visit [to Dimona] early this summer and another visit in June 1964, and thereafter at

---

[20] National Security Archive, George Washington University, http://www.gwu.edu/~nsarchiv/israel/documents/hebrew/index.html.

[21] Israel State Archive, *Israel and the Bomb*, 132–36, accessed April 4, 2010, http://www.gwu.edu/~nsarchiv/israel/documents/hebrew/index.html.

intervals of six months...and that our scientists have access to all areas of the Dimona site...and that sufficient time be allotted for a thorough examination. Knowing that you fully appreciate the truly vital significance of this matter to the future well-being of Israel, to the United States, and internationally, I'm sure our carefully considered request will have your sympathetic attention."[22]

Eshkol discussed the situation with his cabinet and suggested. "Maybe we should start by saying that we have a separation plant, we may not do anything with it for a period of half a year, two years, three years, and in the meantime [Kennedy should give us] another form of deterrence." Eshkol was afraid that Kennedy's "man will come and will be told that he can visit anywhere, but when he goes to open something, then Pratt [Dimona's director] will tell him. 'You can't open that.'"[23]

Kennedy again wrote to Eshkol on August 26, "You have suggested that an official visit take place toward the end of this year in the pre-startup stage. I am asking Ambassador Barbour to keep in touch with you so that the visit can be arranged at a time when the reactor's core is being loaded and before internal radiation hazards have developed.... Our purpose must be to continue striving toward the effective control of the power of the atom so that it may be used only for the welfare of man. The spirit you have shown in your letter to me is a clear indication that you share the same high purpose." Kennedy followed up with a reassuring message to Eshkol on October 2, 1963, "Our policies have given concrete proof of our determination to see a prosperous Israel securely established.... There is no Near Eastern leader today, whatever his attitude to your nation, who does not fully understand our public national

---

[22] JFK letter to Eshkol, July 5, 1963; Avner Cohen, *Israel and the Bomb* (New York: Columbia University Press, 1999), 153.

[23] Ibid., 168–69.

commitment.... Our capabilities to carry out this commitment are, and will remain, more than adequate to deter or halt swiftly any aggression against Israel or its neighbors."[24]

By then Israel's nuclear weapons program was on hold, partly because of the enormous cost, so that the Israelis had nothing to fear from the upcoming inspection.

Walworth Barbour, the US ambassador to Israel, noted that although Kennedy did not approve of or encourage the Israeli nuclear bomb program, he did nothing to stop it. Barbour saw his job as insulating Kennedy from facts that might force him to act on the nuclear issue, and was reported as saying: "The President did not send me there [Israel] to give him problems. He did not want to be told any bad news."[25]

Kennedy had enough problems with Castro, the Bay of Pigs, and the threat of nuclear war between the Soviet Union and the United States. But he backed his words to protect Israelis with action: sending them urgently needed Hawk missiles.

A disaffected American, Lee Harvey Oswald, assassinated Kennedy in Dallas, Texas, on November 22, 1963.

Warren Bass, a senior fellow in the Council of Foreign Relations, concludes that "the Kennedy presidency, despite the professional Arabists in the State Department, shifted America's Middle East policy toward Israel, selling arms to the Jewish state, fudging inspections of its nuclear initiative, and openly engaging in security cooperation."[26]

In *My Life*, Golda Meir recalled a consoling conversation with Kennedy shortly before his assassination. As they sat talking in the garden of his Florida home, she thought he

---

[24] *Foreign Relations of the United States,* 1961–1963, V. XVIll, DC, GOPO, 2000. http://www.jewishvirtuallibrary.org/jsource/US-Isreal/FRUS8_26_63_html.

[25] Steven Altergood and Hans M. Kristensen, Nuclear Weapons, Israel, accessed April 4, 2010, http://www.fas.org/nuke/guide/israel/nuke/.

[26] *Publishers Weekly* review of Warren Bass, *Support Any Friend,* 2003.

might not know much about the Jews and their three-thousand-year history of survival against great odds. So she gave him a history lesson, concluding with, "If we should lose our sovereignty again, those of us who would remain alive – and there wouldn't be many – would be dispersed once more. But we no longer have the great reservoir we once had of our religion, our culture, and our faith. We lost much of that when six million Jews perished in the Holocaust.... If my generation [lost our sovereignty] then we would go down in history as the generation that made Israel sovereign again, but didn't know how to hold onto that independence."

Kennedy then leaned over, "took my hand, looked into my eyes and said very solemnly, 'I understand, Mrs. Meir. Don't worry. Nothing will happen to Israel.' And I think that he did truly understand."[27]

Discussing the president with *New York Times* foreign correspondent C. L. Sulzberger in Tel Aviv on July 24, 1968, Ben-Gurion said, "I met Kennedy three times. First he came here before he was president.... He did not make much of an impression. Then, in 1960, I met him in Washington, even before he was nominated as his party's presidential candidate. He was so young-looking that I couldn't seriously think he stood a chance of being nominated, much less elected. Then I met Kennedy the last time in 1961 in New York.... I could see by then that he was a great man."[28]

A memorial to JFK (Yad Kennedy), in a "peace forest" has been created seven miles from downtown Jerusalem. It consists of a sixty-foot-high building in the shape of a stump of a tree that has been cut down – symbolizing a life cut short. Inside is a bust of JFK, and in the center of the building is an eternal flame.

---

[27] Golda Meir, *My Life* (New York: G. P. Putnam Sons, 1975), 311–13.

[28] C. L. Sulzberger, *An Age of Mediocrity* (New York: Macmillan, 1973), 448.

Lyndon Baines Johnson

1908–1973

- ✪ Thirty-sixth president, 1963–1969
- ✪ John F. Kennedy's vice president, he assumed the presidency after Kennedy's assassination
- ✪ Served in all four elected federal offices of the United States: congressman, senator, vice president, and president

Lyndon Baines Johnson was about to be born during a thunderstorm on August 27, 1908. The nearest doctor was twenty miles away, so his grandfather, Sam Sr., forded a river on horseback to bring back a midwife. When they returned, it was too late: LBJ, as he became known, was already out in the world and, in the words of his aunt, Jessie Johnson Hatcher, "as wide awake as a little owl."[1]

LBJ grew up with a brother and three sisters in Johnson City, named after his forebears. His paternal grandfather influenced his early and positive attitude toward Jews. As a Christadelphian Church member, Samuel Early Johnson Sr.

---

[1] Louis Gomolack, Interview with Jessie Johnson Hatcher, unpublished doctoral thesis, Scripps Library, University of Virginia, December 31, 1969.

taught LBJ to consider God's chosen people as friends, and to help them any way he could. LBJ also developed a personal and emotional connection to Israel from childhood conversations with his aunt Jessie, also a Christadelphian, as well as a member of the Zionist Organization of America.[2]

She recalled telling him "to always remember this. Don't ever go against Israel, because Israel as a nation was given to them by God. They are the only nation that God recognized as His own. They are God's people."[3] She told an interviewer, "When Lyndon was little, the Jews were scattered around. But after that they were told they would be gathered back to the land, and that's their land, and in their hands now. Nobody is going to take it away from them. Truman made them a nation, and as I say, they're there for good."[4]

Of Scots-Irish and English descent, LBJ was a member of the Disciples of Christ Church, believing, like most devote Protestants, that Jesus is the son of God, and their personal savior.

His father, Sam, was a Democratic member of the Texas House of Representatives. Both Sam and his father sought clemency for Leo Franks, a young Jew sentenced to death for the rape and murder of a thirteen-year-old girl. Given persuasive evidence that Franks was innocent, the judge reduced his sentence to prison for life, but in 1915 a mob kidnapped and killed Franks. Since the Johnsons had sought clemency for him, enraged Ku Klux Klan members threatened to kill Sam. So Lyndon's father hid in a cellar while several uncles stood guard with shotguns until the KKK sought other victims. An LBJ speechwriter stated that "Johnson often cited Leo Frank's lynching as the source of his opposition to anti-Semitism."[5]

---

[2] Ibid.

[3] Ibid.

[4] Ibid.

[5] Louis Gomolak, "Prologue: LBJ's Foreign Affairs Background, 1908–1948," unpublished doctoral thesis, University of Texas, 1989.

He proudly watched his father in action in the legislature, representing the poor and downtrodden against big-business, the trusts, and those in power.

LBJ was a teenager in 1922 when his father lost the family's ranch to creditors, and the once-prosperous family began to live close to poverty even though Sam kept his seat in the legislature for a time. He wound up as foreman of a road-building crew. LBJ reacted badly to his father's failure and went wild. One morning his mother found him in bed with a broken nose and bloody shirt, after a night of boozing and brawling. The family hoped to tame him by packing him off to college, but LBJ left by car for California with three school friends in search of fun and fortune.

Fun and fortune eluded him in California, where he picked grapes, washed dishes, and worked as a laborer and elevator operator, hungry much of the time. He briefly worked in the San Bernardino office of his attorney cousin who arranged divorces for the Hollywood crowd. LBJ returned home broke and a somewhat reformed character and, to his parents' relief, began to study at Texas Teachers College in San Mateos, where he majored in history, headed the debate team, and graduated in 1930 with a BS degree. After college he taught public speaking in Sam Houston High School, Houston, Texas. But politics was a stronger magnet than teaching, and he enthusiastically campaigned for a congressional candidate, who returned the favor by getting him a job in Washington as a congressman's aide.[6]

While briefly studying law at Georgetown University in 1934, LBJ met twenty-one-year-old Claudia Taylor, daughter of a Texas landowner. She was known as Lady Bird, a childhood nickname a nurse gave her because she was as pretty as a lady bird. LBJ showed his penchant for politics – and maybe

---

[6]   Lyndon Johnson Presidential Library.

for shock tactics – by giving her as an engagement present a book entitled *Nazism: An Assault on Civilization*. It didn't hurt: they married two months later, after LBJ bought her a $2.50 wedding ring from Sears.

In 1937 LBJ, an FDR supporter, ran against nine other contenders to represent Texas in the US House of Representatives and won easily.

By 1938, realizing that the Nazis were hell-bent on destroying Europe's Jews, he resolved to save as many as possible.

Alice Glass, an attractive, intelligent, and compassionate redhead in her mid-twenties, with whom he was having an affair, played an important part in his mission. The future wife of LBJ's patron and enthusiastic supporter, Charles Marsh, a wealthy newspaper publisher, Glass idolized Lyndon Johnson and believed that he would save the world. One of their joint efforts was to help Erich Leinsdorf, a twenty-three-year-old Jewish musician about to be deported to his homeland, Austria. In a letter on his behalf, Congressman Johnson wrote that the US had "a holy mission to provide a peaceful haven for musical geniuses...from persecution and racial bias." LBJ arranged for him to travel to Havana, Cuba, from where the quota for would-be immigrate to America had not yet been filled. Leinsdorf was then allowed to re-enter the United States, where he became a citizen and a distinguished conductor of the Boston Symphony Orchestra. He credited LBJ with saving his life.[7]

Jim Novy, a Jewish businessman in Austin, was another of LBJ's partners in rescuing Jews from Hitler's Europe. Thirty-five years later, at a dinner for LBJ at an Austin synagogue, Congregation Agudas Achim, Novy explained how it came about. In 1938, he told LBJ, then a congressman, that he and his sons were going to Poland and Germany. LBJ then asked

---

[7] Ibid.

him to get as many Jews out as possible, as things were going to get very difficult for them. "He gave me a personal introduction to the American Embassy in Poland," Novy told the congregation, "and called long distance to guarantee their support, and to see that anyone qualified to immigrate be given a visa without delay. As a result, forty-two people were brought out of Poland and Germany."[8]

In what was known as Operation Texas, writes historian James Smallwood, LBJ "used both legal and illegal means to smuggle hundreds of Jews into Texas" through the port of Galveston. By using "fake passports and fake visas from Cuba, Mexico, and other Latin American countries...Johnson smuggled...Jews into Texas." Then he temporarily hid them in the Texas Youth Administration building (he had recently been a director of the organization)."[9]

On December 10, 1941, three days after the Japanese attack on Pearl Harbor, LBJ joined the US Naval Reserve, and as a lieutenant commander flew over hostile territory in New Guinea. When his plane was shot at he kept cool under fire. Eventually, FDR ordered him back to Congress and then, with his old partner Jim Novy, he collected large sums of cash to buy weapons for Jewish underground fighters in Palestine, shipping them in crates marked "Texas Grapefruit."[10]

LBJ was among those who accepted General Eisenhower's invitation to inspect a concentration camp. He was devastated by what he saw, and returned home with an overpowering feeling of revulsion and horror at what he had witnessed. The enormous cruelty of the Nazis had a lasting effect on him.[11]

---

[8]   Notes for speech at a dedication dinner to LBJ, December 30, 1963, Papers of Jim Novy, LBJ Library.

[9]   "Operation Texas: Lyndon B. Johnson's Attempt to Save Jews from the German Nazi Holocaust," LBJ Library, Claudia Anderson, Supervisory Archivist, May 19, 2008.

[10] Ibid.

[11] Eban, *Personal Witness*, 388.

Three years later, in 1948, now the father of two young daughters, Lynda Bird and Luci Baines, he ran for the US Senate and won. He was serving his third term in the Senate when, in 1960, he became President Kennedy's vice president. After Kennedy's assassination in 1963 and LBJ's assumption of the presidency, he assured Israeli diplomat Abba Eban, "You have lost a very good friend, but you have found a better one."[12]

With LBJ in the White House, Israeli's military fortunes received a greater boost than even JFK had provided. Days after his inauguration, he attended the dedication of an Austin synagogue, where his friend Jim Novy said of him, "We can't thank him enough for all the Jews he got out of Germany during the days of Hitler."[13]

Both Egypt and Israel had agreed on UN observer-peace-keepers to be stationed between them in the Sinai, but Egyptian president Nasser persuaded UN secretary-general U Thant to withdraw them, and on May 22, Nasser announced that he was closing the Straits of Tiran to prevent Israeli ships from using the Red Sea to reach the Israeli port of Eilat.

Israeli foreign minister, Abba Eban, told LBJ that his country had three options: do nothing and face strangulation; fight and defeat the Egyptians; or rely on the international community to solve the problem. The British had already proposed that the principal maritime powers should declare their intention to keep the Straits of Tiran open. What did LBJ think of that? LBJ deplored the withdrawal of UN forces from the Sinai and the threatened closing of the waterway, and told Eban that he preferred a UN solution. If that failed, he would adopt the British proposal. Though sympathizing with the Israelis' plight, LBJ warned them not to attack the saber-rattling Egyptian forces. He also told Israeli prime minister Eshkol, "I cannot accept any responsibilities on behalf

---

[12] Novy notes.

[13] LBJ Library, www.lbjlibrary.org.

of the United States for situations which arise as a result of actions on which we are not consulted."[14] Although anxious to help Israel, he said that "without Congressional approval I am nothing but a six-foot-four-inch Texan friend of Israel."[15]

When Nasser massed his troops on the border and threatened to attack, Israel launched a lightning preemptive strike, destroying the Egyptian air force, and winning the war in an astonishing six days.

During the war, Israeli planes and gunboats attacked the USS *Liberty*, an American spy ship in the Mediterranean, killing thirty-four and wounding 171 Americans. Was it an accident or deliberate? The question is still fiercely argued, over forty years later. LBJ gave the Israelis the benefit of the doubt that it was a tragic accident in the heat and smoke of battle, although top US officials almost to a man, including Secretary of State Dean Rusk; CIA director Richard Helms; LBJ's special assistant Clark Clifford; former NSA/CIA director Admiral Bobby Inman; as well as the ship's captain, William McGonagle, and the other survivors, were certain that it was deliberate.

Numerous official and unofficial investigations, several books, TV shows, and many articles about it – for or against the Israelis – still left the question open. The results of the latest investigations indicate that it was an accident caused by "friendly fire." Among those convinced that it was an accident is US Senator John McCain, whose father was in charge of the first official but hurried investigation.

LBJ's account of the event was as follows:

> Thursday, June 8, began on a note of tragedy. A morning news bulletin reported that a US navy communications ship,

---

[14] Lyndon Baines Johnson, *The Vantage Point: Perspectives of the Presidency, 1963–1969* (New York: Holt, Rinehart and Winston, 1971), 290–94.

[15] Blitzer, *Between Washington and Jerusalem*, 45.

the *Liberty*, had been torpedoed in the international waters off the Sinai coast. For seventy tense minutes we had no idea who was responsible [the Soviet Union was the chief suspect] but at eleven o'clock we learned that the ship had been attacked in error by Israeli gunboats and planes. Ten men of the *Liberty* crew were killed and a hundred were wounded [LBJ underestimated the casualties]. This heartbreaking episode grieved the Israelis deeply, as it did us. There was a possibility that the incident would lead to even greater misfortune, [possibly bringing the Soviet Union into the war on the side of Egypt] and it was precisely to avoid further confusion and tragedy that I sent a message to [Soviet Union] Chairman Kosygin on the hot line. I told him exactly what had happened and advised him that carrier aircraft were on the way to the scene to investigate. I wanted him to know, I said, that the investigation was the sole reason for these flights, and I hoped he would inform the proper parties. Kosygin replied that the message had been received and the information had been relayed immediately to the Egyptians.[16]

One Israeli explanation came from Chaim Herzog, a man with access to his country's top-secret information. He had been Israeli director of Military Intelligence from 1949 to 1950, defense attaché at the Israeli embassy in Washington from 1950 to 1954, and again director of Military Intelligence from 1959 to 1962. In 1967 he became the first military governor of the West Bank. In his 1982 book, *The Arab-Israeli Wars*, Herzog reported:

> A United States electronic intelligence ship, *Liberty*, was at the onset of the [Six-Day] war off the coast of Sinai and was steaming slowly fourteen miles north-west of El-Arish. The Americans had not notified either of the sides, Israel or Egypt, of the purpose or mission of the ship, or indeed the

---

[16] Johnson, *Vantage Point*, 300–301.

fact that the ship was operating in the area.... [Near] El-Arish the Egyptian forces regrouped and retook some of the positions that had been captured by the Israeli forces. A certain atmosphere of confusion had been created by the situation. On 8 June, fire was directed at Israeli forces in the general area of El-Arish. Israeli forces reported that they had been shelled, presumably from the sea. The Air Force was alerted, and identified a vessel sailing off the coast of Sinai in the general area that had received artillery bombardment. The silhouette of the ship was similar – particularly to a pilot flying at high speed in a jet fighter aircraft – to a silhouette of ships in the Egyptian navy. Without further ado the aircraft attacked the strange naval vehicle, which had not been identified as friendly.... Attempts to imply that this was premeditated attack on the part of the Israeli forces do not stand up to examination, especially having regard to the particular relationship that existed between the Governments of Israel and the United States.... The blame would appear to have been primarily that of the United States authorities, who saw fit to position an intelligence-gathering ship off the coast of a friendly nation in time of war without giving any warning whatsoever and without advising of the position of their ship.[17]

Israeli diplomat Abba Eban, who attended all "intimate consultations" of the Israeli defense and diplomatic leaders, reported that they agreed with LBJ's and Herzog's "friendly fire" conclusion. "The vessel had entered the fighting area to keep Washington in touch with the course of the war. In view of the global responsibilities of the United States, this was a legitimate purpose, but it seemed inevitable that those who took risks would sometimes incur tragic sacrifice. Some American leaders...occupied their minds with various scenarios

---

[17] Chaim Herzog, *The Arab-Israeli Wars: War and Peace in the Middle East* (New York: Random House, 1982), 185, 188.

of motivation. All of them were false. Israel had no interest whatever in preventing the United Sates from knowing what was going on. I can categorically assert that the *Liberty* tragedy was not deliberate."[18]

The Israeli government sent $13 million in humanitarian reparations to the wounded victims and to the families of those killed. And LBJ accepted the Israeli contention that they should hold on to the Arab territory they occupied during the Six-Day War, until the Arab states agreed to a just and lasting peace with Israel, which would include their agreeing to Israel's right to exist. Though the US State Department continued to urge a more evenhanded Middle-East policy, despite frequent Arab threats and attacks on Israel, LBJ remained adamantly pro-Israel and blamed the Egyptians for the war. "If a single act of folly was more responsible for the explosion than any other, it was the arbitrary and dangerous announced intention [by Nasser] that the Straits of Tiran [an Israeli lifeline] would be closed [to Israeli ships and Israeli-bound cargo]."[19]

At the UN in November 1967, the British and Americans drafted resolution 242 against Israel keeping all territories captured during the recent war. A year later, LBJ modified the resolution as follows: "We are not the ones to say where the nations should draw the lines between them that will ensure each the greatest security. It is clear, however, that return to the situation of 4 June, 1967, will not bring peace. There must be secure and...recognized borders...agreed upon by the neighbors involved."[20]

LBJ invited the Israeli embassy's Ephraim Evron to his Texas ranch, known as the Texas White House, and implied that his days were numbered. "If anything happens to me, you shouldn't worry," he said, "because Hubert [Humphrey, his

---

[18] Eban, *Personal Witness*, 422.

[19] LBJ Library, www.lbjlibrary.org.

[20] Ibid.

vice president] will be president and Israel has a no more committed friend than Humphrey."[21]

In January, France imposed a freeze on arms to Israel, and
Israeli prime minister Levi Eshkol called on LBJ at his Texas
ranch to ask for the tanks and fifty of the latest Phantom fighter jets LBJ had agreed to sell to Israel. Soon after, talking with
Arthur Goldberg, his UN ambassador, LBJ confided, "I sure as
hell want to be careful and not run out on little Israel."[22] He
showed the same attitude in a phone conversation with Ike
on June 25, 1967, when LBJ said that Soviet leader Kosygin
"couldn't understand why we wanted to support the Jews –
three million people, when there were 100 million Arabs. I
told him numbers didn't determine what was right. We tried
to do what was right regardless of numbers."[23] And Ben-Gurion noted with satisfaction that the American arms shipments
under JFK were increasing under LBJ and saw it as a reflection
of "Israel's new tight bond with the United States."[24]

A vivid example of LBJ's pro-Israel attitude was shown by
his response to the news that weapons-grade, highly enriched
radium was missing from America's stockpile, and that Israel
was top of the list of the usual suspects. Several investigations
had failed to discover the thief or thieves. Peter Stockton, a
take-no-prisoners congressional investigator, had interviewed
a leading suspect, Rafi Eitan, in East Berlin. Eitan denied that
he had been to the site from which the uranium was missing, until Stockton showed him his signature on documents
establishing his visits there. Eitan then admitted he had
been there in an official capacity, but only to discuss buying
minute amounts of nuclear material used in eavesdropping

---

[21] Terence Prittie, *Eshkol: The Man and the Nation* (New York: Pitman, 1969), 327.

[22] LBJ Library, www.lbjlibrary.org.

[23] Office of the Historian, *The Foreign Relations of the United States, 1964–1968*, vol.
XIV, US Department of State, Soviet Union Document 234, 237.

[24] Kurzman, *Ben-Gurion*, 461.

equipment. Eitan was famous for having led the Mossad team that kidnapped Adolf Eichmann and took him to Israel for his trial and eventual execution. Stockton saw Eitan as a man to be reckoned with and not likely to betray his country if he had in fact stolen the uranium.[25]

Carl Duckett, the CIA's deputy director for science and technology, was surprised by LBJ's initial response to news of the missing uranium, which was, "Don't tell anyone else. Not even [Dean] Rusk [secretary of state] and Robert McNamara [secretary of defense]." Who took it and where it went – if it was stolen – is still unknown. Eventually, the facility was closed, and its remaining nuclear material sent to other facilities.[26]

LBJ was much more concerned about the Vietnam War than missing uranium, so distressed by his failure to bring it to a triumphant conclusion that in 1968 he decided not to run for reelection. He was also frustrated by the active opposition to the war by many Jewish friends and the American Jewish community at large. He complained about it to Abba Eban, "A bunch of rabbis came to see me in 1967 to tell me I ought not to send a single screwdriver to Vietnam but...should push all our aircraft carriers through the Straits of Tiran to help Israel."[27]

In his *The Vantage Point*, LBJ acknowledged what few could doubt – his strong Zionist views: "I have always had a deep feeling of sympathy for Israel and its people, gallantly building and defending a modern nation against great odds, and against the tragic background of Jewish experience."[28]

History Professor Robert Johnson wrote in the *New York Sun* that on March 24, 1968, a week before announcing that

---

[25] Author's interview, February 26, 2010.

[26] Seymour M. Hersh, *The Samson Option: Israel's Nuclear Option and American Foreign Policy* (New York: Random House, 1991), 188.

[27] Eban, *Autobiography*, 460.

[28] Johnson, *Vantage Point*, 297.

he would not run for reelection, LBJ told Arthur Goldberg that he had grown even more sympathetic to Israel's plight as his own political fortunes had declined. "They hadn't got many friends in the world and they're in about the same shape that I am [he had suffered several heart attacks].... The closer I face adversity, the closer I get to them.... Because I've got a bunch of Arabs after me – about a hundred million of 'em, but there are just two million of us. So I understand them a little bit." (When LBJ said "There are two million of us," it appears that he felt such empathy for the Israelis that he thought of himself as one of them.) Professor Johnson believed that LBJ's "policies stemmed from personal concerns – his friendship with leading Zionists, his belief that America had a moral obligation to bolster Israeli security, and his conception of Israel as a frontier much like his own state of Texas. His personal concerns led him to intercede when he felt that the State or Defense Department had insufficiently appreciated Israel's diplomatic or military needs."[29]

On January 22, 1973, he died alone on his Texas ranch from a massive heart attack. He was sixty-four. In February 2009, Jewish Congress Conference members honored Lyndon Baines Johnson as a "Righteous Gentile."

---

[29] "LBJ's Secret Tapes," *New York Sun,* May 28, 2008; LBJ Library, www.lbjlibrary. org.

Richard Milhous Nixon

1913–1994

- ✪ Thirty-seventh president, 1969–1974
- ✪ Congressman for California and Eisenhower's vice president
- ✪ Resigned as president to avoid impeachment

Richard Nixon committed political suicide by recording his White House conversations. When they became public, he was revealed as an anti-Semite who mistakenly thought he could do no wrong, because as president he was above the law. He was both an anti-Semite and a benefactor to the Jews, especially those in Israel. No previous US president provided more arms or money to protect the embattled Jewish state.

Nixon called Henry Kissinger, his secretary of state, "My Jewboy," had Christian evangelist Billy Graham agree with him that Jews controlled the American media, and recorded his many anti-Semitic slurs during his White House conversations, showing special contempt for Jewish political rivals. "Nixon would talk about Jewish traitors, and the Eastern Jewish establishment – Jews at Harvard," recalled his chief of staff, John Ehrlichman, "and he'd play off Kissinger. 'Isn't that right, Henry? Don't you agree?' And Henry would respond, 'Well, Mr. President, there are Jews and Jews.'"[1]

Yet Nixon admired Israeli Jews, especially members of the Israeli Defense Forces and its intelligence agency, the Mossad, which he rated the world's best. Many of his staff, including his speech writer William Safire, were Jews who admired him and were rarely if ever subjected to his anti-Semitic invective.

Few Jews voted for Nixon for his first term in the White House, but he was such a generous supporter and supplier of Israel that his Jewish support shot up from 15 to 35 percent in his 1972 reelection campaign. Among his Jewish backers then was Israel's ambassador to Washington, Yitzhak Rabin.

Richard Milhous Nixon was born on January 9, 1913, in Youba Linda, California, to a lemon farmer, Frank, and a Quaker mother, Hanna, whom he called a saint, and who raised him and his four brothers to follow her religious convictions. His forbears (like LBJ's) were English, Irish, and Scots. When he was nine, the family moved to Whittier, California, where his father ran a combined general store and gas station.

Richard Nixon did well as a leading member of the debate team at school and college, won prizes for public speaking, acted in school plays, and played the organ at Quaker meetings and the piano at parties. When he graduated from Whittier College in 1934, second in his class, he planned to be a lawyer. With that goal, he got a scholarship to Harvard Law School, which his parents couldn't afford, so he went instead to Duke University Law School in North Carolina, on a tuition scholarship, paying for his extra expenses by doing research for the dean at 35 cents an hour.

His father, having had to leave school after sixth grade to help support his family, was determined that his sons should

---

[1] Seymour M. Hersh, *The Price of Power: Kissinger in the Nixon White House* (New York: Summit, 1993), 84.

have a first-class education. As Nixon recalled, "My greatest thrill in those years was to see the light in his eyes when I brought home a good report card." To his father's great delight, in 1937 Nixon graduated from Duke third in his class.[2]

Nixon returned to California to join a Whittier law firm and continued his interest in acting. The first night he joined an amateur group he fell for one of its members, Thelma Catherine "Pat" Ryan, a red-headed truck driver's daughter, who taught typing at Whittier College. That same night, he proposed to her. She persuaded him to wait two years. When they married, on June 21, 1940, they were both twenty-seven.

After the Japanese attack on Pearl Harbor and America's entry into World War II, Nixon enlisted in the US Navy as a lieutenant and served in the South Pacific. Soon after the war's end, he began his political career as a Republican, trying to unseat a popular Democratic incumbent, Congressman Jerry Voorhis, paying for some campaign expenses with wartime poker winnings. His no-holds-barred tactics and debating skill won him the seat.

As a member of a congressional committee charged with investigating the need for the Marshall Plan to help Europe recover from its post-war pains, Nixon went to Europe; he returned a lifelong proponent of foreign aid, convinced that to prevent Western Europeans from turning Communist it was vital to give them economic aid.

Back in the States, appointed to the House Un-American Activities Committee, he earned a reputation as a tough investigator when questioning Alger Hiss, a State Department official suspected of passing secret documents to the Soviets. Though Hiss was not found guilty of spying, he got prison for perjury. Nixon's national prominence persuaded him to run for the Senate against Democrat Helen Gahagan Douglas, and in a bitter fight, he won by a wide margin.

---

[2] Whitney and Whitney, *American Presidents*, 331.

Eisenhower picked Senator Nixon as his running mate for the 1952 presidential race, and the team was swept into office in a Republican landslide. They won again in 1956. As Eisenhower's vice president, Nixon was visiting South America in 1958 when Communist-led mobs jeered at him, "spat on him, and tried to overturn his car and kill him. He showed great courage in the face of these attacks." The following year, while in Russia, "he engaged in a series of informal public debates with the Russian leader, Nikita Khrushchev, on the merits of democracy versus communism," and most Americans believed Nixon won.[3]

In his run for president against Kennedy, he told the Zionist Organization of America, "The United States is committed to the preservation of the independence of Israel, the prevention of armed aggression in the Near East, and...to bring about a stable peace between Israel and the Arab states." He agreed with the statement of John Foster Dulles, the late secretary of state, that "the protection of the State of Israel...is one of the essential goals of US foreign policy."[4]

Narrowly beaten by Kennedy, he returned to his law practice in California. In 1962 he became a partner in a leading Wall Street law firm, preparing for a political comeback by touring the world's trouble spots, including Israel. Although the American embassy in Tel Aviv held a dinner in his honor, most Israeli VIPs dismissed him as a has-been, but among the few who attended was Yitzhak Rabin, by then the Israeli prime minister's chief of staff. Knowing Nixon was just back from Vietnam, he questioned Nixon on the situation there. Afterwards, Rabin took him on a helicopter tour of Israel's military installations. It was the start of their friendship.[5]

---

[3]   Ibid., 36.

[4]   Nixon message to the Zionist Organization of America, August 27, 1960, John T. Woolley and Gerhard Peters, The American Presidency Project, http://www.presidency.ucsb.edu/ws/?pld=25476.

[5]   The Jerusalem Report Staff, David Horowitz, ed., *Shalom, Friend: The Life and*

Joe Sisco, another of Rabin's American friends, believed that Nixon identified with the underdog, "and equated that with Israel's position." He also admired the Israelis as fighters. Sisco once heard Nixon say, "By God, those Israelis are tough, they can take care of the Arabs."[6]

Nixon's perseverance worked. He defeated Vice President Hubert Humphrey and George Wallace to become president in 1968.

During a brief walk in the White House Rose Garden the following spring, Nixon asked Israeli ambassador Abba Eban why friends of Israel did not have more faith in his concern for Israel's interests, and assured Eban that he would veto any UN proposal that threatened Israel's security and would "never let Israel down."[7]

He had a chance to keep his promise when Israel's prime minister, Golda Meir, met him for the first time. She wondered how he would respond to her urgent shopping list: twenty-five Phantom and Skyhawk jet planes, and a low interest rate loan of $200 million a year for five years to help pay for the planes. She recalled in her autobiography, that as she arrived at the White House on September 26, 1969, "Nixon helped me out of the car, and Mrs. Nixon handed me a huge bunch of red roses. There was something about the way the Nixons received me that made me feel at home with them." To her relief, Nixon not only agreed to supply Phantom and Skyhawk aircraft and to lend the money to pay for them at a lower interest rate than she had requested, but he also agreed not to try to inspect the Dimona's nuclear facility. She, in turn, agreed not to test nuclear weapons, though like previous

---

Legacy of Yitzhak Rabin (New York: Newmarket Press, 1996), 62–63.

[6]   Ibid., 63.

[7]   Eban, *Personal Witness*, 481.

Israeli prime ministers she did not acknowledge that Israel possessed them.[8]

In September 1970, Palestinian terrorists hijacked four Western aircraft to Jordan and blew them up in the desert. Jordan's King Hussein struck back, attacking Palestinians in refugee camps and killing thousands. Syria came to the defense of the Palestinians by invading Jordan with three hundred tanks. Hussein then made an extraordinary request: he asked the Israeli air force to attack the Syrian tanks. Almost as unlikely, Israel granted the request, after Nixon had agreed that if the Egyptians supported Syria, the United States Mediterranean fleet would join the battle against them. It wasn't necessary though, because Hussein's own air force drove back the Syrian tanks. As Rabin recalled: "Israel's willingness to cooperate closely with the United States in protecting American interests in the region altered her image in the eyes of many officials in Washington. We were considered a partner."[9]

Protests by Americans against the ongoing Vietnam War increased in the summer of 1971, and Nixon saw Jews as a large part of his opposition. He told Bob Haldeman, his chief of staff, "The Jews are all over the government" and needed to be controlled by putting non-Jews in charge of key agencies. He went on, "Washington is full of Jews and most Jews are disloyal. Generally speaking you can't trust the bastards. They turn on you. Am I wrong or right?" Haldeman heartily agreed: "Their whole orientation is against you, in this administration anyway. And they are smart. They have the ability to do what they want to do – which is to hurt us."[10]

As Henry Kissinger saw it, "the President was convinced that all the leaders of the Jewish community had opposed him throughout his political career. The small percentage of Jews

---

[8]   Meir, *My Life*, 389–93.

[9]   Horowitz, *Shalom, Friend*, 67.

[10] Nixon tapes, National Archives, accessed April 28, 2010, www.archives.gov/.

that voted for him, he would joke, had to be so crazy that they would probably stick with him even if he turned on Israel. He delighted in telling associates and visitors that the 'Jewish lobby' had no effect on him."[11]

Yet Louis Brandeis was the lawyer Nixon most admired; Justice Felix Frankfurter his model as a strict constructionist; Herman Wouk his favorite novelist; a German-Jewish immigrant, Henry Kissinger, his foreign policy adviser and later secretary of state; and an Austrian-Jewish immigrant, Arthur Burns, his chief domestic counselor. Herbert Stein was head of his Council of Economic Advisers; Leonard Garment, his special counsel, and Ed David his chief science adviser. All Jews!

In his memoir *Crazy Rhythm*, Leonard Garment wrote "on an anti-Semitic continuum running from 1 to 100, my personal experience would put Nixon as somewhere between 15 and 20 – better than most, worse than some.... If there was one group he hated with a particular passion it was the Left. Within that group, he reserved a particularly intense hatred for the journalistic Left. Most of all, he hated people who caused personal hurt to himself and his family. For reasons of history, many of these were Jewish, but I do not think that was the defining personal characteristic that got Nixon's bile flowing."[12]

It was an open secret that Yitzhak Rabin favored his friend Nixon during Nixon's successful reelection campaign against Senator George McGovern. Rabin confirmed the rumor when, in a radio interview, he said, "While we appreciate support in the form of words which we are getting from one camp, we must prefer the support in the form of deeds, which we are getting from the other."[13]

---

[11] Henry Kissinger, *Years of Upheaval* (Boston: Little Brown, 1979), 564.

[12] Jason Moaz, "Nixon: The 'Anti-Semite' Who Saved Israel," *Jewish Press*, August 5, 2005, 1.

[13] Horowitz, *Shalom, Friend*, 72.

On October 6, 1973, the Jewish Day of Atonement known as Yom Kippur, the holiest day in the Jewish year, Egypt and Syria launched a simultaneous surprise attack on Israel. The odds were enormously against Israel surviving the onslaught. From the towering Golan Heights, 1,400 Syrian tanks advanced on 180 Israeli tanks below, and near the Suez Canal 600,000 Egyptian soldiers supported by 2,000 tanks and 550 aircraft attacked 500 Israelis with three tanks.

When Nixon ordered a massive emergency airlift to Israel of tanks, helicopters, and other supplies, Golda Meir said that she knew from "past experience with [Nixon] that he would not let us down. He ordered the giant G-5 Galaxies to be sent and the first flight arrived on the ninth day of the war. The airlift not only lifted our spirits but made our victory possible."[14]

Nixon maintained that America's "commitment to the survival of Israel runs deep":

> We are not formal allies, but we are bound together by something stronger than any piece of paper, a moral commitment. It is a commitment that no President in the past has ever broken and which every future President will faithfully honor. America will never allow the sworn enemies of Israel to achieve their goal of destroying it.

> There are strong reasons, other than moral ones for the United States. It is the only nation whose population challenges Japan as the world's best educated. With virtually no natural resources it has built an industrial economy that competes successfully in the world's economy. Its armed forces are among the best in the world. Israel has impressed the world with all of its accomplishments during forty years of war. It will astonish the world with what it can achieve with forty years of peace.[15]

---

[14] Meir, *My Life*, 430; Richard Nixon, *1999: Victory without War* (New York: Simon & Schuster, 1988), 276.

[15] Nixon, *1999*, 276.

At four in the morning on May 15, 1974, members of the Democratic Front for the Liberation of Palestine disguised in Israeli Defense Force uniforms and armed with rifles, hand grenades, and plastic explosives, entered an Israeli high school six miles south of the Lebanese border. They took eighty-two students and several teachers hostage, and threatened to kill all the children unless Israel released twenty-three Arab prisoners and three others, including a Japanese citizen involved in the 1972 Lod Airport massacre.

An Israeli special forces team stormed the building at 5:32 p.m. and in the fighting twenty-two children were killed and more than fifty wounded. All the terrorists were killed. Israeli planes retaliated the next day, bombing offices and training bases of the Palestine Democratic Front and the Popular Front, killing twenty-seven and wounding 138 people in Palestinian refugee camps in southern Lebanon.

Nixon wrote to Golda Meir: "Mrs. Nixon and I, along with all Americans, grieve with you and all the parents and schoolmates of those who died. This senseless act of terrorism has underscored once again the need for true peace in the Middle East. I can assure you that our efforts towards this goal will never waver."[16]

Soon after, Nixon flew to Israel for two days – the first American president to visit Israel – in a vain attempt to rescue his presidency endangered by the Watergate scandal, his efforts to cover it up, and a growing demand among his political enemies to impeach him. Rabin had been appointed Israel's prime minister just two weeks previously, when Nixon called on him in Jerusalem. Afterwards, Rabin sadly remarked, "The fate of one of the most pro-Israel presidents has already been settled."[17]

---

[16] Woolley and Peters, American Presidency Project, http://www.presidency.ucsb.edu/ws/index.php?pld=4211.

[17] Horowitz, *Shalom, Friend*, 78.

In her autobiography published after Nixon's resignation in disgrace, Golda Meir revealed herself as one of his greatest admirers: "However history judges Richard Nixon – and it is probable that the verdict will be harsh – it must also be put on record that he did not break a single one of the promises he made to us."[18] And again:

> At the time when two US diplomats had been murdered in Khartoum he said to me very quietly, "You must know, Mrs. Meir, that I will never give in to blackmail. Never. If I compromise with terrorists now, I shall be risking the lives of more men in the future." He was as good as his word. Then on his visit to Israel in 1974 – when we ourselves had been through the unspeakable outrage of the slaughter of children by terrorists at Ma'alot – Nixon returned to the subject. "I was brought up," he told me, "to abhor capital punishment. I come from a Quaker background. But terrorists cannot be dealt with any other way. You must never give in to blackmail."[19]

Nixon resigned under the threat of impeachment, and Rabin's first visit to Washington as Israel's prime minister was to meet Nixon's successor, Gerald R. Ford, who pardoned Nixon for his illegal activities in trying to cover up the attempted break-in of the offices of a political opponent.

Nixon's wife, Pat, a heavy smoker, died of lung cancer in 1993. He died of a stroke a year later, on April 22, 1994, at eighty-one. His daughters, Tricia and Julie, were at his hospital bedside.

Prime Minister Rabin said of Nixon, "Israel has lost a friend. I lost a personal friend. He was president during the Yom Kippur War, and in the face of the opposition from most of the world, sent military equipment and weapons to Israel."[20]

---

[18] Meir, *My Life*, 436.

[19] Ibid.

[20] *Jerusalem Post International Edition*, April 30, 1994, 5.

Gerald Rudolph Ford

1913–2006

- ✪ Thirty-eighth president, 1974–1977
- ✪ Nixon's vice president, he became president upon Nixon's resignation and granted him a presidential pardon
- ✪ US involvement in Vietnam ended during his presidency

Because he was not elected but took over from President Nixon, who resigned under the threat of impeachment, Gerald Ford, an Episcopalian of English ancestry, is known as "the accidental president." Like most if not all of his presidential predecessors, Ford was raised on the Old and New Testaments, so that he was familiar with the stories of ancient Israel's heroes and villains, its torments and triumphs.

It is hardly surprising, then, that after members of the United Nations proposed to condemn Zionism as racist, President Ford should address members of B'nai B'rith, saying:

From the time I first ran for Congress in 1948, I recognized the justice of Israel's rebirth and its importance to the United

States. I am proud to stand on my consistent 28-year record of support for Israel.... We will fight any measure that condemns Zionism as racism or that attempts to deny Israel her full rights of membership in the United Nations. The United States will stand firm in its commitment to Israel's security and survival.... The shepherd boy, David, was both tough and muscular. It's a good thing that he also had the most advanced weapon system of the day.... And I can tell you, I will continue to seek further progress on the issue of emigration from the Soviet Union.... A free people must not capitulate to terrorism."[1]

Born in Omaha, Nebraska, on July 14, 1913, Ford was sixteen before he first spoke with his father, Leslie King, and found him to be both a carefree, well-to-do man and a contentious, mean, and hot-tempered one.

The cause of their long separation was a traumatic incident when Ford was just sixteen days old, and his father, brandishing a butcher knife, threatened his twenty-year-old wife, baby son, and the nursemaid. A divorce soon followed; his mother remarried and had three more sons. His father remarried and had a second son and two daughters.[2]

Despite the shaky start, Ford said that he had an idyllic childhood. He became an Eagle Scout, excelling as both football player and coach at the University of Michigan, where he helped to support himself by flipping hamburgers and washing dishes. After Michigan and a Yale law degree, he practiced law in Cedar Rapids – until his career was interrupted by World War II.

Learning of the Japanese attack on Pearl Harbor on his car radio, as he headed home from his office; he volunteered

---

[1] Woolley and Peters, American Presidency Project, http://www.presidency.ucsb.edu/ws/index.php?pld=6317&st=B%5C%27nth.

[2] James Cannon, *Time and Change: Gerald Ford's Appointment With History* (New York: HarperCollins, 1994), 13–14.

for the navy the next day. Four months later he was a lieutenant on an aircraft carrier, the USS *Monterey*, where he was
known for being cool under fire and concerned with the crew's
welfare.[3]

After the war he briefly returned to law practice before
launching his political career. Elected to Congress for Michigan in 1948, that same year he married Elizabeth Bloomer
Warren. She was a divorced department store fashion consul-
tant, and former fashion model and dance instructor. They
had three sons and a daughter.

An Isolationist before the war, Ford became an Interna-
tionalist after seeing more of the world. He became convinced
that the US should persuade or pressure the Soviet Union to
let its Jewish citizens immigrate to Israel. His chance to make
that happen came when, on October 10, 1973, Vice President
Spiro Agnew was charged with extortion, tax fraud, bribery,
and conspiracy, and resigned from office. President Nixon
chose Ford to replace him.

When Nixon himself resigned rather than fight impeachment, Ford was sworn in as his successor, on August 9, 1974.
The next day he invited Israel's prime minister Rabin to the
White House and promised to "meet all the commitments
undertaken by the United States towards Israel, and the
continuation of long-range American support in all matters
pertaining to Israel's defense and economic well-being."

Rabin arrived on September 10, 1974. He and Ford were
old friends, having first met when Ford was a congressman
and Rabin Israel's ambassador to the United States. Now, as
leaders of their respective countries, they discussed Israel's
need for arms to replace those used in the Yom Kippur war, as
well as Israel's willingness to work for a lasting peace in the
Middle East.[4]

---

[3] Ibid., 38.

[4] Israel Ministry of Foreign Affairs, vol. 3, 1974–1977.

Just a month later the Soviet Union agreed to let sixty thousand Soviet Jews immigrate to Israel every year. Rabin immediately cabled Ford that the news "is causing great joy to the people of Israel and to Jewish communities everywhere. This achievement in the field of human rights would not have been possible but for your...direct concern and deep interest."[5]

Although the Yom Kippur War of October 1973 was over, there was no peace agreement between Egypt and Israel, and Ford believed that the Israelis were stalling. He complained that "their tactics frustrated the Egyptians and made me mad as hell." Cabling Rabin in early March, he expressed his "profound disappointment over Israel's attitude in the course of the negotiations. Failure of the negotiations will have a far reaching impact on the region and on our relations. I have given instructions for a reassessment of United State's policy in the region, including our relations with Israel, with the aim of ensuring that overall American interests...are protected. You will be notified of our decision."[6]

On March 24, 1975, Ford told congressional leaders of both parties that the "reassessment" meant that for the next six months the United States would not conclude any new arms agreements with Israel. To Rabin that time was one of the worst periods in US-Israel relations. The Senate inevitably counterattacked: seventy-six senators signed a letter of protest, urging Ford to respond favorably to Israel's request for almost $3 billion worth of military and economic support. The following summer months were what Ford called a "war of nerves" or "test of wills" between Israel and America, but on September 1, when an interim agreement between Egypt and Israel was signed, aid to Israel resumed.

That same day Ford wrote to Rabin that Israel's recent agreement to withdraw from vital areas in the Sinai was "an

---

[5] Ibid.

[6] Ibid.

act of great significance on Israel's part in the pursuit of final peace and imposes additional heavy military and economic burdens on Israel.... The US will support the position that an overall settlement with Syria...must assure Israel's security from attack from the Golan Heights.... The US has not developed a final position on the borders. Should it do so it will give great weight to Israel's position that any peace agreement with Syria must be predicated on Israel remaining on the Golan Heights."[7] Israel had captured the Golan Heights from Syria in the 1967 war, following almost twenty years of Syrians shelling Israel's northern communities and frequent Syrian attacks on the Sea of Galilee, the source of much of Israel's fresh water.

Ford offered Rabin a generous aid package, including F-16 warplanes, and promised not to recognize or negotiate with the PLO until it renounced its terror tactics. Israel for its part had to pull back its troops from the Suez Canal. When Israel agreed, it allowed Egypt to reopen the canal closed since 1967, and to operate its Gulf of Suez oil fields.

During a press conference on November 3, 1975, a reporter asked Ford what he thought of the Palestinians' demand for a state of their own, and he replied that they first had to recognize the State of Israel before they could take part in any negotiations about having their own state.

An apparently Soviet-inspired resolution was now brought to the floor of the UN to declare that "Zionism is a form of racism and racial discrimination." Responding to the charge on November 10, Israeli ambassador Chaim Herzog gave the General Assembly telling evidence that the Arabs were the racists. He said:

> I can point with pride to the Arab ministers who have served in my government, to the Arab deputy speaker of my parliament, to Arab officers and men serving of their own volition

---

[7] Yitzhak Rabin, *The Rabin Memoirs* (New York: Malboro Books), 256.

in our border and public defense forces frequently commanding Jewish troops; to the hundreds of thousands of Arabs
from all over the Middle East crowding the cities of Israel
every year, to the thousands of Arabs from all over the Middle
East coming for medical treatment into Israel, to the peaceful coexistence which has developed; to the fact that Arabic
is the official language in Israel on a par with Hebrew, to the
fact that it is as natural for an Arab to serve in public office
in Israel as it is incongruous to think of a Jew serving in any
public office in an Arab country, indeed being admitted to
many of them. Is that racism? It is not! That is Zionism.

Who would have believed that in this year, 1975, the mali-
cious falsehoods of *The Elders of Zion* would be distributed
officially by Arab governments? Who would have believed
that we would today contemplate an Arab society which
teaches the vilest anti-Jewish hate in kindergartens. We are
being attacked by a society which is motivated by the most
extreme form of racism...expressed so succinctly in the words
of the leader of the PLO, Yassir Arafat, in his opening address
at a symposium in Tripoli, Libya, when he said, "There can
be no presence in the region other than the Arab presence."

For us, the Jewish people, this resolution based on hatred,
falsehood, and arrogance, is devoid of any moral or legal
value. For us, the Jewish people, this is no more than a piece
of paper and we shall treat it as such.[8]

With that, Herzog tore the resolution in two.

President Ford had also deplored the resolution and
instructed Daniel Patrick Moynihan, his UN representative, to indicate exactly what he thought of the resolution.

---

[8] Accessed April 22, 2010, http://www.zionismisrael.com/hdoc/Herzog_Zionism_
1975.htm.

Moynihan said: "The United States...does not acknowledge, it will not abide by, it will never acquiesce in this infamous act."[9]

Supported overwhelmingly by Arab and Muslim representatives, the resolution passed by 72 votes to 36, with 32 abstentions.

In stark contrast, talking to members of the American Jewish Committee on its seventieth anniversary, on May 13, 1976, Ford said: "I commend the spirit with which you have translated Jewish concerns into concern for all humanity.... When 6 million Jews were so cruelly murdered in World War II, the victim was not only the Jewish people but civilization itself. On my visit to the notorious Auschwitz concentration camp last summer, I saw the words vividly written, 'Never again.' This must apply to all genocide – either physical or cultural."

Turning to what he called "Israel's dilemma," Ford said,

> In moving toward peace, Israel is asked to relinquish territory – a concrete and essentially irreversible step – in return for basically intangible political measures. But it is only in willingness to dare to exchange the tangible for the intangible that hostility can be ended and peace attained.... Our role in supporting Israel honors our heritage. America remains the real hope for freedom throughout the world. We will remain the ultimate guarantor of Israel's freedom. If we falter, there is no one to pick up the torch.... We will remain steadfast in our dedication to peace and to the survival of Israel.[10]

In his bid to be elected president, when his unelected term was up, Ford defeated his Republican rival Ronald Reagan, but

9 Moynihan's response, UN General Assembly Resolution 3379, Mideast Web, accessed April 22, 2010, http://www.mideastweb.org/3379.htm.

10 The American Jewish Committee, May 12, 1976, accessed April 22, 2010, http://www.jewishvirtuallibrary.org/jsource/US-Israel/Ford_Israel4.html.

he lost in the presidential race itself to Democratic contender Jimmy Carter.

Ford died at age ninety-three in his Rancho Mirage home in California on December 26, 2006. Some suggested that he was less friendly to Israel than Johnson, Nixon, George W. Bush, or Clinton. Yet Yitzhak Rabin, who knew him well, considered Ford to be a good friend with the interests of Israel at heart. A year after Ford's death, the American Jewish Committee recalled that he "had continued the strong American tradition of bipartisan support for Israel and had explained that his commitment to the security and future of Israel is based upon basic morality as well as enlightened self-interest. Our role in supporting Israel honors our heritage."[11]

---

[11] Ibid., January 3, 2007.

Jimmy Carter

1924–

⊕ Thirty-ninth president, 1977–1981

⊕ Georgia state senator and governor of Georgia

⊕ As president, moderated negotiations that led to a historical peace treaty between Egypt and Israel

A persistent critic of Israel's treatment of Palestinian Arabs, Jimmy Carter is not only a longtime supporter of Israel as a dynamic democracy that shares American values, but was able to broker an elusive but lasting peace between Israel and Egypt, for which, in 2002, he won the Nobel Peace Prize.

Jimmy Carter was born to Earl Carter Sr. and Lillian Gordy Carter in Plains, Georgia, on October 1, 1924. Their marriage was a classic case of opposites attracting: Earl was a conservative peanut farmer and a segregationist; Lillian was a liberal, a registered nurse who gave health care to the poor, joined the Peace Corps at age sixty-eight, and worked for two years as a nurse in an Indian village.

After studying at Atlanta's Georgia Tech in 1942, Jimmy Carter entered the US Naval Academy, where he learned to fly, and graduated as an ensign in 1946, ranked 59th out of

820 fellow students. Soon after, the twenty-one-year-old Carter married his sister Ruth's best friend, eighteen-year-old Rosalynn Smith. Continuing his navy career, he took graduate courses in nuclear physics while a gunnery and electronics instructor aboard battleships *Wyoming* and *Mississippi*, and in the Pacific aboard the submarine USS *Pomfret*.

His courage was tested in 1952, when a Canadian experimental nuclear reactor went out of control and he volunteered for the team that put their lives on the line to safely disassemble the reactor.

That same year, at twenty-eight, he became an engineering officer aboard the atomic-powered submarine USS *Sea Wolf*, commanded by the almost legendary Admiral Hyman Rickover, the son of Polish Jews. Almost alone, this determined and outspoken perfectionist had persuaded a reluctant Navy to build nuclear-powered submarines. Carter acknowledged that Rickover, a Christian convert, had a profound effect on his life – perhaps more than anyone except his parents, "because of his insistence on perfection." And Carter resolved to emulate his hero.[1]

When his father died of cancer in 1953, he left the navy to live with his wife and their three children in Plains, Georgia, where he helped his widowed mother run the Carter farm and studied advanced farming methods. Ten years later, in 1963, he started his political career as a Democratic senator in the Georgia state legislature, where he was appalled to find that the public interest was often defeated by lobbyists representing special interests. After four years he ran for governor against segregationist restaurant owner Lester Maddox, losing by some twenty thousand votes out of a million cast.

Since his return to Plains, Carter, as a born-again Christian, had been a regular churchgoer and Sunday school

---

[1] Whitney and Whitney, *American Presidents*, 387.

teacher in his Baptist church. He had also made frequent trips throughout Georgia and other states hoping to convert others to his faith. In his second bid for governor, Carter defeated Lester Maddox. During his brief inaugural address, as the first southern governor to oppose segregation, he set the tone of his future commitment to human rights: "Every adult illiterate, every school drop-out, and every untrained retarded child is an indictment of us all. The time for racial discrimination is over."[2]

He and Rosalynn toured Israel in May 1973 as guests of Prime Minister Golda Meir's government and discussed with her, Yitzhak Rabin, Moshe Dayan and the chief of Israeli intelligence, Simon Bar-Lev, the strength of Israel's military as a defense against its hostile neighbors.

The following year, on October 27, 1976, as the Democratic presidential candidate, he denounced the Arab boycott of American businesses that traded with Israel as an absolute disgrace, and promised to "do everything I can as President to stop the boycott.... It's not a matter of diplomacy or trade with me; it's a matter of morality."[3]

The fifty-two-year-old Carter was part of the Democratic landslide victory, overwhelmingly defeating Nixon's brief successor, Gerald Ford. Jews in Carter's administration included a US representative at the UN; Harold Brown, secretary of defense; Michael Blumenthal, secretary of the Treasury; Arthur Burns, chairman of the Federal Reserve Board; Stuart Eizenstat, chief speechwriter and chief domestic affairs adviser; Morris Dees, Justice Department; James Schlesinger, head of the Energy Department; William Hyland, adviser on European affairs; Simon Lazarus, presidential aide; David Tatel, head of the Civil Rights Division; Arthur Fleming, US civil

---

[2] Ibid., 389.

[3] Jimmy Carter, *Keeping Faith: Memoirs of a President* (New York: Bantam, 1982), 277.

rights commissioner; Jule Sugarman, federal civil rights commissioner, and Madeleine Albright (although she didn't yet know that she was of Jewish descent) as secretary of state.

Early in Carter's presidency, PLO terrorists blew up two American planes in the Jordan desert, murdered an American ambassador and eleven Israeli athletes at the Munich Olympic Games, and, after hijacking an Air France plane with many Israeli passengers, held them hostage in Entebbe, Uganda. They were freed in a daring rescue by Israeli Defense Forces, during which Yoni Netanyahu, brother of future Israeli prime minister Benjamin Netanyahu, was killed.

Carter believed that there was "no way to escape the realization of how intimately and intertwined are the history, the aspirations, and the fate of the two long-suffering peoples, the Jews and the Palestinian Arabs.... The Palestinians are suffering from...homelessness, scattered as they are throughout many nations, and their desire for self-determination and their own national homeland has aroused strong worldwide support."[4]

Determined to be a peace-broker and finalize the interim peace agreement between Israel and Egypt, on February 14, 1977, just three weeks after becoming president, he sent Secretary of State Cyrus Vance to Israel, where Prime Minister Yitzhak Rabin told him that "for real peace" Israel would "make territorial compromises in all sectors." But the agreement would have to be with Jordan, because the PLO as a terrorist organization was not an acceptable partner. Vance then flew to Egypt, where President Anwar Sadat welcomed American involvement in the peace process.[5]

---

[4] Benjamin Netanyahu, *A Place among the Nations: Israel and the World* (New York: Bantam Books, 1993), 206, quoting Jimmy Carter's *The Blood of Abraham: Insights into the Middle East* (University of Arkansas Press, 1993), 112–13.

[5] Gilbert, *Israel*, 475–76.

Should anyone assume that Carter's support for a Palestinian homeland would be at Israel's expense, he said: "We have a special relationship with Israel. It's absolutely crucial that no one in our country or around the world ever doubt that our number one commitment in the Middle East is to protect the right of Israel to exist, to exist permanently, and to exist in peace."[6]

During his first visit to Carter at the White House on March 7, 1977, Rabin told him that Israel's conditions for peace with the Egyptians and the Palestinians were as follows: Israel would return most of the Sinai to Egypt, and later withdraw from most of the West Bank. Israel would then accept a combined Jordanian-Palestinian state, but not a separate Palestinian state. After dinner, when they left the guests for a one-on-one conversation, Rabin was shocked, according to his wife, Leah, when Carter said, "Now, Mr. Prime Minister, tell me what you really think." Rabin replied, "We had long talks today. I don't have two agendas or opinions. I have only one and you have heard all about it today."[7]

The lack of rapport between the two men explains that night's diary entry by Carter:

> I've put in an awful lot of time studying the Middle East question and was hoping Rabin would give me some outline of what Israel ultimately wants to see achieved in a permanent peace settlement. I found him very timid, very stubborn, and also somewhat ill at ease.... When we went upstairs with just the two of us I asked him what Israel wanted me to do when I met with the Arab leaders and if there was something specific, for instance, that I could propose to Sadat. He didn't unbend at all, nor did he respond. It seems to me that the Israelis, at least Rabin, don't trust our government or any

---

6 White House, May 12, 1977.

7 Gilbert, *Israel*, 476.

of their neighbors. I guess there's some justification for this mistrust, I've never met any of the Arab leaders, but am looking forward to seeing if they are more flexible than Rabin.[8]

In his memoir published five years later, Carter says that he knew Rabin was extremely intelligent and courageous, so that it was an unpleasant surprise to find that an Israeli leader he expected to be among the most likely to be willing to discuss ideas for peace, was so reticent. In fact, he wrote, it almost "caused me to think again about whether we should launch another major effort for peace."[9]

Throughout the spring of 1977, Carter infuriated Jews by linking the sale of F-15 fighter planes to Egypt and Saudi Arabia with the sale of F-15 planes already promised to Israel. So that when Menachem Begin replaced Rabin as prime minister, Carter anticipated with trepidation their planned meeting because he was warned that they would not get along. To his relief, he found Begin congenial and deeply religious – doubtless the way Carter regarded himself. That night, he noted in his diary: "Begin is a very good man, and though it will be difficult for him to change his position, the [Israeli] public opinion polls show that the people there are quite flexible, and genuinely want peace. My own guess is that if we give Begin support, he will prove to be a strong leader, quite different from Rabin."[10]

As with Rabin, Carter took Begin upstairs in the White House for a private conversation, when Begin promised to keep an open mind on controversial matters and confided that he and Egypt's Sadat were planning to meet. According to a Rabin biographer, Michael G. Kort, Sadat's distrust of Israel had been considerably reduced when the Mossad warned him

[8] Carter's personal diary, March 7, 1977.
[9] Carter, *Keeping Faith*, 280.
[10] Ibid., 290.

of an assassination plot against him and gave the names and addresses of his would-be killers.

Carter emphasized his pro-Israel credentials in a speech to the Democratic National Committee on October 22, 1977: "A few days ago in a conversation with about thirty members of the House of Representatives, I said that I would rather commit suicide than hurt Israel.... If I should ever hurt Israel, which I won't, I think political suicide would automatically result, because it is not only our Jewish citizens who have this deep commitment to Israel...that ties us together in an irrevocable way."[11]

A month later, Sadat astonished the political world by telling his parliament that he was willing to go...even to the Knesset in search of peace – but only if the invitation came directly from President Carter. So Carter sent Sadat the invitation, and also enclosed a letter from Begin inviting Sadat to speak to the Knesset. Begin warned Carter not to be too optimistic, pointing out that over the past twenty-nine years, six Israeli prime ministers had offered to go anywhere to meet Arab leaders for the sake of peace, without result.

When Sadat arrived in Jerusalem on November 20, 1977, cheering crowds waving Egyptian flags greeted him, and his first words to Begin were, "No more war. Let's make peace." And Golda Meir said, "We have been waiting for you a long time." Sadat replied, "The time has come."[12]

The PLO disagreed. On March 11, 1978, PLO terrorists near the northern Israeli border with Lebanon murdered thirty-eight Israelis, including thirteen children. Three days later, Israeli troops invaded Lebanon from the area where the terror attack occurred, killing over a thousand people as they drove the PLO many miles back from the border. Concerned that the Israelis had used US weapons in the counterattack, Carter

---

[11] Democratic National Committee, October 22, 1977.

[12] Gilbert, *Israel*, 492.

called for the Israelis to withdraw from Lebanon and for the establishment of a UN peacekeeping force between the Lebanese and Israelis.

Begin again went to the White House on March 21, while the Israelis were still in Lebanon, but apparently this wasn't discussed during the Carters' private supper with Begin and his wife, Aliza. Instead, Begin spoke of his life as leader of Betar, a Zionist youth movement in Poland, and how he had been falsely charged by Soviet intelligence with being a British agent and sentenced to eight years in the Gulag. He spoke, too, of the murder in the Holocaust of his parents and his only brother.

This helped Carter to understand Begin's views on Israel. Even so, when they went to Carter's office for an intense sometimes emotional discussion about the Middle East, Carter was baffled by Begin's inflexibility and sensitivity. For example, Begin said that he had been "wounded in the heart" because Carter had not praised him sufficiently for his offer to withdraw from the Sinai; Begin asserted that Sadat's visit to Israel had been just "a grand gesture" and that the Egyptian president really wanted an independent Palestine and Israel's complete withdrawal from the West Bank. Carter asked what more Begin would do for peace. To which, according to Carter's diary, Begin said nothing more than he had already proposed.

In May, when Begin returned to the White House to commemorate Israel's thirtieth birthday, Carter promised that America would always support Israel and announced the formation of a committee to establish an American memorial to Holocaust victims.

To reassure those who feared that Carter's admiration for Sadat might have weakened his support for Israel, he said on May 26: "There need be no concern among the Israeli people nor among Jews in this country that our Nation has changed

or turned away from Israel."[13] He invited the Israeli and
Egyptian leaders to join him at Camp David, Maryland, on
September 4, 1978. Both accepted. Three weeks before the
start of the negotiations, the Israeli Cabinet agreed to establish three more settlements. Carter then cabled Begin: "These
illegal unilateral acts in territory presently under Israeli occupation create obstacles to constructive negotiations. The
repetition of these acts will make it difficult for the President
to reaffirm publicly the US position regarding the 1967 borders with minor modifications."[14]

Begin arrived at Camp David on September 5, 1978, and
told Carter that Israel's security was the most vital issue and
that this would be the first time in over two thousand years
that his country and Egypt had discussed their mutual interests. On the second day, Sadat insisted that Egypt and all other
Arab nations must get back every inch of their land that Israel
had won in battle, with possible minor modifications of West
Bank borders.

With the three leaders and their aides present, Sadat read
out all the time-worn Arab demands and charges against the
Israelis. Begin listened with a straight face to the end. After a
shocked silence, Carter broke the tension by telling Begin that
if he signed the document as written it would save a lot of
time, and they all roared with laughter.

On day three, Begin insisted that Sadat's demands
threatened Israel's existence. Sadat wanted an independent
Palestinian state. Begin didn't.

By day five, Carter felt that his task was to convince Begin
to change his public and private commitments of a lifetime:
his dedication to the establishment and preservation of his
country – for which he had fought against the British as leader
of the Jewish underground, the Irgun. But Begin was deeply

---

[13] Ibid., May 26, 1978.
[14] Ibid., August 17, 1978.

religious, with a firm belief that the entire West Bank was an indivisible part of Israel, which Israel had liberated in the Six-Day War, and should be maintained with a Jewish majority and an Arab minority. Carter sympathized with Begin, but had resolved to take a hard-line to persuade him to modify his views.

On day eight, Carter angrily accused Begin of being ready to give up the chance of peace with Israel's formidable enemy, Egypt; the unimpeded access to international waterways; free trade and diplomatic recognition; Arab acceptance of an undivided Jerusalem; security for his country, and the world's approval; just to keep a few illegal settlers on Egyptian land (the Sinai).

Day ten ended with Carter's "heartbroken" realization that the apparently irreconcilable differences between the two nations were so insignificant compared with the enormous advantages of peace.

Day eleven, Carter was desperate when told that Sadat had packed and wanted a helicopter to take him back to Washington. He rushed to Sadat's cabin, and warned him that he would be blamed for the failure of the peace talks, damage his reputation as the world's foremost peacemaker, be admitting the fruitlessness of his celebrated visit to Jerusalem, and that "his worst enemies in the Arab world would be proved right in their claims that he had made a foolish mistake." When that didn't move him, Carter asked him to stay for a few more days, after which, if there was no progress, everyone would leave at the same time.

He stayed.

Day twelve, Sadat agreed that the Jews should retain the Western Wall, and that Egypt would exchange ambassadors with Israel within nine months of signing a peace treaty. Most importantly, Sadat accepted a compromise that separated the requirement that Israel withdraw from the Sinai from any agreement to give up land on the West Bank, Golan Heights, and Gaza.

Day thirteen, the exhausted negotiators flew to Washington where, in the East Room of the White House, at 10:15 p.m. on September 19, 1978, Begin, Carter, and Sadat signed the Camp David Accords.[15]

As blueprints for a final peace treaty, the first accord called for five more years of ongoing negotiations, taking into account "the legitimate rights of the Palestinian people, and their just requirements," after which their permanent status in the West Bank and Gaza would have to be resolved. As historian Martin Gilbert pointed out, "This was the first time that Israel conceded what were essentially the national aspirations of the Palestinians, hitherto regarded as former Jordanians, or Arabs who happened to live in and around [such cities as Hebron, Ramallah, Bethlehem, and Jenin], whose loyalties were primarily to their families and regions. This was a major step forward for Israel, and one which the Palestinians were in due course to use to the fullest advantage."[16]

In the second accord, Israel agreed to completely withdraw from the Sinai to an internationally recognized border with a large buffer zone between the Israeli and Egyptian armies, and to give up all its settlements, airfields, oil wells, and military bases in the Sinai. In return, Egypt would normalize relations between the two countries – after technically being at war with each other for thirty years – and establish diplomatic, cultural and economic relations with Israel. To compensate for its loss of Sinai airfields, the US agreed to build three military airfields for Israel in the Negev.

Carter solved the roadblock over the future of Jerusalem by persuading each man to agree to disagree in an exchange of letters, and to leave it for others to settle the problem. So Begin

15 Carter, *Keeping Faith*, 327–402.
16 Gilbert, *Israel*, 492.

wrote that Jerusalem was the indivisible capital of Israel, and Sadat wrote that Arab East Jerusalem was an indivisible part of the West Bank, which should be returned to Arab sovereignty.

Several months later Carter flew to Jerusalem, where to compensate for its lost Sinai oil he promised to supply Israel with oil for the next fifteen years. While in Israel, he went with Begin to Yad Vashem for a service at the Holocaust memorial, which made it easier for him to understand Begin's extreme caution concerning Israel's security. Then they went to the graves of the founder of modern Zionism, Theodor Herzl, and Begin's political mentor, Zionist Ze'ev Jabotinsky.[17]

Next stop for Carter was Cairo, where he persuaded Sadat to exchange ambassadors with Israel, to provide an oil pipeline from the Sinai wells to Israel, and to try to reduce the anti-Begin insults in the Egyptian press. Soon after, Begin and Sadat joined Carter in Washington, and on March 26, 1979, signed the peace treaty on the White House lawn.

Despite his many pro-Israel statements and actions, many Jews believed Carter to be biased in favor of the Arabs. What few of them knew is that he was about to give Israel reconnaissance photos taken by America's most recent and valuable military secret – the KH11-satellite orbiting the earth every hour and thirty-six minutes, taking amazingly clear pictures of whatever lay below. Even America's closest allies, the British, were shown some of these photos but only on a need-to-know basis. But as investigative reporter Seymour Hersh discovered, in March 1979, Carter decided to give Israel "access to any satellite intelligence dealing with troop movements or other potentially threatening activities as deep as one hundred miles inside the boarders of neighboring Lebanon, Syria, Egypt, and Jordan.... Israeli leaders, not surprisingly, viewed the secret

---

[17] Carter, *Keeping Faith*, 421–23.

KH-11 agreement as a reaffirmation of respect and support from the Carter administration."[18]

In April 1979, at Sadat's invitation, Begin visited Cairo and phoned Carter to say that it had been wonderful. Tens of thousands of Egyptians had lined the streets cheering and waving as he drove by. "I am very moved," Begin said. "I left my car for a while to the disturbance of the Egyptian Secret Service, and went into the crowd, which was crying, 'We like you, we love you.' It was absolutely wonderful."[19]

That same month Carter persuaded the Russians to free three Jewish political prisoners – who then went to Israel – in exchange for commuting the sentences of two Soviet spies who had worked in the United Nations.

As well as Middle East peace, Carter had wrestled with another enormous problem: how to free Americans held hostage in Teheran by Iranian militants. His failure did not help his reelection campaign that summer of 1979. Nor did the admission of younger brother, Billy, to a Senate investigation committee, that the Libyan government paid him $20,000 as their agent. Although Billy denied that he had tried to influence his brother, the committee reported that his actions were "contrary to the interest of the President and the United States."[20]

When Americans voted for their next president, Carter had been negotiating with the Iranian government for over a year in a futile attempt to free the American hostages in Teheran.

In November 1980, Jewish Americans nationwide voted equally for Carter and his challenger, Ronald Reagan – each getting 40 percent of their votes. However, the public at large voted overwhelmingly for Reagan. Not until it was clear that

[18] Hersh, *Samson Option*, 3–5.
[19] Carter, *Keeping Faith*, 428.
[20] Whitney and Whitney, *American Presidents*, 409.

Carter would lose to Reagan, did the Iranians begin serious discussions and the first freed hostages only flew from Iran on the day of Reagan's inauguration.

On October 6, 1981, Sadat paid with his life for making peace with Israel, gunned down by Egyptian army officers opposed to the peace treaty. Carter and his wife, together with former presidents Ford and Nixon, and Prime Minister Begin, attended Sadat's Cairo funeral.

Out of office in 1982, Carter became the third US president to win the Nobel Peace Prize, the two previous winners being Theodore Roosevelt and Woodrow Wilson. That year Carter and his wife, in partnership with Emory University, founded the Carter Center. Its motto is "Waging Peace, Fighting Disease, Building Hope." Its purpose is "to advance human rights, alleviate human suffering, strengthen democracy, mediate and prevent conflicts, and monitor elections around the world." Since then Carter and fellow members of the center have traveled to more than seventy nations to carry out their mission.[21]

Carter also wrote several books, the most controversial being *Palestine: Peace Not Apartheid*, and explained that by using the word apartheid in the title he did not intend to imply that Israel had a racist policy in the West Bank, but that its treatment of the Palestinians there was inhumane. The *Publishers Weekly* review echoed many others: "Carter assigns ultimate blame to Israel, arguing that the country's leadership has routinely undermined the peace process through its obstinate, aggressive and illegal occupation of territories seized in 1967. He is decidedly less critical of Arab leaders, accepting their concern for the Palestinian cause at face value, and including their anti-Israel rhetoric as a matter of course, without much in the way of counter-argument."[22]

---

[21] Carter Center, accessed April 10, 2010, www.cartercenter.org.

[22] *Publishers Weekly*, December 13, 2006.

His critics also contend that when Israel built its protective wall, he focused on its intrusion into what Palestinians called their land, and did not mention that the wall has substantially reduced terrorist attacks inside Israel.

In a more recent book, *We Can Have Peace in the Holy Land: A Plan That Will Work*, Carter proposes the involvement of the international quartet, Russia, the United Nations, the European Union, the United States, together with Iran, Syria, Hezbollah, and Hamas. He suggests the following points: (1) Israel's right to exist – and to live in peace – must be recognized and accepted by the Palestinians and all other neighbors. (2) The killing of innocent people by suicide bombs or other acts of violence cannot be condoned. (3) Palestinians must live in peace and dignity, and permanent settlements on their land are a major obstacle to this goal."[23]

On a mission to the Middle East in 2008 with a group called the Elders, Carter spoke with Hamas leaders and took them at their word that they wanted peace with Israel, while they were doing little or nothing to stop rocket attacks on Israel, with the exception of one ceasefire lasting several months. On this trip he got a warm welcome from the Arabs, but the Israelis gave him the cold shoulder. To Jews, the name Elders is an emotionally disturbing reminder of *The Protocols of the Learned Elders of Zion*. This long-since discredited anti-Semitic work of propaganda claims that Jews plan to control the world and subjugate non-Jews. After the Koran, this book, which demonizes Jews, is said to be the most popular book in the Muslim world.

Responding to some of Carter's statements, Israeli prime minister Benjamin Netanyahu was amazed that "the Arab-inspired myth of 'Israeli expansionism' persists, even though in 1979, in pursuit of peace at Camp David, Israel willingly

---

[23] Jimmy Carter, *We Can Have Peace in the Holy Land: A Plan That Will Work* (New York: Simon and Schuster, 2009), 1.

agreed to give up 91 percent of the territory it had won in a war of self-defense against Egypt, land containing billions of dollars of investments and the oil fields that it had developed and that met most of its energy needs. No victor in recorded history has behaved similarly. What other nation would give up its oil supply and become dependent on imported oil for the sake of peace?"[24]

---

[24] Netanyahu, *Place among the Nations*, 141.

Ronald Wilson Reagan

1911–2004

- ✪ Fortieth president, 1981–1989
- ✪ Took office at age sixty-nine, the oldest man to be elected president
- ✪ Previously governor of California, as well as a radio, film, and television actor

Ronald Reagan is the only professional actor to become president, though cynics might say that they're all actors. He had also been head of a union, the Screen Actors Guild. Working in Hollywood for some twenty years, he interacted with many Jews on both sides of the camera and had a jocular relationship with his Jewish boss, Jack Warner, head of Warner Studios. While Reagan was yet to become a Zionist, Warner was already one when, in 1938, at the request of American Zionist leaders, he called on Joseph Kennedy, the US ambassador in London, and urged him to support the Balfour Declaration. Warner had already closed all his movie offices in Germany after Nazi thugs had murdered Joe Kauffman, his Berlin representative.[1]

As for Reagan, he would prove himself to be pro-Jewish long before he entered politics and as president was an outstanding supporter of Israel.

Reagan's ancestors came from Tipperary in Ireland, and as a boy his father, Jack, had encountered bigotry against his people in America, including seeing such forbidding store signs as "No dogs or Irishmen allowed." Jack grew up to be a lapsed Catholic, an alcoholic shoe salesman with the gift of the gab and with a lifelong dream to own a shoe store. Reagan's mother, Nell, a seamstress of Scots-Irish descent, filled in for her husband when he was too drunk to work. As a devout Disciple of Christ, she taught her two sons that God had a plan for everyone and that the greatest sin was racial bigotry. Friends and relatives called her a saint. Though Reagan's father was nominally a Catholic and his mother a member of the Disciples of Christ Church, as an adult Reagan chose to be a Presbyterian. His brother, Neil, was three when Ronald was born on February 6, 1911, in Tampico, Illinois, increasing its population to 821. Three years later, the family moved to Dixon, a larger community eighty miles west of Chicago. There his father took a step toward his dream job, as part-owner of a general store.

At seven, Ronald got perfect marks in arithmetic and spelling, with a 97 percent average in his final report. He was a high school football star and president of the student council. Those schooldays, he recalled, were the happiest of his life, though overshadowed by his father's boozing. In his autobiography, he tells how, just after his eleventh birthday, in 1922, when his mother was away on a sewing job, he was approaching home from a basketball game at the Y to find his father

---

[1]   Jack Warner with Dean Jennings, *My First Hundred Years in Hollywood: An Autobiography* (New York: Random House, 1965), 249, 274.

"lying like a corpse in the snow, his arms outstretched, flat on his back. He was drunk, dead to the world...I felt myself fill with grief for my father. Seeing his arms spread out as if he were crucified – and indeed he was [presumably by his addiction] – his hair soaked with melting snow, snoring as he breathed, I could feel no resentment against him. I bent over him...got a fistful of his overcoat. Opening the door, I managed to drag him inside and get him to bed."[2]

Reagan attended Eureka College during the Great Depression of the early 1930s, but to him they were idyllic days. Being a strong swimmer, he was both captain and coach of Eureka College's swimming team, and for seven summers used his talent as a lifeguard at nearby Lowell Park. There he achieved an amazing record – saving seventy-seven people from drowning in the river. Equally amazing, only one of them, a blind man, ever thanked him.

As a sports enthusiast, he was delighted to get a job as a radio sports announcer at WOC in Davenport, Iowa, then at a bigger station, WHO in Des Moines. With his father's gift of the gab and his play-by-play accounts of football and baseball games, he developed a wide following. On a trip to Pasadena, California, in 1937 to cover the Chicago White Sox at spring training, he took a tour of a movie studio, and emerged so star-struck that he asked a talent agent to represent him. The agent phoned a Warner Brothers casting director to say, "Max, I have another Robert Taylor sitting in my office." To which Max Arrow replied, "God only made one Robert Taylor," but agreed to see Reagan.[3]

Studio boss Jack Warner offered the twenty-six-year-old radio announcer a seven-year contract, and Reagan accepted. He loved acting, especially in cowboy movies, and after a few years as a leading man he bought his parents a California

---

[2] Ronald Reagan, *An American Life* (New York: Simon & Schuster, 1990), 99–100.

[3] Ibid., 33.

home, hired his father as his secretary, and married actress Jane Wyman. They had a daughter, Maureen, and an adopted son, Michael, before divorcing after eight years.

Coming from a family who regarded racial bigotry as a great sin, it's hardly surprising that, as his biographer Edmund Morris reports, Reagan almost got into a fistfight at a Beverly Hills party with a fellow guest who made anti-Semitic remarks. And on learning that Jews were excluded from his Lakeside Country Club, he resigned and joined Hillcrest Club, which had a large Jewish membership.[4]

During World War II, Reagan was assigned to processing documentary films of the various fighting fronts. His empathy for Jews intensified when, toward the war's end, he saw several secret Signal Corps films of Nazi concentration camps. One he never forgot showed German families who had been ordered "to see for themselves the unspeakable inhumanity of their countrymen.... Some were laughing and enjoying themselves, as if they were on an outing.... Then you followed the villagers through the camp and the cameramen switched between them and the horrors they were witnessing. Soon their reactions had changed completely: the men began to grow stooped and their faces turned ashen, many women began crying, some fainted and others turned away from the camera and began vomiting."[5]

Reagan remembered that after World War I many Americans had dismissed reports of German atrocities as Allied propaganda, so he kept several World War II concentration-camp films to refute anyone who denied the camps existed. Sure enough, after the war, he was entertaining a movie producer and his wife at his home when the producer remarked that he doubted accounts he had heard of Nazi atrocities.

---

[4]   Edmund Morris, *Dutch: A Memoir of Ronald Reagan* (New York: Random House, 1999), 208.

[5]   Ibid., 208–9.

Reagan then screened a newsreel of Jews in concentration camps, and his now distressed and better-informed guests cried at the sights.[6]

In 1952, Reagan married actress Nancy Davis, a love-match that lasted and produced a son and daughter, Ron and Patti. Having resumed his acting career and his work as president of the Screen Actors Guild, he was faced with countering Communists trying to control Hollywood studios for propaganda purposes. As Reagan recalled, "We met for so many long hours each day to try and keep the studios open in the face of the long communist-inspired attempt through labor troubles to dominate the industry."[7]

When his opponents threatened to have acid thrown in his face to ruin his looks and end his career, the police kept a twenty-four-hour watch on his house and gave him a gun, which he carried in a shoulder holster for several months.[8]

Getting more deeply involved in politics, he gave a televised speech promoting conservative Barry Goldwater for president, which led to Reagan being the conservative choice to unseat Pat Brown, California's two-term Democratic governor. Brown went on the attack with a TV commercial in which he told an audience of children: "I'm running against an actor, and you know who killed President Lincoln, don't you?"[9]

Reagan defeated Brown by 58 percent to 42, and inherited a state government that was broke. As governor he backed a law allowing California banks and savings institutions to invest in State of Israel Bonds, and during the Six-Day War of 1967, he was the featured speaker at a pro-Israel rally in Los Angeles's Hollywood Bowl.

---

[6] Ibid., 99–100.

[7] Whitney and Whitney, *American Presidents*, 413.

[8] Reagan, *An American Life*, 108, 111.

[9] Ibid., 149.

On the strength of his achievements as governor, he ran for president in 1979. Talking to members of B'nai B'rith during his campaign against incumbent Jimmy Carter, Reagan said, "Since the rebirth of the State of Israel, there has been an ironclad bond between that democracy and this one."[10] He won the election with 489 electoral votes to Carter's 49. Forty percent of Jews voted for him and forty percent for Carter. However, Brooklyn's Orthodox Jews voted overwhelmingly for Reagan.

On March 30, 1981, John Hinckley fired a bullet into Reagan's lung within an inch of his heart. Hardly able to breathe, coughing blood, losing consciousness, and afraid that he was dying, he quipped to Nancy as she entered his hospital room, "Sorry, honey, I forgot to duck." Nineteen days later he was back at his desk in the Oval Office. His would-be assassin went to a mental hospital. Reagan wrote in his diary, "I owe my life to God and will try to serve him in any way I can."[11]

In June, three months later, Iraq's dictator, Saddam Hussein, had followed up his threat to destroy Israel by building a nuclear reactor at Osirak, twelve miles southeast of Baghdad. But it didn't last for long. Israeli pilots flying American F-16s destroyed it. It was obvious why they had done it, so that when Reagan's national security adviser, Richard Allen, asked him, "Why d'you suppose they did it?" he replied, "Well, boys will be boys." According to Allen, although Reagan protested in public, he "was delighted...very satisfied. It showed that the Israelis had claws, a sense of strategy, and were able to take care of problems before they developed."[12]

That summer of 1981, terrorists murdered an Israeli diplomat in London, and the PLO had launched cross-border

---

[10] Mitchell G. Bard, "Myths & Facts Online: US Middle East Policy," Jewish Virtual Library, http://www.jewishvirtuallibrary.org/jsource/myths/mf21.html.

[11] Reagan, *An American Life*, 203.

[12] Hersh, *Samson Option*, 8–9.

attacks on Israel from southern Lebanon. Israeli ground and air forces responded by attacking PLO targets. Reagan approved the UN Security Council resolution calling for the withdrawal of all Israeli troops, but only after the PLO ended its cross-border attacks. This seemed possible in September, 1982, when US ambassador Phillip Habib arranged the evacuation of the PLO from Lebanon. Reagan then called for direct negotiations between Israel and the Arab states to discuss autonomy for the Palestinians, but not an independent state. Jerusalem was to remain an undivided city, with its final status to be negotiated.

Meanwhile, with Reagan's blessing, his ardently pro-Israel UN ambassador, Jeane Kirkpatrick, had vetoed over a dozen anti-Israeli UN resolutions. In 1982 Israel had responded to Reagan's military and political support by voting in the UN with the United States more often than any other country. During Hanukkah, on December 4, 1983, Reagan spoke of Kirkpatrick's work to members of the Jewish Community Center of Greater Washington: "We are making sure that Israel is not hurt in the United Nations. Ambassador Kirkpatrick is our watchdog on this, and let me assure you, one thing about Jeane, she's a very determined woman. But just so no one gets any ideas, let me be blunt: if Israel is ever forced to leave the UN, the United States and Israel will leave together...." Like several previous presidents he was concerned with the mistreatment of Russian Jews and told the meeting, "We know that the emigration of Jews from the Soviet Union is practically stopped. They're constantly ridiculed, harassed, beaten, and arrested by the Soviet authorities. It is no exaggeration to say their entire Jewish population feels it's under siege.... In their struggle we must not forsake them. We will not remain silent."[13]

---

[13] Woolley and Peters, The American Presidency Project, http://www.presidency. ucsb.edu/ws/index.php?pld=40832.

As he spoke Reagan was involved in a secret mission to fly thousands of Ethiopian Jews facing starvation in Sudanese refugee camps to safety in Israel. Reagan's rapport with the Soviet Union's Mikhail Gorbachev – who apparently did not share the anti-Semitic views of many fellow Russians – allowed the CIA-sponsored "Operation Joshua" and " Operation Moses," headed by Reagan's vice president, George Herbert Walker Bush, to rescue and settle in Israel some ten thousand Ethiopian Jews. That delighted Jews worldwide.

Soon after, Jews were outraged by Reagan's decision to visit Bitburg, a West German military cemetery where SS officers guilty of war crimes were buried. Even his wife could not dissuade Reagan from going, because he didn't "think it right to keep punishing every German for the Holocaust, including generations not yet born in the time of Hitler."[14]

In his diary for April 28, 1985, he wrote: "I'm worried about Nancy. She's uptight about the situation and nothing I can say can wind her down. I'll pray about that, too." He had only been informed that SS men were buried there after he had promised West Germany's vice chancellor, Helmut Kohl, that he would go there. He tried to diminish criticism by also agreeing to visit the site of a former concentration camp.

Middle East expert Wolf Blitzer believed that Reagan was motivated "by the legacy of the Holocaust, despite his controversial decision in 1985 to go through with his visit to Bitburg. The message had repeatedly been brought back to him since entering the White House that Israel was established only after six million Jews perished during World War II. Every year, for example, he had participated in some ceremony commemorating the Holocaust. He seems genuinely moved, as does his wife, Nancy. 'The security of your safe havens, here and in

---

[14] Reagan, *An American Life*, 379–80.

Israel, will never be compromised,' he promised some 20,000 Holocaust survivors at the ceremony in 1983."[15]

Should anyone doubt Reagan's Zionist credentials, he proved them wrong when, ten years after the UN General Assembly had condemned Zionism as racist, Reagan told a UN conference on Israel, Zionism, and the United Nations, that "he would support any move to repeal the resolution." (It wasn't repealed until December 16, 1991.)

After suffering from Alzheimer's disease – so did his mother – Reagan died in 2004 at age ninety-three, in his California home. The American Israel Public Affairs Committee (AIPAC) eulogized him as "a beacon of hope and optimism, a steady hand guiding America toward a vision of peace and prosperity.... Rising above party and politics, President Reagan articulated the views of the United States when he said in September, 1984, 'We who are friends of Israel; may differ over tactics, but our goal remains always unchanged: Permanent security for the people of that brave state. In the great enterprise, the United States and Israel stand forever united.' By the conclusion of President Reagan's time in office, the US and Israel regularly conducted joint military training."[16]

Though Reagan never visited Israel, Mitchell G. Bard, webmaster for the Jewish Virtual Library, stated: "Ronald Reagan will be fondly remembered as perhaps the most pro-Israel president in history."[17]

---

[15] Blitzer, *Between Washington and Jerusalem*, 242.

[16] AIPAC Press Release, June 8, 2004.

[17] "Reagan's Legacy on Israel," Israel Insider, June 25, 2004, http://web.Israelinsider.com/Views/3779.htm.

George Herbert Walker Bush

1924–

- ✪ Forty-first president, 1989–1993
- ✪ Served as vice president, congressman, ambassador, and director of Central Intelligence Agency
- ✪ As president, in Desert Storm, played a leading role in freeing Kuwait from Iraqi invaders

President George Herbert Walker Bush had a distinct advantage in dealing with both Arabs and Israelis in the Middle East. Through his business and political career he developed closer and more influential Arab contacts – in Jordan, Egypt, and Saudi Arabia – than any previous US president, including Carter. He took Egypt's President Mubarak to an Orioles game in Baltimore and discussed with Saudi Arabia's King Fahd their experiences when they were both heads of their countries' respective intelligence services. The Oval Office was invariably open to the Harvard-educated Prince Bandar bin Sultan, Saudi Arabia's colorful ambassador to the United States. They met so frequently that someone asked if the prince was a member of Bush's Cabinet.[1]

Early in his political career as director of the CIA, Bush had also developed rapport with leaders of Israel's government and intelligence agencies. Then, as Reagan's vice president, he played a major role in helping thousands of endangered Ethiopian Jews find a safe home in Israel. As president, he further served the Zionist cause by successfully and enthusiastically voting to revoke a United Nations resolution equating Zionism with racism.

Born in Milton, Massachusetts, on June 12, 1924, Bush was the second son of Prescott Bush – a Yale graduate, businessman, and eventually a US senator for Connecticut – and Dorothy Walker. They were both Episcopalians of English ancestry. Graduating from prestigious Philips Academy in 1942, on his eighteenth birthday George joined the US Navy to train as a bomber pilot. In early 1943 he got his wings as one of the navy's youngest pilots.

On a bombing run in the Pacific, Japanese anti-aircraft fire disabled his Grumman Avenger, and the plane headed for the water. He yelled at his two crewmen to bail out, then parachuted safely into the ocean. He was the sole survivor, floating on a life raft until a US submarine rescued him. Rejoining his squadron in the Philippines, he flew fifty-eight combat missions, and was then sent home for Christmas 1944. Just over a week later he married his high-school sweetheart, Barbara Pierce. Like the Reagans, it was a love-match that lasted. The first of their five children, and a future president, George Jr., was born in the summer of 1946.

The war over, Bush followed his father to Yale, majored in economics, and became a member of the secret society Skull and Bones. Limited to fifteen members a year, the society is

---

[1] William Simpson, *The Prince: The Secret Story of the World's Most Intriguing Royal: Prince Bandar bin Sultan* (New York: Regan/HarperCollins, 2006), 23.

reputed to have an initiation ceremony in which the new-comer tells the other fourteen members details of his sexual history. In its vow of secrecy it has been compared to the Mafia. Its purpose, however, seems more benign: to massage its members' egos and encourage them to become the nation's leaders, and lifelong, loyal, and supportive friends. And, of course, keep its secrets. Apparently, at least one member was Jewish, because, according to the *Jewish Press*, Bush "fought successfully for Jews to be allowed into the exclusive Skull and Bones Society."[2]

Graduating from Yale in 1948, he became a partner in various Texas oil companies and made a fortune. In 1952, his father, a partner in an investment banking firm, was elected US senator for Connecticut, holding the seat until 1962. The year Prescott Bush left the Senate, his son, George, was elected Republican Party county chairman. In 1969, hooked on public service, he resigned as chairman and chief executive officer of the Zapata Off-Shore Oil Company to devote his life to poli-tics. His chance came when he won a seat in a newly created Houston district and moved with his family to Washington, DC, to serve in the US House of Representatives. He soon had his eye on the Senate. Twice failing to get there, in 1971 he accepted President Nixon's offer to be the US ambassador to the United Nations, where he served for two years before becoming chairman of the Republican National Committee.

Nixon had just made his memorable trip to China, and had for the first time officially recognized that country's Com-munist government. When China was admitted to the United Nations, Bush was still there as the US ambassador.

Soon after, when Vice President Gerald Ford replaced the disgraced Nixon, he offered Bush the newly created post of chief US liaison officer in China, which Bush enthusiastically

---

2   Jason Maoz, "Writing About Presidents," *The Jewish Press*, August 27, 2008, http://www.jewishpress.com/pageroute. do/255451.

accepted. Thirteen months later, in 1976, Ford recalled him to head the discredited CIA, accused of keeping government activities under wraps to hide political scandals. In less than a year as CIA director Bush testified at fifty-one Congressional Committee hearings held to expose CIA failings and to enact radical reforms.

President Reagan chose Bush as his vice president in 1981 and made good use of him on a massive rescue mission. This work began after a violent coup in Ethiopia, in which some twenty-five hundred Ethiopian Jews were killed, seven thousand made homeless, and the country's Emperor Selassie escaped to Jerusalem. The rebel leader outlawed Judaism, and his followers monitored and harassed the surviving Jewish religious leaders and imprisoned many Ethiopian Jews falsely accused of being Zionist spies. Anxious to rescue the surviving Ethiopian Jews, Israeli prime minister Begin got into the good graces of the new dictator by agreeing to sell him arms. Then, when the deal was underway, Begin asked him to let two hundred Ethiopian Jews leave the country in an Israeli military jet that had just emptied its cargo of weapons, and was about to return to Israel. The plan worked. The two hundred Ethiopian Jews left for Israel.

This was the beginning of a mass exodus known as Operation Moses. To escape from famine and religious persecution in war-torn Ethiopia, many refugees had made a long and dangerous journey on foot across the border to Sudan. There, Israeli planes waited at secret locations to fly them to their new homeland. In six weeks, between November 1984 and January 1985, almost eight thousand Ethiopian Jews were secretly flown to Israel.

Unfortunately, the *Washington Jewish Week* and the United Jewish Appeal publicized the ongoing secret rescue mission, causing Arab nations to pressure Sudan to stop the exodus. This left over fifteen thousand Jews, mostly women, young children, and the sick, stranded in a hostile Ethiopia. It was then that Vice President Bush spearheaded Operation Joshua, the 1985 rescue of Ethiopian Jewry. The three-day secret operation airlifted an additional eight hundred Jews from Sudan to resettlement in Israel.[3]

In the summer of the following year, President Reagan sent Bush on a brief trip to investigate the prospects for peace in the Middle East. While in Jordan, Bush played tennis with Prince Hassan, whom he described as "a little guy in height but he weighs a ton as a tennis partner." After the game they discussed a Jordanian plan "to computerize Jerusalem's multi-faceted history." On his return, he reported that Israeli prime minister Shimon Peres genuinely wanted peace between Jordan and Israel.[4]

Elected president in 1989, Bush faced the problem of how to deal with Iraq's Saddam Hussein, who was threatening to destabilize the Middle East. A brutal dictator, hated by many of his countrymen, Saddam so feared assassination that he never slept in the same place two nights running. Only his security detail – not even his head of Intelligence – knew his hiding places. Doubtless still smarting from the Israelis' destruction of his nuclear reactor, Saddam declared on April 2, 1990, "I swear to God we will let our fire eat half of Israel [presumably by using his chemical weapons] if it tries to wage anything against Iraq."[5]

Just over two weeks later he said that war against Israel would not end until all Arab territory was restored to the Arabs, and that he intended to launch chemical weapons at Israel. On June 18, 1990, he told an Islamic conference in Baghdad that Palestine had been stolen and urged the Arab

---

[3]   *Encyclopedia Judaica* (Gale Publishers, 2008), s.v. "Bush, George Herbert Walker."

[4]   George Bush, *All the Best: My Life in Letters and Other Writings* (New York: Scribner, 1999), 350.

[5]   Reuters, April 2, 1990.

world to "recover their usurped rights in Palestine and to free Jerusalem from Zionist captivity."[6]

Hungry for oil, money, and access to the ocean, on August 2, 1990, Saddam ordered eight thousand Republican Guards to invade Kuwait, their small oil-rich neighboring kingdom to the south. While the Iraqi invaders were torturing, raping, and killing fellow Arabs, about a thousand Palestinians marched together, shouting, "Saddam, you hero, attack Israel with chemical weapons."

Bush doubted that this would be the end of Saddam's aggression and noted in his diary his distress at accounts of Iraqi atrocities against the Kuwaiti population.[7]

Saddam's threats against Israel, spurred Bush to upgrade the Israelis defense capabilities by sending them two Patriot air defense units as protection from Iraqi missiles. Suspecting that Saudi Arabia, rather than Israel, would be Saddam's more immediate victim, Bush had its King Faud shown the top-secret evidence: US satellite photos of advancing Iraqi troops approaching the Saudi border, some less than a mile away. Because Faud's own forces were dangerously outmatched against Saddam's one million battle-tested troops, seven hundred military planes, and six thousand tanks, Bush offered to help defend Saudi Arabia, and Faud accepted. Bush's friendship with Arab leaders paid off. Over the next several months, with UN approval, he built a coalition of thirty-four nations, including Egypt, Kuwait, Morocco, Oman, Qatar, Saudi Arabia, and Syria.

However, Bush faced an even greater challenge than getting Arabs to join him to fight fellow Arabs: how to keep Israel out of the war. Saddam continued to threaten to attack Israel if Israel attacked Iraq – and it was almost certain that Saddam would keep his word. The Israelis always responded

---

6   Ibid., April 18, 1990.

7   Associated Press, August 12, 1990.

to attacks, and it was virtually certain that if Saddam lived up to his threats to attack Israel, Israelis would fight back. Inevitably, Arab nations in the coalition would then drop out, rather than fight a war with Israelis as allies. Fearing such an event, Bush made a secret phone call to Israeli prime minister Shamir, asked him not to respond to Saddam's anticipated attacks, and explained why. Reluctantly, Shamir agreed.

In December 1990, Saddam warned that if the United States moved against Iraq, "Tel Aviv would receive the next attack, whether or not Israel takes part."[8]

Bush approved a top-secret phone link between the Pentagon's operation center and the Israeli Defense Forces in Tel Aviv to warn the Israelis when the war was about to start and of potential Iraqi attacks on Israel. Then, on January 17, 1991, President Bush launched Operation Desert Storm to free Kuwait.

As expected, on the second night of the war, Saddam fired seven Scud missiles (short-range ballistic missiles) at Israel. During the war, all told thirty-nine Iraqi Scuds killed, by some miracle, only two Israelis. The Scuds also damaged some 3,300 Tel Aviv buildings, while Palestinians greeted the explosions by cheering in the streets and from their rooftops, undermining Israeli hopes that they were willing to make peace.

US General Colin Powell, chairman of the Joint Chiefs of Staff and the mastermind of Desert Storm, praised Shamir for showing "a special brand of statesmanship in resisting heavy pressure...to strike back. The forbearance of the Israelis, in the face of intense provocation, going completely against their grain, in my judgment helped keep the coalition intact."[9]

To reward Israel, Bush ordered special-ops troops into Iraq to destroy Scud launching sites and sent Patriot anti-missile missiles to protect Israeli cities from future attacks.

---

[8]   Reuters, December 26, 1990.

[9]   Ibid.

Although Shamir kept Israel out of the fighting, he did offer Bush the use of its hospitals, and American ships en-route to the battle were welcomed at Haifa's port for repairs and maintenance. After an intense thirty-eight-day bombing campaign, ground forces took over and crushed the Iraqi military in just forty-two days, driving Saddam's forces out of Kuwait and killing tens of thousands of them, while American casualties were 137 killed and seven missing in action. Although forced out of Kuwait, Saddam remained in power in Iraq. To those who complained that Bush had ended the war prematurely, he replied: "We had defined the mission: it was not to kill Saddam Hussein; it was certainly not to occupy an Arab nation; it was to end the aggression against Kuwait."[10]

In the summer of 1991, Bush again turned his attention to Ethiopia, where rebels had driven Ethiopia's dictator out of the country and replaced him with an acting president. Bush persuaded the new leader – during the ongoing civil war in Ethiopia – to let thousands more Ethiopian Jews immigrate to Israel for humanitarian reasons. A two-day airlift known as Operation Solomon followed and employed thirty-four El Al jumbo jets and Hercules C-150s. All the planes' seats were removed to make more room – and 14,324 refugees were rescued – two of them born on their journey to freedom.

During the operation, Shamir phoned Bush aboard Air Force One to thank him for his and Secretary of State James Baker's efforts. Then, at a Rose Garden ceremony to recognize the American diplomats who had helped in the airlift, Bush said, "For all of us here today, and I think for all the Jews around the world, this was an event of emotional proportions. And I just want you to know that I share in that emotional

---

[10] Colin Powell with Joseph E. Persico, *My American Journey* (New York: Ballantine Books, 1996), 512.

feeling that something wonderful has happened."[11] Today, some ninety-four thousand Ethiopian Jews live in Israel.

After Operations Moses and Solomon, Bush tried to advance the Arab-Israeli peace process by sending a secret letter to Syria's President Assad on June 1, 1991, assuring him that America would guarantee the security of any border on the Golan Heights to which Israel and Syria agreed. Assad was not interested.

Still hoping to reconcile Jews and Arabs, on October 31, 1991, he co-sponsored with the Soviet Union's Gorbachev a Middle East Peace Conference in Madrid, also attended by representatives of Europe, Syria, and Jordan. Bush persuaded Israel's Shamir to let Palestinian representatives attend, breaking a forty-three-year-old taboo (since the birth of Israel) against Arab and Jewish politicians publicly talking directly to one another – with the exception of the few words between Begin and Sadat. In Madrid, Shamir invited his Arab counterparts to meet him in Israel to negotiate peace, but they refused to modify any of their non-negotiable demands. Nevertheless, two years later Israel and Jordan would sign a peace treaty and Israel and the Palestinians would sign the Oslo Accords, another small step on the rocky road to peace.

On December 16, 1991, Bush voted with the majority to revoke the UN's long-standing "Zionism is Racism" resolution. "To equate Zionism with the intolerable sin of racism," said Bush, "is to forget history and to forget the terrible plight of the Jews in World War II, and indeed throughout history."[12]

Prime Minister Yitzhak Rabin replaced Shamir in 1992, and Bush invited him and his wife, Leah, to his summer home

---

[11] Public Papers of the President, http://bushlibrary.tamu.edu/research/research.php.

[12] James A. Baker III with Steve Fiffer, *"Work Hard, Study. . .And Keep Out of Politics!": Adventures and Lessons from an Unexpected Public Life* (New York: Putnam's, 2006), 303, footnote.

in Maine for a weekend together. At a news conference afterwards, on August 11, Bush said:

> We agree one thousand percent that our goal goes beyond that
> of ending the state of war. What we seek is a real peace, codi-
> fied by treaties, characterized by reconciliation and openness,
> including trade and tourism. It must be a comprehensive
> peace on all fronts, grounded in UN Security Council Resolu-
> tions 242 and 338, born of direct negotiations.

> Israel is no longer stigmatized so unfairly by the UN reso-
> lution equating Zionism with racism. Literally hundreds of
> thousands of Jews from Ethiopia and from the former Soviet
> Union now make their homes in Israel; and this more than
> anything else, is what the Jewish state is all about. In this
> regard, I am extremely pleased to grant up to ten billon dol-
> lars in loan guarantees. [Bush had held up the ten billion
> dollar loan, as he believed that extending West Bank settle-
> ments was an obstacle to peace. Prime Minister Shamir had
> disagreed. When Rabin, Shamir's successor, agreed to freeze
> settlement expansion, Bush gave Israel the loan.][13]

Bush and Rabin met again in the White House a month
later, when Bush promised to maintain Israel's qualitative
military edge in the Middle East by sending Israel Apache and
Blackhawk helicopters. The two also agreed for their armed
forces to cooperate on technology upgrades.

At a B'nai B'rith International Council meeting on September 8, 1982, Bush called anti-Semitism "an evil idea with
an ugly history.... In the end anti-Semitism and prejudice
mock and threaten the basic principles upon which the United
States is founded."[14]

---

[13] Public Papers of the President, http://bushlibrary.tamu.edu/research/research.php.
[14] Ibid.

Despite significant triumphs abroad, Bush had reneged on his "no new taxes" pledge. In debates with Democratic presidential contender Bill Clinton, Bush seemed out of touch with people's everyday concerns. Consequently, Clinton won with 62 percent of the popular vote.

William Jefferson Clinton

1946–

- ✪ Forty-second president, 1993–2001
- ✪ Attorney general and governor of Arkansas
- ✪ As president led NATO in helping Kosovo achieve freedom from Serbian domination

Bill Clinton's father, William Jefferson Blythe Jr., died before he was born and his stepfather was a wife- and child-beating drunk. Three months before Bill's birth, in Hope, Arkansas, on August 19, 1946, his traveling salesman father was killed in a car crash. When Bill was still a baby, his widowed mother, Virginia, went to Louisiana to complete her nursing studies while his grandparents took care of him.

His mother returned to Arkansas with a nurse's diploma, and in 1950, when Bill was four, she married Roger Clinton. The family then moved to Hot Springs, Arkansas, where Virginia had another son, Roger Clinton Jr. Despite a sometimes horrific home life, where he tried to protect his mother and young brother from his violent, alcoholic stepfather, Clinton rose above it, sustained and encouraged by a mother who adored him and buoyed by the teaching at his Baptist Sunday school.

He excelled at school, was an avid reader, especially of biographies of heroic American Indians. At Sunday school, he accepted that he was a sinner and needed Christ to save him, and at ten, in 1956, he and a friend, Bert Jeffries, were baptized.

Bill was a promising debater and a popular student leader. At fifteen, he legally changed his name from Blythe to Clinton. At seventeen, as a delegate for Boys Nation, a group that taught youngsters the American electoral system, his handshake in the White House Rose Garden with President Kennedy inspired him to "study and get ready, and perhaps my time will come."[1]

After high school, he took a course in International Studies at Georgetown University, partly paying for the tuition by working as an intern for Arkansas senator William Fulbright, the powerful chairman of the Senate Foreign Relations Committee. In the early 1960s, Fulbright had stopped Israel from illegally funding the American Zionist Council, whose goal was to spread pro-Israel information throughout the United States. On the other hand, Fulbright proposed guaranteeing American military support if needed to defend Israel's borders and independence within the territory that it held before the 1967 war. As a former Rhodes scholar, Fulbright encouraged Clinton to follow in his successful footsteps, and to Clinton's delight he won the prestigious scholarship to England's University College, Oxford. There he became friends with another Rhodes scholar, the Jewish-American Robert Reich – destined

---

[1] Clinton, *My Life*, 62.

to be one of the many Jews in Clinton's cabinet. After Oxford, Clinton headed for Yale Law School.

In 1968, Clinton's stepfather was dying of cancer and the two were reconciled. Clinton had even grown to love him.

After Yale, he taught law at the University of Arkansas in Fayetteville, while Hillary Rodham – a fellow attorney with whom he had fallen in love at Yale – went to Boston to join the legal staff of the Children's Defense Fund. In 1974 Clinton failed in his attempt to be a US representative, but was compensated by Hillary's return to Arkansas, where they married in 1975. Bill is of English descent, Hillary of French Canadian, Scottish, and Native American descent, and they have a daughter, Chelsea.

In 1975, Clinton became Arkansas's attorney general. Two years later, at age thirty-two, he was elected the state's governor, the nation's youngest governor. As governor he promised to reform the failing school system by insisting that schoolteachers pass a standard teaching test before starting or continuing to teach – a promise he kept, despite fierce opposition from many teachers.

At Hillary's urging they traveled to Israel in 1980 with a Baptist church group, spending time in Jerusalem, following in the steps of Christ, and visiting the Sea of Galilee and other sites where he was said to have been crucified, buried, and resurrected. They saw the Western Wall and Muslim holy sites, including the Al-Aqsa Mosque and the Dome of the Rock, from which Muslims believe that Mohammed rose to heaven on his horse. They climbed to Masada where, as Clinton wrote in his autobiography:

> A band of Jewish warriors, the Maccabees, withstood a long, furious Roman assault until they were finally overcome and entered the long pantheon of martyrs [by killing themselves rather than be taken prisoner]. Atop Masada, as we looked

down on the valley below, Dr. W. O. Vaught [their tour guide and pastor of the Clintons' Immanuel Baptist Church] reminded us that history's greatest armies, including those of Alexander the Great and Napoleon, had marched through it and that the Book of Revelation says that at the end of time, the valley will flow with blood. The trip left a lasting mark on me. I returned home with a deeper appreciation of my own faith, a profound admiration for Israel, and for the first time, some understanding of Palestinian aspirations and grievances. It was the beginning of an obsession to see all the children of Abraham reconciled to the holy ground in which our three faiths came to life.[2]

In 1985 Clinton played a major role in national politics by responding for the Democrats to President Reagan's State of the Union address.

Shortly before Clinton's friend and counselor, Baptist Minister Vaught, died on Christmas Day, 1989, he had predicted that Clinton would become president and a good one, and told him that he must remember above all that God would never forgive him if he didn't stand by Israel. "He believed," Clinton wrote, "that God intended the Jews to be at home in the Holy land. While he didn't disagree that the Palestinians had been mistreated, he said the answer to their problem had to include peace and security for Israel."[3]

As the Democratic presidential candidate in 1991, Clinton challenged incumbent President Bush, who, after his success in the Gulf War in Iraq, seemed unbeatable, especially when the media spotlighted Clinton's twelve-year extra-marital affair, his draft evasion during the Vietnam War, and an experiment with marijuana at Oxford. Hillary stuck with him and he pressed on, campaigning vigorously, focusing on the

---

[2] Ibid., 294.
[3] Ibid., 353–54.

failing economy, gaining twenty-three pounds, and losing his voice – but winning the election.

He even outdid his hero JFK, who chose the best and the brightest Jews for his administration, by appointing more Jews than any other US president before or since. Among them were Madeleine Albright (who discovered to her surprise that she had Jewish grandparents); Robert Rubin, secretary of the Treasury; Alan Greenspan, chairman of the Federal Reserve Bank; Robert Reich, labor secretary; Richard Holbrooke, assistant secretary of state for European Affairs and chief negotiator or the Balkan conflict; Sandy Berger, head of the National Security Council; Rahm Emanuel, director of political affairs; Dennis Ross, special envoy to the Middle East; Martin Indyk, assistant secretary of state; Dan Glickman, secretary of agriculture; Bernie Nausbaum, White House counsel; Stuart Eizenstat, undersecretary of commerce and US ambassador to the European Union; and Ira Magaziner, another friend from Oxford, senior adviser on policy development.

On September 9, 1993, Israeli prime minister Yitzhak Rabin phoned about secret talks in Oslo, Norway, in which Israel and the PLO had agreed to sign the Oslo Declaration of Principles, intended to reconcile Israel's desire for peace and security with the Palestinians' desire for a national home. Under the agreement, Israel gave the Palestinians responsibility for health, education, welfare, taxation, and tourism in the West Bank. They would have self-rule, first in Gaza and Jericho, and negotiations would follow for self-rule in the rest of the territories. The Israel Defense Forces would leave heavily populated places in the territories, and Israelis living in the West Bank and Gaza would be allowed to stay under Israeli protection. After the agreement had been in force three years the future of Jerusalem would be negotiated.

With the PLO agreeing to renounce violence and to recognize Israel's right to exist, a provisional peace agreement was to be signed on the White House lawn, on the desk used by Begin and Sadat to sign the 1978 peace treaty between Israel and Egypt.

The Bible was never far from Clinton's thoughts or reach when dealing with matters of life or death. Unable to sleep the night before he was to meet Arafat and Rabin, he leafed through the Bible, and happened to turn to the book of Joshua. This inspired him "to rewrite some of my remarks and to wear a blue tie with golden horns, which reminded me of those Joshua used to blow down the walls of Jericho. Now the horns would herald the coming of peace that would return Jericho to the Palestinians."[4]

As he wrote in his autobiography, Clinton was impressed by Rabin, "even before meeting him in 1992, but that day, watching him speak at the ceremony and listening to his argument for peace, I had seen the greatness of his leadership and his spirit. I had never met anyone quite like him, and I was determined to help him achieve his dream of peace."[5] Afterwards, at Clinton's private dinner with Rabin, the Israeli leader said that he now believed that the territories Israel had occupied since 1967 were not needed for his country's security and in fact made it less secure.

But the Oslo agreement did not lead to peace, and for the next seven years Clinton devoted much time and energy to end the violence and reconcile the conflicting dreams of both peoples. On what he called "a mission inspired by a dream of peace," Clinton visited Sadat's tomb in Cairo on October 26, 1994; flew to Aqaba for the signing of the Israel-Jordan peace treaty, for which President Bush had laid the way; then he left for Israel to address the Knesset. There, he explained US policy: "Our role in war has been to help you defend yourself. That is what you have asked. Now that you have taken the

---

[4]   Ibid., 542.
[5]   Ibid., 679.

road to peace, our role is to help you to minimize the risks of peace."[6]

Early in 1995, Edgar Bronfman Sr., president of the World Jewish Congress, encouraged Clinton to investigate the mystery of the "Nazi gold," which the Nazis were rumored to have stolen from Jews and hidden in Swiss banks during World War II. Clinton chose Stuart Eizenstat, US ambassador to the European Union, to undertake the investigation. Over the next several years the talented and tenacious investigator battled with fiercely resistant representatives of European countries and Swiss banks. At first they denied their guilt, then reluctantly admitted the truth, but understated how much looted gold they possessed. Eizenstat eventually retrieved several billion dollars for Holocaust victims and their families, many of them Americans, as well as compensation for Jews and non-Jews forced to work in Nazi slave-labor camps.

Clinton's efforts were recognized in a White House ceremony in the Fall of 1995, when Rabin, before returning to Israel, presented him with the United Jewish Appeal's Isaiah award. Ten days later, on November 4, after addressing a pro-peace rally in Tel Aviv, as Rabin was getting into his car, a young Jewish law student opposed to giving land for peace, killed him with two bullets in the back.

Clinton was grief-stricken. As he wrote in his autobiography, "Rabin and I had developed an unusually close relationship, marked by candor, trust, and an extraordinary understanding of each other's political problems, and thought processes. We had become friends in that unique way people do when they are in a struggle that they believe is great and good. With every encounter I came to respect and care for him more. By the time he was killed, I had come to love him as I had rarely loved another man."

---

[6] Ibid.

He and Hillary, with former presidents Bush and Carter, attended Rabin's funeral on Mount Herzl, where Clinton said, "Look at the leaders from all over the Middle East and the world who have journeyed here today for Yitzhak Rabin and peace. Now it falls to us who love peace and all of us who loved him, to carry on the struggle to which he gave life and for which he gave his life."[7]

Shimon Peres succeeded Rabin and brought Clinton promising news at their first meeting: before the imminent Israeli elections, Israel planned to hand over to the Palestinians Gaza, Jericho, several other major cities, and 450 West Bank villages, and to release one thousand Palestinian prisoners.[8]

The following spring, Hezbollah terrorists were firing rockets into Israel from Southern Lebanon. Israel responded by launching a ground and air attack on Lebanon. At month's end, Peres and Clinton signed an anti-terrorism agreement that included $50 million for joint efforts to reduce Israel's vulnerability to suicide bombings.

The following year at the start of Clinton's second term, the Israelis replaced Peres with hard-liner Benjamin Netanyahu, who hit back at persistent Lebanese terrorists with Operation Grapes of Wrath. When the two met in mid-February, 1997, Clinton realized that Netanyahu's and Rabin's problems were identical: "to give up something concrete – land, access, jobs, an airport – for something far less tangible."[9] Clinton also discussed the situation with Arafat, who resented what he saw as his having to end all violence and then wait for Netanyahu to honor his commitments.

During his exhaustive attempts to bring peace to the Middle East, Clinton was being questioned about his affair with Monica Lewinsky, a Jewish-American White House

---

[7]   Horowitz, *Shalom Friend*, 255–56; Clinton, *My Life*, 679.

[8]   Clinton, *My Life*, 689.

[9]   Ibid., 747.

intern. Ashamed and embarrassed, he denied it. On January 20, 1998, while the FBI was interrogating Lewinsky, Clinton and Netanyahu began to discuss plans for a phased Israeli withdrawal from parts of the West Bank and Gaza, if Israel could be confident that peace and security would follow.[10]

The next day, Arafat arrived at the White House, and Clinton told him of Netanyahu's withdrawal plans and asked him to make a serious attempt to prevent terrorist attacks. Arafat ridiculed Netanyahu's proposals as "peanuts," threatened a possible "explosion of violence," and demanded a large initial withdrawal of Israelis from the disputed territories. Disappointed, Clinton said, "I don't accept what Netanyahu is offering, but I also can't accept what you are demanding."[11]

Clinton survived the Lewinsky scandal, the threat of impeachment, was forgiven by his wife, and returned to the political fray.

On Israel's fiftieth birthday, April 30, 1998, Clinton cabled Netanyahu: "Faced with daunting challenges, but rich with spirit and determination, the Israeli people have created a vibrant democracy, made unprecedented advances in education and technology, built a prosperous economy, and concluded peace agreements with some of its neighbors (Jordan and Egypt).... We are proud of the strong bond we have forged with Israel.... Together, we can make real the vision of an Israel at peace with her neighbors, sharing with them genuine, lasting security and prosperity. Mazel Tov."[12]

Although Arafat and Netanyahu had publicly expressed tough positions for a final peace treaty, Clinton hoped to bring them together at a meeting at Wye River Plantation, Maryland, in October 1998. Netanyahu brought his foreign minister,

---

[10] William J. Clinton Presidential Library, White House's Virtual Library, http://www.clintonlibrary.gov/links.html.

[11] Clinton, *My Life*, 815.

[12] Jewish Virtual Library.

Ariel Sharon, with him. Sharon was the most hard-line of the Likud ministers and had called the provisional 1993 peace agreement national suicide for Israel. Clinton advised Netanyahu to offer Arafat land, the opening of Gaza airport, a safe route between Gaza and the West Bank, and a port in Gaza, so that Arafat would be in a stronger position to fight terror. He again asked Arafat to increase his efforts in fighting terror, and to get the Palestinian National Council to delete from its charter the section calling for Israel's destruction.

But Arafat was reluctant to comply, afraid that because Palestinians throughout the world were eligible to vote on such a proposal, and would vote against it, this would jeopardize his leadership role.

Jordan's King Hussein, who was being treated for cancer at the Mayo Clinic, appeared briefly at the Wye negotiations, where he said that the differences between the Palestinians and Israelis were trivial when weighed against the fruits of peace. Arafat hardly agreed, demanding that Israel free one thousand of its Palestinian prisoners. Netanyahu was willing to free five hundred, but only if Arafat "took care of a certain prominent Palestinian," and arrested thirty "killers" of Jews (a terrorist leader and thirty Palestinians identified as having murdered Israelis in terror attacks). Arafat asked how he was supposed to "take care" of the Palestinian: "Just execute him?" When Netanyahu replied, "I won't ask, you won't tell," Clinton seemed infuriated by this apparent allusion to his controversial gays in the military policy. He got up from the table and walked out, yelling, "This is outrageous! This is despicable! This is just chicken shit! I am not going to put up with this kind of bullshit!"[13]

He returned after almost an hour. Then, by working all through the rest of the night they reached a partial agreement:

---

[13] Madeleine Albright, *Madam Secretary: A Memoir* (New York: Mirimax Books, 2005), 315–16.

Palestinians would get more land on the West Bank, a seaport and airport in Gaza, safe passage between the West Bank and Gaza, and – at Albright's compromise suggestion – the release of 750 prisoners, and economic assistance. Israel would get greatly improved cooperation in preventing terror attacks – Palestinians would jail those Israel identified as the source of violence and terror attacks – the goal of destroying Israel would be removed from the Palestinian charter, and final status talks would soon begin.

After Arafat and Netanyahu signed the promising agreement, King Hussein told Clinton that he had been friends with nine American presidents, "but on the subject of peace... never – with all the affection I have for your predecessors – have I known someone with your dedication, clear-headedness, focus and determination."[14] At one session Clinton had worked forty hours straight without sleep.

Albright saw the agreement as a way station along the road of a comprehensive peace between the Israelis and Palestinians."[15]

When Clinton and Hillary flew to Israel in December 1998, he said that he would be requesting Congress to approve $1.2 billion for Israel's security needs. The next day he went to Gaza, cut a ribbon at its new airport, and was about to address a Palestinian National Council meeting, when most delegates stood and raised their hands in support of removing the destroy-Israel provision in their charter. But the charter remained intact.

Five months later, the Israelis voted Netanyahu out of office and Labor leader Ehud Barak, Israel's most decorated soldier, took his place. That November, on the fourth anniversary of Rabin's murder, Norway's prime minister hoped to help the peace process through a conference in Oslo. Clinton

---

[14] Clinton, *My Life*, 819.

[15] Albright, *Madam Secretary*, 318.

joined Arafat, Barak, Peres, and Rabin's widow, Leah, there and left feeling that Arafat and Barak would agree to a final peace plan by the year 2000. With that high hope, on January 3, 2000, Clinton arrived in Shepherdstown, West Virginia, to launch peace talks between Syria and Israel. Barak was willing to return the captured Golan Heights to Syria, even though some eighteen thousand Israelis were living there, but only if Israel could maintain early-warning equipment on the Heights to prevent surprise Syrian attacks. Clinton assured Barak that he would sign a security agreement with Israel. But at the crunch, Barak hesitated, having learned that many Israelis, especially recent Russian immigrants, were adamantly opposed to giving up the Golan Heights. Consequently, he decided to wait until he had more public support. So, those talks failed.[16]

Clinton next tried to end the Israeli-Palestinian conflict with a summit at Camp David in July 2000, where Arafat stated his terms for peace: most of the West Bank and Gaza, complete sovereignty over the Temple Mount and East Jerusalem, except for the Jewish neighborhoods, and the right of Palestinian refugees to return to Israel. Taking their relatives and children into account there might be some four million of them.

After conferring with Barak, Clinton told Arafat that he could probably get 91 percent of the West Bank, a swap of land near the West Bank and Gaza, a Palestinian capital in East Jerusalem, sovereignty over the Muslim and Christian quarters of the Old City, planning, zoning and law-enforcement authority over the eastern part of the rest of Jerusalem, and custodianship over the Temple Mount. Because Arafat insisted on sovereignty over all East Jerusalem, including the Temple

---

[16] Clinton, *My Life*, 819.

Mount, Clinton believed that the PLO leader was afraid to make any compromises: it was all or nothing.

At 3 a.m. on the fourteenth day of the talks, Clinton asked Arafat if he would accept "effective control" rather than "sovereignty" over the Temple Mount and all East Jerusalem, with "full sovereignty" of East Jerusalem's outer neighborhoods, "limited sovereignty" over the inner ones, and "custodial" sovereignty of Haran. Arafat said no. Both sides essentially agreed over how Jerusalem's affairs should be handled, but split over who would have sovereignty. Arafat wanted to continue the negotiations, but still gave no indication that he was ready to compromise. And that was the end of Camp David.

Clinton and his Middle East adviser, Dennis Ross, eventually wrote of Barak's generous offer that Arafat rejected. But Palestinians and their supporters have a different version of events, especially exactly what the offer entailed. It didn't help that during the negotiations, a Jordanian soldier had gone berserk and killed seven Israeli schoolgirls on a field trip near the border with Israel. King Hussein immediately went to Israel and apologized. That diffused the tension, but violence again erupted when Israel decided to build new housing in an Israeli settlement on the edge of East Jerusalem.[17]

After Arafat left the talks, an exasperated Clinton blamed him for the failure of the negotiations, and when interviewed by Israel TV on July 27, 2000, he said: "I would hope that any President would honor America's historic commitment to Israel, and our decades of involvement in the Middle East and our attempt to be fair to the people of the region, including the Palestinians. I don't know if anybody else will ever put the time in on this that I have, and have the kind of personal, almost religious conviction I have about it."

---

[17] The White House, Office of the Press Secretary, http://www.clintonlibrary.gov/links.html.

Asked how the Israeli and Palestinian leaders had been able to resist his charm and fail to come to an agreement, Clinton replied, "I'm afraid my charm and reasoning abilities cannot compare with the thousands of years of history that go to the core and the identity of the Israelis and Palestinians as regards Jerusalem."

Ten weeks before his presidency ended, Clinton again met Arafat in the Oval Office and said that he had done everything he could to "get the Palestinians a state on the West Bank and Gaza while protecting the security of Israel." Clinton believed that "after all my efforts, if Arafat wasn't going to make peace, he owed it to me to tell me, so that I could go to North Korea to end another serious security threat." Arafat pleaded with him to stay, saying that if they didn't achieve a peace treaty now it would be at least five years before there was another opportunity. Clinton was anxious to go to North Korea to get it to end its long-range missile program and so couldn't postpone his trip to re-engage with Arafat.[18]

But on his return, two days after the November presidential election (after which the US Supreme Court was to choose Republican George W. Bush as the next president, rather than Clinton's vice president, Al Gore), Clinton did speak with Arafat in the White house. "I've got ten weeks left in office," Clinton said, "and want to use that time to produce a comprehensive agreement, a historical agreement, a real reconciliation. I want you to have your own state. I know the complexity of the issues, but I think you can do it. I want to know from you, Chairman Arafat, if you are with me. Can you commit yourself to me in this endeavor?" Arafat replied, "I count on you, Mr. President. I think we can do it together, and we will follow any move you want to take."[19]

---

[18] Clinton, *My Life*, 929.

[19] Albright, *Madam Secretary*, 496.

On December 20, the last-chance talks began between Israeli and Palestinian negotiators at Bolling Airforce Base. Three days later the talks were going nowhere, so Clinton called Arafat and Barak to his Cabinet Room and presented them with his own nonnegotiable "parameters" for advancing the discussion. He gave them five days to accept. If either refused, then the negotiations were over. To make sure that there was no misunderstanding, Clinton slowly read out his nonnegotiable parameters. He recommended that 94 to 96 percent of the West Bank should go to the Palestinians, with a land swap from Israel of 1 to 3 percent. The land kept by Israel would include 80 percent of the settlements. Israeli forces should withdraw over three years while an international force gradually took over. A small Israeli force should stay in the Jordan Valley for an additional three years, under the control of an international force.

This force would patrol the borders and deter terrorist attacks. The Israelis would keep their early-warning system in the West Bank with a Palestinian liaison present. If there was an imminent and demonstrable threat to Israel's security, a system would be in place for emergency deployments in the West Bank.

Although the new Palestinian state would lack an army, it would have a strong security force, sovereignty over its air space, with allowances made for Israel's training, and operational needs. As for Jerusalem, the Palestinians should control the Muslim and Christian neighborhoods (East Jerusalem and parts of the Old City), with sovereignty over the Temple Mount and Haran.

For their part, the Israelis would control Jerusalem's Jewish and Armenian neighborhoods, with sovereignty over the Western Wall and the holy areas, of which it is a part, with no excavations allowed around the wall or under the Temple Mount without mutual consent. Palestinian refugees displaced by the 1948 war and since would have the new Palestinian state as their homeland, while the possibility should be kept open that Israel might accept some of them, depending on its laws. Special attention should be given to the Palestinian refugees living in Lebanon. There should be an international effort to compensate refugees and help them find homes in their new state, as well as in their present homes, in other countries willing to accept them, or in Israel.

Clinton's final point was that if the agreement was accepted it must clearly mark both the end of conflict and all violence. And he proposed a new UN Security Council resolution to accept this peace agreement, together with the final release of Israel's Palestinian prisoners.

When Arafat asked for clarifications, Clinton suspected he was simply playing for time and phoned the Egyptian leader, Mubarak, and read him the "parameters" for peace. Mubarak praised them as historic and promised to urge Arafat to accept them.[20]

On December 27, 2000, Barak's cabinet endorsed the parameters, with reservations, all of which were within the parameters and consequently subject to negotiation. Clinton was elated with the news that in exchange for peace, Israel had agreed to accept a Palestinian state in about 97 percent of the West Bank and all of Gaza. Meanwhile, he had been phoning several Arab leaders urging them to persuade Arafat to accept the deal. All agreed that it was fair.

Not hearing from Arafat, Clinton invited him to the White House on January 2, but to the president's bitter disappointment, Arafat now wanted to change the parameters so that the Palestinians would have fifty feet of the Western Wall. But Clinton insisted that, for security reasons, the entire wall must be in Israel.[21]

---

[20] Clinton, *My Life*, 936–37.
[21] Ibid., 943.

Arafat was also reluctant to give up the right of Palestinian refugees to return to Israel. Clinton pointed out that Israel had agreed to take some from Lebanon, but would never agree to the unrestricted return of Palestinian refugees because, judging by their high birthrate, they would soon outnumber Jews, making the Jews a minority in their own country.

Clinton believed that Arafat insisting on the refugees' right of return to Israel was the deal breaker. Secretary of State Albright thought that the Palestinians had rejected the best peace offer they'd ever get. Or, as she put it, "They wouldn't yield a dime to make a dollar."[22] Just before Clinton left office, Arafat thanked him for his hard work and called him a great man. "I am not a great man," the angry, disappointed, and frustrated Clinton replied. "I am a failure, and you have made me one."[23]

In his autobiography, Clinton concluded that "Arafat's rejection of my proposal after Barak had accepted it was an error of historic proportions. Some believe that when there is a peace treaty it will look a lot "like the proposals that came out of Camp David and the six long months that followed."[24]

Palestinian-Arab author Said K. Aburish agrees with Clinton. In his biography of Arafat, he called him the master of double-talk, for whom the end justified the means, and whose "descent into dictatorial ways has created a Palestine Authority which suppresses the Palestinian people and does not represent their aspirations."[25]

---

[22] Albright, *Madam Secretary*, 497.

[23] Ibid., 944.

[24] Ibid., 944–45.

[25] Said K. Aburish, *Arafat: From Defender to Dictator* (London: Bloomsbury, 1998), 524.

Madeleine Albright believed that Arafat's interest in his own survival explained his reluctance to cooperate, his fear that "if he said yes, he would be killed."[26]

The conventional wisdom is that in working for a secure and peaceful Israel, Clinton took on an impossible task, since Arafat never wanted peace and he was unlikely to play a significant role in a peaceful Palestinian state, a view also held by former CIA director George Tenet, who took part in the negotiations with Arafat.

Even while out of office for more than ten years, former president Clinton continued to pursue his role as a Middle East peace broker. At the World Economic Forum in Davos, Switzerland, in 2011, Clinton noted that the Arab world was in turmoil after the revolutions in Tunisia and Egypt, and urged Israel to make peace with the Arabs, because the Jewish state would never have a better partner than the present Palestinian leadership, and because both sides wanted it. He said, "If I were in Israel and had any influence I'd want to make the deal now."[27]

---

[26] Albright, *Madam Secretary*, 497.

[27] *Jerusalem Post*, January 28, 2011.

George Walker Bush

1946–

- ⚬ Forty-third president, 2001–2009
- ⚬ Son of President George H. W. Bush and governor of Texas
- ⚬ With twenty other allied nations, he launched the war on Iraq that deposed Saddam Hussein

When *Washington Post* reporter Bob Woodward asked President George W. Bush if he sought his father's advice before invading Iraq, he replied, "You know he is the wrong father to appeal to in terms of strength. There is a higher father that I appeal to."[1]

Years before, in 1983, when George's father was president, he had visited his parents in the White House. In his daily Bible reading he had come across the passage in the New Testament which said that only Christians went to heaven, and in discussing religion with his mother, Barbara, he mentioned the Christians-only reference. She couldn't believe it, but, to make sure, phoned her spiritual adviser, Billy Graham. The

---

[1] Bob Woodward, *Plan of Attack* (New York: Simon and Schuster, 2004), 421.

evangelist agreed that George had quoted the Bible accurately, but cautioned them, "Don't play God. Who are you two to play God?" That same year, campaigning to be Texas governor, the subject of his religion came up, and he repeated to *Austin American-Statesman* reporter Ed Herman the conversation about heaven with his mother, adding that the lesson he had learned was to listen to the New Testament but not to be harshly judgmental.[2]

When Bush was governor of Texas and about to visit Israel with his wife and several other governors, a trip sponsored by the National Jewish Coalition, the same reporter asked what he would say to Israeli Jews about who gets to heaven. Bush wisecracked that he'd tell them they were all going to hell. This aroused the ire of Abraham Foxman, president of the Anti-Defamation League, who failed to see the joke and asked Bush to clarify his views.

"I am troubled that some people were hurt by my remarks," he replied. "I never intended to make judgments about the faith of others. Judgments about heaven do not belong in the realm of politics or this world; they belong to a Higher Authority. In discussing my own personal faith as a Christian, I in no way meant to imply any disrespect or denigrate any other religion. During my four years as governor, I have set a positive tone that indicates my respect for individuals from all faiths, all backgrounds, and all walks of life." Foxman welcomed his reply and called the matter closed.[3]

Bush's belief that Jews are unlikely to join him in heaven did not deter them from joining his administration. His ambassador to Israel, Daniel Kurzer, was a Jew, so were his ambassadors to Denmark, Hungary, Italy, Singapore, Slovakia, and Uruguay, respectively, Stuart Bernstein, Nancy Brinker,

---

[2] Eric Fingerhut, "Bush Clarifies His Stand on Jews, Heaven," *Jewish World Review*, December 29, 1998.

[3] Ibid.

Mel Semble, Frank Lavin, Ron Weiser, and Martin Silverstein. His White House press secretary, Ari Fleischer, is an Orthodox Jew.

Being a Republican and Evangelical Christian, it was a safe bet that he would be strongly pro-Israel. He was. Some even rate him a more fervent supporter than any previous president, though it would be hard to top Truman, LBJ, or Clinton.

Born in New Haven, Connecticut, on July 6, 1946, a year after the end of World War II, George was the first of five children. He was an enthusiastic baseball player at his high school, Phillips Academy, where he was also head cheerleader in his senior year. He followed his father to Yale, as his father had followed his, graduating in 1968 with a BA in history. Like his father, he became a member of the secret society Skull and Bones. Though a mediocre student, he played on Yale's top Rugby team.

During the Vietnam War, he served as a lieutenant in the Texas Air National Guard, flying Convair F-102s. Following an honorable discharge from the Air Force Reserve on November 21, 1974, he graduated from Harvard Business School, then joined his father's oil business.

For years he had been a heavy drinker and the life of the party, and on September 4, 1976, the police arrested thirty-year-old Bush for driving under the influence. He pleaded guilty, was fined $150, and had his driving license suspended for two years. During that time, at a backyard barbecue, he met and fell for Laura Welch, an attractive librarian and school teacher. She accepted his marriage proposal three months later, and he left his Episcopal Church to join her Methodist Church in Midland, Texas.

The next year, following his father and grandfather into politics, he ran for the US House of Representatives, but failed to be elected. Still he was doing well in his business career, having started his own oil company, Bush Exploration, which merged with Spectrum 7 in 1984. That year the Bushes' twin daughters, Barbara and Jenna, were born.

Encouraged by his wife and fortified by his faith, in 1986 Bush quit drinking, worked on his father's presidential campaign, and in 1988 moved with his family from Texas to Washington, DC.

After his father's election, he again showed his business acumen by becoming co-owner of the Texas Rangers baseball team, whose games he often attended.

In December 1990, he went on an all-expenses-paid Mediterranean cruise in return for giving a lecture about his baseball team. Among the other passengers were hundreds of the world's leading economists, politicians, and academics. Israel's Shimon Peres spoke on the Middle East and was impressed by two fellow lecturers. As he recalled, one was Simeon of Saxe-Coburg-Gotha, Bulgaria's exiled king, who was later elected its prime minister. "The other lecturer was a charming Texan who told his audience how he had bought and managed a Texas baseball team. His name was George W. Bush." The economists among the passengers would surely have been interested to know that Bush bought his share of the Rangers for $800,000, and sold it five years later for $15 million.[4]

The new multimillionaire again felt the pull of politics and in 1994 defeated popular Democratic incumbent Anne Richard in a no-holds-barred fight to become the forty-sixth governor of Texas; he was reelected four years later with 69 percent of the vote, the first Texas governor to be elected for two consecutive terms. Among the bills he signed was one allowing Texans to carry concealed weapons. He increased

---

[4]   Michael Bar-Zohar, *Shimon Peres: The Biography* (New York: Random House, 2007), 422–23.

funding to teach the dangers of alcohol and drugs, and raised teachers' salaries, which resulted in improved students' test scores. He also signed a memorandum proclaiming June 10 "Jesus Day" – when Texans were asked to help the needy.

During the previously mentioned trip to Israel with his wife and fellow governors, he saw the West Bank and Golan Heights from a helicopter. His tour guide, Foreign Minister Ariel Sharon, impressed Bush with his "marvelous sense of history." In his bird's-eye view of the area he was astonished at how tiny Israel was compared to its Arab neighbors. Sharon showed him that before the Six-Day War, at its narrowest point, Israel was just nine miles wide. When they landed on the Golan Heights Bush realized what a rich prize it was for the security of people in northern Israel. He "saw democracy firsthand in Israel," and in Jerusalem he prayed at the Western Wall. Afterwards, he and his wife dined with Benjamin Netanyahu, and then watched the Knesset in action.[5]

Back in the United States, his reelection as governor and contacts with foreign leaders gave him the confidence to run for the White House. As a presidential candidate addressing an AIPAC conference in May 2000, he called America and Israel "brothers and sisters in the family of democracy," and reminded his listeners:

> While the distance between Dallas and Galveston is 270 miles, the distance between Israel and Saddam Hussein's Iraq is only 250 miles. As the world learned to its horror back in 1991 [during Desert Storm], those 250 miles can be crossed in a matter of 12 minutes by a Scud missile.... Who could forget the sight of millions of Israelis wearing gas masks to protect themselves in case those Scud missiles were carrying chemical weapons.... Saddam's attacks were the act of a tyrant without mercy.... My advice is to keep speaking, keep

---

[5] Michael Abramowitz, *Washington Post*, January 19, 2008.

working, keep fighting for your principles. This nation, the land of Israel, the Middle East and the world are better for it.

Having won the presidential election, Bush welcomed Ariel Sharon to the White House on March 20, 2001, where the Israeli prime minister spoke of the frequent terrorist attacks on Israelis, the most recent the fatal drive-by shooting of a father of six. When Sharon suggested that Palestinian terrorists should be removed from society, Bush's response, according to one witness, was, "You need not elaborate."[6]

Soon after, at the UN, Bush announced his support for a two-state solution – an Israeli and a Palestinian state. Sharon welcomed US help as "a mediator or honest broker," but pointed out that to reach a final settlement "the two parties themselves would have to resolve their problems."[7]

On May 3, Bush told American Jewish Committee members that his government would "stand up for our friends in the world. And one of our most important friends is the State of Israel.... At the first meeting of my National Security Council, I told them a top foreign policy priority is the safety and security of Israel. My administration will be steadfast in supporting Israel against terrorism and violence, and in seeking the peace for which all Israelis pray."

Not if Arafat had his way. After the failure of Clinton's Camp David peace negotiations, Arafat had threatened to continue the five-month-old uprising "until we see the Palestinian flag on the wall of Jerusalem."[8]

Aware of how Arafat had disappointed Clinton, Bush did not invite the Palestinian leader to the White House and

6 Israel Ministry of Foreign Affairs.
7 Anita Miller, Jordan Miller, and Sigalit Zetouni, *Sharon: Israel's Warrior-Politician* (Chicago: Academy Chicago Publishers and Olive Publishing, 2002), 421.
8 Ibid., 365.

rejected an effort to arrange an informal handshake with him while they were both in the UN building.

Before the end of May 2001, Sharon announced a unilateral cease-fire and ordered Israeli troops only to fire their weapons if their lives were in danger. He then told the Palestinians, "Peace will only be achieved through talks. Stop the violence and accept us as a serious and responsible partner for reaching peace."[9] Bush phoned him the next day to say that he'd "welcome a similar statement from the Palestinians."[10]

Instead, on the morning of May 25, a member of Hamas drove his truckload of explosives toward an Israeli army post in Gaza. Soldiers fired at the truck, blowing it up and killing its driver. They found a videotape among the debris, in which the terrorist had recorded his intention to kill Israelis. That same afternoon, two Palestinians drove their explosive-laden car into a crowded bus in the coastal town of Hadera, blowing themselves up and injuring sixty-three Israelis. Uncharacteristically, Sharon did not retaliate.

On September 11, 2001, Saudi Arabian terrorists flying hijacked American passenger planes destroyed Manhattan's World Trade Center, killing 2,973 people and injuring over 6,000. In a simultaneous attack on the Pentagon they killed 55 military personnel and 70 civilians, and injured 106.

Stepped-up terrorist attacks in Israel drove the Israeli cabinet to declare Arafat no longer relevant. Bush also lost the little faith he had in Arafat as a partner for peace after January 3, 2002, when Israeli commandos seized a Palestine Authority–owned freighter in the Red Sea with over fifty tons of Iranian- and Russian-made weapons, including rockets intended to arm Palestinian terrorists.

Consequently, on June 24, 2002, in presenting his new plan for Middle East peace to be achieved within three years,

---

[9]   Ibid., 423.
[10] Ibid., 426.

Bush called for a new Palestinian leadership. His plan required the Israelis to stop settlement activity in the West Bank and Gaza, and as the violence subsided, Israel should give peaceful Palestinians freedom of movement, free the frozen tax revenues owed to the Palestinians, and see that it got into the right hands. Then Israel would be expected to support a viable and credible provisional Palestinian state and, after improved security, to withdraw to positions held before September 2000. Eventually, after the question of Jerusalem and the future of Palestinian refugees had been resolved, the Israelis would withdraw to secure and recognized borders.

For their part, the Palestinians had to create a democracy based on tolerance and liberty, with a free market system, a new constitution that separated the powers of government, and a new legal system that punished both terrorists and criminals. They had to elect new leaders not tainted by terrorism, which, of course, meant getting rid of Arafat. Lebanon and Syria would also have to renounce terrorism.[11]

The Quartet, consisting of the United Nations, Russia, the United States, and the European Union, endorsed Bush's Middle East peace plan.

In November 2002, Bush warned members of Congress that although the war on terrorism was going well, "the biggest threat is Saddam Hussein and his weapons of mass destruction. He can blow up Israel and that would trigger an International conflict."[12] Misled by the CIA and several European intelligence agencies, themselves duped by unreliable sources, Bush believed that Saddam had weapons of mass destruction. And three weeks before the allied invasion of Iraq, he told Holocaust survivor Elie Wiesel, "If we don't disarm

---

[11] Jewish Virtual Library, and John Podhoretz, *Bush Country: How Douba Became a Great President While Driving Liberals Insane* (New York: St. Martin's Press, 2004), 211–15.

[12] Woodward, *Plan of Attack*, 186.

Saddam Hussein, he will put a weapon of mass destruction on Israel and they will do what they think they have to do [presumably retaliate] and we have to avoid that."[13]

The war against Saddam's regime, known as the Gulf War or the Second Iraq War, began with a massive bombing of Baghdad on March 19, followed by a ground attack led by the United States with a coalition of British, Australian, Danish, Polish, and Spanish forces, later joined by contingents from thirty-six other countries.

The war officially ended on May 1, 2003, when the Iraqi army surrendered and the occupation began. The cost to the United States was 4,439 soldiers killed and 32,633 seriously injured.

After hunting for Saddam Hussein for eight months, American troops of the 44th Infantry found the man who built fifty-five palaces as his legacy hiding in a hole in the ground. After a lengthy trial, his countrymen hanged him.

With Iraq no longer an immediate threat to Israel, on June 4, 2003, Bush, ever the optimist, hoped to advance the elusive Middle East peace process. He joined Jordan's King Abdullah, Palestinian Authority Prime Minister Abbas, and Prime Minister Ariel Sharon in Jordan, where he said, "In Iraq, a dictator who funded terror and sowed conflict has been removed, and a more just and democratic society is emerging." He praised Abbas for moving toward creating a democratic state, and Sharon for his "pledge to improve the humanitarian situation in the Palestinian areas and to begin removing unauthorized Jewish outposts immediately.... Both prime ministers here agree that progress towards peace also requires an end to violence and the elimination of all forms of hatred and prejudice and official incitement, in schoolbooks, in broadcasts, and in the words used by political leaders."[14]

---

[13] Ibid., 320.

[14] June 4, 2003. Jordanian Embassy, Washington.

During his presidential reelection campaign, in the summer of 2004, Bush told members of AIPAC's Policy Conference:

> Followers of the terrorist ideology executed an elderly man in a wheelchair, Leon Klinghoffer, and pushed his body off a ship into the sea. They kidnapped journalist Daniel Pearl and cut his throat, because he was a Jew. The enemy...have declared war on the civilized world – and war is what they got.... For the sake of peace and security we have ended the regime of Saddam Hussein...Iraq now has an independent judiciary, a free market, a new currency, more than 200 newspapers in circulation, and schools free of hateful propaganda.... I supported the plan announced by Prime Minister Sharon to withdraw military installations and settlements from Gaza and parts of the West Bank. It is a bold, courageous step, that can bring us closer to the goal of two states, Israel and Palestine, living side by side, in peace and security.... Anti-Semitism is not a problem of the past: the hatred of the Jews did not die in a Berlin bunker [with Hitler's suicide]. In its cruder forms it can be found in some Arab media, and this government will call upon Arab governments to end libels and incitements.... The demonization of Israel, the most extreme anti-Zionist rhetoric, can be a flimsy cover for anti-Semitism, and contribute to an atmosphere of fear in which synagogues are desecrated, people are slandered, folks are threatened. I will continue to call upon our friends in Europe to renounce and fight any sign of anti-Semitism in their midst."[15]

Despite frequent enthusiastic applause from the AIPAC members, in his reelection campaign Bush won only 24 percent of the Jewish vote, while his Democratic opponent, John Kerry, got 76 percent. Still, Bush won the election.

---

[15] Bush's address to AIPAC, May 16, 2004, http://www.jewishvirtuallibrary.org/jsource/US-Israel/bushaipac2004.html.

In the fall of 2004, Arafat was rushed to a Paris hospital in a coma and died soon after, on November 11. French doctors who treated him could not determine what caused his death.

The following year, in August 2005, Sharon ordered Israeli soldiers to remove 9,480 Israeli settlers from Gaza and from four West-Bank settlements, some by force. The fate of Gaza was now in the hands of its Palestinian inhabitants – who, in their first election, voted Hamas into power, the terrorist group dedicated to Israel's destruction.

Ariel Sharon suffered a stroke on January 4, 2006, and was put in an induced coma in a hospital, where he remains. His deputy, Ehud Olmert, who replaced him, had known Bush since 1998 when Olmert was Jerusalem's mayor and Bush was governor of Texas. The two met in the White House on May 22 and recalled Sharon's contributions to peace. Olmert returned home to a desperate situation. Hezbollah terrorists in Lebanon had launched an anti-tank missile attack on Israeli soldiers in two autos patrolling the Israeli side of the border. They killed five Israelis and wounded several. The terrorists took the bodies of two men to Lebanon. Not knowing they were dead, five more Israeli soldiers died in a rescue attempt.

Olmert ordered a massive reprisal attack on the Hezbollah forces in southern Lebanon. Fierce fighting went on for thirty-four days with Israel using tanks and planes, destroying much of southern Lebanon.

The UN brokered a ceasefire, and the decimated Hezbollah forces claimed victory. Bush disagreed, saying at a press conference on August 21, 2006: "The Hezbollah suffered a defeat in this crisis." To ensure the peace held, he approved the UN decision to provide an international force of peacekeepers as a buffer between southern Lebanon and northern Israel. He blamed the arming of Hezbollah by Iran and Syria for causing civilian Lebanese war. He had no doubt that Iran's goal was "the destruction of Israel":

We can only imagine how much more dangerous this conflict would have been if Iran had the nuclear weapon it seeks.... What's very interesting about the violence in Lebanon and the violence in Iraq and the violence in Gaza is this: These are all groups of terrorists who are trying to stop the advance of democracy. They're trying to thwart the will of the millions who simply want a normal, hopeful life.... After the Hezbollah launched its rocket attacks on Israel, I said this is a clarifying moment. It's a chance for the world to see the threats of the 21st century, the challenge we face.[16]

During their White House conversation on June 19, 2007, Bush assured Israel's new prime minister Olmert of his commitment to maintaining Israel's military superiority in the Middle East, and said that he was working on a ten-year agreement with Israel proposed during Sharon's previous visit.

In the waning days of his presidency, early in January 2008, Bush flew to the Middle East, where he met Israeli and Palestinian leaders in Jerusalem and Ramallah. On his return, although his quest for peace still eluded him, he remained optimistic, speculating that there could be a Palestinian state by year's end. During his last State of the Union address on January 28, 2008, he portrayed America as "standing against the forces of extremism in the Holy Land, where we have new cause for hope. Palestinians [in the West Bank] have elected a president [Abbas] who recognizes that confronting terror is essential to achieving a state where his people can live in dignity and peace with Israel. Israelis have leaders who recognize that a peaceful, democratic Palestinian state will be a source of lasting security."[17]

Bush traveled to Israel with his wife to celebrate the country's sixtieth birthday on Thursday, May 15, 2008, when he

---

[16] Bush White House press conference, August 21, 2006.

[17] Robert Malley, *New York Review of Books*, June 25, 2006, 83.

told the Knesset that his one regret was that Sharon, "one of Israel's greatest leaders is not here to share this moment.... America is proud to be Israel's closest ally and best friend in the world.... Israel's population may be just over seven million, but when you confront terror and evil, you are 307 million strong, because the United States of America stands with you."

The history major then recalled a historic moment on the eve of Israel's independence:

> The last British soldiers departing Jerusalem stopped at an old building in the Jewish Quarter of the Old City. An officer knocked on the door and met a senior rabbi. The officer presented him with a short iron bar – the key to the Zion gate – and said it was the first time in eighteen centuries that a key to the gates of Jerusalem had belonged to a Jew. His hands trembling, the rabbi offered a prayer of thanks to God, "Who had granted us life and permitted us to reach this day." Then, he turned to the officer and uttered the words Jews had awaited so long: "I accept this key in the name of my people."

After the speech, Knesset members remarked that Bush seemed to be more of a Zionist than their own prime minister, Olmert, and that Bush seemed to be the one person who would achieve Zionist aspirations.[18]

With Iran's apparent plan to build nuclear weapons and its threats to wipe Israel off the map, Bush approved an Israeli plan – if diplomacy failed – to attack Iran's nuclear missile sites. According to London's *Sunday Times*, a senior Pentagon official stated in the summer of 2008: "It's really all down to the Israelis. The [Bush] administration will not attack Iran. This has already been decided. But the president is really

---

[18] Jewish United Fund News, May 15, 2008, www.juf.org/news/default.aspx.

preoccupied with the nuclear threat against Israel, and I know he doesn't believe that anything but force will deter Iran."[19]

George W. Bush ranks high on the list of American presidents who gave ardent and effective support to Israel.

He was succeeded by a Democrat, Barack Hussein Obama, America's first African-American president, and the first to be born in Hawaii.

---

[19] John Little, "President Bush Backs Israeli Plan for Strike on Iran," *Sunday Times*, Timesonline, London, July 13, 2008, http://www.timesonline.co.uk./tol/news/world/.

Barack Hussein Obama

1961–

- ✪ Forty-fourth president, 2009–
- ✪ First African American US president
- ✪ Ordered the successful killing of terrorist leader Osama bin Laden and played a leading role in overthrowing Libyan dictator Muammar Gaddafi

Barack Hussein Obama had been president for seven months by July 2009, when a *Jerusalem Post* poll showed that only 6 percent of Israeli Jews regarded his administration as pro-Israel. Yet 78 percent of Jewish Americans had voted for him to be president, and many of his White House staff and advisers were pro-Israel Jews. Why the big difference? Many Israelis resented his administration's opposition to their building for natural growth in settlement blocs, and its refusal to differentiate policies regarding construction in unauthorized outposts, settlement blocs close to the Green Line, and Jerusalem's suburbs.[1]

---

[1] Gil Hoffman, "Post Poll: Obama Still in Single Digits," *Jerusalem Post*, July 19, 2009, http://www.jpost.com/Israel/Article.aspx?id=171849.

Yet many Jewish Americans backed him because he had been a consistent supporter of Israel during his entire political career. In the Illinois state senate he co-sponsored a bill authorizing Illinois to invest in Israel bonds. As a US senator for Illinois, he always voted in favor of foreign aid to Israel. He was the lead sponsor of an act urging President George W. Bush to persuade Palestinian leaders to bar terrorist groups from voting in Palestinian elections. He pressured the European Union to add Hezbollah to its list of terrorist groups, and called for the US to support Israel in the UN Security Council. He voted for fully funding defense aid for Israel, including Arrow missiles. He also voted for the US-Israel Energy Act and against recognizing Hamas until it recognized Israel. And Obama approved Israel destroying a probable Syrian nuclear reactor under construction. He believed Jerusalem should be Israel's capital pending its final status, and, during the 2006 Israel-Lebanon War, he supported Israel's right to defend itself against Hezbollah's rockets.[2]

America's first African American president had an unconventional and conflicted childhood. At a time when marriage between whites and blacks was illegal in twenty-two states, he was the son of a white Christian mother – Ann Dunham, a teenager from Kansas, with Midwestern values – and a black Kenyan father, also Barack, a charismatic, self-assured, highly intelligent agnostic. His parents met as fellow students in a basic Russian-language course at the University of Hawaii, and married when his father was twenty-three and his mother was eighteen. Ann didn't yet know it, but her husband was already married to another woman in Kenya and had a son by her.

Barack Hussein Obama was born at Hawaii's Kapolani Medical Center on August 4, 1961. Barack Obama Sr. left

---

[2] On the Issues and Jews for Obama, www.ontheissues.org/.

them to get a Harvard degree in economics before returning to his native Kenya, where he fathered two more children by his first wife. When Ann discovered she had been married to and deserted by a bigamist, she divorced him in 1964.

The single mother and her two-year-old son lived with her parents in Honolulu, where her mother, the family's money-maker, was vice president of a local bank, while her father, a former furniture salesman, tried to sell life insurance. Soon after her divorce, Ann married an Indonesian student also at the University of Hawaii, and in 1967, when Sukarno, Indonesia's military dictator, recalled all Indonesian students living abroad, Obama and his mother went with him to Indonesia. But, as Obama told a reporter, "Other than my name and the fact that I lived in a populous Muslim country for four years when I was a child, I have very little connection to the Islam religion."[3]

For three years Obama attended a Catholic school and in his fourth he studied at a secular government-run school, while his mother taught English to Indonesian businessmen at the American embassy. Her encouragement spurred his ambition: he told a teacher he wanted to become president in order to make everyone happy, but did not say of which country. He returned to Hawaii when he was about seven to continue his studies in America while living with his maternal grandparents.

He was ten when he last saw his father, who was making a month-long and final visit to Hawaii in 1971. Obama told schoolmates that his African grandfather was like a king, and his father the prince of a tribe of battling warriors, and that he might take over some day, but only after his father settled the feuds and recovered from a serious car crash. In fact he had been in a car crash, but despite his injuries he

---

[3] Associated Press, February 29, 2008.

was high-spirited and resilient, charming everyone with his cultured British accent, deep, resonant voice, and striking good looks. Obama's proudest memory of that visit was when classmates enthusiastically applauded his father's account of newly independent Kenya free from British rule.

About that time, Obama's mother also arrived back in Hawaii with her daughter – his half-sister, Maya – fathered by her Indonesian husband, whom she eventually divorced. The three of them shared a small apartment. Obama attended the prestigious Puhahou, a college preparatory school in Hawaii, and worked in his free time at a Baskin-Robbins Ice Cream store while his mother studied for her Masters degree in anthropology.

Obama tells in his memoir, *Dreams From My Father, A Story of Race and Inheritance*, that after three years in Hawaii, his mother was about to return to Indonesia for field work. When she suggested that he go with her and Maya in order to attend the international school there, "I immediately said no.... I had arrived at an unspoken pact with my grandparents: I could live with them and they'd leave me alone so long as I kept my troubles out of sight."[4]

Obama's grandfather, a Christian who favored the inclusive Unitarians, taught him that confidence was the secret of success. His grandfather also occasionally wrote poetry, "listened to jazz, and counted a number of Jews he'd met in the furniture business as his closest friends."[5]

As a teenager, conflicted by the reactions of others to his multi-racial heritage and depressed by his father's absence, he used alcohol, marijuana, and cocaine. He now considers this his greatest moral failure, and says he overcame it after his teenage years.

---

[4] Barack Obama, *Dreams From My Father: A Story of Race and Inheritance* (New York: Crown, 2004), 75.

[5] Ibid., 17.

After preparatory school, Obama studied at Occidental College in Los Angeles, and in 1981 at Manhattan's Columbia University, majoring in political science and specializing in international studies. After a year at Columbia, twenty-one-year-old Obama was making breakfast in his cramped apartment when his Aunt Jane phoned from Kenya to say his father was dead.[6]

Graduating from Columbia with a BA in 1985, he worked as a research assistant for a multinational company, then for consumer advocate Ralph Nader in Harlem, trying to persuade City College's minority students of the importance of recycling.

Because he missed his father, he sometimes conjured him up in his dreams as a loving but mysterious presence. In 1988, he had saved enough cash to make his first trip to Kenya, hoping to learn more about the real man. There he discovered that his father had been a polygamist (which is permissible under Islam), with four wives and at least eight children.

In his memoir Obama does not mention his father's tragic end. But it was unearthed by a *London Daily Mail* reporter, who revealed that Obama Sr. had accused Kenyan president Jomo Kenyatta's administration of corruption and nepotism. In response, Kenyatta had fired him from his influential government job and seized his passport, making him a prisoner in his own country. Without prospects and facing poverty, he disintegrated into an alcoholic and caused several drunk-driving crashes, once killing another driver. In a later crash he broke both legs, which eventually were amputated. Even so, he was about to marry a woman pregnant with his eighth child, when he died in another drunk-driving episode at age forty-six.[7]

---

[6] Ibid., 5.

[7] Sharon Churcher, "A Drunk and a Bigot," *London Daily Mail*, January 27, 2007, http://www.dailymail.co.uk/home/index.html.

Obama "is haunted by his father's failure," said a family friend. "He grew up thinking of his father as a brilliant intellectual and a pioneer of African independence, only to learn that in Western terms he was basically a drunken lecher."[8] Obama's cousin, Said Hussein Obama, told a reporter: "We have assured Barack that his father was a loving person, but it was difficult for him to reconcile with his father's drinking and simultaneous marriages."[9]

Before leaving Kenya, Obama sat beside his father's grave and wept.

His mother, who had returned to America from Indonesia, told her disillusioned son to remember the positive qualities he had inherited from his father. He decided to follow her advice by becoming a community organizer and activist, concerned with the welfare of the underprivileged. To prepare for this he studied at Harvard Law School, where in his second year eighty fellow law students elected him the first African American editor of the *Harvard Law Review* – because he was extremely bright, wrote well, and was fair to those with differing views.

In his summer vacations he worked at the law firm of Sidley and Austin in Chicago where, in 1989, he met and dated his future wife, Michelle Robinson, an attorney of considerable promise.

In 1991, thirty-year-old Obama graduated from Harvard Law School with a JD *magna cum laude* and began to work as a community organizer on Chicago's south side. Two fellow organizers were Jewish, and he was attacked for associating with them. "So," as he recalled, "I've been in the foxhole with Jewish friends."[10]

---

8   Sally Jacobs, "A Father's Charm, Absence," *Boston Globe*, September 21, 2008.

9   Churcher, "A Drunk and a Bigot."

10 Jeffrey Goldberg, "Obama on Zionism and Hamas," *Atlantic Monthly*, May 12, 2008, http://www.theatlantic.com/international/archive/2008/05/obama-on-zionism-and-hamas/8318.

Michelle left the Chicago law firm in 1992 to be executive director of a non-profit organization, and she and Obama were married by the controversial clergyman Jeremiah Wright. For the next twelve years Obama worked as a civil rights attorney, taught constitutional law at the University of Chicago Law School, and served three terms in the Illinois senate from 1997 to 2004, when voters sent him to the US Senate. During those years he and Michelle had two daughters, Malia and Sasha.

On his first trip to Israel in 2006, as a US senator, he visited residents of the beleaguered southern town of Sderot, who had been terrorized by more than a thousand rockets Hamas had fired from Gaza. Eventually the Israelis retaliated by an attack on Gaza. Much of the world deplored Israel's military response to the terrorist attacks, but not Obama. While in Sderot, he said, "If somebody was sending rockets into my house where my two daughters sleep at night, I'm going to do everything in my power to stop that. And I would expect Israelis to do the same thing."[11]

During Obama's presidential campaign in the summer of 2008, Jeffrey Goldberg of the *Atlantic Monthly* asked him what he thought of Zionism. He said that a young Jewish American camp counselor who had been to Israel had shaped his views when he was a child in the sixth grade:

> He shared with me the idea of returning to a homeland and what that meant for people who had suffered from the Holocaust, and he talked about the idea of preserving a culture, when people had been uprooted with the view of eventually returning home. There was something so powerful and compelling for me, maybe because I was a kid who never entirely felt like he was rooted. That was part of my upbringing, to be

---

[11] Roni Sofer, "Obama Visits Sderot, Warns of Nuclear Iran," Ynet News, July 23, 2008, http://www.ynetnews.com/articles/0,7340,L-3572036,00.html.

traveling and always having a sense of values and culture but wanting a place. So that is my first memory of thinking of Israel. And that was mixed with a great affinity for social justice that was embodied in the earliest Zionist movement.[12]

Running against Republican Senator John McCain for the US presidency in 2008, Obama's performance in their debates raised his credibility. Speaking to a mostly Jewish audience in Cleveland, Ohio, in February 2008, Obama said:

> Here's my starting orientation: Israel's security is sacrosanct. Point number two is that the status quo, I believe, is unsustainable over time. So we're going to have to make a shift from the current deadlock that we're in. Number three: For it to remain a Jewish state, any negotiated peace between the Israelis and Palestinians is going to involve Palestinians relinquishing the right of return as it has been understood in the past. It also means they will have to figure out how do we work with a legitimate Palestinian government to create a Palestinian state that is sustainable. When Israel launched its counterattack against Hezbollah in Lebanon during the summer of 2006, I was in South Africa...and I was asked by the press what did I think? And I said, if somebody invades my country, or is firing rockets into my country, or kidnapping my soldiers, I will not tolerate that. And there's no nation in the world that would.[13]

In the presidential election, Obama won 78 percent of the Jewish vote. He backed up his pro-Jewish and pro-Israel rhetoric by being the first US president to host a Seder in the White House for his Jewish friends and staff (in both 2009 and 2010).

---

[12] Jeffrey Goldberg, *Atlantic Monthly*, May 12, 2008.

[13] *New York Sun*, February 25, 2008, http://www.nysun.com/national/.

He appointed many Jews to his staff, among them David Axelrod, senior adviser; Rahm Emanuel, chief of staff; Lee Feinstein, foreign policy adviser; Elena Kagan, solicitor general of the United States (later his approved choice for the US Supreme Court); Jack Lew, deputy secretary of state; Eric Lynn, Middle East policy adviser; Dennis Ross, special adviser for the Gulf and South East Asia; Mara Rodman, foreign policy adviser; Dan Shapiro, head of the Middle East Desk at the National Security Council; James B. Steinberg, deputy secretary of state; and Lawrence Summers, director of the National Economic Council. Even more telling was his choice of Joe Biden, who had publicly proclaimed that he was a Zionist, as his vice president.

At a joint press conference on May 19, 2009, after White House discussions with Prime Minster Netanyahu, who called their meeting "extraordinarily friendly and constructive," Obama said, "When it comes to my policies towards Israel and the Middle East...Israel's security is paramount and I repeated that to Prime Minister Netanyahu." They had also discussed the danger of Iran's "potential pursuit of a nuclear weapon," and had "an extensive discussion about the possibilities of restarting serious negotiations on the issue of Israel and the Palestinians."

Netanyahu responded by calling Obama "a great leader of the United States, a great leader of the world, a great friend of Israel, and someone who is acutely cognizant of our security concerns.... I share with you very much the desire to move the peace process forward. I want to start the peace negotiations with the Palestinians immediately [and] to broaden the circle of peace to include others in the Arab world."[14]

---

[14] White House Oval Office, May 18, 2009, Office of the Press Secretary.

In the summer of 2009, when Obama gave a much-anticipated speech in Cairo, the *New York Times* published the responses of several Mideast experts:

David Newman of Ben-Gurion University in Beersheba: "President Obama is putting Israel and the Muslim world on the spot. He is telling them all that it is time to implement all their declarations and do something practical instead of continuing to play verbal one-upmanship."

David Kuttab, a Palestinian journalist and former Princeton University professor of journalism, saw Obama as accepting "the international consensus by declaring settlement in the Palestinian territories 'Illegitimate.' A major shift in US foreign policy. 'The US does not accept the legitimacy of continued Israeli settlements,' he told the cheering Egyptian attendees."

David Gordiss, author of *Saving Israel: How the Jewish People Can Win a War That May Never End*, believed that "President Obama assumed positions virtually identical to those of Israel's political center – namely that the Palestinians must renounce violence and recognize Israel's right to exist, while Israel must cease settlement building and permit a Palestinian state to arise. Benjamin Netanyahu's problem is that it's difficult to distinguish between President Obama and Tzipi Livni. And in Israel's recent elections, Livni and her Kadima Party won more votes than anyone else."[15]

After Israel's twenty-two-day incursion into Gaza in January 2009, a UN fact-finding mission submitted what is known as the Goldstone Report and concluded that Israelis had committed war crimes by deliberately targeting civilians. The Obama administration considered the Goldstone Report flawed, because among other things it had failed to mention that Hamas had provoked the war by firing thousands of rockets

---

[15] The Editors, *New York Times*, Opinion Pages, June 4, 2009, http://roomfordebate. blogs.nytimes.com/2009/06/04/what-obama-said-what-the-mideast-heard/.

from Gaza into Israel. Obama himself had seen some of the damage caused by those rockets when he had visited Israel. His UN ambassador, Susan Rice, called the Goldstone Report "unbalanced, one-sided, and basically unacceptable." Another thing the report failed to mention was that before their attack, the Israelis had dropped thousands of leaflets from the air and made thousands of phone calls to warn Gaza's civilians where the attacks would take place.

On November 3, 2009, the US House of Representatives supported Obama, voting 344 to 36 to condemn the Goldstone Report. Then, Dr. Goldstone himself retracted the charge against Israel. In an op-ed piece published in the *Washington Post* of April 1, 2011, he conceded that he had been mistaken and that it was not Israeli policy to target civilians.[16]

Soon after the initial Goldstone Report, Obama had invited Netanyahu to the White House where he reaffirmed America's strong commitment to Israel's security and discussed joint security measures, the problem of Iran, and how to energize the Middle East peace process.

Obama won the Nobel Peace Prize in 2009 for his words rather than his deeds, which he acknowledged.

Buoyed by having helped to stop the Irish from killing each other, Obama's optimistic Middle East envoy George Mitchell predicted a peace treaty between the Israelis and the Palestinians within two years.[17]

In March 2010, the PLO authorized their leader, President Mahmoud Abbas, to restart indirect peace negotiations with Israel for four months, dropping a previous precondition that Israel must stop building settlements. That same month,

---

[16] JTA, September 23, 2009, http://www.jta.org/news/article/2009/09/23/1008097/us-pledges-to-quash-goldstone; Richard Goldstone, "Reconsidering the Goldstone Report on Israel and War Crimes," *Washington Post*, April 2, 2011, op-ed, http://www.washingtonpost.com/opinions/ reconsidering-the-goldstone-report-on-Israel-and-war-crimes/2011/04/01/AFg111JC//2011/04/01/AFg111JC_seory.html.

[17] *The Jerusalem Post*, January, 2010, http://www.jpost.com/.

an AIPAC Policy Conference gave Obama's secretary of state, Hillary Clinton, a standing ovation when she said: "For President Obama, for me, and for his entire administration, our commitment to Israel's security and Israel's future is rock solid, unwavering, and forever."[18]

However, when Israeli prime minister Netanyahu received a frigid reception at the White House – because he refused to agree to freeze settlement building – Obama's critics charged that rather than living up to his pro-Israel statements he was trying to improve US ties with the Arab world.

The critics were half right. He was trying to improve US-Arab relations, but not at the expense of the Jewish state. This was made clear after the May 31, 2010, Israeli attack on an aid flotilla trying to break the blockade of Gaza. Despite the subsequent international anti-Israel outcry and attempt in the United Nations to censure Israel, Obama sided with Israel.

Martin Indyk, formerly Bill Clinton's ambassador to Israel and now vice president and director of foreign policy at Brookings Institution, an independent Washington think tank, said that "Obama embraces the core policy of his predecessors Clinton and George W. Bush: the US will give Israel unwavering diplomatic and military support even as tensions test their relationship."[19]

A *Jerusalem Post* poll, taken in March 2010, had shown that 9 percent of Israelis believed that Obama was pro-Israel, and 48 percent that he was pro-Palestinian. A *Haaretz*-Dialog poll taken that same month showed that 56 percent of Israelis do not believe that Obama is anti-Semitic or hostile to Israel, nor that he is "striving to topple Netanyahu." A large majority considered him "fair and friendly." The *Jerusalem Post* is a

[18] United States State Department. http://www.state.gov/secretary/rm/2010/03/138722.htm.

[19] Nicole Gaouette, "Obama's Israel Policy Showing No Difference with Clinton-Bush," *Businessweek*, June 14, 2010.

right-leaning newspaper and *Haaretz* leans to the left, which might explain the discrepancies.

A CNN poll taken between March 19 and 21, 2010, showed that 39 percent of Americans see Israel as an ally, 41 percent as friendly but not an ally, 12 percent as unfriendly, and 5 percent as an enemy.

At a White House press conference on July 6, 2010, Netanyahu characterized reports of the ties between Israel and the United States being damaged as "just dead wrong." Obama stressed "unwavering" American support for Israel, and both spoke of their mutual desire for the Israelis and Palestinians to have face-to-face peace negotiations. To enhance its support for Israel, the US is helping to develop "David's Sling," a defense system to counter medium-range rockets, and Obama has asked Congress for $205 million to provide another defense system known as "Iron Dome."[20]

In response to revolutions in Tunisia, Egypt, and Libya, and attempts to overthrow the governments in Yemen and Syria, in February 2011 President Obama ordered a complete review of America's Middle East policy "that emphasizes political and economic reforms to bolster US allies now threatened by the protest movement sweeping the region."[21]

And during his reelection campaign in July 2012, Obama cited the "ruthless" and deadly attack by a suicide bomber who killed five and injured more than thirty Israeli tourists in Bulgaria, and the upheaval in Syria, as reasons to fortify support for Israel.[22]

One outcome of the turmoil is predictable: Israel will remain the one truly democratic country by Western standards in the Middle East. And, if history does repeat itself, it will remain the only consistently loyal US ally in the area.

---

[20] White House press conference.

[21] Peter Nicholas and Paul Richter, *Los Angeles Times*, February 25, 2011.

[22] Reuters, July 19, 2012.

Bibliography

Aburish, Said A. *Arafat: From Defender to Dictator.* London: Bloomsbury, 1998.

Adams, Charles Francis, ed. *Works of John Adams.* Boston: Little, Brown, 1854.

Adams, John Quincy. *Diary.* Massachusetts Historical Society.

Adler, Cyrus, and Aaron Margaith, *With Firmness in the Right: American Intervention on Behalf of the United States; Diplomatic Actions Affecting Jews, 1840–1945.* New York: The American Jewish Committee, 1946.

Albright, Madeleine. *Madam Secretary: A Memoir.* New York: Miramax, 2003.

Alteras, Isaac. *Eisenhower and Israel: US-Israel Relations, 1953–1960.* Gainsville, FL: University of Florida, 2003.

Ambrose, Stephen. *Eisenhower: Soldier and President.* New York: Simon & Schuster, 1990.

American Heritage Book of Presidents and Famous Americans. New York: Dell, 1987.

Angle, Paul M., ed. *The Lincoln Reader.* New Brunswick, NJ: Rutgers University Press, 1947.

Baker, James A. III, with Steve Fiffer. *"Work Hard, Study...And Keep Out of Politics!" Adventures and Lessons from an Unexpected Public Life.* New York: Putnam, 2006.

Baker, John H. *James Buchanan.* New York: Times Books, 2004.

Baldwin, Neil. *Henry Ford and the Jews: The Mass Production of Hate.* New York: Public Affairs, 2001.

Barber, James D. *The Presidential Character: Predicting Performance in the White House*. Upper Saddle River, NJ: Prentice Hall, 1972.

Bar-Zohar, Michael. *Ben-Gurion*. Ramat Gan, Israel: Zemora-Bitan, 1987.

———. *Shimon Peres: The Biography*. New York: Random House, 2007.

Basler, Roy P. *The Collected Works of Abraham Lincoln*. New Brunswick, NJ: Rutgers University Press, 1955.

Bass, Warren. *Support Any Friend: Kennedy's Middle East and the Making of the US-Israel Alliance*. New York: Oxford University Press, 2003.

Begin, Menachem. *The Revolt*. New York: Nash, 1977.

Bein, Alex. *Theodore Herzl: A Biography*. New York: World, 1962.

Ben-Ami, Yitshaq. *Years of Wrath; Days of Glory*. New York: Robert Speller & Sons, 1982.

Ben-Gurion, David. *Israel: A Personal History*. New York: Funk & Wagnalls, 1971.

Benson, Michael T. *Truman and the Founding of Israel*. Westport, CN: Praeger, 1997.

Blackstone, William M. *Palestine for the Jews*. New York: Arno, 1997.

Blitzer, Wolf. *Between Washington and Jerusalem: A Reporter's Notebook*. New York: Oxford University Press, 1985.

Brian, Denis. *Pulitzer: A Life*. New York: Wiley, 1985.

———. *The Seven Lives of Colonel Patterson: How an Irish Lion Hunter Led the Jewish Legion to Victory*. Syracuse, NY: Syracuse University Press, 2008.

Bundy, McGeorge. *Danger and Survival*. New York: Vintage, 1990.

Burleigh, Anne Husted. *John Adams: Man of Braintree.* Piscataway, NJ: Transaction, 2009.

Burns, James MacGregor. *Roosevelt: The Soldier or Freedom, 1940–1945.* New York: Harcourt Brace Jovanovich, 1970.

Bush, George. *All the Best: My Life in Letters and Other Writings.* New York: Scribner 1999.

Butterfield, L. H., ed. *Diary and Autobiography of John Adams.* Cambridge, MA: Harvard University Press, 1962.

Cannon, James. *Time and Courage: Gerald Ford's Appointment with History.* New York: HarperCollins, 1994.

Carter, Jimmy. *The Blood of Abraham.* Boston: Houghton Mifflin, 1985.

———. *Keeping Faith: Memoirs of a President.* New York: Bantam, 1982.

———. *Palestine: Peace Not Apartheid.* New York: Simon & Schuster, 2006.

———. *We Can Have Peace in the Holy Land: A Plan That Will Work.* New York: Simon & Schuster, 2009.

Charnwood, Lord. *Abraham Lincoln.* New York: Henry Holt, 1917.

Clifford, Clark, with Richard Holbrook. *Counsel to the President: A Memoir.* New York: Random House, 1991.

Clinton, Bill. *My Life.* New York: Knopf, 2004.

Cohen, Naomi W. *Jacob H. Schiff: A Study in American Jewish Leadership.* Hanover and London: Brandeis University Press, 1999.

The Collected Works of Abraham Lincoln. New Brunswick, NJ: Lincoln Association, 1933.

Crum, Bartley. *Behind the Silken Curtain: A Personal Account of Anglo-American Diplomacy.* New York: Simon & Schuster, 1947.

Davis, Moshe, ed. *With Eyes Towards Zion: Scholars Colloquium America-Holy Land Studies*. New York: Arno Press, 1977.

Dimont, Max I. *The Jews of America: The Roots History and Destiny of the Jews of America*. New York: Simon & Schuster, 1978.

Downes, Randolph C. *The Rise of Warren Gamaliel Harding, 1885–1920*. Columbus, OH: Ohio State University Press, 1970.

Druks, Herbert M. *John F. Kennedy and Israel*. Westport, CN: Praeger, 2005.

Durant, John and Alice. *Pictorial History of American Presidents*. New York: A. S. Barnes, 1955.

Dye, Ira. *Uriah Levy: Reformer of the Antebellum Navy*. Gainsville, FL: University Press of Florida, 2006.

Eban, Abba. *An Autobiography*. New York: Random House, 1977.

———. *Personal Witness: Israel through My Eyes*. New York: Putnam, 1992.

Dayan, Moshe. *Story of My Life: An Autobiography*. New York: Warner Books, 1977.

Eisenhower, Dwight D. *Crusade in Europe*. Garden City, NY: Permabooks, 1952.

———. *The Papers of Dwight David Eisenhower*. March 8, 1956. Edited by Louis Galambos and Daun van Ee. Baltimore, MD: John Hopkins University Press, 1996.

Evans, Eli N. *Judah P. Benjamin: The Jewish Confederate*. New York: The Free Press, 1988.

Ferrell, Robert H. *Off the Record: The Private Papers of Harry S. Truman*. Columbia, MO: University of Missouri Press, 1997.

Frankel, Jonathon. *The Damascus Affair*. New York: Cambridge University Press, 1977.

Garment, Leonard. *Crazy Rhythm*. New York: Times Books, 1997.

Gilbert, Martin. *Churchill and the Jews: A Lifelong Friendship*. New York: Holt, 2008.

Golden, Peter. *Quiet Diplomat: A Biography of Max Fisher*. New York: Cornwall Books, 1982.

Goodwin, Doris Kearns. *No Ordinary Time: Franklin and Eleanor Roosevelt, the Home Front in World War II*. New York: Simon & Schuster, 1994.

Hart, Gary. *James Buchanan*. New York: Times Books, 2005.

Heckscher, August. *Woodrow Wilson: A Biography*. New York: Scribner's, 1991.

Hersh, Seymour M. *The Dark Side of Camelot*. Boston: Back Bay Books, 1998.

———. *The Price of Power: Kissinger in the Nixon White House*. New York: Summit, 1993.

———. *The Samson Option: Israel's Nuclear Arsenal and America's Foreign Policy*. New York: Random House, 1991.

Hertzberg, Arthur. *The Jews in America*. New York: Columbia University Press, 1998.

Herzog, Chaim. *The Arab-Israeli Wars: War and Peace in the Middle East*. New York: Random House, 1982.

Hoover, Herbert. *Memoirs of Herbert Hoover: Years of Adventure, 1874–1920*. New York: Hollis and Carter, 1932.

Hoover, Herbert and Hugh Gibson. *The Problems of Lasting Peace*. New York: Doubleday Doran Company, 1942.

Horowitz, David, ed., and the *Jerusalem Report* staff. *Shalom, Friend: The Life and Legacy of Yitzhak Rabin*. New York: Newmarket Press, 1990.

Hudson, James H. *The Founders on Religion*. Princeton, NJ: Princeton University Press, 2007.

Humes, James C. *Confessions of a White House Ghostwriter: Five Presidents and Other Political Ventures.* Washington, DC: Regnery, 1996.

Hyamson, Albert M. *Palestine: The Rebirth of an Ancient People.* New York: Knopf, 1917.

Indyk, Martin. *Innocent Abroad: An Intimate Account of American Peace Diplomacy in the Middle East.* New York: Simon & Schuster, 2009.

Jefferson's Works. Vol. 4. Library of Congress.

Johnson, Lyndon Baines. *The Vantage Point: Perspectives of the Presidency, 1963–1969.* New York: Holt, Rinehart & Winston, 1971.

Karp, Abraham J. *From the Ends of the Earth: Judaic Treasures of the Library of Congress.* New York: Rizzoli, 1991.

Kessler, Ronald. *Sins of the Father: Joseph P. Kennedy and the Dynasty He Founded.* New York: Warner Books, 1996.

Kissinger, Henry. *Years of Upheaval.* Boston: Little, Brown, 1979.

Kleeman, Rita Halle. *Gracious Lady: The Life of Sara Delano Roosevelt.* New York: D. Appleton Century, 1935.

Klein, Philip S. *President James Buchanan: A Biography.* University Park, PA: Pennsylvania State University Press, 1962.

Kurzman, Dan. *Ben-Gurion: Prophet of Fire.* New York: Simon & Schuster, 1983.

Leech, Margaret. *In the Days of McKinley.* New York: Harper and Brothers, 1999.

Lengel, Edward. *General George Washington: A Military Life.* New York: Random House, 2007.

Lipset, Seymour Martin. *American Exceptionalism: A Double-Edged Sword.* New York: W.W. Norton, 1997.

Markus, David. *Abraham Lincoln and the Jews.* Self-published, 1909.

y, Bernard, ed. *Jefferson Himself*. Boston: Houghton Mifflin, 1942.

McCullough, David. *Truman*. New York: Simon & Schuster, 1992.

Meir, Golda. *My Life*. New York: Putnam, 1975.

Meisler, Stanley. *United Nations: The First Fifty Years*. New York: Atlantic Monthly Press, 1997.

Miller, Anita, Jordan Miller, and Sigalit Zetouni. *Sharon: Israel's Warrior-Politician*. Chicago: Academy Chicago Publishers, 2002.

Miller, Merle. *Plain Speaking: An Oral Biography of Harry S. Truman*. New York: Berkley, 1977.

Morris, Edmund. *Dutch: A Memoir of Ronald Reagan*. New York: Random House, 1999.

———. *Theodore Rex*. New York: Random House, 2001.

Netanyahu, Benjamin. *A Place among the Nations: Israel and the World*. New York: Bantam, 1993.

Nixon, Richard. *The Memoirs of Richard Nixon*. New York: Grosset & Dunlap, 1978.

———. *1999: Victory without War*. New York: Simon & Schuster, 1998.

Noah, Mordecai. *Discourses on the Restoration of the Jews*. New York: Harper & Brothers, 1845.

Obama, Barack M. *Dreams from My Father: A Story of Race and Inheritance*. New York: Crown, 2004.

O'Brien, Michael. *John F. Kennedy: A Biography*. New York: St. Martin's Press, 2005.

Peres, Shimon. *Battling for Peace: A Memoir*. New York: Random House, 1995.

Peres, Shimon, with Arye Noar. *The New Middle East*. New York: Henry Holt, 1993.

Peres, Shimon, with David Landau. *Ben-Gurion: A Political Life*. New York: Schocken, 2011.

Podhoretz, John. *Bush Country: How Dubya Became a Great President While Driving Liberals Insane*. New York: St. Martin's Press, 2004.

Powell, Colin, with Joseph Persico. *My American Journey*. New York: Random House, 1995.

Prittie, Terence. *Eshkol: The Man and the Nation*. New York: Pitman, 1969.

Rabin, Yitzhak. *The Rabin Memoirs*. New York: Marboro, 1979.

Reagan, Ronald. *An American Life*. New York: Simon & Schuster, 1990.

Rigden, John S. *Rabi: Scientist and Citizen*. New York: Basic Books, 1987.

Roosevelt, Theodore. *An Autobiography*. Cambridge, MA: De Capo Press, 2000.

―――. *The Letters of Theodore Roosevelt*. Volume 8. Cambridge, MA: Harvard University Press, 1954.

Roth, Cecil, ed. Standard Jewish Encyclopedia. Garden City, NY: Doubleday, 1959.

Rusk, Dean. *As I Saw It: A Secretary of State's Memoirs*. London: I. B. Tauris, 1991.

Seibert, Jeffrey. *I Done My Duty: The Complete Story of the Assassination of President McKinley*. New York: Heritage Books, 2001.

Sharman, Harold. *The First Rabbi*. Santa Barbara, CA: Pangloss Press, 1907.

Snetsinger, John. *Truman, the Jewish Vote and the Creation of Israel*. Stanford, CA: Hoover Press, 1974.

Simpson, Brooks. *Ulysses S. Grant: Triumph over Adversity, 1822–1885*. New York: Houghton Mifflin, 2000.

Simpson, William. *The Prince: The Secret Story of the World's Most Intriguing Royal; Prince Bandar bin Sultan*. New York: Regan / HarperCollins, 2006.

Sobel, Robert. *Coolidge: An American Enigma*. Washington, DC: Regnery, 1990.

Stadiem, William. *To Rich: The High Life and Tragic Death of King Farouk*. New York: Carroll & Graf, 1991.

Steinberg, Alfred. *The Man from Missouri: The Life and Times of Harry S. Truman*. New York: St. Martin's Press, 1962.

Steiner, Franklin. *Religious Beliefs of the Presidents: From Washington to F.D.R.* Amherst, MA: Prometheus Books, 1996.

Sterling, Colonel Edward W., as told to Thomas Sugrue. *Sterling of the White House*. Chicago: Peoples Book Club, 1946.

Straus, Oscar S. *Under Four Administrations: From Cleveland to Taft*. Cambridge, MA: Houghton Mifflin, 1922.

Strum, Philippa. *Louis D. Brandeis: Justice for the People*. New York: Schocken Books, 1984.

Sulzberger, S. L. *An Age of Mediocrity, Memoirs and Diaries 1963–1972*. New York: Macmillan, 1973.

Summers, Mark. *Rum, Romanism and Rebellion: The Making of a President, 1884*. Chapel Hill, NC: University of North Carolina Press, 2000.

Townsend, Colonel T. W. *Our Martyred President: Memorial Life of President McKinley*. Memorial volume, 1901.

Trials of War Criminals before the Nuremberg Military Tribunals. Volume 12. 1951–1952, Washington, DC: US Government Printing Office,

Truman, Harry S. *Truman Diary*. March 19, 1948. Truman Library. Truman Papers, President's Secretary's Files.

———. *Years of Trial and Hope*. Garden City, NY: Doubleday, 1950.

Truman, Margaret. *Harry S. Truman.* New York: William Morrow, 1972.

Tuchman, Barbara. *The Proud Tower: A Portrait of the World before the War, 1890–1914.* New York: Bantam Books, 1979.

Urolsky, Melvin I., and David W. Levy. *Letters of Louis D. Brandeis.* Norman, OK: University of Oklahoma Press, 2002.

Warner, Jack, with Dean Jennings. *My First Hundred Years in Hollywood.* New York: Random House, 1965.

Weisgal, Meyer W., and Joel Carmichael, eds. *Chaim Weizmann: A Biography by Several Hands.* New York: Atheneum, 1963.

———. *Chaim Weizmann, Statesman and Scientist: Builder of the Jewish Commonwealth.* New York: Dial Press, 1944.

Whitney, David C., and Robin Vaughn Whitney. *The American Presidents.* Garden City, NY: Doubleday, 1973.

Wise, Isaac M. *Reminiscences.* Cincinnati, OH: Leo Wise and Company, 1901.

Wolf, Simon. *The American Jew as Patriot, Soldier and Citizen.* Philadelphia , 1875.

Woodward, Bob. *Plan of Attack.* New York: Simon & Schuster, 2004.

Young, Mel, ed. *Uriah: Uriah Phillips Levy, Captain, USN, and the Naval Court of Inquiry.* Lanham, MD: University Press of America, 2009.

Index

Abbas, Mahmoud, 369, 385
Abdul Hamid II (sultan), 144
Abdullah (king), 369
Abilene, 244
Abraham, 117
Abulafia, Moses, 64
Aburish, K., 359
Adams, Abigail Smith (wife of John), 26, 54
Adams, Henry, 29
Adams, John Quincy, 50, 52, 53–57
Adams, John, 2–3, 19, 26–31, 36, 38, 52, 54
Adams, Louisa Catherine Johnson (wife of John Quincy), 53
Adirondack, the, 161
Agnew, Spiro, 301
Ahlwardt, Hermann, 157–59, 185–86
Ahmadinejad, Mahmoud, 8
Albany, 78
Albright, Madeleine, 310, 347, 353, 359
Alexander II, 124
Alexander III, 143, 144, 145
Alexandria (Egypt), 65
Algeria, 41, 43
Algiers, 42
Allen, Richard, 328
Alpena (MI), 154
Alteras, Isaac, 245–46, 259
Amara, Ibrahim, 62–63, 64

Aqaba, 233, 348
Arabia, 4. *See also* Saudi Arabia
Arafat, Yasser, 11, 304, 348, 350, 351, 352, 353, 354–55, 356, 357–60, 366, 367, 371
Ararat, 55
Argentina, 152
Arizona, 79
Armenia, 166–67
Armistead, Mary, 70
Arnold, Benedict, 22, 23
Arrow, Max, 325
Arthur, Chester A., 127, 130–34, 169
Arthur, Ellen Herndon, 132
Arthur, Malvina, 131
Arthur, William, 131
Assad, Hafez al-, 340
Atlanta, 102, 142, 307
Auschwitz, 219, 305
Austin, 279, 281
Austin, Warren, 234
Australia, 198
Austria, 210, 279
Austria-Hungary, 169

Baghdad, 7, 203, 336
Bahrain, 1
Baker, James, 339
Baldwin, Stanley, 209–10
Baltimore, 35, 72, 90, 102, 332
Bancroft, George, 86

Bandar bin Sultan (prince of
    Saudi Arabia), 11, 332–33
Barak, Ehud, 353, 354, 355,
    356, 357–58, 359
Barbary, 44
Barbour, Walworth, 273, 274
Barboursville (VA), 78
Bard, Mitchell G., 331
Barkley, Alben, 268
Bar-Lev, Simon, 309
Barton, Clara, 134
Baruch, Bernard, 181
Basle, 147, 151
Bass, Warren, 274
Beersheba, 384
Begin, Aliza, 314
Begin, Menachem, 312, 314,
    315–17, 319, 320, 340, 348
Belgium, 144
Belize, 51
Bell, Alexander Graham, 123, 130
Belle Grove Plantation, 40
Belmont, August, 86
Ben Abraham, Michael Boiaz
    Israel. See Cresson, Walter
Ben Eliyahu, Eitan, 14
Ben-Gurion, David, 7, 12,
    248–49, 237, 249, 251, 252,
    254–55, 256, 257, 258, 263,
    265, 268–70, 272, 286
Ben-Horin, Eliahu, 202, 204
Benjamin, Judah P., 82,
    85, 89–90, 101, 106,
    107–8, 109, 110
Berger, Sandy, 347
Berle, Adolf, 213
Berlin, Irving, 252
Bernstein, Herman, 201
Bernstein, Stuart, 362

Bethlehem, 317
Biddle, Anthony Drexel, Jr., 213
Biden, Joe, 13, 383
Birchard, Sardis, 118, 122
Bishop, Robert, 141
Bitburg (W. DE), 330
Blackstone, William, 3,
    143–47, 148, 151
Blaine, James G., 133,
    144, 145, 146–47
Blitzer, Wolf, 330
Blumenberg, Leopold, 102
Blumenthal, Michael, 309
Blythe, William Jef-
    ferson, Jr., 343
Bolling Airforce Base, 356
Booth, John Wilkes, 103–4
Boston, 19, 46, 190,
    192, 263, 345
Braddock, Edward, 18
Bradlee, Ben, 261
Braintree (MA), 26
Brandeis, Louis, 172, 178–81,
    183, 186, 187, 295, 202,
    209, 211, 215–16, 223
Branigar, Thomas, 251
Breckenridge, Clifton, 138
Briggs, Vernon, 154
Brinker, Nancy, 362
Britain, 4, 8, 12, 28, 49, 54,
    109, 144, 177, 199, 215,
    225, 253, 258, 261, 270
Britton, Elizabeth Anne, 185
Britton, Nan, 185
Bronfman, Edgar, Sr., 349
Brown, Harold, 309
Brown, Pat, 327
Brunswick (ME), 84

Bryan, William Jennings, 151, 171, 175
Bryce, James, 166
Buchanan, James, 88–91
Buchanan, James, Sr., 89
Bucharest, 117
Buchenwald, 247
Buffalo, 55, 83, 135, 153
Bulgaria, 144, 387
Bundy, McGeorge, 270
Burns, Arthur, 295, 309
Burns, Robert, 93
Bush, Barbara, 364
Bush, Barbara Pierce (wife of George H. W.), 353, 361
Bush, Dorothy Walker, 333
Bush, George Herbert Walker, 9, 11, 330, 332–42, 346, 348, 350
Bush, George W., 8, 306, 356, 361–74, 376, 386
Bush, Jenna, 364
Bush, Laura Welch (wife of George W.), 363
Bush, Prescott, 333, 334
Butler, Benjamin F., 86
Byron, Lord George Gordon, 93

Cairo, 31, 318, 320, 384
California, 78, 116, 291, 292, 326
Camp David (MD), 315, 321, 354–55
Canada, 8, 46
Cardozo, Benjamin, 202
Carlisle (PA), 89
Carter, Billy, 319
Carter, Earl, Sr., 307

Carter, James, 9, 13, 306, 307–22, 328, 350
Carter, Lilian Gordy, 307
Carter, Rosalynn Smith, 308, 309, 320
Carter, Ruth, 308
Cass, Louis, 79
Cedar Rapids (IA), 300
Chapman, Dr. 88
Charles City (VA), 70
Charles I (king), 29
Charleston (SC), 19, 50, 54, 97
Chaytor, Edmund, 166
Chicago, 21, 116, 143, 227, 380
China, 198, 199, 246, 272, 334
Christ, 2, 33–34, 169, 225, 277, 344
Churchill, Winston, 183, 202–3, 216, 221
Cincinnati, 62, 78, 100, 116, 122, 142, 168, 169
Clarksburg (WV), 120
Clemenceau, Georges, 182
Cleveland, 382
Cleveland, Frances Folsom, 136
Cleveland, Grover, 135–40, 146, 205, 223
Clifford, Clark, 230, 234, 235, 236–37, 282
Clinton, Chelsea, 345
Clinton, Hillary Rodham, 345, 346, 350, 353
Clinton, Roger, 343
Clinton, Roger, Jr., 343
Clinton, Virginia, 343
Clinton, William Jefferson [Blythe], 9, 13, 306, 342, 343–360, 363, 366, 386
Cochrane, Sir Alexander, 45

Cohen, Avner, 266
Coleman, Anne 88
Cologne, 55
Colorado, 79
Columbus, 113, 139
Comte d'Estaing, 22
Concord, 19
Connecticut, 253, 334
Constantinople, 65, 67
Conway, Eleanor Rose, 40
Coolidge, Calvin, 190–96
Coolidge, Calvin, Jr., 193
Coolidge, Grace Goodhue,
    191–92, 193, 196
Coolidge, Victoria, 191
Cortelyou, George, 153
Coughlin, Charles, 10
Cox, James, 182, 187
Cozolgosz, Leon, 153, 154
Craig, Elijah, 40
Crawford, William, 46, 50
Cresson, Walter, 70–71
Crossman, Richard, 5
Crum, Bartley, 6, 229, 233
Cuba, 153, 160
Cyrus (king), 239–40
Czechoslovakia, 237, 238, 262

D'Este, Carlo, 245
Dakota Territory, 156
Damascus, 62, 63–65, 67
Dana, Francis, 53–54
Darrow, Clarence, 175
Davenport (IA), 325
David, Ed, 295
Davis, Jefferson, 82, 85,
    106, 107, 109
Davis, Valma, 85
Davos (CH), 360

Dayan, Moshe, 241, 309
de Camangiano, Tomaso,
    62, 63, 67
de Kalb, Baron, 195
De La Motta, Jacob, 37, 38
de Lafayette, Marquis, 46
de Leon, Jacob, 195
Decatur, Stephen, 42
Dees, Morris, 309
Delano, Sara, 206
Delaware (OH), 118
Dembitz, Lewis, 95
Denison (TX), 244
Denmark, 144, 362
Des Moines, 325
Detroit, 180, 201
Dewey, Thomas, 238
Dickson, Harold Rich-
    ard Patrick, 5, 221
Dimona, 12, 256, 266, 267,
    270, 271, 272, 293
Dineen, Joe, 261
Dixon (IL), 324
Dodd, William, Jr., 206, 207
Dominican Republic, 210–11
Donegal (IE), 88
Douglas, Helen Gahagan, 291
Douglas, Stephen, 95
Drayton, William Henry, 20
Dreyfus, Alfred, 146, 161
Dubois, W.E. B., 175
Duckett, Carl, 287
Dulles, John Foster, 253,
    256, 259, 292
Dunham, Ann, 376
Dunkirk, 227

Eban, Abba, 239, 244,
    281, 284, 287, 293

Eddy, William, 220
Egypt, 1, 7, 12, 65, 302–3,
    252, 257, 264, 268–69,
    270, 272, 281, 283, 296,
    302, 303, 307, 310, 311,
    312, 315–18, 322, 332,
    337, 348, 351, 360, 387
Ehrlichman, John, 290
Eichmann, Adolf, 287
Eilat, 281
Einstein, Albert, 5
Eisenhower, David Jacob, 244
Eisenhower, Dwight David, 8,
    12, 222–23, 228, 243–59,
    264, 267, 269, 272, 278, 292
Eisenhower, Ida, 243–44
Eisenhower, John, 253, 257
Eisenhower, Mamie, 247, 257
Eisenhower, Milton, 251
Eitan, Rafi, 286–87
Eizenstat, Stuart, 309, 347, 348
Elath, Eliahu, 237, 242
Ellis Island, 173
Elting, Howard, Jr., 216
Emanuel, Rahm, 347, 383
Entebbe (UG), 310
Epictetus, 33
Erie County (NY), 135
Eshkol, Levi, 272, 273, 281, 286
Ethiopia, 335, 339
Etting, Reuben, 35
Evarts, William, 123, 124
Evian (FR), 210
Evron, Ephraim, 285
Ezekiel, Jacob 69

Fahd (king), 332, 337
Fairfax, Thomas, 17
Fairfield (VT), 131

Faisal (prince), 232
Fanmich, Wolf, 172–73
Fay, Theodor, 90
Fayette (WV), 98
Fayetteville (AR), 346
Feinstein, Lee, 383
Feldman, Myer, 266, 268, 271
Fielding (DE), 248
Fillmore, Abigail Powers, 81, 83
Fillmore, Caroline McIntosh, 83
Fillmore, Mary, 83
Fillmore, Millard, 81–83, 85
Fillmore, Nathaniel, 81
Fillmore, Phoebe, 81
Finn, James, 67
Fischel, Arnold, 97
Fish, Hamilton, 115
Fisher, Max, 257–58
Fleischer, Ari, 363
Fleming, Arthur, 309
Florida, 109, 274
Folsom, Oscar, 136
Ford, Elizabeth Bloom-
    er Warren, 301
Ford, Gerald Rudolph, 298,
    299–306, 309, 320, 334–35
Ford, Henry, 10, 174–75
Forrestal, James, 235
Forsyth, John, 65
Foster, John, 124
Foxman, Abe, 362
France, 12, 46, 49, 57, 82,
    144, 146, 194, 215, 227,
    253, 258, 262, 286
Francis Joseph (emperor), 144
Frankfurt (DE), 251
Frankfurter, Felix, 182,
    211, 223, 295
Franklin (PA), 89

Franklin, Benjamin, 2, 22, 28
Franklin, Leo, 174
Franks, David, 21–23
Franks, Leo, 277
Fredericksburg (VA), 17, 49
Frelinghuysen, Frederick, 133
Fremont, John, 89
Frieder, Alex, 245, 246
Frieder, Philip, 246
Fry, Varian, 215
Fulbright, William, 344
Fuller, Melville, 144

Galena (IL), 112
Galveston, 280
Garfield, Abram, 126
Garfield, Eliza, 126
Garfield, James A.,
    126–30, 132, 184
Garfield, Lucretia Rudolph, 127
Garment, Leonard, 295
Gates, Robert, 14
Gaza, 1, 13, 15, 252, 317, 347,
    350, 353, 354, 356, 368, 370,
    371, 372, 381, 384–85, 386
Geneva, 134
George (king), 21
Georgia, 50, 109, 308, 309
Germany, 12, 76, 144, 181, 206,
    213, 221, 227, 262, 272,
    279–80, 324
    West, 8
Gettysburg (PA), 102, 257
Gibbons, James (cardinal), 145
Giddon, Jon, 66
Gilbert, Martin, 317
Glass, Alice, 279
Glazer, Simon, 188
Glickman, Dan, 347

Goebbels, Joseph, 212
Golan Heights, 296, 303,
    317, 340, 354
Goldberg, Arthur,
    267, 286, 288
Goldberg, Jeffry, 381
Goldstein, Israel, 252
Goldstone, Richard, 385
Goldwater, Barry, 327
Gompers, Samuel, 190–91
Goodman, A. H., 90
Gorbachev, Mikhail, 330, 340
Gordiss, David, 384
Gore, Al, 356
Gotheil, Gustav, 152
Graham, Billy, 289, 361
Grand Island (NY), 55
Grant, Jesse Root, 111
Grant, Julia Boggs
    Dent, 112, 117
Grant, Ulysses S., 98–99, 102,
    110, 111–17, 123, 184
Greece, 75, 144, 262
Greenspan, Alan, 347
Greenville (East TN), 105
Gregory, Captain, 47
Grynszpan, Herschel, 212
Guiteau, Charles, 129

Habib, Philip, 328
Haifa, 12, 339
Haldeman, Bob, 294
Halleck, H. W., 99–100
Hamilton, Alice 206
Hamlin, Hannibal, 108
Hanks, John, 93
Harari, David, 64
Harding Florence King
    DeWolfe, 185, 189

Harding, Warren Gama-
liel, 183–89, 192
Harrison, Anna Tuthill Symmes
(wife of William Henry), 68
Harrison, Benjamin,
138, 141–47, 184
Harrison, Caroline Scott
(wife of Benjamin), 142
Harrison, John Scott, 141
Harrison, William
Henry 68, 141
Hart, Emmanuel, 89
Hassan (prince), 336
Hatcher, Jessie John-
son, 276, 277
Havana, 279
Hawaii, 374, 377, 378
Hawthorne, Nathaniel, 84
Hay, John 163, 165
Hayes, Lucy Ware Webb,
119–20, 125
Hayes, Rutherford B., 118–25,
149, 150, 169, 184
Hearst, William Randolph, 152
Hebron, 317
Hedjaz, 213
Helms, Richard, 282
Hemingway, Ernest, 165
Henderson, Loy, 228, 230, 235
Herman, Ed, 362
Herndon, William, 92, 104
Hersh, Seymour, 318
Herter, Christian, 266
Hertzberg, Arthur, 38
Herzl, Theodor, 3, 75, 137,
146–47, 151–52, 266, 318
Herzog, Chaim, 283–84, 303–5
Hill, Robert, 144
Hillsborough (NH), 84

Hinckley, John, 328
Hines, Walter, 200
Hirsch, Baron Maurice, 185
Hiss, Algier, 291
Hitler, Adolf, 9, 10, 12, 206,
207, 208, 212, 216, 217,
218, 227, 238, 240, 246,
261, 263, 268, 279, 281
Hitti, Philip, 6
Holbrooke, Richard, 347
Hollywood, 327
Home, Charles Francis, 226
Honolulu, 377
Hooe, George Mason, 71
Hoover, Alan, 199
Hoover, Herbert, 4, 12,
196, 197–204
Hoover, Herbert, Jr., 199
Hoover, Jesse Clark, 198
Hoover, Lou Henry, 198
Hope (AR), 343
Horowitz, Phineas, 102
Hot Springs (AR), 343
House, Edward, 183
Houston, 278, 334
Hull, Cordell, 207–8, 261
Hulme, Joseph, 57
Humbert (king), 144
Humphrey, Hubert, 285, 293
Hungary, 362
Hurlbut, Stephen, 112
Hussein (king), 10, 294,
352, 353, 355
Hyde Park (NY), 205
Hyland, William, 309

Ibn Saud, 5, 11, 221–22, 229, 230
Iccioto, Isaac, 64
Illinois, 93, 102

Independence (MO), 240
India, 215, 266
Indiana, 102
Indianapolis, 142, 147
Indochina, 246, 377
Indyk, Martin, 347, 386
Inman, Bobby, 282
Iran, 8, 13, 320, 321, 372, 373–74
Iraq, 5, 7, 12, 204, 237, 328,
    336–39, 364, 369, 370, 372
Irwin, Elizabeth Ramsey, 141
Isle of May (West Indies), 45
Israel, 1, 2, 7–8, 9, 10,11–12,
    13–14, 237–39, 241–42, 250,
    252–57, 258, 263–64, 265–74,
    277, 281–88, 292–93, 295,
    296–97, 299–300, 301–4, 305,
    306, 307, 309, 310–18, 320–21,
    324, 327–30, 331, 335, 336–41,
    344, 345, 347, 350, 351–60,
    361, 362, 365–71, 372–74,
    375–76, 381–82, 383–87
Italy, 8, 262, 362

Jabotinsky, Ze'ev, 318
Jackson (MS), 112
Jackson, Andrew, 50, 58–60,
    61, 62, 89, 91, 233
Jackson, Rachel Donel-
    son Robards, 59
Jacobson, Eddie, 226,
    232–33, 239, 241
Jaffa, 235
Jane (Obama's aunt), 379
Japan, 8, 216, 227, 228
Jay, John, 22
Jefferson, Martha Wayles
    Skelton, 33
Jefferson, Peter, 32

Jefferson, Thomas 2, 23, 28,
    31, 32–38, 39, 40, 49,
    52, 70, 194–95, 223
Jenin, 317
Jericho, 347, 350
Jerusalem, 6, 31, 66, 116, 117,
    137, 201, 210, 217, 262,
    264, 297, 317–18, 328,
    354–55, 357, 371, 372,
    373, 375
    East, 13, 318,
    354, 355, 357
Joel, Joseph, 120, 122
Joel, Rutherford B. Hayes, 122
Johnson City (TX), 276
Johnson, Andrew, 105–10
Johnson, Claudia [Lady Bird]
    Taylor (wife of Lyndon), 278
Johnson, Eliza McCardle
    (wife of Andrew), 105
Johnson, Jacob, 105
Johnson, Louisa Catherine, 54
Johnson, Luci Baines, 281
Johnson, Lynda Bird, 281
Johnson, Lyndon Baines, 9, 11,
    12, 257, 276–288, 306, 363
Johnson, Mary, 105
Johnson, Robert, 288
Johnson, Sam Early, Jr., 277
Johnson, Sam Early,
    Sr., 276–77
Johnson, Sarah Bush, 92–93
Joly, Maurice, 175
Jonas, Abraham, 94, 95
Jonas, Joseph, 94
Jones, Elizabeth, 48
Jordan, 4, 7, 11, 214,
    237, 294, 310, 332,
    336, 340, 350, 369

Josephson, Manuel, 24
Josephus, 126
Judea, 31

Kagan, Elena, 383
Kahler, Erich, 5
Kahn, Julius, 153
Kalisch, Samuel, 178
Kansas, 95
Kansas City (KS), 188
Kansas City (MO), 241
Kaskel, Cesar, 99, 114
Kauffman, Joe, 324
Kaufmann, Sigmund, 95
Kendrick, Anna, 84
Kennan, George, 235
Kennedy, Caroline, 264
Kennedy, Jacqueline
    Lee Bouvier, 264
Kennedy, John, Jr., 264
Kennedy, John Fitzgerald, 9, 12,
    257, 260–75, 281, 292, 344
Kennedy, Joseph, 211,
    260–62, 323
Kennedy, Robert, 263
Kentucky, 92, 98, 112, 114, 127
Kenya, 379–80
Kenyatta, Jomo, 379
Kerry, John, 370
Khartoum, 298
Khrushchev, Nikita, 292
Kiev, 146
Kinderhook (NY), 61, 67
King, Leslie, 300
Kirkpatrick, Jane, 7–8, 329
Kishinev, 162–63
Kissinger, Henry, 289–
    90, 294, 295
Klinghoffer, Leon, 370

Klutznick, Philip, 250
Knabenshue, Paul, 201
Kneher, Frederick, 102
Knox, Jane, 75
Knox, John, 75
Kohl, Helmut, 330
Kook, Abraham Isaac, 193–94
Kort, Michael G., 312
Kosygin, Alexei, 283, 286
Kurzer, Daniel, 362
Kutner, Henry, 99
Kuttab, David, 384
Kuwait, 337, 338–39

Lacy Bagallay, Herbert, 213
LaGuardia, Fiorello, 207–8
Lamar, Joseph, 180
Lancaster (PN), 89
Lansing, Robert, 181, 183
Lantos, Tom, 219
Lavin, Frank, 363
Lawley, Francis, 85
Lawrence, T. E., 202
Lazarus, Simon, 309
Lebanon, 4, 6, 41, 43, 237,
    262, 297, 313–14, 328, 350,
    358, 368, 371, 372, 382
Lee, Robert E., 77, 102, 121
Leech, Margaret, 148
Leeser, Isaac, 62, 67
Leinsdorf, Erich, 279
Levi, Louis, 163
Levy, C. M., 104
Levy, Leonard, 171
Levy, Uriah, 44–47, 49, 50–52,
    56, 59–60, 62, 71–72,
    82, 86–87, 90–91, 97
Lew, Jack, 383
Lewinsky, Monica, 350–51

Lexington, 19
Libya, 1, 387
Lincoln, Abraham, 8, 83, 91,
    92–104, 106, 107, 108, 109,
    110, 112, 120, 128, 150
Lincoln, Mary Todd, 95, 103
Lincoln, Nancy, 92
Lindsay, Sir Ronald,
    212, 213, 214
Lithuania, 143
Livni, Tzipi, 384
Locke, John, 35
Loeb, William, Jr., 161
London, 54, 55, 199, 256
Longfellow, Henry Wad-
    sworth, 84, 163
Los Angeles, 379
Louis XIII (pope), 170
Louisiana, 82, 95, 106, 161
Louisville, 78, 95
Lovett, Robert, 235, 236–37
Lynchburg (VA), 121
Lynn, Eric, 383

Ma'alot, 298
MacArthur, Douglas, 245
MacDonald, Malcolm, 262
Maddox, Lester, 308, 309
Madison, Dolly, 40
Madison, James (father), 40
Madison, James (son), 20–21,
    35, 39–47, 49, 53, 77, 194
Madrid, 22, 340
Magaziner, Ira, 347
Maine, 341
Manhattan, 43, 158,
    160, 164, 204
Manila, 246
Mann, Thomas, 208

Marie Christiana (queen
    regent), 144
Marion (Blooming Grove,
    OH), 184, 186
Marseilles, 22
Marsh, Charles, 279
Marshall, George, 7,
    235, 236, 247
Marshall, Louis, 186, 200
Martin, Thomas, 40
Marx, Joseph, 36, 37
Maryland, 35, 102, 121
Masada, 345–46
Massachusetts, 19, 56,
    127, 190, 192, 263
Mayer, Daniel, 149, 152
McCain, John, 282, 382
McCarthy, Joseph, 261
McCone, John, 271
McGonagle, William, 282
McGovern, George, 295
McKinley, Ida Saxton, 150, 154
McKinley, Nancy, 148
McKinley, William, 3, 144,
    148–154, 160, 161, 165, 184
McKinley, William, Sr., 148
McNamara, Robert, 287
McNutt, Paul V., 246
Meade (PN), 148
Medoff, Rafael, 240
Meir, Golda, 270–71, 272,
    274–75, 293, 296,
    297, 298, 309, 313
Meriato, Giovanni, 64
Mesopotamia (IQ), 4, 192
Mexico, 101, 280
Meyer, William, 102
Miami, 14, 226
Middletown (CT), 119

Middletown (MD), 121
Midland (TX), 363
Miehorn, Rose, 162
Miller, Julian H., 167
Milton (MA), 333
Minthorn, Hulda, 198
Mississippi, 77, 98, 112, 161
Missouri, 224, 226, 227, 240
Mitchell, George, 385
Mobile, 102
Monk, Henry Wentworth, 100
Monroe, Elizabeth Kortright, 49
Monroe, James, 41, 42, 47,
    48–52, 53, 90–91
Monroe, Spence, 48
Montefiore, Moses Haim, 66, 67
Monterey, 77, 78
Monticello, 32
Montreal, 21
Moores (midshipman), 56
Moos, H. M., 108
Mordecai, Alfred, 102
Mordecai, Goodman, 103
Morgan, J. P., 145
Morgenthau, Henry, Jr.,
    182, 207, 217, 218
Morocco, 337
Morris, Edmund, 163, 326
Morris, Robert, 21, 194
Moscow, 146
Moses, 2, 103
Moses, Alfred Huger, 109
Mount Vernon, 17, 18, 25
Moynihan, Daniel Patrick, 305
Mubarak, Hosni, 332, 358
Muhammad Ali, 65, 66
Munich, 310
Mussolini, Benito, 10

Nader, Ralph, 379
Nadich, Judah, 248–49
Napoleon Bonaparte, 37
Napoleon, Louis, 82
Nasser, Gamal Abdul,
    252–53, 255, 259, 268,
    269, 281, 282, 285
Nausbaum, Bernie, 347
Nazareth, 238
Nebraska, 95
Negrin, Suleiman, 63
Netanyahu, Benjamin, 13, 14,
    321–22, 350, 351–52, 353,
    364, 383, 384, 385, 387
Netanyahu, Yoni, 310
Netherlands, 53, 54, 144, 194
Neuchatel (CH), 90
Neumann, Emanuel, 201
Nevada, 78
New Guinea, 280
New Haven, 363
New Jersey, 178, 253
New Mexico, 79
New Orleans, 59, 93, 101, 102
New Salem (IL), 93, 94
New York City, 30, 55, 104,
    131, 155, 157–58, 159, 171,
    193, 206, 208, 244, 249,
    251
    port of, 59, 89, 131
New York State, 65, 102,
    160, 206, 238, 253
Newman, David, 384
Newman, Leopold, 102
Newport, 23
Nicholas II, 138
Nicolayson, John, 66
Niles (OH), 148
Niles, David, 230, 237

Nixon, Frank, 290
Nixon, Hanna, 290
Nixon, Julie, 298
Nixon, Richard Milhous, 9,
    12–13, 258, 266, 289–98,
    301, 306, 320, 334
Nixon, Thelma Catherine "Pat"
    Ryan, 291, 297, 298
Nixon, Tricia, 298
Noah, Mordecai, 2, 30–31,
    36, 38, 41, 42–44, 47,
    49, 50, 54–55, 59, 75
Nones (major), 195
North Africa, 8–9, 246–47
North Bend (OH), 141
North Carolina, 58
North Korea, 356
North Rhodesia, 262
Northampton (MA), 192, 196
Norwich (UK), 63
Novy, Jim, 279–80, 281
Nussbaum, Max, 204

Oak Park (IL), 3
Obama, Barack, Sr., 376–77
Obama, Barack Hussein,
    1, 13–15, 375–387
Obama, Malia, 381
Obama, Michelle Robin-
    son, 380, 381
Obama, Said Hussein, 380
Obama, Sasha, 381
Odessa, 139
Ohio, 102, 119, 120, 121–22,
    148, 150, 151, 184, 186
Oklahoma, 226
Olmert, Ehud, 371, 372, 373
Omaha (NE), 300
Oman, 337

O'Meara, Barry, 37
Oregon, 74
Oslo, 347, 353
Osirak (IQ), 328
Oswald, Lee Harvey, 274
Oxford (OH), 141
Oyster Bay (Long Island), 167

Paducah (KY), 99
Palestine, 2, 3–6, 12, 67, 70,
    71, 114, 100, 143, 163,
    167, 137, 144, 145–46, 147,
    151, 172, 188, 192–93, 197,
    201–4, 211–12, 213–14,
    217, 220, 221–22, 227,
    228, 229–35, 239, 241, 248,
    249–50, 262, 263, 265, 278
Palm Desert (CA), 257
Palmerston, Lord, 66–67
Paris, 22, 37, 54, 117, 182, 244
Parisburg (VA), 121
Pasadena, 325
Pasha, Sherif, 64, 65
Patterson, John Henry, 165–66
Patton, George, 249
Pearl, Daniel, 370
Peixotto, Benjamin
    Franklin, 117
Pennsylvania, 102,
    173, 185, 253
Peres, Shimon, 14, 271–72,
    336, 350, 354, 364
Peters, Andrew, 190
Pharaoh, 2, 29, 158
Philadelphia, 19, 20,
    22, 23, 62, 180
Philippines, 153, 170, 246
Phillips, Carrie, 185

Pierce, Benjamin (grandfather), 84
Pierce, Benjamin (son), 84
Pierce, Franklin, 84–87, 89
Pierce, Jane Means Appleton, 84, 85, 87
Pinkos, Henry, 124
Plains (GA), 308
Plymouth (VT), 191, 196
Point Pleasant (OH), 111
Poland, 76, 143, 172, 210, 213, 263, 279–80
Polk, James, 73–76, 79, 89
Polk, Samuel, 75
Polk, Sarah Childress, 75, 76
Port Conway (VA), 40
Portugal, 53, 144, 215
Potter, Peter, 46–47
Powell, Colin, 338
Pratt (Dimona director), 273
Preston, Thomas, 27–28
Puerto Rico, 153
Pulitzer, Joseph, 102, 136, 152

Qatar, 337
Quebec, 21
Quincy (IL), 94
Quincy (MA), 26, 31, 54

Rabi, I. I., 267
Rabin, Leah, 311, 340, 354
Rabin, Yitzhak, 9, 13, 290, 292, 294, 295, 297, 298, 301–3, 306, 309, 310, 311–12, 340, 341, 347, 348, 349–50, 353
Ramallah, 317, 372
Rancho Mirage (CA), 306
Randolph, Jane, 32
Raphael, Otto, 159–60
Raphall, Morris, 104

Reagan, Jack, 324
Reagan, Maureen, 326
Reagan, Michael, 326
Reagan, Nancy Davis, 327, 328, 330
Reagan, Neil, 324
Reagan, Nell, 324
Reagan, Patti, 327
Reagan, Ron, 327
Reagan, Ronald, 9, 12, 306, 319–20, 323–31, 333, 335, 336, 346
Reed, Thomas, 144
Reich, Robert, 344–45, 347
Reid, Ogden, 267
Ribicoff, Abe, 267
Rice, Susan, 385
Richard, Anne, 364
Richmond, 62, 101, 109
Rickover, Hyman, 308
Riegner, Gerhardt, 216, 218
Rifkind, Simon, 249
Riga, 41
Rio de Janeiro, 56
Riss, Jacob, 157
Robertson, Donald, 40
Rockefeller, John D., 144
Rockefeller, William, 144
Rodman, Mara, 383
Romania, 116, 137, 144, 188, 210, 262
Roosevelt, Alice Lee (wife of Theodore), 156
Roosevelt, Anna, 156
Roosevelt, Edith Kermit Carow (wife of Theodore), 156–57
Roosevelt, Eleanor (wife of Franklin), 206, 208

Roosevelt, Franklin Delano, 4–5, 6, 12, 59, 186, 202, 205–23, 228, 230, 247, 260, 262, 279, 280
Roosevelt, James, 206
Roosevelt, Theodore, 8, 153–54, 155–67, 170, 171, 174, 175, 178, 206, 320
Root, Elihu, 170
Rosenman, Samuel, 213
Rosenwald, Julius, 186
Ross, Dennis, 347, 355, 383
Rothschild family, 59
Rothschild, James de, 64
Rubin, Robert, 347
Rush, Benjamin, 68
Rusk, Dean, 231–32, 235, 267, 282, 287
Russell, William, 144
Russia, 1, 53, 54, 76, 100, 124, 129, 132–33, 137, 143, 144, 145–46, 152, 159, 163–64, 165, 166, 172–73, 292, 233, 321, 368

Sadat, Anwar, 11, 310, 311, 312–13, 314–17, 318, 319, 320, 340, 348
Saddam Hussein, 328, 336–38, 365, 368–69, 370
Safire, William, 290
Said, Nuri, 203
Saloman, Edwin S., 114
Salomon, Edward, 102
Salomon, Haym, 20–21, 194
Salomon, Moses, 64
Salvador, Francis, 19–20
San Bernadino (CA), 278
San Francisco, 117
San Mateos (TX), 278

San Remo (IT), 4
Saratoga Springs (NY), 117
Sardinia, 91
Saudi Arabia, 5, 11, 220, 312, 332, 337
Savannah, 37, 103
Schiff, Jacob, 138–39, 172, 182, 185
Schlesinger, James, 309
Schneerson, Hayim, 114–17
Scott (General in Chief), 72
Sderot, 381
Seeligson, Henry, 77–78
Seixas, Moses, 23–24
Semble, Mel, 363
Servia, 144
Seward, William H., 79–80
Shadwell (VA), 32
Shakespeare, William, 93, 225
Shamir, Yitzhak, 338, 339, 340, 341
Shanghai, 246
Shapiro, Dan, 383
Sharett, Moshe, 241, 244
Sharon, Ariel, 352, 364, 366, 367, 369, 371, 372
Shenandoah Valley, 17
Sheperdstown (WV), 354
Sheridan, Philip, 121
Sherman, William T., 98
Silver, Abba Hillel, 186, 230, 252, 254
Silverman, Samuel, 216
Silverstein, Martin, 363
Simeon of Saxe-Coburg-Gotha, 364
Simpson, Hannah, 111
Simpson, Joseph, 72–73

Sinai Desert, 253, 258,
    281, 283–84, 303, 311,
    314, 316, 317, 318
Singapore, 362
Sisco, Joe, 293
Slovakia, 362
Smallwood, James, 280
Smith, Al, 200
Smith, Jesse, 189
Socrates, 33
Soetoro, Maya Kassandra, 378
Solomon, Adolphus, 134
South Africa, 382
Soviet Union, 10, 236, 237, 252,
    255, 257, 262, 264, 283, 300,
    301, 302, 329–30, 340, 341
Spain, 153, 215
Spanier, Louis, 78
Speer, Elizabeth, 89
Springfield (IL), 94
St. Helena, 37
St. Louis, 99
St. Petersburg, 124, 129,
    132, 146, 173
Stalin, Joseph, 221
Stanton (VA), 178
Stanton, Edwin, 110
Stark County (OH), 150
Staten Island, 122
Stein, Herbert, 295
Steinberg, James B., 383
Stevenson, Adlai, 251
Stockton, Peter, 286–87
Straits of Tiran, 281, 285, 287
Straus, Oscar, 136–38,
    165, 171, 186
Strauss, Louis, 200
Strong, William, 157
Sudan, 336

Sugarman, Jule, 309
Sukarno, 377
Sullivan, John L., 169
Sulzberger, C. L., 275
Summerhill (NY), 81
Summers, Lawrence, 383
Susskind, David, 240
Swanson, Gloria, 260
Sweden, 144, 219
Switzerland, 82, 218
Syria, 1, 4, 7, 31, 62–65, 237,
    262, 294, 296, 303, 321,
    337, 340, 354, 368, 387

Taft, Alphonso, 169
Taft, Helen Herron, 168, 169
Taft, Louisa Torrey, 168, 169
Taft, William Howard, 10,
    168–76, 179, 180, 184, 188
Tampico (IL), 324
Tatel, David, 309
Taylor, Margaret Mack-
    all Smith, 78
Taylor, Sarah Dabney
    Strother, 78
Taylor, Richard, 78
Taylor, Zachary, 76, 277–80, 82
Teheran, 319
Tel Aviv, 237, 256, 275, 292, 338
Tenet, George, 360
Tennessee, 75, 98, 106,
    107, 110, 112, 113
Texas, 74, 95, 244, 285,
    286, 334, 371
Thant, U, 281
Thomas, Lorenzo, 110
Thompson, Dorothy, 251
Tiensin, 199
Tilden, Samuel, 122–23

Tipperary (IE), 324
Transjordan, 4. *See also* Jordan
Trieste, 207
Tripoli (LY), 304
Truman, Bess Wallace,
    226, 240, 241
Truman, Harry S., 5, 7, 10, 11,
    12, 59, 76, 223, 224–42, 244,
    250, 261, 263, 277, 363
Truscott, Lucian, 249
Tunis, 1, 30, 41, 42, 43, 44, 49
Tunisia, 360, 387
Turkey, 65, 76, 100, 165,
    136, 171, 181, 192, 262
Tydings, Willard, 211
Tyler, John (father), 70
Tyler, John (son), 69–73
Tyler, Julia Gardiner, 70
Tyler, Letitia Christian, 70

Ukraine, 188
Uruguay, 362
Utah, 78

Van Buren, Abraham, 61
Van Buren, Hannah Hoes, 61
Van Buren, Maria, 61
Van Buren, Martin, 3,
    60, 61–67, 74, 79
Van der Kemp, F. A., 29
Vance, Cyrus, 310
Vaught, W. O, 346
Vermont, 126, 193
Victoria (queen), 109, 144
Vienna, 152, 169
Vietnam, 292
Viner (family), 225
Virginia (state), 33, 35,
    41, 49, 104

Virginia (territory), 17, 18
Voltaire, 29
von Dirksen, Herbert, 261
von Steuben, Friedrich
    Wilhelm, 195
Voorhis, Jerry, 291

Wallace, George, 293
Wallenberg, Raoul, 219–20
Walton (NY), 161
Warburg, Felix, 200
Warner, Jack, 323, 325
Washington, Augustus, 16
Washington, DC, 74, 96, 110,
    114, 115, 134, 129, 151,
    181, 294, 298, 318, 334, 364
Washington, George, 1,
    16–25, 28, 53, 93
Washington, Martha Curtis, 18
Washington, Lawrence, 17
Washington, Mary, 16
Webb, Joseph, 121
Webster, Joseph Dana, 113
Weiser, Ron, 363
Weizmann, Chaim, 5, 229, 232,
    233, 234, 235, 239, 264
Weizmann, Vera, 264
Welles, Sumner, 216–17
West Bank, 311, 317, 320, 341,
    347, 350, 351, 352, 353,
    354, 356, 357, 368, 370, 371
West Branch (Iowa), 198
West Point, 22
West Virginia, 120
Westmoreland County (VA), 48
Wheeler (family), 241
White, Allen, 189
Whittier (CA), 290, 291
Wiesel, Elie, 247, 368–69

Wigner, Eugene, 267
Wilbusky, Jacob, 160
William II (emperor), 144
Williamsburg (VA), 33, 48, 69
Williamson, Andrew, 20
Willkie, Wendell, 6, 229
Wilson, Edith Gault, 179, 183
Wilson, Ellen Louise Axson, 179
Wilson, Jesse, 177
Wilson, Woodrow, 3, 174,
    175, 177–83, 186,
    199, 200, 223, 320
Winchester (VA), 121, 150
Wise, Isaac Mayer, 74, 78,
    79, 100, 108, 168–69
Wise, Leo, 187
Wise, Stephen, 152,
    179–80, 182, 186–87,
    209, 216, 217, 218
Witherspoon, John, 40

Wolcott, C. P., 113
Wolf, Simon, 114, 151
Wolsey, Louis, 186
Woodward, Bob, 361
Wouk, Herman, 295
Wright, Edwin, 238–39
Wright, Jeremiah, 381
Wye River Plantation (MD), 351
Wyman, Jane, 326
Wyoming, 79

Yemen, 1, 5, 387
Yorba Linda (CA), 290
Yulee, David, 106

Zacharie, Isachar, 97–98,
    100–102, 103
Zangwill, Israel, 152
Zeilsheim, 248–49